Religious Education
and
Human Development

Religious Education
and
Human Development

*The Relationship Between Studying Religions
and Personal, Social and Moral Education.*

Michael Grimmitt

Contains a common core RE Curriculum for PSME and GCSE
with 120 Curriculum Units for classroom use illustrated
by Schemes of Work on Christianity, Hinduism, Islam,
Judaism and Sikhism.

McCRIMMONS

Dedicated with love to my three daughters,
Gabriela, Jodie and Amy.

First published in Great Britain in 1987 by
McCRIMMON PUBLISHING CO LTD
Great Wakering   Essex   England

© Copyright 1987 Michael Grimmitt

ISBN 0 85597 401 X

Typeset and printed in Hong Kong by
Permanent Typesetting & Printing Co Ltd

Contents

Acknowledgements
See also Page 424

Grateful acknowledgements are made to the respective publishers for permission to include quotations or extracts from the following books:

Aberdeen University Press: Henriksson, B, *Not for Sale* (1983).

Faber & Faber: Berger, P, *The Social Reality of Religion* (1969).

Falmer Press: Hull, J M (ed), *New Directions in Religious Education* (1982); *Studies in Religion and Education* (1984).

General Synod Board of Education: Martin, B, & Pluck, R, *Young People's Beliefs* (1977).

Harrap/UNESCO: Wall, W D, *Constructive Education for Adolescents* (1977).

Hodder & Stoughton: Lawton, D, *Social Change, Education Theory and Curriculum Planning* (1973); Felderhof, M C (ed), *Religious Education in a Pluralistic Society* (1985).

Islamic Academy: Halstead, J M, *The Case for Muslim Voluntary Schools* (1986).

Penguin Books: Berger, P, *A Rumour of Angels* (1970), *Facing Upto Modernity* (1979).

Pitman Publishing: Postman, N, & Weingartner, C, *Teaching as a Subversive Activity* (1969).

Religious Experience Research Unit: Robinson, E, *The Original Vision* (1981).

Routledge & Kegan Paul: Kitwood, T, *Disclosures to a Stranger* (1980); Weil, S, *Waiting on God* (1951).

SCM Press: Bonhoeffer, D, *Letters and Papers from Prison*—The Enlarged Edition (1971).

Unwin Hyman Ltd: Frith, N, *The Legend of Krishna* (1975).

Every effort has been made to acknowledge sources upon which the author has drawn, but pardon is sought and apology made for any oversights and a correction will be made in any reprint.

Preface

In his paper entitled 'Education and human development', Richard Peters comments:

> *First, by what criteria are we to determine that someone is developing as a person in distinction from mathematically, scientifically and so on? Second, how are these more specialised forms of development related to personal development? This is not simply a speculative problem that it might be fun to solve; it is one of considerable practical importance.*[1]

This book is an exploratory study of the contribution religious education can make to pupils' learning, especially to their personal, social and moral development. At a time when 'Personal, Social and Moral Education' (PSME) courses are fast becoming a feature of the secondary school curriculum, most notably in the fourth and fifth years, and these courses are beginning to vie with religious education for timetable time, or, more often, incorporate religious education within them, it is desirable that some attempt is made to identify what, if anything, the study of religions contributes to the personal development of pupils. Being able to identify this contribution might then place religious education teachers in a stronger position when negotiating either to keep their subject out of integrated PSME courses or to incorporate it into such courses on terms which are supportive of religious education's interests and concerns and which permit its identity and integrity to be preserved.

In pursuing this issue I have found it necessary to draw on insights from a number of disciplines which, until now, have not been a particular feature of the work of religious educators—most notably the sociology of knowledge and philosophical anthropology. I cannot claim to be expert in either field, but, as I hope this book will show, in thinking about the nature and aims of religious education in our modern, plural, multi-faith society, both these disciplines are particularly illuminating not only of the circumstances in which human beings develop but also of the means by which they do so. I have also found these disciplines a useful ally in formulating a critique of much contemporary theory and practice in religious education, especially when they fail to connect with, and so meet, young persons' needs to make sense of their everyday life and experience and further their capacities for personal decision-making.

Although I have retained the use of chapters to organise the contents of this book, most are rather longer than conventional chapters and incorporate at least three main sections. My reason for following this format is that in each chapter I introduce and develop a number of issues related to a central concept which I believe has an important bearing on any conception of religious education. None of these central concepts, although applicable to religious education, is exclusive to it: all have implications for our understanding of education itself. For this reason I have been prepared to undertake excursions into areas of wider educational concern, though I hope I succeed in the final chapter of Part One of the book in applying what I have learned from these excursions to an understanding of 'The Concerns of Religious Education'. Part Two is entirely devoted to curriculum units and schemes of work derived from the conception of religious education which I propose in Chapter Six and which illustrate the 'The Adolescent Life-World Curriculum' and 'The Religious Life-World Curriculum' which are the outcomes of this exploratory study.

While in many ways the present work represents a development of the approaches to religious education contained in my book *What Can I Do in RE?*, the genesis of some of the ideas contained in this study was a project on teaching Christianity which Garth Read and I undertook between September 1974 and December 1975, when I was Director of the Regional Religious Education Centre at Westhill College, Birmingham, and which we intended to develop into a comprehensive programme for religious education for pupils aged 5–16. Although after that date, when Garth returned to Australia, our collaborative efforts ended and have not been resumed, some aspects of the project were taken up by the Queensland Religious Education Curriculum Project and, more recently, have been incorporated into what has been designated 'The Westhill Project'. The present work takes up some of these earlier ideas and for the first time re-works them into a comprehensive theory of the relationship of religious education to human development. It incorporates some of my earlier research papers, most notably my 1978 lectures to the Australian Association for Religious Education, and contributions I have made to various publications over the last six years. Substantially, however, the work draws on ideas on which I have been working during the past three years.

I would like to take this opportunity to thank the many people in this country and abroad who have encouraged me to persist with this work and whose comments and constructive criticisms have greatly inspired me to do so. Closer to home, I owe a considerable debt of gratitude to Dr John Hull for his willingness to share not only his profoundest thoughts with me but also his tea and his coffee. Few are blessed with so brilliant a mind and so generous a spirit in a person who is both friend and colleague. I am also grateful to Professor Robert Dearden, my head of department, for his interest in my work and for his readiness to comment on earlier drafts of this book and on the final manuscript. I would also like to thank Professor Philip Taylor, Dean of the Faculty of Education, for doing likewise and especially for putting me in the way of books I might otherwise never have come across. Finally I would like to say to Carol, my wife, that she has surpassed her own infinite capacity for tolerance and patience in the past three years by demurring so rarely to my unsocial hours of work and my neglect of family and home. Without her unfailing support this book could not have been written.

Michael Grimmitt
University of Birmingham,
April, 1987.

Who am I?

Who am I? They often tell me
I would step from my cell's confinement
calmly, cheerfully, firmly,
like a squire from his country house.

Who am I? They often tell me
I would talk to my warders
freely and friendly and clearly,
as though it were mine to command.

Who am I? They also tell me
I would bear the days of misfortune
equably, smilingly, proudly,
like one accustomed to win.

Am I then really all that which other men tell of?
Or am I only what I know of myself,
restless and longing and sick, like a bird in a cage,
struggling for breath, as though hands were
compressing my throat,
yearning for colours, for flowers, for the voices of birds,
thirsting for words of kindness, for neighbourliness,
trembling with anger at despotisms and petty humiliation,
tossing in expectation of great events,
powerlessly trembling for friends at an infinite distance,
weary and empty at praying, at thinking, at making,
faint, and ready to say farewell to it all?

Who am I? This or the other?
Am I one person today, and tomorrow another?
Am I both at once? A hypocrite before others,
and before myself a contemptibly woebegone weakling?
Or is something within me still like a beaten army,
fleeing in disorder from victory already achieved?

Who am I? They mock me, these lonely questions of mine.
Whoever I am, thou knowest, O God, I am thine.

Dietrich Bonhoeffer, June 1944.

(Letters and Papers from Prison—The Enlarged Edition,
SCM Press, 1971)

PART ONE

Towards a theory of
religious education's
contribution to
human development

Chapter One

Value assumptions and the curriculum

Introduction: the need to examine value assumptions

Given the fact of cultural, religious and ideological pluralism, and recognising the value-laden nature of any educational enterprise, the task of establishing an acceptable basis for teaching religion in schools—one which enables the study of religions to conform to educational principles while preserving the integrity of those religions which are the objects of study—is an essential prerequisite to the formulation of curriculum proposals. That task, however, demands that we give close attention to the value assumptions which underlie our view of religious education, especially to those which underpin our view of how education and religion are related to each other and what contribution the study of religion makes to pupils' learning.

But as we seek to identify, examine and justify the value assumptions which support our curriculum proposals we find ourselves caught up in a chain of infinite regress. Value assumptions underlying the curriculum are related to value assumptions underlying our general theory of education and these are reified within the formal structure of educational institutions and systems. Value assumptions underlying our general theory of education are related to an amalgam of value assumptions which a society makes about the nature, function and status of knowledge, the relationship of knowledge to human development and the relationship of the individual to society. These value assumptions, in turn, reflect, through the values and beliefs embedded in its culture, that society's value assumptions about the nature and destiny of human beings and the significance of human life.

As teachers, the times when our value assumptions are likely to be most apparent are when we address such basic questions as 'What shall I teach?', 'How shall I teach it?' and 'When shall I teach it?'. There is, however, another question which we often tend to overlook: 'Why should I teach it?'. This is the question which challenges us to reflect carefully on our value assumptions. If we stay with that question long enough, we will find ourselves needing to become involved in some complicated and controversial issues before we are able to formulate a reasonable response. The problem may be presented by way of a diagram and three more questions:

Figure One: The ideological and cultural context of curriculum decision-making

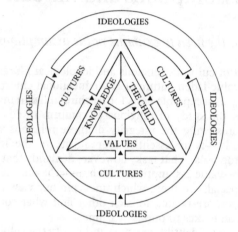

1. What knowledge is worthwhile and how is it selected, transmitted and acquired?
2. What values are important and how are they selected, transmitted and acquired?
3. What understanding of childhood and how children learn should inform educational aims and practices?

How we understand the concept of education and decide upon the shape and purpose of the curriculum will, I suggest, depend upon our particular assumptions about *knowledge, values* and the *child*. I think we need to find ways of bringing our views about these into dialectical or creative tension so that, like the sides of an equilateral triangle, each is held in place by its equal relationship to the other two. In trying to achieve this, we also need to be conscious of the ideological and cultural framework through which we view this triangle and the influence this exerts on our thinking.

Although this task demands the exercise of reason, I think we should be aware that finding a solution is not just a matter of rationality; it also involves our feelings and personal histories. In other words, in trying to answer these three questions we will, I suggest, need to reflect on the particular set of personal circumstances which causes us to feel more at ease with one view than another, even though the logic of that view cannot necessarily be demonstrated to be superior to that of another. For example, coming to hold an *absolutist* view of knowledge and values or a *relativist* view is not just a matter of weighing *pros* and *cons* in a detached sort of way; it also involves us considering why we feel the position we have chosen is to be preferred. Similarly, in comparing and contrasting competing *ideological* perspectives (including religious ones) which may predispose us to accept, for example, one view of the child (or of religion, politics, morality and education) as opposed to another, we may find ourselves needing to reflect on such questions as: Why is it that some people are conservative in their views while others are liberal or radical?; Why are some teachers and parents authoritarian in their attitudes to children while others are permissive?; Is it merely a matter of being rational about our choices or, if not, how do we acquire our attitudes and values?; Are we the person we are as a result of the conscious exercise of choice or because we unconsciously become the person that others have made us? Similarly, how do we decide between the view that teachers are 'professional ideologists engaged in the trans-mission of a variety of know-how wrapped up in a massive inculcation of the ideology of the ruling class' or that they are 'guardians of quality, standards, abiding cultural, moral and spiritual values and excellencies transcending class and politics'?[1] How do we decide whether schools should implement educational policies which are designed to stratify people economically and socially or policies which ensure an equitable distribution of power and economic resources? How do we decide be-tween the views that the curriculum should be 'discipline-centred' or 'child-centred', 'academic' or 'social'; that religious education should nurture religious faith or promote an objective, critical attitude towards religion?; that moral education should inculcate particular moral values or present values in a neutral or impartial manner recognising them to be controversial?

I have deliberately phrased these questions rather starkly as either-or questions and I recognise that different views are not necessarily mutually exclusive. While this may be the case, the fact remains that unless we are prepared to press towards greater clarity and precision in our response to such questions we are unlikely to reflect critically on the 'taken-for-granted' assumptions which underlie our day to day activi-ties as teachers. As I indicated earlier, there is a necessary connection between the assumptions underpinning the curriculum and how we implement it and a chain of assumptions linking the work and life of schools with particular estimates of the nature and value of human life. If it is our intention that the period of schooling should, in some way, connect with the needs human beings experience in the rest of their lives and that the curriculum should serve to improve their competence in personal decision-making, it is important that we recognise the limitations placed upon these goals by our uncritical acceptance of certain views of the curriculum, including current views about the nature and purpose of the religious education curriculum. In illustration of these points, I wish to consider in this chapter, first, how alternative conceptions of knowledge have different implications for our understanding of the aims of education, the form and content of the curriculum and our role as teachers, and then do the same exercise in relation to alternative conceptions of values and of childhood and learning. In this manner I hope to identify the issues which need to be addressed when seeking to provide an educational rationale for religious education and to formulate curriculum proposals within this subject.

1. Knowledge

For the purpose of this illustration we can distinguish two different conceptions of knowledge. The two conceptions may be defined as:

Knowledge as Type A: Knowledge as objectively existent, external to the knower, presented through certain 'disciplines', 'public traditions' or 'common culture' and there to be discovered, mastered and learnt.

Knowledge as Type B: Knowledge as a social construct, socially-related and socially relative.

A brief description of the grounds upon which these conceptions are based will, I hope, enable us to clarify the assumptions underlying them—assumptions which are implicit in certain conceptions of education, the curriculum and 'personal development' and which we are inclined, at least in relation to Knowledge as Type A, to accept uncritically.

(i) Knowledge as Type A

The conception of knowledge as impersonal, explicit and permanent, objectively existent and external to the knower has been most powerfully impressed on Western minds by the Idealist, Rationalist and Empiricist traditions of philosophy. Idealism began with Socrates and Plato and was developed by Rationalist philosophers like Spinoza, Leibnitz and Berkeley, and also by Kant and Hegel. Plato makes a distinction between knowledge and belief and restricts knowledge to the apprehension, by means of a sort of intuition, of 'Ideas' or 'Forms' which stand outside the ever-changing world of everyday things. He equates knowledge with acquiring Truth about the 'noumenal' or non-phenomenal world, such Truth being eternal and changeless. The Rationalists regard knowledge as analogous to the grasping of mathematical truths and have sought to identify 'universal' or 'necessary' truths of a *propositional* kind. Such truths, ideas or principles are grasped by the mind, whereas matter is known through the senses which are to be distrusted. It is in engagement with such universal and unchanging ideas that mind is constituted.

The Empiricist account of knowledge, associated with Locke and Hume, while also holding that knowledge is objective, impersonal and unchanging, reverses the roles that the Idealist/Rationalist tradition gives to reason and sense experience. The function of reason is to coordinate the findings of experience, for reason, apart from sensory experience, is unable to yield any knowledge. The order and regularity with which experiences occur allow generalisations or laws about the world to be made. These generalisations do not constitute a body of necessary truths but contingent conclusions depending upon how the world happens in fact to be. A body of knowledge can thus be built up which gives substantial information about the world, and this knowledge, although contigent upon the world as it happens to be, exists independently of the knower. We have here the basis of scientific method and the scientific paradigm of objectivity, although Karl Popper has shown how a Rationalist model can equally well be used to define and formulate science and the scientific method.

It is of interest to note how Kant argues that we can only experience the world as we do on the assumption that it is a causal system operating in time and space. The phenomenal world, he holds, appears to us as it does, not because that is necessarily how it actually is but because certain forms and categories of the mind structure our experience and give it a framework of necessity. He thus accepts that the act of knowing occurs by means of a transaction between mind and experience which, to all intents and purposes, generates 'objective' knowledge of the phenomenal world. He discounts the possibility of the noumenal world, or world of 'Ideas' being directly knowable.[2]

(a) Knowledge as Type A and Educational Theory

There can be little doubt that theories of knowledge derived from the Idealist, Rationalist and Empiricist traditions have had the greatest influence on Western conceptions of education and still do. At this point I will not attempt to consider the pervasive influence that the scientific method, derived from Empiricism, has had on the curriculum, except to note that if any conception of knowledge is responsible for convincing our pupils that we live in a knowable, understandable and quantifiable world, and that knowledge is a body of 'objective facts' capable of being 'proved true', it is this one. Instead I will give some attention to considering the influence the Rationalist tradition has had, and continues to have, on our thinking about education and the curriculum, and, since the early seventies, about religious education.

During the last twenty-five years, philosophy of education in the United Kingdom has been dominated by the work of Richard Peters, Paul Hirst and Robert Dearden—all, at one time or another, holding posts in the University of London Institute of Education and working within the Rationalist tradition using the tools of conceptual analysis. Although an over-simplification, the main assumptions about knowledge that underpin their work may be stated as follows:

1. There are certain facts, truth and knowledge (called 'givens' by the early Wittgenstein) which have universal applicability.
2. These facts, truth and knowledge are independent of ourselves.
3. These facts, truth and knowledge are expressed and known through language and are differentiated into 'forms of knowledge' or 'disciplines', each form having its own distinctive logical structure, its own central concepts ('key' or 'organising' concepts), its own truth criteria (or forms of verification), and its own mode of expression.

(b) Paul Hirst's account of Forms of Knowledge

Of the various attempts to apply this conception of knowledge to education and the curriculum, probably the most celebrated is that of Paul Hirst, who, in his 1974 version,[3] distinguishes seven fundamentally distinct forms:

1. Formal logic and mathematics.
2. The physical sciences.
3. 'Truths of a mental or personal kind.' (In previous versions this form was referred to as 'human sciences' and then as 'our awareness and understanding of our own and other people's minds', which, at one point, included history).
4. Moral judgment and awareness.
5. Aesthetics (literature and fine arts).
6. Religion.
7. Philosophy.

Hirst and Peters define a 'form' as being identified by the 'fundamental, ultimate or categoreal concepts of a most general kind which other concepts in the category presuppose'[4]. For example, 'space', 'time', 'cause' are the categoreal concepts of the physical sciences which are presupposed by such concepts as 'acid', 'electron' or 'velocity'. 'God' might be a central concept of the religious form of thinking in a way in which 'prayer' is not, because 'prayer' presupposes 'God'. Thus, the distinctive characteristics of the various forms of knowledge are determined by:

1. Certain concepts unique to the form and not reducible to any other form;
2. These and other concepts that denote, if perhaps in a very complex way, certain aspects of experience, form a network of possible relationships in which experience is understood'[5];
3. Objective tests peculiar to the form and by which its statements can be validated against experience as truth claims.

Hirst comments:

The labels I have used for distinct forms of knowledge are to be understood as being strictly labels for different classes of true propositions. . . .[6]

With Peters, he adds:

That other domains ought, in due course, come to be distinguished, is in no sense being prejudged; for the history of human consciousness would seem to be one of progressive differentiation. The categorisation that is at present being suggested may, in fact, be inaccurate in detail. Be that as it may. What we are suggesting is that within the domain of objective experience and knowledge, there are such radical differences of kind that experience and knowledge of one form is neither equatable with, nor reducible to, that of any other form.[7]

Hirst next applies his theory of the structure and organisation of knowledge to the selection of curriculum objectives. He sees the curriculum in terms of limited objectives derived from the forms of knowledge. It is his view that the traditional subject-based timetable is likely to be the most efficient method of organising content to meet these objectives. Thus be believes that the curriculum should reflect the formal characteristics of each kind of knowledge.

On the basis of the Idealist/Rationalist assumption that 'mind' is constituted and developed through its engagement with these kinds of knowledge because they are the fundamental categories of all truth-seeking activities, Hirst, in company with Peters and Dearden, understands education as the initiation of pupils into these forms of knowledge which he sees as necessary and 'worthwhile' in themselves. Thus we have the grounds upon which some, including myself, have argued for the inclusion of the study of religion in the school curriculum.[8]

(c) Philip Phenix's account of Realms of Meaning

An alternative analysis of the structure of knowledge is offered by the American educationist Philip Phenix. He argues that what characterises human beings is that they are 'essentially creatures who have the power to experience *meanings*. Distinctively human existence consists in a pattern of meanings'.[9] He suggests that it is possible to distinguish six 'realms of meaning' or six distinctive ways in which human beings come to terms with, and make sense of experience. These are:

1. *Symbolics* — neutral tools of communication such as language, mathematics and symbolic forms such as gestures and rituals.
2. *Empirics* — factual descriptions of the physical world and of living things (including human beings).
3. *Aesthetics* — the arts, eg, music, the visual arts, the arts of movement and literature.
4. *Synnoetics* — direct awareness we have of people as persons (eg, our understanding of what it is to be a person in relation to other persons).
5. *Ethics* — meanings that express obligations.
6. *Synoptics* — history, philosophy and religion — that realm concerned with constructing a coherent pattern which includes all other realms of meaning, eg, religion is concerned with the whole of life, seen from a religious perspective.

From this analysis of 'meanings' Phenix moves on to consider its implications for education. In doing so, however, he pays particular attention to the *function* of meaning in everyday life. He observes that the human situation is such that humankind is always threatened by forces that destroy meanings, and when this occurs, values, purposes and understandings give way to attitudes of futility, frustration and doubt. Thus meaning is under a perennial threat. He identifies four contributory factors which, in modern industrial civilisation, endanger meaning. These are: the spirit of criticism and scepticism; the depersonalisation and fragmentation of life caused by extreme specialisation; the mass of knowledge that modern man is required to assimilate; and the rapid rate of change in the conditions of life which result in feelings of impermanence and insecurity.[10] Consequently, Phenix defines education as 'the process of engendering essential meanings'.[11]

Phenix's analysis of meanings does not fit comfortably within that conception of knowledge derived from Rationalism. It reveals strains of Existentialist thought, and his analysis of the psycho-social context within which human beings experience meanings places it outside the bounds of philosophical thinking and on the boundary between *Knowledge as Type A* and *Knowledge as Type B*. This is why it has a more obvious relevance than that of Hirst's to an understanding of personal and social development. His fourth realm of meaning, which he calls 'Synnoetics', is especially applicable and I will be considering a possible application of it in Chapter Four to what I call the development of 'moral, religious and spiritual consciousness'. In the meantime we should note the characteristics which Phenix gives to synnoetic meaning. As is the case with all six realms, the selection and organisation of experience in this realm is of a distinctively different, logical kind from the others. It is Phenix's view that whereas knowledge in symbolics, empirics and aesthetics, for example, requires *detachment* so that the knower stands apart from what he or she knows, knowledge in synnoetics requires *engagement*. In other words, knowledge in symbolics, empirics and aesthetics is *objective*, or external to the knower, but synnoetic meanings are *subjective* and give rise to *personal knowledge*. To put it another way, language, science and art are concerned with *essences*, while personal knowledge is *existential*, concerned with the concrete existence of the individual. What results from the synnoetic realm of meaning is, therefore, *intersubjective* awareness (ie, meanings relating subjects to subjects) and *intrasubjective* awareness (ie, self-knowledge and self-awareness)—the means by which individuals make sense of themselves. Phenix comments that personal knowledge of this sort is not developed through formal instruction but is largely a product of social experience and the nature of the common life.[12] I will also return to a consideration of this view in Chapter Four. Finally we should note that he sees religion falling into the realm of meaning he calls 'Synoptics', a realm which refers to meanings that are comprehensively integrative. He writes:

> *Religion is concerned with ultimate meanings, that is, with meanings from any realm whatsoever, considered from the standpoint of such boundary concepts as the Whole, the Comprehensive, and the Transcendent.*[13]

(ii) Knowledge as Type B

We come now to a consideration of the conception of knowledge as 'a social construct, socially-related and socially relative'.[14] In moving from *Knowledge as Type A* to *Knowledge as Type B* we are moving from a philosophical approach to the problem of knowledge to a sociological one. Something of the difference between the ways in which philosophers and sociologists approach and understand curriculum problems is very well illustrated by Tony Beecher's fable of the butterflies and the caterpillars.

> *Once upon a time, the secret garden of the curriculum was presided over by butterflies. They tended it neatly, albeit in a rather distant and formal way. Their concern was to impose order on the untidiness of nature, to identify logical categories and lay bare the underlying structures. But because they always looked upon the garden from aloft, they failed to notice what was happening at ground level. Unseen at first, but soon more obviously, the garden was invaded by caterpillars. They were not at all impressed by the overall effects which the butterflies had worked hard to bring about; they saw things from a more earthy point of view. Their concern was with reality at close quarters, with the day to day activities and routine transactions which gave the garden character. They ate their way steadily through any foliage which obscured their vision. The butterflies hovered above, angry but impotent; and soon the neat, formal garden was transformed into a flourishing but untidy wilderness.*[15]

Unlike philosophers, sociologists—especially social phenomenologists and symbolic interactionists—are not concerned to differentiate between valid and invalid assertions about the world, nor are they concerned with 'theoretical knowledge' as such. Their interest is in everything that passes for 'knowledge' in society, frequently called 'everyday knowledge'. In attempting to understand this everyday knowledge in terms of how it works, questions about the origin and validity of such knowledge are put to one side or 'bracketed'. For this reason philosophers have reservations about their claim to be 'sociologists of knowledge' and would prefer them to be known as 'sociologists of belief'.

One of the central axioms of the sociology of knowledge is that the relationship between human beings and society is a dialectical one. That is, not only are human beings in society, but society is in human beings—in their thought, in their way of organising their existence as a meaningful, coherent process. Indeed, one of the central interests of social phenomenologists is how human beings create meaning and order out of an apparently meaningless universe. Peter Berger, the American sociologist, explains this dialectical relationship as follows:

> *Society is a dialectic phenomenon in that it is a human product, and nothing but a human product, that yet continuously acts back upon its producer. Society is a product of man. It has no other being except that which is bestowed upon it by human activity and consciousness. There*

can be no social reality apart from man. Yet it may also be stated that man is a product of society. Every individual biography is an episode within the history of society which both precedes and survives it. . . . What is more, it is within society, and as a result of social processes, that the individual becomes a person, that he attains and holds onto identity and that he carries out the projects that constitute his life. . . . .

The fundamental dialectic process of society consists of three movements or steps. These are externalisation, objectivation *and* internalisation. . . *Externalisation is the ongoing outpouring of human being into the world, both in the physical and mental activity of men. Objectivation is the attainment by the products of this activity (again physical and mental) of a reality that confronts its original producers as a facticity external to and other than themselves. Internalisation is the reappropriation by man of this same reality, transforming it once again from structures of the objective world into structures of the subjective consciousness. It is through objectivation that society becomes a reality* sui generis. *It is through internalisation that man is a product of society.*[16]

The idea that human beings construct reality is a logical extension of the view that society and the individual are dialectically linked. Social phenomenologists draw our attention to the sociological fact that it is our location within a particular social, cultural or ideological context which provides our life with shape and meaning—not only in its external features but also in its internal features, our own interior experience or 'life-world'. We are not born 'human' but are made 'human'. We are shaped by the circumstances of our birth—its time in history, its location within a particular ethnic, cultural, ideological and religious setting. We are shaped by our experience of others—parents, siblings, peer groups, work mates, marriage partners, authority figures. We internalise facts, values, beliefs and attitudes and in making them our own are made by them. We are shaped in the image of that reality, or that view of the human which is 'normative' in a given time in a given place. In this sense we are all human beings of our time. We are all shaped in terms of the cultural models of the human which are part of our social, cultural and ideological inheritance. Even if we seek to reject such models, we cannot remove ourselves from their shaping influence; we react against something not against nothing and the starting-points of our lives are never changed by the courses we choose to follow, but continue to exert an influence on the choices we make.

On this view, the way in which meanings are assigned to a common 'objective' world is through a common interpretational system, ie. sets of categories and typicalities through which definitions, descriptions and explanations of the world are given. The chief and most powerful way in which these categories and typicalities are organised or given meaning is through language. Postman and Weingartner put it like this:

> As studies in perception indicate, we do not get meaning from things, we assign meaning. But beyond this, there is a growing understanding that the meaning we assign is a function of the pattern of symbols through which we order and relate whatever it is we are dealing with. In other words, whatever is out there isn't anything until we make it something and then it 'is' whatever we make it. Most of our 'making something' activity, of course, consists essentially of naming things. Korzybski reminded us that whatever we say something is, it is not. But in a certain sense, whatever we say something is, it is. Because we have said it, and because of having said it, we will perceive it.[17]

Postman and Weingartner also refer to Korzybski's use of the term 'projection', meaning that we transfer our own feelings and evaluations to objects outside us.

> For example, we say, 'John is stupid' or 'Helen is smart', as if stupidity and smartness were characteristics of John and Helen. A literal translation of 'John is stupid' might go something like this: When I perceive John's behaviour, I am disappointed or distressed or frustrated or disgusted. The sentence I use to express my perceptions and evaluations of these events is 'John is stupid'. Note how the 'I'—the involvement of the perceiver—has been removed by a grammatical peculiarity. Our grammar has forced us to 'objectify' our feelings, to project them onto something outside our skins. 'Stupidity' is a grammatical category. It does not exist in nature. Yet we imagine that it does because our language has put it there.[18]

As we saw earlier, another way in which meanings are assigned, or the 'objective' world is given meaning, is through the classification of experience into 'forms of knowledge' or 'disciplines'. The points that Postman and Weingartner make about language are equally applicable to the 'disciplines', namely that they do not exist independently of those who have put them there. The sociologists of education who embrace a symbolic interactionist position are very critical of the assumptions which underlie rationalist analyses of knowledge. A not infrequently voiced criticism is that 'an academic curriculum' imposes 'middle class values' on pupils.[19] This criticism is based on the view that what counts as 'knowledge' can never be more than what particular social groups label as such. 'Forms of knowledge' therefore are no more than socio-historical constructs of a particular time involving canons of thought which dominant social groups (such as upper middle class academics) regard as necessary and worthwhile. An academic curriculum may be seen, consequently, as a form of indoctrination into middle class values;

an initiation into those values and beliefs which characterise the life-styles of those who are in control of education. In other words, the rules governing language and knowledge result in the domination of some people over others. Although it may be easy to become impatient with this sort of view, the truth remains that we are not always conscious that how we select, structure and teach content involves us in making judgments not only about what is desirable in the experience of our pupils, but also judgments about the direction in which they should develop as growing human beings and how they should understand and behave in the world. In short, in our teaching we prescribe the model of our pupils' understanding of reality and humanity, which is the model by which *we* understand it.

And many would say, 'Yes!—and that's how it should be! Isn't one of the fundamental intentions of teaching that of transforming children's realities—of giving them new ways of understanding the world, and developing in them new kinds of awareness and skill? And in order to do this, don't we have to influence the way in which children think?' Most certainly we have to do this, but the social phenomenologists are saying: 'If knowledge at all levels becomes relativised, the possibility of absolute knowledge is denied. Human beings can no longer be certain of anything. The cosmos offers no absolute confirmations. Relativity and uncertainty are facts of life. How then can you proceed in your teaching as if all things are fixed and there is only one way of understanding reality? Your task is not to impose your particular construct of reality on the children you teach; it is rather to assist them in restructuring their realities through a "negotiation" of meaning. And the syllabus of content and the methods of teaching should be designed to encourage and facilitate this process of "negotiation".'

The sociology of knowledge, then, treats as problematic (or 'problematises') the definitions and categories of knowledge that usually go unquestioned by those who teach and transmit them. In so doing, it challenges the criteria by which 'worthwhile' and 'necessary' knowledge are identified, it questions the way in which knowledge is organised in the curriculum, it condemns the uncritical manner in which pupils acquire knowledge and it is scornful about the status of 'success' in the educational enterprise as a whole. Again, although an oversimplification, we can set out the main assumptions underlying this conception of knowledge and their implications for education and the curriculum as follows:

1. Human beings enter into agreements or transactions in order to establish what is to count as fact, truth and knowledge.
2. These agreements vary; only the agreements are absolute whereas the content is relative.

27

3. At one level, these agreements reflect the dominant cultural and ideological assumptions of a society, or at least the assumptions of those who have power. At another level, these agreements reflect the individual's accumulation of experiences from birth to maturity.

4. The concern of the curriculum is for teachers and pupils to engage co-operatively in those activities which 'produce' knowledge— namely questioning, defining, observing, classifying, generalising, verifying, applying, valuing, and deciding upon criteria for what is to count as knowledge.

5. It is very difficult to give a single definition of 'education' as this is also seen to be 'problematic' and subject to the same processes as knowledge. The following statement by Paulo Freire is consistent with this view:

Education is *'the problematisation of the world of work, products, ideas, convictions, aspirations, myths, arts, science: the world, in short, of culture and history which is the result of relations between human beings and the world. To present this human world as a problem for human beings is to propose that they 'enter into' it critically, taking the operations as a whole, their action and that of others on it. It means 're-entering' the world through the 'entering into' of the previous understandings which may have been arrived at naively because reality was not examined as a whole. In 'entering into' their own world, people become aware of their manner of acquiring knowledge and then realise the need to know even more.'*[20]

(iii) *Some implications of these different conceptions of knowledge for our own reflections on education, the curriculum and its contribution to pupils' personal development*

The apparent conflict between these two conceptions of knowledge and the contrasting views of education and the curriculum which derive from them illustrate the need for us to become more attuned to the idea of discerning truth within the creative tension of dialectic rather than attributing truth to one of two mutually exclusive alternatives. Let us see if there is something we can learn from both these conceptions which provides us with fresh insights upon which we can draw in thinking about the nature and purpose of education and the structure of the curriculum.

I think we can learn from the social phenomenologists that in a society such as ours everyone has to cope with *multiple realities* and that 'reality' is not adequately defined only by reference to the Rationalist's 'forms of knowledge' or 'disciplines'. The thesis that reality is a social construct places *Knowledge as Type A within* the framework of *Knowledge as Type B* where it exists alongside other realities, especially *interpersonal* and *intra-personal realities* such as those represented by Phenix's 'Synnoetic' realm of meanings. Bringing the 'forms of knowledge' within a framework of reality which is socially constructed does not rule out that such knowledge is 'objective' as compared with inter-personal and intra-personal knowledge which is 'subjective'. It does, however, deny that such knowledge is 'absolute' and not subject or relative to the social processes which create it. At the same time, the incorporation of the 'forms of knowledge' alongside other realities raises, in a helpful way, the issue of their relationship to 'everyday knowledge'.

Traditionally, schools have been concerned with academic knowledge but not with everyday reality which has been discounted and viewed, at best, as irrelevant, and, at worst, as ignorance and error. The thesis that reality is a social construct proposes that different perceptions of reality are varieties of truth as opposed to varieties of error. An educational process which isolates or segregates 'academic knowledge' or 'truth' from the social 'life-world' of the pupils does not assist them in valuing that world or reappraising it but expects them to abandon it for an alternative social 'life-world'. It is significant that R S Peters uses a Platonic image when he argues that education is concerned to bring 'the barbarian outside the gates. . . inside the citadel of civilisation'.[21] Here he is indicating that the superiority of certain kinds of human activity are based on appeals to cognitive content, seriousness and intrinsic value; by implication other human activities, such as those which fall outside the Rationalist's categorisation of knowledge, are of no interest to, and have no consequence for, the educator. As we have seen, the sociologists of education are particularly critical of this view, stressing that it ignores the relationship which exists between human thought and the social context within which it exists and has value. In keeping with this emphasis, they concentrate their attention on the pupils' existing knowledge—what rationalist philosophers define as ignorance. Here, then, we have competing estimates of what knowledge and values are 'worthwhile'.

But what is the point of this disagreement? I think it is this. Education *does* things to people; it is a form of socialisation and human shaping; it is the means by which a particular model of the human being is perpetuated in and through individuals. The model which the traditional academic curriculum perpetuates is of the 'educated man' who, in the words of Peters, is 'someone who is capable of delighting in a variety of pursuits and projects for their own sake and whose pursuit of them and general conduct of his life is transformed by some degree of all-round understanding and sensitivity'.[22] This is the ancient Greek idea of a 'liberal' education for 'free' men which, in the words of Paul Hirst, was

29

so called 'because they saw it as freeing the mind to function according to its true nature, freeing reason from error and illusion and freeing man's conduct from wrong'.[23] This conception of a liberal education came into prominence in England in the nineteenth century and has continued to provide a pattern for the aims of education ever since. It is significant that the title of the paper in which Hirst first distinguished the forms of knowledge is 'Liberal education and the nature of knowledge'.[24]

Writing in 1950, some seventeen years before Berger and Luckmann proposed their 'Social Construction of Reality' thesis, M V C Jeffreys described the liberal education tradition as one in which 'knowledge, learning, personal development are good in themselves' and declared that 'the nobility of the educational process ought not to be degraded, nor its full reach short-circuited, by the subordination of ultimate aims to immediate utilities'. However, he also commented that 'at its best the liberal ideal has affirmed the full and balanced development of the personality. . . at its worst is has provided a dignified camouflage for a good deal of scholastic humbug'.[25] The criticisms of the sociologists of education, although coming from roots very different from those of Jeffreys, are similar. They point to the preponderance of elitist values and elitist ways of thinking represented by the academic curriculum and argue that 'success' in the educational system is evaluated only in terms of how many pupils can be socialised into these values. Thus, despite its ideals of equality, the educational system severely disadvantages working class children and, ironically, those who do 'succeed' are so re-socialised in the process that there is minimal correspondence between their social 'life-worlds' and the social 'life-worlds' of other members of their social class. But even more significant is the criticism that although studying academic disciplines (thought to be 'intrinsically worthwhile' by educators and teachers) may be expected to promote certain desirable habits of mind, such as critical judgment and rationality, which have some application to the pupils' tasks of ordering and giving meaning to their own 'life-worlds', does this expectation justify the exclusion from the curriculum of any consideration of those other forms of experience which constitute their present realities and which are more directly relevant to their situations? Denis Lawton expresses the same point as follows:

> Bearing in mind the fact that academic knowledge accounts for only a small part of what should be studied as knowledge in a society, we should radically re-examine the traditional secondary school curriculum to judge whether it is still the best possible means of transmitting knowledge (as we have defined it) in a system which is not catering for an elite but for the whole population.[26]

My final comment relates to the notion of defining what is worthwhile in terms of its *intrinsic* worth. Although central to the Idealist/Rationalist tradition, the concept of knowledge having *intrinsic* worth has questionable validity within the thesis that reality is a social construct. This adopts a *functional* view of knowledge. Knowledge is generated and preserved because it provides a working hypothesis for living; when it ceases to do this, it ceases to have social and personal significance, except, perhaps, as content for the history of ideas. Accordingly, knowledge is defined not in terms of its *intrinsic* worth but in terms of its *instrumental* worth—in terms of what it does. This stress on the instrumental, functional character of knowledge reinforces the notion that knowledge is socially relative—not only relative to the society that values it but of relative value within that society according to the importance attached to what it does. The same argument can be advanced in respect of education and the curriculum. Education's worth is assessed in terms of its functional value in a society, by what it achieves. The same is true of the curriculum. The value of the curriculum cannot be assessed in terms of the *intrinsic* worth of each of the disciplines which constitute it but rather in terms of their *instrumental* value in contributing to the achievement of certain educational goals. Teaching disciplines, because of their capacity to promote skills and abilities which have application in the life of the individual, may involve considerable changes in both the selection of content and in teaching styles. This observation is particularly pertinent to teaching religion, and I will be examining it more closely in later chapters.

2. *Values and culture: an introductory note*

The controversies which exist in relation to knowledge and its status exist equally in relation to values. Indeed, much of what has been said in the previous section about knowledge can be said about values. For example, values, like knowledge, cohere within a framework of culture and ideology and are major determinants of a society's sense of identity and cultural continuity. But in a society as complex as ours, what are those values? The rapid growth of the modern, technological, plural, multi-cultural/multi-faith societies makes this a most important question. Where a multiplicity of ethnic and social groups co-exist within a single society, each with their own conceptions of reality and their own values, beliefs and identities, the development of a sense of relationship and coherence between these groups to form a single society may well be dependent upon their participation in a 'common culture' and their adherence to a set of common or 'core' values. But how may these be identified and what status may be attached to them? If schools are to participate in fostering a sense of community within a multi-cultural setting, they will need to give careful attention to the values which they espouse.

But the identification of a common core of values is only part of the problem. Even if such values could be identified, how are they to be treated within the curriculum? Are they to be taught as moral absolutes, rather in the manner that *Knowledge as Type A* is treated? An alternative perspective, derived from the sociological analysis of values, might be that we should cease to think of values as entities with some kind of existence of their own, and think of *valuing* as an activity in which all human beings engage. In this sense, values derive their validity from the actual choices and decisions which individuals make; they are validated by acts of commitment which involve the restructuring of personal experience in such a way as to affirm what the individual finds of value. But there is a considerable danger in personalising and relativising values in this manner; it erodes the essential context within which values cohere, namely culture. If culture is defined as 'the totality of typical life-forms of a community, including its spiritual/intellectual system and especially its scale of values',[27] it is apparent that in recent decades European culture has been undergoing an atomisation due to the impact of modernity, secularisation, technologisation, the pluralism of Western liberal democracies and the increasing influence of non-European cultures. This has accelerated the tendency for values to be both relativised and individualised. This presents a major threat to cultural traditions, traditional values and, of course, to traditional religion. It raises the difficult question of what happens in a society when traditions break down because they are felt to be meaningless, especially by young people. What is to be the response of the schools to this situation? How are they to maintain their traditional role as agents of cultural transmission? Do teachers respond to this situation by adapting to it—and if so how?—or resisting it—and, if so to what end?

There are some who hold that 'the structures and methods of education must help to sustain the traditional values of society',[28] and that it is both desirable and possible to relate traditional values and traditional religion to the new situations and experiences which are the products of technological, industrial and social change. There are others, however, who hold that new values are emerging and that these are positive and life-enhancing in so far as they are representative of a movement away from an imperialistic and materialistic culture within which traditional values have become trapped and which is undergoing a 'crisis of legitimation'.[29] On the latter view, the emergence of new values is seen to herald the renewal of culture, as may be discerned within new political and religious groups which are opposed to the most typical features of the industrial/technological society, namely to its goals of competitive economic strength, to its exploitation and spoilation of natural resources, its fierce defence of the superiority of the Western way of life and its adulation of masculine toughness.[30] If, as is argued, such movements represent a deliberate attempt to promote values which sustain and further the growth of the human spirit and contribute to the achievement of human dignity, even though they may appear to be in conflict with traditional values, their existence cannot be ignored and the values they espouse cannot be disregarded.

But our response to 'value change', like our response to the issue of the status of knowledge, will be influenced by factors beyond the rational. We have already noted how feelings and personal histories may predispose us towards acceptance of a particular perspective or reinforce our attachment to a particular value position. Another powerful influence on our value position, however, is one which derives from our participation within certain social structures. Our membership of a social class, a profession, a community of faith or a political party are particularly obvious examples. Whereas individuals have beliefs or opinions which they use to conduct their lives, organised collections of people have 'ideologies' or systems of thought which serve the interests of the group. It is important, therefore, that these brief, preliminary observations about values and culture (to which I will be giving more detailed attention in Chapter Three) are now linked with a consideration of some of the ways in which our thinking about education and the curriculum is subject to ideological influences.

3. Ideological influences on educational values

(i) The concept of ideology

In recent times there has been a concern on the part of certain social theorists and sociologists of education[31] to draw attention to the 'social and political embeddedness of the educational system . . . and to suggest ways in which issues of power, ideology and control are implicated in educational arrangements'.[32] They have stressed that curricula and pedagogy do not exist in abstraction from social and political contexts and are not ideologically neutral but *value laden*. In other words, decisions taken about the content of the curriculum reflect particular views about the desirability of preserving certain political, social, economic, religious and professional interests supportive of a particular type of society. Such views are given coherence by their relationship to (a) a world-view or world picture of what is happening in human life, (b) central values and goals that are considered desirable in human life, and

(c) an image of the process of social change (or of maintaining the *status quo*) and the particular tactics deemed appropriate for achieving this according to the world view, values and goals.[33] The combination of (a), (b) and (c) constitutes an *ideology* or system of thought. It is important that we recognise, however, that an ideology is a *socially founded* thought system, not a set of opinions shared by a number of individuals, and that it operates through social structures. Ben Cosin offers the following explanation of the relationship between ideology and social structure and how ideology relates to education:

> . . . *since social structures operate in a different manner from individuals, it will not be surprising if the systems of belief which enable them to carry on also operate differently from the opinions of individuals. . . . When we find systems of ideas working in a social structure and helping to keep it going, we describe it as an* ideology; *we refer to it as the ideology of that structure . . . We may expect to find systems of thought perpetuating themselves within the system of education. Those who take part in education do not necessarily absorb in a passive way what they are told, but still the descriptions, explanations and evaluations which they acquire are largely constructed from within the educational system rather than invented from scratch . . . One reason for studying social structure is plainly that the better you know about the factors which influence you, the more likely you are to be able to control them rather than merely be their playthings . . .[34]*

In his research into ideological conflict in inner-city schools, Gerald Grace distinguishes between conservative, liberal and radical ideologies which inform teacher behaviour.[35] To provide a summary of his descriptions of the essential characteristics of each ideological perspective may assist us in identifying and assessing the extent to which ideological influences have a bearing on our own thinking about the purpose of schools and the aims of the curriculum and which may predispose us towards certain values and attitudes.

Conservative ideologies, according to Grace, emphasise the rule of law and discipline, strong leadership, clearly defined roles, a hierarchy of power, and define 'good teaching' as a reassertion of the absolutes of 'standards' and of 'received cultural forms'. *Liberal ideologies* offer various alternative standpoints; 'liberal pragmatism' sees the problem of inner-city schools as one of technical inefficiency, which can be repaired through better management, and low expectations of teachers for the achievements and behaviour of pupils, which can be improved through increased pedagogical optimism; 'liberal romanticism' looks to a more progressive and relevant curriculum with teaching addressed more to the needs of the child and with opportunities for self-expression overcoming alienation, pupil resistance and problems of under-achievement; 'liberal social democracy' holds that inequalities in society at large can be met by positive discrimination in favour of deprived areas and the creation of urban community schools as the means of generating active and responsible local democracy. *Radical ideologies* see the problem arising from the processes of cultural and personal domination in which schools are engaged. They hold that the crisis will continue until they cease to be essentially custodial and authoritarian and until they employ a practice based upon a relativist and non-hierarchic view of knowledge, and encourage 'the practice of freedom' rather than continue to engage in 'an enterprise of cultural invasion and domination'. Finally, *Marxist ideologies* claim that the schools are repro-ducing the social relations of a capitalist mode of production and are a crucial part of the 'ideological state apparatus'. Teachers should reject professionalism, make common cause with pupils and workers and work to raise political consciousness.

It is not difficult to see that implicit in these different ideologies are different conceptions of the human being, human society, the purpose of schools and the curriculum, and the role of the teachers. In other words, teachers are subject to the influences of conflicting 'ideologies of education'.

(ii) Ideologies of education

Although to my mind education is not an ideology but only subject to ideological influence, some writers have attempted to identify and describe 'ideologies of education' and to indicate their particular im-plications for curriculum theory and construction. For example, Cosin identifies four ideologies which he regards 'as constituting the bulk of thinking about education in this country—at least in England'.[36] These he describes as *Elitist/Conservative* (having a concern for the mainte-nance of the established standards of cultural excellence through tradi-tional methods of selection); *Rationalisation/Technocratic* (having a con-cern for the vocational relevance of education); *Romantic/Individualist* (having a concern for the development of all the individual's innate abilities); and *Egalitarian/Democratic* (having a concern for the princi-ple that all have an equal right to be educated).

Denis Lawton[37] distinguishes between *Classical* and *Romantic* ideologies of education and summarises their different characteristics and the attitudes which they seek to promote by means of two juxta-posed lists:

Classical	Romantic
Subject-centred	Child-centred
Skills	Creativity
Instruction	Experience
Information	Discovery
Obedience	Awareness
Conformity	Originality
Discipline	Freedom

He shows how the two ideologies might be polarised on questions of knowledge and the curriculum:

Classical	*Romantic*
Objectives: Acquiring knowledge	*Processes*: 'Living' attitudes and values
Content: Subjects	*Experience*: Real-life topics and projects
Method: Didactic instruction Competition	*Method*: Involvement Co-operation
Evaluation: By tests (teacher-set) and examinations (public and competitive)	*Evaluation*: Self-assessment (in terms of self-improvement)

Lawton refers to another set of classical and romantic pairs put forward by Malcolm Skilbeck:

Classical	Romantic
Standards	Expression
Structure	Style
Unity	Diversity
Excellence	Excellences
Rationality	Experience
Culture	Subcultures

Standards are externally imposed by 'society', whereas expression is unique and individual; structure is concerned with established concepts and processes of the disciplines, style is personal; unity is socially defined, diversity is a move away from norms and social consensus; excellence assumes one agreed set of standards, excellences assumes a variety of views; rationality means working according to the rules, experience implies individual freedom from rules; curriculum based on culture is monolithic, one based on subcultures is pluralistic.[38]

William Reid, a British curriculum theorist, distinguishes four 'perspectives on the curriculum' each indicative of a different set of assumptions about 'the nature of human society and how it intersects with the lives of its members'.[39] *The Systemic Perspective* has as one of the main objects of curriculum studies the search for efficient ways of planning, implementing and evaluating curricula. Objective data, including the measurement of abilities and attitudes, statistical representations of trends, logistics of school organisation, and so on, are used in the design of universal paradigms and models for curriculum development. It is assumed that the solution of curriculum problems is dependent upon rational procedures which are universally applicable, and that the method's scientific approach enables curricular questions to be treated in a *value-free* manner.

In contrast to the systemic theorist whose thinking is rooted in existing social forms, radical thinking relates to what would exist in the aftermath of fundamental social change. *The Radical Perspective* thus places stress on explaining the determinants of the curriculum and raising 'revolutionary consciousness' as a first step towards the transformation of society. Only afterwards can attention be given to matters of curriculum design.[40]

Whereas the systemic and radical curriculum theorists are concerned in their different ways with questions of the 'macro-structure' of society, those who adopt *The Existential Perspective* concentrate on the mind of the individual who experiences the curriculum. Reid comments:

For them, the reality of life consists not in classes, capitalism or hegemony, on the one hand, nor in the administrative processes and established structures, on the other, but in the relationship of the individual consciousness to the external world.[41]

The intention here is to promote an exploration, through existential analysis, of those features of the individual's experience which constitute personal awareness of identity or 'autobiography'.[42] Reid sees existential curriculum theory as essentially psychological in character, allied to humanistic, introspective psychology which is the opposite of objectivist, psychometric psychology favoured by systemic theorists.

Finally, curriculum theorists who adopt *The Deliberative Approach* argue that the central concern of curriculum studies should be to improve the teacher's capacity, both individually and collectively, to make good decisions about teaching and learning, and that it is possible for this to be done in a scholarly and theoretical way. The assumptions of the deliberative position are diametrically opposed to those of the radical perspective while sharing the exploratory outlook of the existential perspective.

They comprise an emphasis on the individual as a morally responsible person, a belief in the possibility of improvement through working with present institutions, and in the efficacy of consensual approaches to the identification and solution of problems[43]

(iii) Ideological influences on religious education

Although, as we noted earlier, the dominant influence on the study of the religious education curriculum during the last fifteen years or so has been that of a rationalist philosophy of education, the 'objectives' approach to curriculum development in religious education which has followed from this has fallen short of the scientific and systematic rigour which Reid identifies as central to *The Systemic Perspective*.[44] It may be the case, however, that the other three perspectives which Reid describes can be more appropriately related to a contemporary understanding of the nature, aims and content of religious education and be better able to stimulate the development of the subject's educational potential. In this book, for example, I am attempting to engage in 'curriculum deliberation' as a means of identifying criteria for curriculum decision-making and for choosing teaching strategies in religious education. But while being influenced by the *Deliberative Perspective*, I take seriously the importance given by *The Radical Perspective* to recognising the social, cultural and ideological determinants of the curriculum (hence this opening chapter), and, as will be especially apparent in the later chapters, follow *The Existential Perspective* in stressing that it is the contribution that the study of religion can make to self-awareness and self-knowledge which constitutes religious education's major educational value. What I will be considering carefully in Chapter Six is how the conception of religious education which I will be putting forward is subject to ideological influences and how the value assumptions which underlie it can be justified. At this point, however, in illustration of how conceptions of religious education *are* subject to conflicting ideological influences I propose to consider two different conceptions of the subject and then to comment on the value assumptions underlying each of them.

(a) Religious education: conception one: the value assumptions of 'Religious Absolutism'

In the 1930s and 1940s, when it could be assumed that the beliefs and values contained within the Christian revelation provided not only the essential underpinning of English culture but the basis for communal life, including that of the schools, there could be but one conception of religious education—that of instructing pupils in the Christian faith, inducting them into the Christian interpretion of human experience, and inculcating in them Christian values. The value assumptions of this conception are clear and unambiguous. It is a conception of religious education in which Christian values and beliefs are accorded an absolute status and provide a norm against which other values and beliefs are to be assessed. We can also note that it is a conception of religious education which accords to theology an absolute status over and against the secular disciplines of education. The relationship which is thus envisaged between religion and education is an imperialistic one in which Christian values and beliefs are applied to education and exercise a normative function within the educational enterprise. It is a conception of religious education which is informed by what we might call an ideology of 'Christian Absolutism' and, as such, it is entirely resistant to the notion of religious beliefs and values becoming relativised in order to accommodate the study of religions within the curriculum to educational principles and procedures. Indeed, it is a conception of religious education which recognises no difference or distinction between Christian nurture and religious education and holds to the view that the task of the school in relation to religious teaching is identical with that of the Christian church.[45] Additionally we should note that, although I have placed this conception of religious education within the historical context of England in the 1930s and 1940s, by substituting 'Islam' or 'Islamic' for 'Christian' I have provided an adequate description of the value assumption of 'Religious Absolutism' that underlies the Islamic conception of education and religious education and which accounts for the present demands by Muslims in England for Muslim schools and Islamic religious education in state schools.

But when, as is now the case, a number of identifiably different religious traditions exist in parallel in the context of a society which also embraces a variety of secular stances and which is characterised by a predominantly secular consciousness, the divine authority by which particular values and beliefs are given an absolute and normative status in one religious tradition cannot be assumed to be prescriptive for the others. Similarly, if education is by nature *contextual*—that is, it exists, operates and participates in a specific social, cultural and ideological context—it cannot accommodate itself to the specific values of one religious tradition among many, even if, as it is sometimes argued, that tradition has a special relationship to the incipient culture of that society or meets the felt needs of an ethnic minority. Under such conditions, a conception of religious education which is based on assumptions of 'Religious Absolutism' must be questioned and alternative conceptions which are able to accommodate religious and ideological pluralism must be found.

(b) Religious education: conception two: the value assumptions of 'Religious Equality'/'Neutrality'

An alternative conception of religious education which has received widespread support in the last fifteen or so years seeks to treat all religious views and beliefs *within the context of education* as 'claims' of equal value and as characteristic forms of religious experience. It is a conception which is informed by those principles which are derived from a phenomenological approach to the study of religions. Supporters of a phenomenological approach argue that because learners are required to distance themselves from their own pre-suppositions and beliefs (by 'bracketing' them), the study can be 'objective' and yet directed towards an understanding of the subjective consciousness of the religious adherent, something which is essential if a religion is to be understood as it is felt to be by those who practise it.[46] Furthermore, they argue, a phenomenological approach does not impose a 'construct' of its own upon a religion; its concern is to elucidate a religion's own self-understanding. The religions are studied from the standpoint of the adherent, not from some position outside them. In so far as this is the intention, the method of study itself is believed to be 'neutral' or value-free. On this basis, *for the purpose of study*, all religious views and beliefs are judged to be 'truth claims' of equal value.[47] This conception of religious education, which is informed by what we might call an ideology of 'Religious Equality' or 'Religious Neutrality', accepts, therefore, that the *relativisation* of religious values and beliefs (ie, treating them as equal claims to truth) is an inevitable consequence of studying religions within a secular educational context.

The notion that a phenomenological approach provides a neutral way of treating religions while recognising that each is distinctive and unique has, however, been criticised by some academics and members of different faiths as damaging to religion.[48] Their principal objection is that the approach 'domesticates' religion by reducing it to a secular academic discipline or to an expression of human behaviour and by equating 'religious understanding' with a way of interpreting or categorising human experience. They point out that for religious adherents their religion is a vehicle for revealed, eternal Truth and they, as believers, are in the presence of Truth. Their religion is not a way of living in the world—a 'stance for living'; neither is it a set of religious responses to questions imposed by the human condition—a 'belief system'; nor is it a way of interpreting and categorising human experience—a 'form of knowledge'. Neither can their religion be known or judged by its capacity to fulfil truth tests based on criteria other than the Truth within their religion. It is this Truth, not a 'truth claim', which is the object of study. Furthermore, there can be no question of studying a religion for some instrumental purpose other than that of gaining greater insight into Truth and strengthening one's commitment to it. 'Religious understanding' can only be meaningful if it refers to the level of consciousness of one's awareness and knowledge of God and of one's dependence upon Him. In this sense a method of studying a religion can be neither 'objective' nor 'neutral'. Neither can it proceed on the assumption that all religious views are claims of equal value, for this is contrary to a religion's self-understanding and its understanding of other religions.[49] The following statement by Professor Syed Ali Ashraf, director general of The Islamic Academy in Cambridge, illustrates the incompatibility of the value assumptions of the phenomenological approach with those of 'Religious Absolutism':

> . . . the secularist state schools (are) creating non-believers in spite of religious education. All subjects are taughts from a secularist point of view. Children are encouraged to be critical of their own traditions and values and even of faith. Doubts are encouraged. Whereas a Muslim teaches a child to pray to God for forgiveness and to strengthen his/her faith, the rationalist teacher teaches the student to explore on his/her own or with reference to other faiths and ideologies. The Islamic method of removing doubts and the strengthening of faith is completely ignored. It is desirable for a Muslim child to be open-minded and be ready to admit the truth of other religions and ideologies, but it would be wrong to be critical of one's own religion without any norm to judge which is true and which is false. . . . . . We want Muslim children to acquire that norm of judgment from Islam.[50]

Another way of expressing these objections, then, is to say that a method of study which claims to be objective and neutral imposes its own ideological perspective on the religions being studied. In so far as it may only be possible for one ideology to be criticised from the standpoint of another ideology, so, it may be argued, descriptions of ideologies (and of religions) reflect the standpoint from which they are described. Because these objections challenge the 'taken-for-granted' assumptions of many religious education teachers that the phenomenological approach provides the only satisfactory rationale for religious education in state schools[51], I will give closer attention to the arguments

of its critics. In the United Kingdom, the views of Bishop Lesslie Newbigin may be taken as typical of this viewpoint.

Newbigin says of the *Birmingham Agreed Syllabus* (1975) that it regards all religions and ideologies from the point of view of a secular,
liberal inhabitant of the Western capitalist, post-Christian world'[52]. His
further criticism is that the ideological stance of the syllabus is 'concealed from view' and yet what will be communicated to pupils 'will be
the ideology which informs the syllabus, which is as much one of the
possible "stances for living" as Marxism or Christianity'. Finally he
asserts: 'There is no standpoint which is above all standpoints.' What
observations might be made on these criticisms and comments?

Firstly, in asserting that 'there is no standpoint which is above all
standpoints', Newbigin would appear to be agreeing with the view that
curricula and pedagogy do not exist in abstraction and are not ideologically neutral but value-laden. In other words, we can suppose he
would agree with the view that any educational stance we may adopt
towards the study of beliefs and values in the curriculum, or, indeed,
towards the place of religious values in education itself, cannot purport
to be either 'neutral' or 'objective'. That the syllabus has an ideological
stance is not, therefore, at issue, for this would be true of any syllabus;
so Newbigin's objections appear to be (a) to the *particular* ideological
stance adopted by the syllabus and (b) to the way in which this is 'concealed from view'. Are these objections reasonable? A close examination of the Introduction to the Agreed Syllabus reveals two statements
which are of relevance to this question.

The syllabus should thus be used to enlarge and deepen the pupils'
understanding of religion by studying world religions, and by exploring
all those elements in human experience which raise questions about life's
ultimate meaning and value. This involves informing pupils in a de-
scriptive, critical and experiential manner about what religion is, and
increasing their sensitivity to the areas of experience from which a reli-
gious view of life may arise. It should stimulate within the pupils, and
assist them in the search for, a personal sense of meaning in life, whilst
enabling them to understand the beliefs and commitments of others.[53]

. . . Second, the tendency when looking at world religions was towards
a comparison of other faiths with one considered as self-evidently supe-
rior to the rest; whereas the approach now is to study them objectively
and for their own sake. . .'[54]

Taking the second quotation first, we note that pupils are to study
world religions 'objectively and for their own sake'. We have already
recognised that no method of study can be without some presupposi-

tions and that value-free methods are, in fact, value-laden. If in using the word 'objective' the framers of the syllabus are claiming that the study can be value-free, they are mistaken and Newbigin is correct in pointing this out. The phrase 'for their own sake' presents several problems. If in using this phrase the framers are excluding any possibility of pupils gaining educational value *beyond* that of understanding the religions they study, this is inconsistent with the stated intention that studying religions should 'stimulate within pupils, and assist them in the search for, a personal sense of meaning in life . . .'. Similarly, if by using this phrase they are implying that pupils through religious education in schools come to understand and experience religion in exactly the same way as do adherents studying a religion 'for its own sake' within a faith community, they are contradicting the stated view of the syllabus that religious education is 'subject to the same disciplines as other areas of study' in the school curriculum and that it is 'directed towards a critical understanding of the religious and moral dimensions of human experience and away from attempting to foster the claims of particular religious standpoints'.[55] There is a strong probability, however, that all that the framers intend to convey by the phrases 'to study them objectively and for their own sake' is that the *ideological* (ie, the educational) stance of the syllabus is not comparative or proselytising. We may assume that Newbigin would support such a stance as a necessary one within any educational, as opposed to faith nurturing, process.[56]

With regard to the first quotation, the statement that studying religions means 'informing pupils in a descriptive, critical and experiental manner about what religion is . . .' indicates the compatibility of the syllabus' assumptions with those of the phenomenological approach which we examined earlier. One suspects, therefore, that Newbigin's objections are not directed only to the Birmingham Agreed Syllabus but to the phenomenological approach itself. He clearly has profound reservations about the capacity of this approach to provide an understanding of 'what religion is'. But the use of the phenomenological approach is a consequence of taking the study of religion outside the context of the faith community and placing it within the context of secular education. What is seen to 'domesticate' religion is not, therefore, just the use of this method of study but the restrictions which education places on religion by bringing it within the constraints of the secular curriculum. What is at issue here, therefore, is how education should relate to religion and what contribution the study of religion should make to pupils' learning. Clearly there is divergence between the opinions and expectations of some members of the faith communities and those of the secular educators. Let us consider this problem in more detail.

(c) The problems presented by placing the study of religion within the value-laden context of education

As we have seen, education is not a value-free process; nor does it seek to create a value-free context within which to engage in, for example, the study of religions. The value-laden context of education derives from its intention to bring about changes in the way in which pupils understand themselves and the world; thus, educational aims and objectives are, by nature, value-laden; they cannot be value-free or 'neutral' and remain educational. When we seek to place the study of religions within this context we are faced, therefore, with a difficult question, namely, how are we to treat something which is inherently value-laden (ie, a religious belief/value system) in a context which itself is value-laden with value assumptions which are not necessarily compatible with those of religion and religions?

Neither of the two conceptions of religious education we have considered—one based on assumptions of religious absolutism and the other on assumptions of religious equality/neutrality—provides an adequate answer to this question. For example, the first conception requires that the values which inform education are the values of a particular religion. This is clearly unacceptable. The aims and objectives of religious education in the state schools cannot be religious, nor can they be determined solely by aims which are internal to religion. The second conception of religious education, rather than solving the problem, only accentuates its complexity. The value assumptions of religious equality/neutrality are derived not from education but from the application of phenomenological method to the study of religion. These assumptions, like the method itself, are seen by critics to impose a perspective on the religions being studied which is contrary to their self-understanding and subsequently misrepresents them. Their view is that the use of phenomenological method, therefore, is unable to promote *understanding* of a religion, for a religion can only be understood from the inside. The implication of this view is that any method or context of study which does not share the value and belief assumptions of the religion being studied can only produce a distorted understanding of that religion; thus the study of religion cannot be subject to those critieria which education as a normative, discriminatory concept requires. This view must ultimately lead to adopting a position which necessitates agreement with the first conception of religious education which we have already judged to be unacceptable.[57]

But the second conception of religious education is not without its difficulties also for educationists. In requiring the beliefs and values of the pupils to be 'bracketed' as well as the beliefs and values of the religions being studied, the use of phenomenological method effectively invalidates the educational process. This is because the descriptive and non-evaluative nature of phenomenological study is incompatible with the critical and evaluative nature of educational enquiry. For pupils to gain personally from the study, education must enable them to relate what they learn to their own experience and to become aware of the ways in which their own perceptions of what they are studying influence their understanding. This is precisely what the use of phenomenological method (as it is commonly applied in religious education) cannot permit because it infringes its requirement that procedures for studying religion are neutral. If value-laden educational objectives are effectively excluded by the use of this method, what is the educational value of studying religions in this manner? It is not surprising that there is confusion over what may be regarded as legitimate educational aims for religious education if this conception of the subject is adopted.

To return to Newbigin's criticisms, there are some indications that he is prepared to tolerate a phenomenological approach to the study of religions in school provided that 'the pretence of neutrality' and 'the insistence on "objectivity"' are dropped and that the 'ideology which underlies this Syllabus' is exposed for critical examination. In illustration of this point he says:

> If. . . I try to study Hinduism and all the other religions from—so to speak—an equal distance, as this Syllabus suggests, then I must also undertake the study of the ideology which underlies this Syllabus, and must answer the question: 'What are the grounds for believing that this way of looking at Hinduism is true, as against the Hindu way of looking at Hinduism?'[58]

Rather than weakening the case for the retention of the place of religion within education, Newbigin's suggestions may indicate, it seems to me, a possible way forward in strengthening it. If ideology exerts so profound an influence on human thought and behaviour, and if education, because it is contextual, cannot be ideologically neutral, then it may be argued that a fundamental task of schools and their curricula is to promote in pupils increased consciousness of ideological influence on their attitudes and values and on the way they see the world and themselves. Religions are important and powerful ideologies existing alongside their secular alternatives in our plural society, but it is probably true, as Newbigin concedes, that a secular point of view 'is naturally accepted by the majority of the inhabitants of this corner of the world as being simply "how things really are"'. While it is the responsibility of education to encourage pupils to be critical of their own perspective by, for example, confronting them with alternative perspectives such as those of the world's great religions and ideologies, it does not necessarily follow that the study itself cannot proceed from a perspective which is consistent with the dominant ideological assumptions of the majority of our pupils. That this perspective is 'our particular cultural model' which inhabitants in other parts of the world will only recognise as 'myth' is not in itself an adequate reason for substituting an alternative ideological perspective, such as a Christian or Muslim one, with which the majority of pupils will be less familiar. It is essential, however, that the perspective from which religions and ideologies are studied is not 'concealed from view'; indeed, far from claiming that the study is objective, neutral or value-free, it must be disclosed for what it is—a *secular* study of religion, drawing upon a variety of disciplines, including psychology, sociology, phenomenology, history and theology, and governed by those educational principles which relate to the manner in which all subject disciplines in the curriculum, including religion, should be investigated (ie, in a manner which assists the development of cognitive perspective or rationality, promotes understanding of the structure and procedures of the discipline, recognises the integrity, autonomy and voluntariness of the pupil, and so on).

Although the application of certain phenomenological techniques to the area of study enables, within the limitations of the method, religious faith, as understood by adherents, to be described and expressed, how pupils come to understand this will inevitably be influenced by the fact that the study is taking place within the context of a secular educational enterprise with an ideological perspective which is significantly different from those of the religions being studied and with goals determined by essentially secular values and assumptions rather than religious ones. The problem that this educational *use* of religion raises for the faith communities is to decide whether it is more desirable to exclude the study of religion from schools altogether because religious beliefs cannot be conveyed in a manner which enables the pupils' understanding of them to be identical to that of adherents, or whether it is more desirable that pupils should have some opportunity to explore religious beliefs and values even though their understanding of them may, in some respects, differ from those of adherents. If there is a price to be paid for establishing a relationship between education and religion, then, it seems to me, that cost has to be met by the religions, not by education. It is a matter for the faith communities to consider whether that cost is too great.

(iv) Religions as ideologies

As the previous section illustrates, personal religious faith can be an influential factor in predisposing us to support one conception of religious education and to oppose another. But the 'synoptic' function of

46

religious belief means that just as theological assumptions may influence our view of the nature of religious education, its content and its methods of study, so too can they predispose us to accept, for example, certain views of the nature of knowledge, the nature of childhood, and the nature and aims of education. The conflict that can exist between religious ideologies and between religious and secular ideologies with regard to the principles of education is very well illustrated by J M Halstead in his book *The Case for Muslim Voluntary-Aided Schools*,[59] viz:

A contrast between the principles of Islamic education and Western secular education (as perceived by Muslims)

Principles	Islamic model	Secular model
Aim of education	The good man	The rational man
Highest personal values	Spiritual wisdom	Material well-being, happiness
Nature of morality	Divine law	Relativism or subjectivism
Focus of values	Community of believers	Individual fulfilment
Nature of reality	Unity (of God, humanity, religion and knowledge)	Diversity and pluralism
Attitude to man	God's earthly vicegerent.	A self-sufficient being
Attitude to knowledge	A form of worship	A goal in itself
Source of knowledge	Revelation	Reason, the experimental method
Foundation of belief	Authority	Rational autonomy
Attitude to belief	Certainty	Doubt, critical openness
Approach to religion	Commitment, faith	Scepticism
Valued state of mind	Submission, reverence	Pride, ambition
View of multiculturalism	Moral chaos	Healthy pluralism

It is not my intention to comment on these irreconcilably opposite perspectives within the scope of this exploratory study; suffice it to say that other than by means of Muslim parents having recourse to legislation permitting them to withdraw their children for Islamic religious instruction, the state schools of a pluralist democracy cannot embrace as 'educational principles' what are, for one religion, tenets of faith. In many ways there are parallels to be discerned in this situation with that which obtained in the second half of the nineteenth century when some of the Christian churches made similar demands of state school education. There have, of course, always been tensions between conservative, liberal and radical religious views, both within the religions, between the religions and between the religions and the secular ideologies. What divides religious opinion is the fundamentally different responses that religious traditions and religious denominations make to change. Engagement with change is a necessary feature of all living religions in order to ensure their survival, and in this sense no religion is a static, fixed system of beliefs or ritual practices. *Conservatives* hold that in the face of change the tradition must be preserved, taught and developed for the sake of the eternal truths it contains. *Liberals* hold that religious beliefs must evolve and develop in response to changing circumstances, and that the tradition must undergo constant reform and renewal if it is to retain its validity as a vehicle of truth. *Radicals*, as represented, for example, by Christian liberation and feminist theologians, hold that the tradition must be purged of those elements which support certain types of oppressive relationships in society and which are antithetical to human freedom and dignity; they stress the importance of faith finding its fullest expression in contemporary social and political movements, especially those offering a radical critique of what a society takes to be 'normative' views of the human. A further religious response to change, and one that often follows a period when liberal views have been widely held, is that of fundamentalism. *Fundamentalists* often hold that the tradition has been compromised by attempts to accommodate change, and that in order to restore the true faith the tradition must revert to its original form and all later interpretations and practices be repudiated. Fundamentalism, like the emergence of religious cults and sects, is normally expressive of the desire for the renewal of absolute values and absolute standards in religion. In so far as the major religious and secular institutions may have moved away from these, fundamentalism represents the re-assertion of the need for acceptance of a total religious authority, such as is now occurring in certain Islamic states.

In functional terms, a 'religious view of life' is a 'religious ideology' sharing many of the characteristics of 'political ideology'. For example, both provide 'synoptic meaning' which encompasses the whole of life and predisposes those committed to the ideology to hold only to views which are consistent with its tenets or beliefs. While each type of ideology constitutes a very powerful reactionary, progressive or revolutionary force in its own right, when—as occasionally happens—religious and political ideologies fuse together, they can exert a most potent influence in the life of the individual and, under certain circumstances, in society. Contrasting examples would be the combination of conservative religious and political ideologies sustaining a policy of racial apartheid and the combination of radical religious and political ideologies sustaining a bloody revolution to overthrow it. In both cases education will be seen as an important instrument for effecting ideological conversion and so extending the ideology's influence in pursuit of its utopian goal.

In the United Kingdom, the only formal aspect of a state school's social structure which has retained a direct relationship to religion and religious values is its provision for religious education and school worship. This has the effect of limiting both the positive and negative effects of religious ideology within the life of the school. With regular school worship now in decline and a tendency for upper secondary school religious education to lose its identity within integrated personal, social and moral education courses, the influence of religious values on education is likely to be even weaker in the future than at present. This situation makes it all the more important that those who seek to preserve the place of religious values in education are scrupulous in their concern to reconcile the presence and expression of such values in the curriculum and the ethos of the school with the demands of an educational process which is committed to the principles of critical openness, rationality and respect for individual conscience. We have already considered the necessity of religious education conforming to these educational principles, and here we should recognise that if it fails to do so it jeopardises its place in the formal curriculum. That state schools should still be required by law to provide an act of worship for pupils at the beginning of each school day seems to me to be wholly indefensible from an educational point of view and carries with it at least two added dangers. Firstly, it perpetuates, quite unjustifiably, the mistaken notion (so apparent in television 'reports' on and discussion of religious education) that religious education is the natural extension of this faith nurturing activity. Secondly, it places the majority of the pupils in a false relationship with religion and religious faith and one which is entirely inconsistent with the relationship which religious education seeks to foster between pupils and this area of study. It would be unfortunate if the association in the public mind between school worship and classroom religious education meant that the strong claims to educational legitimacy of the latter were contaminated by the untenable position of the former. It is clear that whereas the religious education clauses of the 1944 Education Act possess a flexibility which enables religious educa-

49

tion to respond positively to the changing circumstances of our society and are, therefore, worthy of retention and preservation, this is not so of the worship clauses. Thus, as a vehicle for the communication and exploration of religious values within an educational context, school worship has little to commend it.

This then leaves only the individual religious believer—teacher or pupil—as a mediator of religious values within the life of the school, and here we must assume that this will be by way of personal example rather than by a process of overt evangelism. While it is important that all teachers have a carefully formulated value stance, it does not follow that this should be prescriptive of the value stance of the school or restrictive of the values to be encountered through the curriculum. A guiding principle here might be that the teacher's own value position should not prevent them from fulfilling their task of encouraging pupils to formulate their own. Such a principle is easily stated but not always easily applied, not least because it reflects a position which is antithetical to some conceptions of the nature and demands of personal religious faith. How far individual teachers are able to agree with such a principle (and, of course, with any other of the suggestions made in this book) will depend in large measure upon their own theological assumptions. The maintenance of the educational integrity of a process which brings children and young people into contact with religions and religious beliefs is dependent upon teachers being willing to make a *professional* commitment to fulfilling that process's educational goals. The willingness of teachers who hold to a religious faith to meet this requirement, however, will be conditional upon their willingness and ability to develop a coherent 'theology of education' in which the demands of their religious faith and those of education are reconciled.[60]

4. The child

Postman and Weingartner suggest that teachers reveal the way in which they understand the human mind by the metaphors they use when describing what they do for a living. They comment:

For example, there is the type of teacher who believes he is in the lighting business. We may call him the Lamplighter. When he is asked what he is trying to do with his students, his reply is something like this: 'I want to illuminate their minds, to allow some light to penetrate the darkness.' Then there is the Gardener. He says: 'I want to cultivate their minds, to fertilise them, so that the seeds I plant will flourish.' There is also the Personnel Manager, who wants nothing more than to keep his students' minds busy, to make them efficient and industrious. The Muscle Builder wants to strengthen flabby minds, and the Bucket

Filler to fill them up. . . . The Potter wants to mould minds, the Dietician to feed minds, and the Builder to provide minds with a sound and sturdy foundation.[61]

Behind each of these metaphors lie certain assumptions about the child and about 'learning' and 'teaching'. Indeed, one could say that ideologies of education are most easily identified by the metaphors they employ to define childhood.[62] For example, we have already noted the existence of a 'Romantic' ideology of education which has as its central concern the development of an individual's innate abilities and which includes amongst its characteristics an emphasis on creativity, experience, discovery, awareness, originality and freedom. This ideology is usually traced back to the romantic philosophy of Rousseau (1712–1778) with its all-pervading notion that children should be allowed to develop 'naturally, as Nature intended, unsullied by the corrupting influences of society'. Such a view is based on the assumption that children possess within themselves 'natural goodness' and are born, in Wordsworth's words, in 'freedom and innocence' and have an uncorrupted nature which, if they are allowed to follow their natural impulses, will realise itself in adult life in the form of human perfection.[63] In the nineteenth century this view of childhood reached its peak in the educational writings of Friedrich Froebel (1782–1852) which are full of metaphors drawn from the language of gardening. For Froebel, the expert teacher, like the expert gardener, provides the right environment for the seeds of perfection which lie within the child to unfold and grow towards perfection and unity with God and Nature.[64]

That this philosophy derives from certain theological premises, largely pantheistic or deistic, and is imbued with a mystical element, is very apparent. It is a 'natural theology' which is in sharp contrast to that of the Calvinistic type, itself very influential from the sixteenth to the middle of the nineteenth century, which derives from the entirely different premise that the nature of the child is depraved and corrupt, inherently sinful and given to wilfulness and idleness.[65] Thus, in this latter model, natural innocence is refuted and the child's nature is thought to need 're-forming' by bringing it under the influence of teachers (who have, of course, already been 're-formed' themselves) who have the responsibility of ensuring that the child rapidly acquires a moral state characterised by humility, industry and obedience. This state is to be achieved through corrective treatment involving moral and religious instruction and, as necessary, discipline and punishment. Ultimately, however, the child's 're-formation' (ie, salvation) is dependent upon the grace of God.

In outlining these divergent views of childhood I am not wishing to infer that, in the form in which they arose, they continue to provide viable conceptions of the child today. Indeed, speculation on the 'nature' of the child, in the sense that it was an important issue in earlier centuries, has now been replaced by an altogether more scientific emphasis on discovering how children learn and, in the light of these discoveries, devising strategies by which they may best be taught. Teachers are no longer expected to seek answers to their questions about children and pedagogy in the realms of metaphysics and theology but to turn to the authoritative discipline of psychology in its various forms—developmental, behaviourist, psychoanalytic and so on.

It is, of course, very important that due regard is given to the cognitive theories of, for example, Piaget and Bruner when devising curricula and learning experiences, and to the operant conditioning theories of Skinner when considering issues of motivation, control and teaching strategy. Similarly, in thinking about the personal development of pupils and trying to understand what happens to young people during adolescence, reference to the theories of Erik Erikson is a *sine qua non* for teachers. What we are offered by these psychologists, however, are closer to theories of human *behaviour* than to theories of human *nature*. These theories, although not necessarily addressed directly to the question 'What is the nature of childhood?', have assumed, at least in the popular mind, the status of theories of human nature, and consequently are sometimes used to support or reinforce certain ideological conceptions of education in a manner which may not have been intended by their originators. In illustration of this point, and as a way of raising issues about children, learning and teaching which are germane to the task of examining our own assumptions, especially about personal development, I will consider in detail a *behaviourist* theory of human behaviour and the conception of human nature which it may be seen to support and promote.

(i) Behaviourist psychology and human behaviour

'Behaviourism' as a 'school' of psychology gained its impetus from the work of J B Watson (1878–1958) who, reacting against attempts to explain human actions by reference to unconscious motives, as proposed by Freud, or to instincts, placed stress upon the systematic observation of behaviour and the explanation of such behaviour in terms of cumulative conditioning. Watson thus sought to place the study of human behaviour on a strictly scientific basis—in short, to develop a 'science of behaviour'. In his book *Beyond Freedom and Dignity*, B F Skinner, the foremost exponent of behaviourism today, indicates that such an approach requires that:

> . . . . *the autonomous agent* (ie, presumably, the human being) *to which behaviour has traditionally been attributed is replaced by the*

environment—the environment in which the species evolved and in which the behaviour of the individual is shaped and maintained.[66]

By controlling the environment in a systematic manner through a system of 'operant conditioning' using schedules of reinforcement (usually rewards, but also punishments), Skinner has demonstrated that human behaviour can be changed to accord with the human behaviour required. That such modifications of human behaviour can be achieved relatively easily is seen to indicate that human behaviour (and, by implication, human nature—although behaviourists avoid this term) is infinitely malleable and that its form and expression at any one time is a product of the conditioning influence of culture. Skinner's thesis in *Beyond Freedom and Dignity* is that, given the capacity to design and create an entire culture which can eradicate, through its conditioning influence, all those features of human behaviour which militate against the common good, human beings cannot be afforded the freedom or dignity of absolute autonomy in a totally individualistic sense.[67] A concomitant of this thesis is that the mental life of human beings is as conditioned by their environment or culture as is their overt, physical behaviour. Indeed, in his book *About Behaviourism*, Skinner states that 'mental life and the world in which it is lived are inventions'.[68] On this view, human beings are passive mechanisms responding in a predictable way to their immediate environmental circumstances.

The principles of Skinner's behaviourism have been applied successfully to learning in schools, most notably in the field of programmed instruction. By sequencing content into a series of small and related steps, each requiring a response from the pupil, programmes maximise the probability of successful learning taking place and, at the same time, increase the learner's motivation by giving immediate feedback of positive results. Such programmes allow pupils to learn at their own pace and, in the case of the more sophisticated 'branching' programmes now available on computer software, cater for individual differences in the characteristics of the pupil, including certain types of needs such as the need to succeed and gain approval.

When the content is amenable to sequencing and the learning outcome is clearly predictable, there is little doubt that the use of operant conditioning techniques greatly increases the probability of successful learning taking place, although the reponses that are encouraged are inevitably repetitive and mechanical. These types of responses, however, are consistent with the behaviourist's view that human beings are passive mechanisms responding in a predictable way to their environment. As we might expect, then, these techniques have little to contribute to the promotion of imagination, creativity, critical thinking, self-awareness and a capacity for personal decision-making, for all these

53

styles of thinking and learning are only valued within a view of human beings as autonomous agents of their own thinking and behaviour. It is, therefore, with both interest and concern that we note that, in recent years, the principles of behavioural psychology have been applied to classroom management and used 'to promote good classroom discipline'.[69] Because what is commonly referred to as 'behaviour modification' has implications for the behaviour of the teacher as well as that of the pupils, and, more especially, because its principles imply a way in which relationships between human beings are to be established, maintained and understood, anyone who is concerned about the contribution of education to pupils' personal and social development should give some attention to work currently being undertaken in this field.

(a) The theoretical basis of the behavioural approach to 'positive teaching'

In recognition of the importance which is attached to positive reinforcement of 'good behaviour' (through rewards of praise and tokens), some exponents of behaviour modification prefer to use the term 'positive teaching'.[70] Wheldall and Merrett characterise the behavioural approach to teaching as being based on several assumptions which they summarise as follows:

1. *The concern of psychology (and hence of teaching) is with the observable. This means that teachers who adopt the behavioural approach concern themselves with what a child actually does, ie, his behaviour, rather than speculating about unconscious motives or the processes underlying behaviour.*
2. *For the most part, what people do is assumed to have been learned as a result of the individual interacting with his environment, rather than being inherited at birth. This does not mean that behavioural psychologists and teachers do not believe in genetic inheritance or that they do believe that anybody can be taught to do anything given time. Rather they believe that genetics or biological endowment may set the limits for what an individual can learn, but that behaviour is still the result of learning.*
3. *Learning means change in behaviour. This follows from the first point really. The only way we know (that we can know) that learning has taken place is by observing a change in a child's behaviour.*
4. *Changes in behaviour (ie, learning) are governed primarily by the 'law of effect'. This means that children (and adults, and other animals for that matter) learn on the basis of tending to repeat behaviours which are followed by consequences which they find desirable or rewarding; similarly they tend not to repeat behaviours, the consequences of which they find aversive or punishing.*

5. *Behaviours are also governed by the contexts in which they occur. In any situation some behaviours are more appropriate than others and we learn which situations are appropriate for which behaviour. If a child's behaviour is appropriate for the circumstances in which it occurs it is likely to be rewarded; if it occurs in inappropriate circumstances reward is less likely and the behaviour may lead to punishing consequences. As a result of this we rapidly learn not only how to perform a certain behaviour, but when and where to perform it.*[71]

(b) 'Positive teaching' in practice

Given this theoretical basis, how does 'positive teaching' work in practice? In looking at this question we are not concerned with its application to academic learning but rather with the way in which it may be used to promote 'good classroom discipline' (which, of course, is important if academic learning is to take place) and contribute to pupils' personal and social development. Having witnessed my own students applying the principles of positive teaching in the classroom during Teaching Practice and achieving quite remarkable results, I have no doubts that it 'works', at least in relation to establishing good classroom order and discipline. On these occasions classes (some of them with a history of disruptive behaviour) were divided into teams (usually three teams per class) and an attitude of competition between the teams was encouraged by the promise of an end of term 'prize' (unspecified) for all members of the winning team. Positive reinforcement of required behaviour (such as staying in one's seat, not shouting out, answering questions, working quietly at prescribed tasks, producing a good standard of work, etc) was effected by the very frequent and regular use of praise supported by the awarding of points to the teams. A large chart with columns for each team was fixed prominently to the blackboard and the student teachers recorded points for the appropriate team as and when they were awarded during the lesson. Initially, points were awarded very frequently, as many as two a minute, but gradually, after the schedule had been in use for some weeks, the frequency with which points were awarded was decreased. Awarding points was interspersed with the use of other 'reinforcers' such as smiles, nods of approval, exclamations of delight, etc, and encouraging and appreciative remarks were addressed regularly to individuals and teams when full attention was achieved or the class was working quietly. Both individuals and teams were commended as appropriate. A good answer or contribution from a pupil was rewarded by his or her team being given a point.

The effects of using the 'positive teaching' technique, as I have already indicated, were dramatic. Pupils who were previously unruly, having little motivation to work or behave, suddenly became attentive, well-behaved and hard working. They entered quickly into the spirit of the competition and were quick to censure any of their peers who 'let the team down'. The standard of their work and contribution to lessons noticeably improved; indeed, on one occasion a class of fifteen-year-old boys, working in teams producing a series of short scenes from the *Ramayana*, were prepared to sing, for the benefit of the class, the hymns of praise to Rama that they had written and composed themselves. This was a class of whom their regular teachers had despaired of ever teaching anything! The prize (of Mars bars) was duly awarded to everyone in the class at the end of the term and was accepted appreciatively, although by then the need for extrinsic motivators, including points, had greatly diminished.

(c) The teacher as behaviour modifier

What can we make of this? Firstly, if, as we noted in our earlier consideration of different conceptions of knowledge, education is a process which is intended to 'transform children's realities', then the act of teaching requires us to design learning experiences which develop children's thinking. Secondly, the process of education is generally recognised to have a wider concern than the development of children's cognitive capacities; it also seeks to contribute to their emotional, moral and spiritual development and, in so doing, plays a part in their socialisation. I do not think these statements about the intentions of education are controversial or contentious. What *is* controversial and contentious is the view held by behaviourists that these intentions can and should be fulfilled by the use of conditioning techniques.

We should recognise, however, that the language which behaviourists use to describe the behavioural approach to learning may prejudice our perception of it. If we talk about 'stimulating', 'extending' or 'developing' children's thinking or about 'encouraging' responsibility and 'fostering' good behaviour, we do not perceive the process of learning and teaching which they imply as being anything but wholesome and ethically laudable. If, however, we hear behaviourists talk about 'conditioning', 'modifying' or 'shaping' children's behaviour (ie, their thinking and social actions) by 'schedules of reinforcement' which may use 'rewards' and 'punishment', then our perception of the process of learning and teaching which we think is implied is of one which is unhealthy and ethically reprehensible. It is also worth noting that whereas we may, with only a few reservations, accept the value of operant conditioning techniques when they are applied to programmed learning of information or to learning a piece of academic knowledge, our reactions may be much more hostile to the view that the same techniques should be used to bring about social learning.

Exponents of the technique are quick to point out, however, that behaviour modification uses no devices that are not commonly used by good and successful parents and teachers. But whereas some adults use approval, rewards and punishments spasmodically, inconsistently and even unconsciously, the application of the behavioural approach involves their use consciously, systematically and consistently whilst at the same time monitoring their effects. They also say that we should not imagine that a lack of knowledge of, or intention to apply the actual techniques of behaviour modification means that teachers are not already engaged in behaviour modification. All teachers exercise a shaping influence on their pupils; it is part of their professional responsibility to do so. The only difference that a precise understanding of the technique and a conscious intention to apply it makes to teachers is that it enables them to influence their pupil's social learning more successfully and efficiently.

We may not, however, be much heartened by this latter point. We may feel that even if it is likely, as behaviourists argue, that all teachers modify children's behaviour but do so in an unconscious manner, the fact that teachers *are* unconscious of this ensures that they are not particularly successful in influencing children and, consequently, we need not entertain any ethical anxieties about the situation. But if teachers are taught a technique which enables them consciously to modify pupils' behaviour and which, as a consequence, greatly increases their efficiency in influencing children, then we are more likely to feel that this situation presents considerable ethical problems. The view presented here is an extraordinary one; it is tantamount to saying that we experience ethical anxieties about what teachers do only when those teachers are efficient, not when they are inefficient!

We can, I think, resolve this problem if we separate the issues from the emotivism which tinges our perception of what is involved and what is at stake. It is in the area of social learning, not in the area of information learning, where serious ethical objections to the behavioural approach are most commonly raised. We might distinguish between using the approach to achieve a reasonable level of classroom behaviour among pupils, and using the approach to condition pupils to accept certain *values* and *beliefs* as normative rather than as controversial and open to a variety of different interpretations. In the case of the former I think we may presume that there is a large measure of agreement among teachers (and parents) about what constitutes acceptable classroom behaviour by pupils—not calling out, not throwing books about the room, listening to the teacher and to each other, and so on. Any ethical objections to the use of behavioural techniques to achieve this may be felt to be really rather marginal. (In the illustration given earlier, such objections might surface in questions like, 'Isn't giving Mars bars as prizes for good behaviour equivalent to bribing pupils so that they won't play the teacher up?', or 'Can the use of competition between pupils be justified when we are trying to teach pupils to be co-operative towards each other?'.) In the case of pupils being conditioned to accept certain attitudes, values and beliefs as normative, our ethical objections are likely to be much more substantial. Beliefs and values are, by their nature, controversial; people are united or divided by their adoption of one set of beliefs and, consequently, their rejection of others; while beliefs and values are fundamental to social and personal coherence, they can also be a cause for social division and personal disjuncture. Any attempt to *condition* pupils to accept a *particular* interpretation of experience as normative is inimical to education, not least because it is inimical to encouraging individuals to come to a *conscious* decision to hold particular beliefs for themselves. Thus, although it is certainly possible to condition pupils to hold certain beliefs and values within an educational process, it is not permissible to do so. But, it might be objected, if we show teachers how to use behavioural techniques to achieve good classroom order, what is to prevent them from also using these techniques to indoctrinate pupils in their own beliefs and values?

It is here that we should recognise that the behavioural approach is rather like a sharp axe; it can be used for good or evil, by devil and saint. Despite the claims of its exponents that it is 'ethically neutral', a knowledge of behaviour modification is a powerful means by which an unscrupulous, or just a misguided teacher can indoctrinate pupils in questionable and even personally damaging values and beliefs. Should the formal use of this technique therefore be restricted or prohibited in schools? There is a sense in which behaviour modification cannot be excluded from the process of education. If behaviourists are correct in their assertion that all behaviour is learned as a consequence of individuals interacting with their environment, human beings are constantly modified by their total environment, and that, for children, includes the school and the classroom. It is widely recognised that the 'hidden curriculum' exercises a profound influence on pupils' learning, especially of attitudes and values. In so far as the values which the school regards as normative constitute the hidden curriculum and these are tacitly or indirectly taught through human interaction, how else are they to be learned by pupils (and by teachers) except by a process of cumulative conditioning? There are strong grounds for school staffs collectively examining the 'messages' which pupils receive from the hidden curriculum, the intention being to identify those values, beliefs and attitudes which are considered worthwhile to human development and to plan how best to expose pupils to them. To seek to organise the hidden curriculum consciously in this manner so that its influence on pupils is consistent rather than spasmodic, planned rather than arbitrary, is to fulfil exactly the conditions upon which successful behaviour modification depends. Are we to restrict or prohibit such conscious planning of the hidden curriculum in schools because the ways in which pupils are exposed to its values may be thought unethical? If so, does it mean that we have to rely on a school's ethos to emerge and influence pupils by chance? Surely it is inconceivable that educational institutions should prefer to rely on chance than to engage in careful planning and efficient means of teaching. But how can something thought to be desirable and necessary for the school community to do collectively, be thought undesirable, unnecessary and even unethical for the individual teacher to do in their own classroom?

A reason for this could be found in the view that teachers acting as a group may be expected to act responsibly in the interests of the school community, but teachers acting on their own may only be expected to act in their own interests. The opportunity for teachers to abuse the trust placed in them that they will act with professional integrity is, of course, always present. But the sense of being a member of a community and profession which has certain expectations of its members exercises a considerable influence on the behaviour of individual teachers (by way of cumulative ideological conditioning?). There is every likelihood, therefore, that instructing teachers in the theory and practice of behaviour modification during their initial training would not, in general, lead to individuals abusing this knowledge but rather, if anything, to their exercising considerable caution in putting it into effect. Exponents of 'positive teaching' techniques do not, of course, envisage teachers applying them privately or in secret. The behavioural approach used by my students on Teaching Practice could hardly have been concealed from the staff of the schools. On the contrary, because of the amount of painstaking observation, identification and monitoring of desired and actual behaviour which must precede and accompany the use of these techniques, there are grounds for believing that teachers who use them are normally inclined to be more open in their intentions and more articulate about what they do in their classrooms than most of their colleagues who favour an 'intuitive' approach.

(d) The long-term effects of behaviour modification on the child's moral and social development

But even if, as I am suggesting, teachers can be expected to use behaviour modification techniques in a responsible manner, what effects does the use of these techniques have upon the pupils? In looking at this

tion I am not so much concerned about the short-term effects—such as the initial impact that the approach may have upon pupils who are unruly in class—but upon the long-term effects that the use of conditioning techniques may have upon the children's thinking and social behaviour. It may be significant that the use of behaviour modification techniques is more in evidence in Special Schools and Special Units than in ordinary schools. As we have seen, the techniques can be effective in establishing 'good classroom behaviour' and so producing suitable conditions in which teachers may teach and pupils may learn. But does the fact that they are effective in this respect validate their use in an educational enterprise which is committed to the promotion of personal autonomy and the exercise of rationality as the basis for personal decision-making? In other words, do these techniques support or undermine basic educational values?

Let us assume that the behaviour to be modified is the child's 'social' behaviour. We might define this as the child's behaviour towards other people, including, for instance, other children, teachers, other members of the school community and members of the wider community of which the school is a part. But how might we define 'acceptable' social behaviour? The lowest common denominator of acceptable social behaviour (commonly called 'good' behaviour) is, I suppose, treating other people as we would wish them to treat us. This involves being courteous and considerate towards them, recognising their rights, respecting their views, feelings, customs, property, and so on. It certainly may be possible to reinforce behaviour in the classroom which approximates in expression to what having respect for others means—speaking politely rather than harshly to others, not mistreating other people's belongings, listening patiently and with interest to other people's views and experiences, etc—but, in its concentration on rewarding pupils' externally acceptable behaviour, what opportunity does the approach provide for pupils to understand the *moral* basis of social behaviour? At best the approach may communicate a 'morality of co-operation'—'I will show you consideration because you are then more likely to show me consideration'. At worst the approach may communicate a 'morality of constraint'—'You will do as I want you to do, and I will reward you when you do'.

The work of cognitive psychologists such as Piaget and Kohlberg provides 'models' of moral development against which we might assess these suggested outcomes of the behavioural approach.[72] Piaget considers that children's moral judgments are too inconsistent to justify the use of 'stages' to classify them. He speaks of there being 'two moralities'—*heteronomous* and *autonomous*. Within the first category he indicates the existence of a type of morality which he designates 'moral realism' or 'a morality of objective restraint'. This is formed in the context of the unilateral relations between child as inferior and adult as superior. The child adapts to the prohibitions and sanctions handed down from the adult and accepts tham as unquestioned 'givens'. Commenting on this 'morality of constraint', John Flavell says:

Hence, the child views wrongdoing in objective rather than subjective terms, is confined to the letter rather than the spirit of the law, and is incapable of seeing morality-relevant acts either in terms of the inner motives of the actor or in terms of the social-interpersonal meaning of the act itself (ie, as a breach of solidarity and mutual trust between group members). For a morality of constraint, it must be the overt consequences alone which count in assessing the wrongfulness of acts, not the inner intentions and motives involved.[73]

The type of morality which Piaget designates a 'morality of co-operation' moves beyond the 'authoritarianism' of a 'morality of constraint' and yet retains features of *heteronomous* morality. Through a wider experience of social relationships, the child perceives the social implications of antisocial behaviour and recognises the benefits of co-operation. There is a growing appreciation of the role of motives in the actions of self and others and experience of co-operation issues in moral judgments based on the concept of equality. Unlike a morality of constraint, a morality of co-operation is motivated from within the child, but individual responses are largely governed by a firm attachment to the principle of reciprocity which requires all to be treated equally. Being 'fair', which is seen to be very important, demands that the basis for co-operation is 'Do unto others as you would have them do unto you', and the basis for punishment is 'An eye for an eye . . .'. This reciprocity, as Kohlberg observes, becomes a matter of 'You scratch my back and I'll scratch yours', not of loyalty, gratitude or justice.[74]

While the seeds of *autonomous* morality may lie within the concept of reciprocity, it is equity rather than equality which governs the formulation of moral judgments in Piaget's final 'stage' of moral development. Social relationships are based on concern and compassion and not solely on a demand for justice and equality. The limitations of given rules and regulations are recognised; situational factors are taken into account; there is an awareness of what an ideal morality would require. Thus 'moral creativity' is possible and the impulse for moral action is completely internalised. On this view, the achievement of 'moral autonomy' is dependent upon the individual being actively engaged in formulating his or her response to social behaviour, guided by the conception of moral action as an autonomous good, not merely accepting passively the required behaviour reinforced by others.

Kohlberg differs from Piaget in believing that moral development is a long continued and complex process rather than a single step from heteronomous to autonomous morality. Over the last twenty years he has produced at least six versions of his six-stage theory arranged within three levels of 'morality'.[75] His first two stages of moral development refer to a morality which has an 'obedience and punishment' orientation and a 'naively egoistic and hedonistic' orientation. Both of these stages fall within the *Premoral or Preconventional Level*. Stages three and four fall within the *Conventional Level*. Stage three refers to a morality which has a 'good boy—nice girl' orientation in which good behaviour is that which pleases and helps others and is approved by them. Stage four morality has an 'authority and social order-maintaining' orientation and has a regard to the earned expectations of others. Level three morality is called *Postconventional or Principled Level* and comprises stage five and stage six moralities. Stage five morality has a 'contractual legalistic' orientation and stage six a 'conscience or universal ethical principle' orientation. The perspective of stage six is described by Kohlberg as 'that of any rational individual recognising the nature of morality or the fact that persons are ends in themselves and must be treated as such'.[76]

The two types of morality which we identified as following from the behavioural approach to social learning—a 'morality of co-operation' and a 'morality of constraint'—both fall within the category which Piaget calls *heteronomous* morality. Kohlberg also uses this term to designate the characteristics of his stage one morality; viz:

> What is right: *to avoid breaking rules backed by punishment; obedience for its own sake; and avoiding physical damage to persons and property*. Reasons for doing right: *avoidance of punishment, and the superior power of authorities*. Egocentric point of view: *does not consider the interests of others or recognise that they differ from the actor's; does not relate two points of view; actions are considered physically rather than in terms of the psychological interests of others*. . .[77]

In many ways, however, the term *heteronomous* could apply to the characteristics of all of Kohlberg's stages of morality with the exception of stage six. Both Piaget and Kohlberg, therefore, would see the type of moral learning which results from applying behavioural techniques to modify social behaviour as low level and, possibly, premoral learning. Piaget in particular would, I believe, have considerable reservations about the value of such learning, particularly as, for him, there is an intrinsic connection between morality and thought. In his book, *The Moral Judgment of the Child*, he states:

> Logic is the morality of thought just as morality is the logic of action.[78]

The 'moral realism' which Piaget identifies in the development of the

62

child's moral reasoning directly parallels the 'intellectual realism' which he identifies in the development of the child's intellectual reasoning. His work on the latter is too well known to require re-statement here,[79] but we should recall that, although during the Concrete Operations stage content should be presented in a way which is consistent with the characteristics of the learner's concrete operational thought, care should be taken not to *reinforce* those characteristics. Indeed, one of the essential tasks of the teacher is to bring children face to face with the inadequacy of their existing schemata and to offer them guidance in the process of abstracting, assimilating and accommodating new experiences and situations. This is precisely what the behavioural approach does not do in relation to social learning; what it does do is to reinforce certain actions which are accepted uncritically as a consequence of certain rewards being attached to their performance. In this respect, the existing schemata of thought (in this case, applied to moral judgment) remain unchallenged and are consequently reinforced. We must conclude, therefore, that the use of behaviour modification techniques to achieve an acceptable level of social behaviour is inimical to the promotion of moral thinking. This is a most damaging criticism of the technique and its rationale.

(e) The child as a behaviour modifier

There is a further point to be made against the behavioural approach which is equally damaging to it. Use of the behavioural approach could be said to produce a 'morality of manipulation'. 'Manipulation' is a word which usually has pejorative connotations when its object is a person. It is not a word that fits comfortably with 'morality'. But I use the word advisedly in order to point to the possibility of a person actually viewing human nature as requiring humans to be manipulated. Let us imagine a situation where children or young people have undergone the form of social learning which we have been considering and, as a consequence, have developed a morality of constraint or a morality of co-operation. If R F Dearden is correct in his criticism that to guide their perception of which reinforcer to choose 'many behaviour modifiers take for granted as universally valid the model of a commercial transaction',[80] then it is highly probable that the type of understanding which these children and young people attach to human relationships will be based on the commercial model. If metaphors from the language of commercialism are applied to the area of inter-personal relationships, we have a situation in which we 'do deals', 'secure a contract', 'make a profit', 'safeguard our assets', 'redeploy' someone or 'make them redundant'. Thus a person's value is not seen in terms of their personal worth but reduced to an 'estimate' of their value to us in achieving what we want. In making these observations I am, of course, assuming that the child imbibes this view unconsciously; but if, as some behaviour modifiers suggest, we were to provide young people with a knowledge of behaviour modification techniques and the skills to apply them in their daily interactions, then we would be equipping them to be very successful operators of a 'morality of manipulation'. Although I am very much in favour of schools providing young people with the skills which will enable them to respond creatively and imaginatively to future experiences, I am pessimistic about the future of a generation which lives by such a morality and depends on such techniques to establish and sustain their relationships with their fellow human beings.

One final comment before concluding this consideration of behaviourism. Wheldall and Merrett state that the principle which underlies behaviour modification is succinctly summarised by Skinner in the following words:

> When he behaves as we want him to behave, we simply create a situation he likes, or remove one he doesn't like. As a result the probability that he will behave that way again goes up, which is what we want.[81]

There are several points which can be made against this principle. I will make only two—one ethical, the other practical. First: when Skinner advocates reinforcing desired behaviour by creating a situation which the pupil 'likes' or removing one which the pupil 'doesn't like', he is providing a prescription for the development of what Kohlberg originally called 'naive instrumental hedonism'—the view that right action consists of that which instrumentally satisfies one's own needs, including the need for pleasure. It would be difficult, if not impossible, to find a single ethical argument why schools should give this view houseroom. Second: our experience of life confirms that human beings are constantly needing to sustain themselves and each other through periods of appalling discomfort, pain, anxiety and fear. The utopian world of *Walden Two*[82] (if it can be called that) bears no relationship to the real world as we experience it. Reinforcing behaviour in a classroom by reducing or removing what pupils do not 'like' is not only to foster unrealistic expectations of life for these pupils, it is to fail to encourage the acquisition of those skills, attitudes and values upon which their capacities to meet future difficulties in their lives will depend. The concepts of 'character', 'mind', 'intelligence', 'consciousness', 'will' and 'conscience' are conspicuously absent by design from the writings of the behaviourists; but when they are also absent from the mind of the teacher, and their development has no place in the aims of education, neither can deny the possibility that they may have contributed to creating a generation of young people who have been morally de-skilled and ethically de-humanised.

(ii) Alternative conceptions of the child and of learning and teaching

Our discussion of behaviourism has led us a long way from Froebel and his metaphors of growth and gardens full of children. Images redolent of the natural world have been replaced by images redolent of the scientific and technological world. The metaphor likening the teacher to a gardener and the child to a plant has given way to a metaphor likening the teacher to a technician and the child to a piece of plastic if not a micro-chip. Had I chosen to explore the cognitive theories of Piaget or Bruner, the psychonanalytic theory of Freud or the analytic psychology of Jung, the psycho-social theories of Erikson or Fromm, or the humanistic psychologies and phenomenologies of Maslow and Rogers, a whole range of alternative metaphors would have emerged, each expressive of different conceptions of childhood, learning and teaching and the role of the teacher, and supportive of different conceptions of which knowledge is worthwhile, which aims should determine the curriculum and how education can contribute to human development. Space permits but one illustration of this point, taken from the writings of Carl Rogers. In *Freedom to Learn* he writes:

> *It seems to me that anything that can be taught to another is relatively inconsequential and has little or no significant influence on behaviour. . . Self-directed learning, truth that has been personally appropriated and assimilated in experience, cannot be directly communicated to another. . . When I try to teach, as I do sometimes, I am appalled by the results, which seem as little more than inconsequential, because sometimes the teaching appears to succeed. When this happens I find that the results are damaging. It seems to cause the individual to distrust his experience, and to stifle significant learning. Hence I have come to feel that the outcomes of teaching are either unimportant or hurtful. As a consequence, I realise that I am only interested in being a learner, preferably learning things that matter, that have some significant influence on my behaviour. . .[83]*

Rogers describes education of the future as follows:

> *Education will not be a preparation for living. It will be, in itself, an experience of living. Feelings of inadequacy, hatred, a desire for power, feelings of love and awe and respect, feelings of fear, dread, unhappiness with parents or with other children—all these will be an open part of the curriculum, as worthy of exploration as history or mathematics.*

In fact this openness to feelings will enable him to learn content materials more readily. His will be an education in becoming a whole being, and the learning will involve him deeply, openly, exploringly, in an awareness of his relationships to the world of others, as well as an awareness of the world of abstract knowledge.[84]

The conception of human nature which emerges from Rogers' writings is strikingly similar to that of Froebel's; as such it is the antithesis of Skinner's conception. Rogers' view is that human beings are basically good, rational, co-operative, constructive, trustworthy and realistic. They do, however, have a potential for aggressive and antisocial behaviour which is provoked by threat to or frustration of basic needs— for love, belonging and security—and is an expression of defensiveness. There is, however, no need to be concerned about controlling people's aggressive, antisocial impulses; given the possibility of fulfilling their basic needs, they will become self-regulatory, balancing their needs against each other. Thus, when the individual—child or adult— is provided with the support of love and acceptance, he or she will adjust towards 'self-actualisation' and his or her potentials will develop constructively, 'as a seed grows and becomes its potential'.[85] The contribution that the teacher makes to this process is to provide the right conditions for learning to take place. Rogers sees these as valuing, accepting and trusting the pupil and establishing an empathetic understanding of him or her. Thus teaching becomes a personal relationship, a spontaneous personal encounter which frees the pupil to learn.

Concluding note

It is, I think, appropriate that I should end this chapter by focusing on the importance of *valuing* both as a stimulus to personal growth and as a skill which pupils need to acquire. Our wide-ranging discussions of knowledge, cultures, ideologies and children have revolved around the issue of values—what value can be attached to this conception of knowledge, to this way of looking at the world, to this way of thinking about children? What we have been attempting to do in this chapter— examine our own assumptions about knowledge, values and the child— parallels, I believe, what we should be helping young people to do in schools—examine the assumptions which underlie their values and lifestyles, their priorities and commitments, and their frames of reference for viewing life and giving it meaning. If we accept that this is something which schools and their curricula should be doing, we will, eventually, have to ask what contribution religious education makes to this process. In the meantime we might reflect on the following words of R A Hodgkin:

> . . . *when people are trying to shape their own values from diverse desires, concepts and experiences, it is a central task of teachers to lead them to the possibility—the necessity—that each one learns as maker or as an artist does, from the conflicts and complexities which exist inside the problem. For these are frontier questions where each person must feel and think existentially and then risk responsible action.*[86]

Chapter Two

What does it mean to be human?

Introduction

In Chapter One I tried to show how our view of education and the curriculum is influenced by ideological and cultural assumptions about the nature and status of knowledge, the values which we regard as important and our conception of childhood and how children learn. Implicit in any of these assumptions, however, are further assumptions about human nature and the value of human life. We saw this most clearly when, at the end of the chapter, we contrasted the views of Carl Rogers with those of B F Skinner. In this chapter I want to begin the task of clarifying the concept of 'human development' by trying to analyse what it means to be 'human'. I do not, however, intend to compare and contrast different views of the nature of 'man',[2] or explore alternative conceptions of the meaning, purpose and value of human life. For one thing this is a daunting task which, if undertaken, would take me far beyond the confines of this exploratory study; and for another, I have some doubts about the value of such an exercise to my purpose of identifying the contribution of formal education in general, and of religious education in particular, to human development. Instead, therefore, I want to consider how far it is possible to put forward a description of 'man' and of how 'man' becomes 'human' which is not based on any particular *beliefs* about man or *beliefs* about 'human nature' but which enables us to recognise why and how beliefs and values are of central importance to human development. The identification of what I will call the '*givens*' of the human condition is a necessary feature of this description. By 'givens' I mean 'universal or necessary truths of an anthropological kind contingent upon the human condition being as it happens to be', or, more simply, 'facts about human life which are *constant*, irrespective of culture and ideology'.

I do not expect the description I offer to be accepted uncritically. In the light of my earlier discussion of ideology, especially my recognition that the fact/value distinction is untenable and that all methods of study are value-laden, how can I claim that my description of 'man' is value-free?—that it has not been influenced by value/belief assumptions? With this in mind I will give close attention to some of the possible objections to my description, especially my inclusion of 'holding beliefs by an act of faith' among human '*givens*'. I will also consider if my description of 'man' is compatible with a religious view of 'man' or if a religious view of 'man' must inevitably challenge it. While I hope that the discussion of these issues will serve to stimulate a more careful examination of our own assumptions about 'belief', 'faith' and 'religion', my intentions go beyond this concern. In seeking to describe how 'man' becomes 'human' I am seeking to identify the process whereby *we* become 'human'. If we are concerned that formal education contributes to the 'human' development of pupils, then it is, of course, necessary that all that we do in schools, including what we teach and how we teach it, is not only informed by the *'process of humanisation'* which we identify but actually contributes to it. Thus a necessary part of our investigation will be to examine the features of human development which psychologists have identified, to see if these concur with, and so confirm, what we have identified as the essential characteristics of humanisation. If this can be shown to be the case, then we can move on to consider how the concept of humanisation can not only provide a basis upon which an educational rationale for teaching about beliefs and values can be constructed, but can also inform the contribution which we are seeking to make to the personal, social, moral, spiritual and religious development of our pupils.

1. Human being and being human

(i) What is 'man'?

Philosophically, in considering this question we are entering an area of thought of unparalleled complexity. In the *Handbook* to his lectures on logic, Kant distinguishes between a philosophy in the scholastic sense and a philosophy in the universal sense. He describes a philosophy in the universal sense as 'the knowledge of the ultimate aims of human reason' or as 'the knowledge of the highest maxim of the use of our reason'. According to Kant, the field of philosophy in this universal sense may be marked off into the following questions:

1. What can I know?
2. What ought I to do?
3. What may I hope?
4. What is man?

He comments:

> *Metaphysics answers the first question, ethics the second, religion the third and anthropology the fourth . . . Fundamentally all this could be reckoned as anthropology, since the first questions are related to the last.*[3]

In other words, Kant is positing that the central question of human philosophising (in both speculative and practical senses) is the question 'What is man?' because all other questions are contained within it. But, as Heidegger pointed out, this is not an anthropological question at all;

it is the question about the essence of existence itself—it is the question about being. Martin Buber rephrases it thus:

> *What sort of being is it which is able to know, and ought to do, and may hope?* . . . *knowledge of the essence of this being will make it plain to me* what, *as such a being, it can know*, what, *as such a being, it ought to do, and* what, *as such a being, it may hope.*[4]

Buber observes, however, that despite the abundance of valuable observations Kant makes *about* man, he never actually raises the question of what man *is*. Nor does he consider the problems that this question sets—such as man's special place in the cosmos, his connection with destiny, his relation to the world of things, his understanding of his fellow human beings, his existence as a being that knows he must die, his attitude in all the ordinary and extraordinary encounters with the mystery with which his life is shot through, and so on. The *wholeness* of man does not enter into his philosophising.

(ii) Who am I?

I am not going to propose that we should now set about answering the question that Kant avoided. That would be too much like fools rushing in where angels feared to tread! Nor do I propose to stay within the area of philosophical anthropology—I am not qualified to do so. Instead, I would like us to personalise Kant's question and locate it within our own existential situations. Let us re-phrase Kant's question like this:-

What is man?
= What does it mean to be human?
= What does it mean for me to be human?
= Who am I?

Although I might be able to avoid Kant's question 'What is man?' on the grounds that I am unqualified in philosophical anthropology, can I avoid the question 'Who am I?' on the same grounds? Is that a question I can put to one side because I am unqualified? Unqualified in what?— in being human?, in being me? I think not; indeed, if I cannot answer that question, who can? Ironically, there are many who would claim to be qualified to answer my question for me. A genealogist, a biologist, a psychologist, even an immigration control officer looking at my passport, could answer my question, 'Who am I?' But their answers would all be partial, fragmentary, incomplete. No one but I myself can begin to deal with my *wholeness*, and the question 'Who am I?' is about my wholeness. Even if I could put together all the fragments of me that experts identified, I would still believe I am more than the sum of my separate parts.[5] And, even if I could, as it were, know myself completely,

I would have a sense of being more than I know! So in trying to know myself in order to answer this question, I encounter the mystery of my being. There is a sense, therefore, in which each of us is groping for the answer to Kant's question about the essence of existence, the question about being, in the experience of our own existence, although few of us do so with the aid of philosophical anthropology. More often than not we only become conscious of ourselves—*self-conscious*—at odd moments, and we rarely follow up such glimpses by consciously engaging in a sustained effort to formulate systematically a more adequate or coherent account of who we are. Whether or not all human beings can and should engage in this quest for *self-understanding* is a question to which I will presently return.

(iii) *What does it mean to be human?*

In the meantime, let us consider the 'Who am I?' question in its more impersonalised form of 'What does it mean to be human?'. Whereas speculation about and reflection on the 'Who am I?' question may lead us to a greater awareness of our own uniqueness as persons, this question prompts us to consider what individuals have in common with other human beings. The question seems to imply that if we search diligently enough we may be able to come up with such a thing as 'universal human nature'. Philosophers have grappled with this notion from Plato onwards and there is an abundance of views on offer. They range from the view that human nature is more or less fixed and constant to the view that human nature is infinitely malleable. They include the view that human nature is unfinished and still striving for completion and perfection. These views are related to that thorny, perennial question of the respective influences of culture and genetic endowment on the way in which human beings are shaped, and, of course, to the question of whether or not human beings can transcend these influences.[6] It would appear, then, that the only unequivocal statement we can make about 'being human' is that it involves being a creature which is able to formulate such questions as these.

Being able to make that statement is, however, significant because others follow from it. For example, if being able to ask questions about our own nature is one of the 'givens' of the human situation, other 'givens' must include being able to seek answers to these questions, or, to put it another way, formulate meanings. On this basis we can say that one of the most characteristic activities of human beings is their involvement in meaning-making and truth-questing. To be human is to struggle for meaning, especially for meaning about the human. This human struggle for meaning has produced many alternative views of what it means to be human, but no single definitive answer which can in some way be proved to be true by reference to incontrovertible evidence or empirically verified fact. In other words, facts about the human being do not in themselves provide an adequate answer to the question, 'What does it mean to be human?'. The 'empirical carpet' runs out from beneath this question and we find ourselves choosing between *beliefs* about the human. Here then is the dilemma posed by the human condition; the formulation of meaning about the human involves us entering what I will call the *arena of faith-responses*. Thus, holding beliefs by an act of faith is not an option in the life of the human being, it is an essential constituent of what it means to be human; it is another human 'given'.

Placed in the arena of faith-responses, what choices do we have?

1. We can accept someone else's understanding of the human and believe that it is true.
2. We can attempt to formulate our own understanding of the human and believe that it is true.
3. We can ignore the question and try to live without thinking about it.

A comment about the third choice is, perhaps, needed. Clearly to ignore the question is to make a choice; for, as Harvey Cox puts it, 'Not to decide, is to decide'. Opting for the third choice, whether consciously or, more often, by default, involves making some value judgment about the human—that, for example, there is really no difference between the nature of human beings and the nature of lower animals, or that having an understanding of what it means to be human is not important to the way one lives one's life. Implicit in these value judgments are, of course, beliefs about the human.

(iv) Humans versus turtles

Let us for a moment contemplate the life cycle of the turtle. When the female turtles have been fertilised, they come out of the sea, crawl up the beach and scoop deep holes in the sand. They each lay approximately two hundred eggs into their holes, cover them with sand and return to the sea. Days later, the eggs begin to hatch. From them emerge hundreds of little turtles. Immediately they begin a perilous journey to the sea. Many are picked off in the first few hours of life by seagulls, and many others fall victim to predators long before they reach maturity. I understand that only four or five percent of turtles actually reach maturity and continue the process I have described.

What is significant in the life cycle of the turtle to our consideration of what it means to be human? Infant turtles do not have to *learn* to be turtles; they *are* turtles. The turtle's nature is fixed; it is genetically programmed to produce an identical set of responses to its condition which are absolutely predictable right from the moment of birth until the moment of death. Like McDougall's self-raising flour, the quality of the turtle's life never varies. 'Turtlehood' provides no possibility for surprises. Like father, like son. To use my earlier metaphor, the empirical carpet never runs out from under turtles and they never need to enter the arena of faith-responses.

What a contrast to the life cycle and nature of human beings! Unlike baby turtles, human babies have to learn what it is to be human, and they learn this from other human beings who have also had to learn it from other human beings, and so on. As we can see from the many different models of the human found in different ages and cultures, human nature is not fixed or programmed; 'humanhood' unlike 'turtlehood' has infinite possibilities for surprises; it is capable of being shaped into many and varied forms. This is not to deny that any genetic coding is present but to recognise that such coding allows for an astonishing degree of influence to be exerted by the social or 'human' environment in the shaping of the human being. Of all the influences this environment exerts upon the shape of human beings, none is so powerful as the *beliefs* which humans hold about themselves. The *Bhagavad-Gita* makes this point well when it says:

> Man is made by his belief. As he believes, so he is.[7]

So, unlike 'turtlehood', 'humanhood' is not totally fixed by forces over which the human has no control. The human being is not programmed to be only one type of being—the animal being which is the lot of all non-human beings. The word 'human', therefore, is not just a word used to distinguish the species 'homo-sapiens' from other primates (because in that sense all human beings are *born* 'human'); it is also used as a value-judgment about the quality of life of which human beings are capable. But wonderful though this may seem, that 'man' can become what he chooses to become, it is also one of the most terrifying features of human existence. Although 'man' enjoys the freedom to create his own nature, he is not able to be *certain* about what that means, because he also has to create its meaning. F H Heinemann describes the human dilemma succinctly when he says:

> The mere fact that we are born men does not imply that we are human. On the contrary, it lulls us into pretence. To be human is not a fact, but a task. . .[8]

(v) The 'givens' of the human condition

I have already defined 'givens' as 'universal or necessary truths of an anthropological kind' which are 'constant, irrespective of culture and ideology'. Let me now summarise those 'givens' which have so far emerged from the above discussion in the following way:

Human beings are creatures which are constrained by their condition to:

(1) Formulate questions about their nature and the nature of their human experience;
(2) Engage in meaning-making and truth-questing;
(3) Formulate beliefs about their nature and the nature of their human experience;
(4) Learn from other human beings;
(5) Commit themselves to particular beliefs about themselves by an act of faith;
(6) Live with uncertainty.

As a consequence of these 'givens' we can add a further 'fact' about human beings, namely that the beliefs human beings hold about themselves exercise a profound influence upon how they and their lives are shaped.

Let us now pursue the search for further 'givens' of the human situation by considering the statement, 'Man is made man by man'.[9] In many ways this looks like a *belief* statement incorporating particular assumptions about the nature of man and the nature of human experience. In this respect it might be said to be a statement which could be paralleled by other *belief* statements, such as 'Man is made man by God'. But is this really the case? Let us break down the first statement into its separate parts and consider what they mean.

Man   — ie, 'homo sapiens', the species—
is made   — becomes or is shaped into the form of the
(Hu)man — ie, acquires 'humanhood' and 'humanness' and its particular manifestation at any given time or in any given place (ie, socio-historical context)
by   — ie, as a result of or through
Man   — ie, interacting with other human beings already holding beliefs about human nature and the desirable characteristics or attributes of the human being.

Is this not a matter of fact? Is this not a constant? Is this not universally and necessarily true of all human experience, irrespective of the different beliefs by which particular cultures, ideologies and religions may *interpret* that experience? If so, then other 'givens' follow from this situation.

Firstly, *interdependence* is a 'given'. There is a necessary interdependence between all human beings. To return to the turtles for a moment, we can recognise that any notion of interdependence between turtles is restricted to the act of fertilisation, and there it is really only a form of dependence. Except for this act, turtles are not interdependent—each turtle by means of its genetic coding is entirely self-sufficient. Adult turtles do not nurture or protect their offspring; indeed they would not even recognise their offspring if they swam into them! Human beings, however, need constant interaction with other members of their species from birth onwards in order to develop their human characteristics and human qualities—indeed, in order to 'produce' their human nature. As accounts of 'wolf-children' of the Romulus and Remus type attest, without such interaction human offspring fail to become 'human'. We should note, too, that human beings can never escape from their interdependence with other human beings even if they try to. We may sever our family, ethnic, cultural and religious ties and seek to reject our origins; we can avoid contact with other human beings by living as a hermit in the middle of a wasteland; but we can never escape their shaping influence on our own 'humanness'—that goes with us as we go. Even the act of rejection underlines the fact of our interdependence; we react against something, not against nothing, and the course we choose is mapped by reference to the course we have already taken. 'Independence', therefore, is only possible within the limits prescribed by the fact of human interdependence.

The same is true of another 'given', *freedom*. The meaning and limits of freedom are also prescribed by the fact of human interdependence. Human beings are not free *not* to be interdependent. A human being's inviolable links with other human beings provide the framework within which freedom is exercised. There is no question of human beings being totally free from such constraints. No human beings are free from the personal, social and cultural circumstances through which they have been made and from which they take their meanings and values. But neither are they programmed by them. Because there is no single, complete answer to the question 'What is man?' programmed into 'man's' being, and because human beings ask that question and offer a variety of answers to it, we have to conclude that human beings enjoy a greater possibility of participating in their own making than any other animal. That possibility is conditional upon *freedom* being a human 'given'.

A third human 'given' follows from *interdependence* and *freedom*, namely *responsibility*. This is the consequence of human beings being free to participate in their own making—they have an inescapable *responsibility* for what they become. Because of what human beings are, and because the way in which they formulate beliefs about themselves and structure their ultimate concerns are the result of their own actions and decisions, responsibility is a human 'given'. In saying this I am not making a value-judgment or expressing a belief about what human beings *ought* to do, I am merely describing a state of affairs, namely that a *causal* relationship exists between what human beings believe and what human beings become. It is in this sense, rather than a moral one, that I am suggesting that responsibility is a human 'given'. Of course, moral questions arise from this state of affairs and human beings find themselves having to make *moral* judgments ('faith-responses') about what they *ought* to believe about themselves and the world, but that is to go beyond our immediate task of trying to identify certain universal constants which are ever present in the human condition and which are, in a sense, *a priori* or *prior to* beliefs.

(vi) Humanisation

But *interdependence, freedom* and *responsibility* are empty terms without a socio-historical context in which they can operate and express agreed meanings. However, this socio-historical context is also a product of the way in which human beings have come to terms with these 'givens'. In other words, the 'givens' of the human situation are such that human beings are constrained to formulate norms about what it means to be human and do so by formulating *beliefs* about human nature and the nature of human interdependence, freedom and responsibility. These norms become enshrined within the culture of a society and are made explicit within particular belief systems, such as ideologies and religions. Individuals are, accordingly, socialised into the norms of their society and may also be initiated into the particular belief systems supporting them. This is how the individual both learns about what it means to be human and is made human.

This account of what I have called the *'process of humanisation'* is compatible with much of what the social phenomenologists are saying when they speak of the 'social construction of reality'. For example, it accords with the dialectical process consisting of the three steps, *externalisation, objectivation* and *internalisation* which provide, as we saw in Chapter One, a way of explaining how human beings produce society and society produces human beings. *Step one*: the experience of coming to terms with the 'givens' of the human situation prompts human beings to formulate beliefs about the human and the human situation (*externalisation*). *Step two*: these beliefs achieve a reality or facticity external to human beings; they become normative (*objectivation*). *Step three*: the individual appropriates the normative beliefs about the human within his or her own subjective consciousness and becomes what he or she believes (*internalisation*). Just as it is through objectivation that a society attains its own culture—its way of being in the world—so it is through internalisation that culture shapes the human person—his or her way of being in the world.

We must ask, however, whether this is an adequate account of humanisation. Does it not, for example, lend strong support to a deterministic way of viewing human beings—the view that human beings are inevitably a product of their culture and have only minimal say in their own shaping? Furthermore, does it not imply that the social structure that produces human nature is equivalent to the genetic structure that produces the fixed nature of turtles? If so, is not the potential human beings have for taking responsibility for their own shape as limited as the potential turtles have for taking responsibility for theirs? In reply I make the following observations.

What human beings become is, inevitably, contingent upon whatever models of the human are enshrined within their socio-historical circumstance. For example, they think through the categories of thought built into the language and culture of their society; they come to meaning through the perspectives of meaning built into their cultural history; they accept as binding upon them certain criteria for the evaluation of their experience.[10] To deny this is to impose upon individual human beings the responsibility for their own learning and to deny them access to the experience and understanding of other human beings. It is to push them back into the wilderness to learn for and by themselves, unaided by the efforts of those who have lived before them or alongside them. If we accept that all learning is social and shared, we also have to accept that 'all men are men of their time'—even those who may also be in advance of it!

(vii) Autobiography

But all 'men' are also different and unique. They are different and unique in the sense that their consciousness—how they see things and the things they see, how they give meaning to things and the things they give meaning to, how they make faith-responses and the actual faith-responses they make—is not only shaped by their cultural history, it is also shaped by their own personal history. Speaking of the shaping influence of one's cultural history, Peter Berger says:

> *Every individual biography is an episode within the history of society which both precedes and survives it . . .*[11]

But a 'biography' is someone else's story of my life; it is different from an 'autobiography' which is my story of my life. My 'autobiography' is my own account of my own struggle to make sense of my own life. It involves me in the task of answering the 'Who am I?' question. That is a question only I can answer because only I have had the experience of being me; and in this sense, although I have a cultural history, I have a personal history too, and it is the latter which makes me different and unique from all other human beings.

Thus, although human beings are participants in giving meaning to an 'objective' world which they share in large measure with others (their cultural history), they also seek to give meaning to their own 'subjective' world which is personal to them (their personal history). Our 'subjective' world (in which we are subjects not objects) provides us with the most influential framework within which we evaluate the claims and counter-claims that the so-called 'objective' world makes upon us, especially its imposition of values and beliefs upon us. This is because our subjectivity (ie, our experience of our selves or our 'self' consciousness) is the unifying factor within our experience. In order to move around the world of objects, to manage our relationships within it, we must be able to manage the disturbances, the sensations and feelings wrought within us by our encounters with the world. It is the integrity of our 'interior' world that is the source of our motivation, or enthusiasm, our response to life.[12] Indeed, it is by way of our interior world (sometimes called the 'life-world') that the claims and counter-claims of the exterior world—the 'things', the 'facts', the 'beliefs', the 'values', etc—are both perceived and assessed as significant and meaningful or otherwise.

Our subjectivity incorporates what might be called *personal vision*, and although this is subject to change, it provides us with a continuing filter for our cognitive, affective and spiritual experiences. Subjectivity thus passes into objectivity through the very presuppositions which govern our perceptions. Such presuppositions are part of our personal vision. The use of terms like 'subjectivity', 'interiority' and 'spirituality' reminds us that men and women are more than the sum of all the biological, social, cultural and ideological influences which shape them, and that they themselves can play a part in shaping the person that emerges from the context of such influences. Playing this part—participating in shaping one's own self and taking responsibility for the person one is becoming—is an expression of the human capacity to choose and is thus a mark of being human and of human being.

Participating in the process of creating personal meaning involves our becoming aware of those cultural forces (especially those beliefs and values which our societies regard as 'normative') that have shaped, and continue to shape us as persons—that have shaped, and continue to shape our self-image and self-identity. Another way of putting this would be to say that in order to find personal meaning I need to 'know' my own 'story'. For example, we would all be hard put to be able to separate the person we are now and the values, beliefs and perspectives that are ours now, from the influence of our personal nurturing experiences within our families and from the continuum of experience which has stretched from our birth to the present. The circumstances of our birth in particular and the experience of our early years of life, our relationships with our parents and our place within the family and other significant social groups, have all been decisive in creating the 'script' of our 'stories'. In this sense our stories have been written by others, as the turtle's story has been written by the genetic coding of the species. But unlike the turtle we as human beings can make our stories our own; we can transform our 'biographies' into 'autobiographies' and in so doing become the author of our own personhood.

(viii) Is this a value-free description of humanisation?

The question to which I now turn is whether this description of humanisation is value-free. In other words, is it a description which is not contingent upon holding certain beliefs about human beings? In so far as I am a human being holding particular beliefs about myself and the world I have come to as a consequence of my interactions with other human beings within a given cultural setting (which, by definition, is value-laden), the structure of my consciousness which has been formed through this interaction and through which I interpret my experience does not permit my thinking to be value-free or value-neutral. As Newbigin has observed, 'Having an "open mind" is not the same as having an "empty mind"'. In this sense, my thinking, like everyone else's, has to proceed in accordance with various axioms which I assume to be self-evident. The argument against any claim that it is possible to provide a description of humanisation which is 'value-free' is, therefore, irrefutatable. The odd thing is, however, that it is the strength of the argument *against* the possibility of 'value-free' thinking that substantiates my claim that, for example, one of the human 'givens' *is* that human beings must interpret their experience by holding beliefs and values about themselves and their situation. It is the objection that human thinking *cannot* be value-free which provides the grounds for asserting that this *is* a human 'given'—a universal and necessary truth of an anthropological kind. In other words, the statement that human beings *must* interpret their experiences by holding beliefs and values about themselves is saying exactly the same as the statement that human beings *cannot* be value-free in their thinking. Both statements are asserting a fact, not a belief, about human life which is 'constant, irrespective of culture and ideology'. If we were to work our way systematically through the other human 'givens' I have suggested, we would, I think, find that each has this same 'factual' basis. Reservations about, or opposition to, my inclusion of 'the necessity of human beings committing themselves to particular beliefs about themselves *by an act of faith'* as a human 'given' may, however, be anticipated. Such opposition may also be critical of my assertion that 'holding beliefs by an act of faith is not an option in the life of the human being, it is an essential constituent of what it means to be human; it is another human "given"'.[13] Because the issue of whether or not human beings have to enter the 'arena of faith-responses' has considerable bearing on how we define the nature and purpose of religious education, the arguments for and against its inclusion as a human 'given' must now receive very careful attention.

(a) The 'reserved' or 'suspended' response to choice

An argument against human beings having to enter the 'area of faith-responses' is as follows. Although formulating questions and struggling for meaning may be human 'givens', and although there are 'alternative views of what it means to be human', it does not necessarily follow that human beings have to enter the 'arena of faith-responses', and consequently this is not a human 'given'. All forms of understanding the human are *partial* and, therefore, not exclusive. This means that we do not have to choose between them. We can, for example, accept a biological-anthropological view *and* an existentialist view of human being. Thus human beings try to understand the human phenomenon by placing it in a number of different contexts or 'provinces' of meaning, so all understanding of the human is of necessity *plural*. In formulating (on page 73) only three choices which human beings have to the dilemma of meaning, and by regarding them as mutually exclusive, I have made the 'faith choice' unavoidable when, in fact, it *is* avoidable. But because all understanding of the human is partial and plural, there is a fourth choice: we can *reserve* or *suspend* our response. We can acknowledge that a final answer to the question 'What does it mean to be human?' cannot be given, so we have to learn to live with the unanswered question. The existence of this fourth choice means that human beings do not have to enter the 'arena of faith-responses'. Furthermore, allowing the meaning question to remain as an 'open' question is consistent with the view that 'human nature is not fixed', 'that to be human is a task', and that humans need 'to live with uncertainty'. Positing that all human beings have to enter the 'arena of faith-responses' is, in fact, to say that human nature *is* fixed.[14]

(b) The concept of choice

I think the issue around which the above argument revolves is how we are to define the term 'arena of faith-responses' and what we are to understand by a 'faith response' and 'holding beliefs by an act of faith'.

Let me say immediately that in using the word 'faith' I am not restricting its reference to religion or religious belief. A 'faith response' is not a response appropriate only to religious belief; it is a response which is equally appropriate to other types of belief—those, for example, of a moral or political kind.[15] I would, however, like to defer attempts to define this response until I have given some attention to the concept of 'choice'.

If we accept that necessity to make meaning is a human 'given' and that human beings respond to this necessity by formulating and holding beliefs, does it not follow that another human 'given' is that human beings are constrained to choose *between* beliefs? I do not think there can be any doubt that this is so even if 'all forms of understanding the human are *partial* and *plural*'. Earlier in this chapter I expressed the view that of all the influences which the environment exerts upon the shape of human beings, none is so powerful as the beliefs humans hold about themselves. We should, however, distinguish between the shaping effect of beliefs which human beings assimilate *unconsciously*—that is, the cumulative effect of their constant interaction with other human beings and their culture—and the shaping effect of beliefs which human beings choose *consciously*. I take it for granted, therefore, that to speak of 'choice' is to speak of *conscious* choice; similarly, to speak of human beings 'holding' beliefs is to speak of their doing so *consciously*.

We might reasonably expect that as human beings increase their capacity to make 'choices' (as a consequence, for example, of their being confronted by specific situations necessitating personal choices to be made, and of their becoming more 'self-conscious'), the shaping influence of their unconsciously assimilated beliefs decreases. Thus, through increasing their capacity to make choices between beliefs, human beings are able to increase their control over their own being and their own futures because it is through the choices human beings make that they are able to take responsibility for what they become. Another way of putting this would be to say that the meaning-making potential of human beings is increased in proportion to their capacity to choose between beliefs. Let us now examine this all-important act of choosing between beliefs. What elements are involved in making a choice? I suggest a *minimum* of two: an *evaluative* element and a *commitment* element, which I see to be in a relationship of mutual interaction and mutual interdependence.

(c) Meaning-making and the 'reserved' or 'suspended' response to choice

The *evaluative* element of choice involves the exercise of rationality and the use of appropriate and reliable means of assessing the evidence and testing the belief as a hypothesis. If, to use my earlier example, we are seeking to evaluate whether or not a particular theoretical perspective provides sufficient understanding to enable us to answer the question 'What is man?', then we may legitimately conclude that it does not and, accordingly, 'reserve' or 'suspend' our response. I am prepared to accept that this is a 'choice' because the 'reserved' or 'suspended' response involves a value-commitment issuing in action, namely a commitment *not* to commit oneself to an 'unreserved' response until understanding is 'complete'. Such a commitment may be seen to be both desirable and necessary in order to ensure that the quest for meaning is pursued with integrity and rigour.

There is a sense, however, in which to hold this position necessitates redefining 'belief'. If we accept the premise that all understanding is partial and plural, then we cannot choose to believe anything until understanding is complete. 'Believing' then becomes synonymous with 'knowing' and 'beliefs' become synonymous with 'facts'. Of course it could be pointed out that determining *when* understanding is 'complete' is a matter of 'belief', thus choosing the 'reserved' or 'suspended' response is also a matter of 'belief'—belief that understanding is still partial and that there is more to be understood. The 'partial and plural understanding' argument could, I presume, also be used when we experience difficulty in choosing between conflicting beliefs of a religious, moral or political kind because the rational arguments for and against each belief appear to balance each other out. In these circumstances we could choose to 'reserve' or 'suspend' our response until such time as new arguments are found which will tip the balance in favour of one belief and against another. When this occurs, however, we are not necessarily committed to an 'unreserved' response; we might decide to 'reserve' our response until such time as more new arguments are found which will restore the balance or tip it the other way! Compelling though this argument may seem, we should recognise that it is supportive of a view of human beings which restricts their understanding of meaning-making activities to the level of empirical verification. Thus, to use my earlier metaphor, it is a view that keeps the 'empirical carpet' firmly beneath our feet.

But let us now examine the 'reserved' or 'suspended' response to choice within the context of what I will call 'personal meaning-making'. How do human beings choose between alternative actions in their personal lives? How do they choose between marrying X or marrying Y, or not marrying at all? How do they formulate a personal belief about what is best for their children? How do they decide upon the goals they are to aim for in their lives? I take it for granted that human beings exercise rationality in deciding between alternative actions, ordering their priorities, and choosing their values. The *evaluative* element of choice whereby the *pros and cons* of each possibility are rehearsed and assessed is as necessary in responding to these questions of personal meaning-making as it is in responding to such a question as 'What is man?'. Here, however, the relationship between *evaluative* and *commitment* elements is more apparent; choice of belief constitutes choice of action; what is believed is to be done. We should note, too, that our understanding of all these 'human' situations is as partial and plural as it is in the situation of evaluating more 'academic' responses. What is more, the choice of action and the belief from which it stems are grounded in human hope, not necessarily in human knowledge, and the future is unknowable. Is a 'reserved' or 'suspended' response a legitimate 'choice' in these circumstances?

Certainly, as we acknowledged earlier, it is a *choice*—not to choose! But is it a choice which issues in action? Does this conscious act of choice involve both *evaluative* and *commitment* elements? In deciding not to choose between marrying X or Y, or not marrying at all, I would, I assume, remain exactly as I am. In deciding not to choose what is best for my children, I would continue to do for them what I am already doing. In deciding not to choose an aim in life, I would continue to take things as they come. Thus the 'action' which results from a 'reserved' or 'suspended' choice is no different from the action which precedes it before the 'choice' is made. This kind of 'choice' brings about no change in commitment; it is a choice in name only. The effects of making a 'reserved' or 'suspended' choice are the same as those which follow from 'ignoring the question and trying to live without thinking about it' (my third choice on page 73). Indeed, the effects of a 'reserved' or 'suspended' choice on personal meaning-making may be compared to the effects which unconsciously assimilated beliefs have upon the individual who does not acknowledge their influence and does not, therefore, examine them critically. The 'reserved' or 'suspended' response, therefore, does not result in human beings exercising more control over their being and future; it 'suspends' their control and diminishes their responsibility for who or what they become. I conclude, therefore, that to 'reserve' or 'suspend' our response to matters of belief on the grounds that knowledge is partial and plural and the future unknowable, is to limit the possibilities of, and potentialities for, our own human development; it is to restrict human beings to what they are; it is to challenge the view that human beings have an 'open' future; it is to deny that human beings are in a state of becoming; it is to assert that human nature is fixed.

(d) *Meaning-making and the 'provisional' response to choice*

Although we should not be surprised that it is sometimes necessary to 'reserve' or 'suspend' our response when choosing between beliefs, we should be surprised if it is always necessary to do so. Human beings *are* able to choose between conflicting beliefs of a religious, moral and political kind and they *are* able to choose between alternative actions in their personal lives. We should not assume that being willing to make such choices signals a breakdown in rationality. We may, for example, find the arguments for one belief more consistent with the evidence than another; we may decide that the authorities or experts who support one belief are more trustworthy or persuasive than those who do not; we may choose to hold a certain belief or choose a particular course of action because we see these to be consistent with certain principles in which we already believe. But making a choice between beliefs does not necessarily commit us to holding a belief for ever. We may accept the premise that all understanding is partial but interpret it to mean that we must regard the beliefs we choose to hold as being *provisional* until such time as our experience enables us to confirm them or otherwise. There is, then, a considerable difference between a 'reserved' or 'suspended' response to choosing between beliefs and a 'provisional' response; the former commits us to waiting for verification before we act, the latter commits us to seeking verification through our actions.

The evaluative element of making a 'provisional' choice between beliefs involves, as we would expect, the exercise of rationality in exactly the same manner as we have already considered. The area of experience within which rationality is exercised, however, is not only that part of human experience and endeavour which is susceptible to the verification procedures of the logical positivists, where only propositions which can be empirically verified or falsified have meaning, all others (except those of a logical or mathematical kind) being considered meaningless. Human life is wider than what is circumscribed by a naturalistic philosophy of science. Thus, the exercise of rationality relates to all of human experience, to all of what it means to be human. It encompasses human needs, aspirations, feelings and beliefs; human experiences of relationship both to the natural world and to other human beings; human experiences of wonder and indifference, fear and hope, loneliness and companionship, meaninglessness and purpose, violence and compassion, love and hate, and so on. In illustration of the difference between a 'reserved' or 'suspended' response and a 'provisional' response to choosing between beliefs, we might ask what it would mean to make a 'provisional' choice in the three situations I introduced earlier—that is, to marry, to bring up children, and to choose an aim in life.

The evaluative element of making a 'provisional' choice would involve me in cataloguing the many possible courses of action that, apparently, are open to me. For example: to marry X or Y, or, indeed, A, B, or C, etc; to co-habit, to have series of casual affairs, etc; to be stricter with my children, or more indulgent, or more demonstrable, etc; to work harder at my job, or less hard, to volunteer for extra responsibility, to refuse more responsibility so that I can spend more time with my family, etc. I might then consider the possible consequences of these actions both for myself and for other people affected by my choice. For example: being married could cost me a lot of money and restrict my freedom and I might not be able to make X happy; being stricter with my children could lead to conflict in the home and my children might feel unloved; working harder and taking more responsibility in my job could improve my chances of promotion but my employers might still expect more, etc. I might then try to relate the different courses of action and their consequences to whatever principles I might already have come to hold as a result of being socialised into them by my upbringing. For example: can the value of marriage be assessed in economic terms?; what responsibility can one have for another person's happiness/unhappiness?; do I have the right as a parent to impose my will on my children?; do my children have rights?; what are the moral obligations of an employee to an employer and vice-versa?; what is my value to my employer?; what is my value to my family?; what is my value to myself?: why are human beings valued? etc. Finally, I might try to see each of these situations in terms of their possible significance to the eventual outcome of my life, my personal future. For example: will making this choice contribute to the achievement of a sense of contentment, peace, personal worth, success, the sense of a life well lived?; what values are worthwhile?; what ought I to do? etc.

This process of evaluating the different choices which are possible within these situations may, of course, remain at the level of speculation. I may be overwhelmed by the complexities of the issues involved and feel unable to make a choice. I may seek ways of postponing a choice until such time as my understanding of the consequences of taking certain actions are clearer to me (ie, a 'reserved' or 'suspended' choice). I may decide to discuss the issues with the different persons involved in the hope of eliminating some of the choices and diminishing the possibility of making the wrong choice. In short, there are many reasons which can be found for not translating evaluation into commitment and so completing the act of choice. What really prevents me from choosing is, however, my recognition that to make a choice—any choice—is to take a *risk*. I have already identified 'to live with uncertainty' as a human 'given' and we have seen how this fact can be used to support the view that human beings must 'learn to live with the unanswered question'. The issue is, however, whether the risk of choosing is somehow preferable to the risk of not choosing. At this point, it seems to me, we are poised on the edge of what I have called the 'arena of faith-responses'. Whatever we do—choose or not choose—is to go beyond the limits of our knowledge and to step off the 'empirical carpet'. But, it could be objected, *to choose not to choose* is to make a decision *not* to step off the empirical carpet and *not* to enter the 'arena of faith-responses'. In reply one could argue that to *choose not to choose* is to decide that meaning has to be limited to those propositions which can be verified or falsified by appeal to empirical fact. But to hold this view of meaning is to *believe* that a scientific paradigm of meaning is the only paradigm of meaning that has truth and certainty. *To believe this is to enter the 'arena of faith responses'* for it is to commit oneself to interpreting one's experience of life in terms of the *tenets of faith* of a scientific hypothesis. That choice constitutes 'holding a belief by an act of faith'. It would appear, then, that human beings have no choice but to make a 'faith-response' to choice. We now need to consider what this means.

(e) Meaning-making and the 'faith' response to choice

An 'act of faith' is, quite simply, the conscious choice of a belief or value. Conscious choice, as we have seen, involves two essential elements, *evaluation* and *commitment*, which, when combined, issue in action. That action of holding a belief and acting in accordance with it is an 'act of faith'. Thus a 'faith response' occurs when the individual, confronted by the necessity of choosing between beliefs as an essential constituent of meaning-making, does so by an 'act of faith'. The boundaries of the 'arena of faith responses' occur at that point at which human beings are constrained to risk acting beyond the limits of their present knowledge either by choosing or not choosing what to do and what to believe. The 'arena of faith responses' is entered whenever the individual acts in accordance with a belief which they hold by an 'act of faith'. Contained within the 'arena of faith responses' are all beliefs which human beings hold about themselves and their world, both systematised and individualistic, including the traditional belief systems of religion and their secular equivalents and alternatives.

Let us pursue our consideration of making a 'provisional' response to choice between beliefs (or between actions which reflect particular beliefs) in the light of the above definitions and statements. The commitment element of choice would involve me in the recognition that the situations confronting me, and the issues which they raise, pose important questions to which I must respond. We should note, however, that my recognition that these questions *are* important will depend upon the values and beliefs which I already hold about myself, about other people and about the world. I may have come to hold these values and beliefs consciously by the process which I have tried to identify. However, we must not lose sight of the influence which unconsciously assimilated beliefs and values have upon our perception of what issues are important to us.

There is a sense in which we are born into other people's 'acts of faith'. The socialising process 'humanises' us in accordance with certain beliefs and values which other human beings (most notably, our 'significant others') hold by 'an act of faith'. In childhood and even beyond it, we accept these as 'how things are' and it is only when we begin to develop the capacity to 'problematise' our experience (a capacity which education should increase) that we are confronted by the need to choose between beliefs and values for ourselves. We should note too that the 'culture' into which we are born is a repository of other people's 'acts of faith', both from the past and the present. We are, accordingly, 'humanised' as 'receptors' of those beliefs and values ('civilising values') which a society has come to embrace as important and necessary in human life and its fulfilment within the context of community. This means that the individual, from the time of birth onwards, lives within the 'arena of faith responses' but does so unconsciously. Thus the individual, in seeking to choose between beliefs, does not do so *in vacuo* but draws upon and so makes conscious the beliefs and values by which he or she has been formed. We encountered the same notion earlier when we noted how the 'scripts' of our lives are largely written by others and that it is through exercising a conscious choice between beliefs that we begin to make our 'scripts' our own. We can now express the same view using the terminology of 'faith'. Our capacity to take responsibility for our own being and personal future is dependent upon our capacity to make 'faith responses'—that is, to choose consciously between beliefs and act in accordance with the beliefs we choose. We thus hold beliefs by 'an act of faith'. But by making a 'faith response', or in holding beliefs by an 'act of faith', we do not eradicate our former 'scripts'; we re-evaluate and re-interpret them in the light of newly chosen goals. This is how human beings engage in the task of meaning-making. Holding beliefs by an act of faith is not, therefore, an option for human beings, it is an essential constituent of what it means to be human: it is another human 'given'.

The commitment element of choosing between beliefs—which issues in 'holding beliefs by an act of faith'—draws deeply, then, on the amalgam of beliefs and values which are the outcome of our individual interactional experiences with our cultural and personal histories. It is, however, the act of making a conscious choice which prompts in us a greater awareness of those forces which have shaped, and which continue to shape us, as persons. The choices we make are, therefore, *self disclosing*. Thus, to return to the three illustrative situations I considered earlier, my decision to marry X, to encourage my children to develop greater independence of thought and action, and my acceptance of additional responsibility in my work, may be a more accurate reflection of the beliefs and values I have assimilated unconsciously from my past than indications that I have reached a level of personal autonomy in choosing between beliefs. But we should not expect or even desire the outcome of choosing consciously to be one in which there is no sense of continuity or coherence between previously assimilated beliefs and values and those which we choose consciously. If this were to be the case, our identities would become fragmented and we would lose the will to live, let alone act. I suggest, then, that the act of choosing is a *selective* one which focuses our attention on particular experiences in our past and which involves us in re-evaluating and re-interpreting those experiences in the light of what we know and believe *now*. An important outcome of this process is, of course, that we become aware of what we knew and believed *then*; thus the act of choosing consciously includes the evaluation of our past 'acts of faith' in terms of their actual outcomes in our lives. It is in the light of such outcomes that we make further 'faith responses', and so the process continues.

It is precisely because the choices we make are 'self disclosing' and enable us to evaluate their shaping effects on our lives that we should think of 'faith responses' as 'provisional' choices. To conceive of the choices we make as committing us to hold certain beliefs for ever is to deny that our futures are open and that we can take responsibility for them. Choosing consciously is a selective act because meaning-making only follows from selecting between alternatives. To hold certain beliefs by an 'act of faith' is to make a provisional commitment to seeking meaning through those beliefs rather than through others.[16] Thus, to make a 'faith response' is to discriminate between different beliefs and to place limits—voluntary limits—on the meanings we can find in our lives. If, however, our experience fails to confirm that the beliefs we have chosen have engendered our lives with meaning, or even the possibility of meaning, then we must be free to reject them and choose others.

The process of making 'provisional' choices is, I think, logically defensible in a way in which making a 'reserved' or 'suspended' choice is not, simply because it is selective. To adopt a 'reserved' or 'suspended' response is to refuse to choose between beliefs and therefore to disengage oneself from the process of selection which is integral to meaning-making. Even the 'partial and plural understanding' argument founders on the grounds that one cannot know when knowledge is complete or how it can be brought together unless one engages in the process of selection, and that requires choices to be made.

But the final indictment of the 'reserved' or 'suspended' response to choice is its failure to take account of 'temporality' and 'mortality' factors which exert such a powerful influence on human consciousness. The only certainty within a world of uncertainty is that human beings die; this is a human 'given'. Thus the time-scale within which the individual can engage in meaning-making is not the same as that in which 'humankind' can do so. Because the 'temporality' and 'mortality' factors have an insignificant influence on the course and progress of the knowledge of humankind it is perfectly reasonable that, within this essentially theoretical sphere of meaning-making, choices are deferred and risks avoided until such time as knowledge has progressed to a point where choices become unnecessary. But within the life of the individual, time is too short to permit the 'reserved' or 'suspended' response to be the norm within meaning-making; choices have to be made and risks have to be taken. If I were to take it as the norm, because of the 'temporality' factor, I would find that what I could have chosen is no longer a choice. For example, as an adolescent I might speculate about what I should do with my youth; if I do not make a conscious choice, the temporality of youth chooses for me and now, beyond my youth, I have no choice. Similarly, in the early years of married life, my wife and I may speculate about having children; if we do not choose (for or against), the temporality of my wife's child-bearing potential chooses for us, and now, beyond it, we have no choice. Both these examples illustrate how *risk* is present both in choosing and in not choosing. To choose *not* to steer one's youth in the direction of a chosen goal is as much a risk as choosing to do so; to choose *not* to have children is as much a risk as choosing to have them. Because we are human within the limits of temporality and mortality, there is always an element of risk (but also of growth) at the level of our deepest commitments by which our identities and self understanding are established and preserved and our ultimate concerns defined and expressed. It is how human beings respond to this fact that determines what meaning they will find in their lives. I have argued that their only response to this dilemma is to hold beliefs about themselves, other people and the world by an 'act of faith'.

The human being's task of making meaning might be compared to the artist's task of painting a picture. The human being has no alternative to holding beliefs other than holding other beliefs; the artist has no alternative to using colours other than using other colours. 'Unbeliefs' like 'uncolours' do not exist; a 'beliefless' human life is as impossible to contemplate as a 'colourless' painting. The task of making meaning involves the human being in choosing between beliefs; the task of painting a picture involves the artist in choosing between colours. The human being who does not choose between beliefs cannot make meaning in his or her life; the artist who does not choose between colours cannot paint a picture on the canvas.

(f) The 'religious faith response' to choice: a brief note

I have already stressed in the foregoing sections of this chapter that in using the terms 'act of faith', 'faith response' and 'arena of faith responses', I am not restricting their reference to religion or religious belief. It is the necessity of human beings 'holding beliefs by an act of faith' which I am proposing is a human 'given', not the necessity of holding *religious* beliefs by an act of *religious* faith. As I have indicated, however, the 'arena of faith responses' contains within it the traditional belief systems of religion, and choosing to hold religious beliefs is as much an option for human beings as choosing to hold beliefs of a naturalistic, moral and political kind. An 'act of faith' or a 'faith response' may, of course, be conceived of in religious terms as well as in naturalistic and humanistic ones, although I would expect the process of making a conscious choice both between religious and non-religious beliefs and between different religious beliefs to remain the same—ie, evaluation and commitment leading to action. I will be considering this in more detail later in this book.

In the meantime we should note that a 'religious' view of 'man' and of the human condition consists of an *interpretation* of human 'being' and human 'nature' using religious categories of thought and understanding which combine to produce a coherent framework of meaning. As we have seen, formulating and holding beliefs is an integral part of the process of making meaning. Thus, the coherence of a theological framework of meaning is determined by the way in which certain beliefs are brought into a relationship with each other. We may speak, broadly, therefore, of religions having their own 'inner logic', or, more broadly (and controversially) of religion having its own 'logic'. Thus it is perfectly feasible for religions to provide a description of 'man' and of the human condition using religious categories of understanding. We should recognise, however, that this 'description' is also *interpretational*; it is an expression of those beliefs and values upon which a religion's inner logic depends and upon which, consequently, its understanding of meaning depends. On this basis, the comprehensive 'systems of meaning' which religions provide belong *within* the 'arena of faith responses' and are *religious* faith responses to the question 'What does it mean to be human?'.

In so far as an anthropological or sociological description of 'man' deliberately seeks to be value-free and not interpretational (and, therefore, does not belong within the 'arena of faith responses'), we would expect there to be divergence between it and a theological description of 'man'. However, because both descriptions are of the same phenomenon—'man' and the 'human condition'—we would, equally, expect there to be a correspondence between them. For example, we would expect both descriptions to include reference to what is enigmatic about human life, but that the anthropological account would restrict itself to pointing *to* the enigmas (ie, the enigmas would be 'bracketed') while the theological account would point *beyond* the enigmas to the ultimate shape of reality which, from religious point of view, makes sense of them. Thus a 'religious' view of 'man' is not necessarily contradictory of an 'anthropological' description of 'man', but goes beyond it by indicating how human beings can transcend the human condition which an anthropological account treats as normative. A *'religious* faith response' to choice involves, therefore, choosing to interpret the conditions of one's life in terms of norms derived from a system of meaning with a transcendent reference point outside the human condition. The cultural form of religions is, in general, a set of symbolic words and acts through which this sense of meaning is conveyed to human beings and which also serve to relate human beings to transcendent reality. To make a *'religious* faith response' is thus to see oneself and to interpret one's experiences in terms of whatever a religion understands to be the meaning and purpose of human life. It is also to place one's 'faith' in that understanding to a point of allowing it to shape one's life.

2. *Who am I?: A psychological perspective*

(i) *Are there universal characteristics of human development?*

We move on now to consider whether the features of 'human development' which psychologists have identified concur with, and so confirm, what we have identified, from an anthropological and sociological perspective, as the essential characteristics of humanisation. I cannot attempt to give detailed attention to the enormous corpus of psychological literature which is relevant to such a consideration, so I will be selective and look for indications that might provide grounds for believing that concurrence can be found. I have already expressed the view that in thinking about the personal development of pupils and trying to understand what happens to young people during adolescence, reference to the theories of Erik Erikson is a *sine qua non* for teachers. Here, however, I do not intend to restrict myself to his work but to draw more generally on the field of developmental psychology. I will, however, preface this by making a single excursion into psycho-social theory of development, using Erikson's work as an example.

Erikson believes that individuals have unique capacities to create their own way of life and sense of personal meaning, but how successful they are in doing so will depend upon the way in which they deal with the essentially emotional crises which further their human development. He sees the human being as an evolving system; in each moment of life development, the individual, in one sense, chooses between opposites and, in another sense, incorporates such opposites in order to create a new and unique life situation. Thus human development occurs as a result of the individual moving from phase to phase and within each phase (of which Erikson identifies eight) experiencing the need to strive to incorporate irreconcilable opposites. So, for example, during childhood, development occurs in a progressive manner in accordance with the way in which the child struggles to achieve:

1. A sense of basic trust while overcoming a sense of basic mistrust (a realisation of hope);
2. A sense of autonomy while combatting a sense of doubt and shame (a realisation of will);
3. A sense of initiative while overcoming a sense of guilt (a realisation of purpose);
4. A sense of industry while fending off a sense of inferiority (a realisation of competence);
5. A sense of identity while overcoming a sense of identity diffusion (a realisation of fidelity).[17]

Erikson sees the progression from a central problem or dilemma of one phase to that of the next as a universal characteristic of human development, although the particular context for the dilemma is culturally defined. It is important to note how each successive phase provides the possibility of new solutions for previous struggles. Thus, Erikson's aetiology of human behaviour and his theory of psychosocial development, although focusing on the *affective* forces which make individuals act, provide a close parallel to the essentially cognitive processes which we have been examining whereby human development is seen to occur as a consequence of individuals being constrained to respond to the dilemma of choosing between beliefs.

(ii) Childhood: belongingness-identity and its inherited visions

In turning now to the field of developmental psychology, I will draw on the work of W D Wall, undertaken while he was Professor of the Psychology of Education and head of the Department of Child Development and Educational Psychology in the London Institute of Education, and published in his authoritative texts *Constructive Education for Children* and *Constructive Education for Adolescents*. Wall has little doubt that:

> . . . . *Young children and most pupils throughout their primary schools (5–11) build up and elaborate their sense of identity and the image they hold of themselves by a feeling of identification with their family, by the kinds of information about themselves which they get from important*

*others, including their teachers and their peers, and by their belonging to
various groups. For the most part, they are largely unaware of themselves in any elaborated sense of self-knowledge; and only late in childhood do they begin to develop empathy with others based on notions of
reciprocity. Their identity is rooted in a primitive sense of belonging—
they define themselves in terms of what they belong to and what belongs
to them. . .[18]*

One of the things that belongs to them is an inherited vision of self,
other people, the world, and so on. This vision, to use the language of
transactional analysis, is the framework of their story or 'script' and it
can be life-enhancing or life-destroying. In *Fully Human, Fully Alive,*
Fr John Powell, SJ, offers some examples of how, for better or for
worse, a child's first tentative vision will, by and large, be that of his or
her parents and family. Some of the 'life messages' Powell suggests are
transmitted to children are:

1. I am loved.
2. I am loved only when I'm good.
3. All people are basically good and decent.
4. Our family and relatives are good: everyone else is suspect.
5. Life is exciting; it is a real adventure.
6. Life isn't easy; it is everyone for himself.
7. Success in life is spelled: M-O-N-E-Y.

He comments:

*Eventually the child will be graduated from the home and family situa-
tion, but the old parental messages will continue to play softly on the
tape recorder of the brain: 'Life is. . . .'; 'Success is. . .'; 'The most
important thing is. . . .'; 'You are. . . .' etc.*

On the subject of 'life messages' about the physical world, he adds:

*Blessed are the children who receive a life-giving, energising vision of
the universe. They will be taught to wonder, to be filled with curiosity,
to admire. Their leisure will be filled with nature walks, stargazing,
planting gardens, bird-watching, and rock and seashell collecting. They
will learn to care for their own pets, to distinguish species of flowers and
trees as well as cloud formations. . . . Sad are the children of parents
who have no time for such 'nonsense'. . . They will only be able to see a
dingy little world.[19]*

Inherited visions of self, others, life, the world, God, etc, are an inevitable consequence of a 'belongingness-identity'—and this is another
'given' of the human situation. Young children need to be given a
'belongingness-identity' in order to have any sense of personal security.
But does that mean that, once given, the child can only explore and give
meaning to life from this inherited position of security? Is it not possi-

ble to seek and find new visions which contradict, enlarge and modify the pictures of life drawn for him or her? Clearly the answer is Yes, it is possible. Fortunately, as we grow up, new influences and other messages come to us from significant other persons. There is a constant turnover of new evidence in our lives.[20] But the extent to which we can respond to this evidence is dependent upon other factors—such as whether we have a capacity to be open and flexible as opposed to being closed and rigid. Personal growth in this respect will be dependent upon the degree of our self awareness—our capacity to reflect on our experience, to re-evaluate it and re-interpret it—and that capacity may be governed by our early childhood experiences.

(iii) Adolescence: an opportunity for reflection on and re-evaluation and re-interpretation of the self

But following the necessarily authoritarian context of childhood, the onset of adolescence provides human beings with a natural opportunity for reflection on, and re-evaluation and re-interpretation of the self. Much has been written, especially by psychologists, about adolescence and its importance to personal development, but teachers, traditionally, have characterised it as a period when young people can be expected to be moody, fretful, disorientated and sometimes extremely antagonistic and fractious towards school and learning. But Wall indicates that all these characteristics are symptomatic of the central adolescent quest for new and more adequate social roles and identities. He comments:

> *Central to this whole process, and in a sense the internal foundation of any genuinely adult maturity, is the acquisition of a series of identities or selves unified by a general concept of who one is and by what standards one is prepared to live.*[21]

He suggests that five selves lead to adult identity:

1. *A physical self:*
    Adolescents have to come to terms with the dramatic changes to their own bodies and develop an acceptance of themselves as they physically appear to themselves and others. As a result of pubertal growth they have to define a new concept of the physical self *and acquire a much modified body image.*
2. *A sexual self:*
    Adolescents have to come to terms with their own sexuality and develop a sexual self *which permits a varied range of relationships with the opposite sex ranging from affectionate indifference to full adult love and passion.*
3. *A vocational self:*
    In order to find an occupation, a job, trade or profession, which will

give them some satisfaction in work and provide economically for their
independence from their family, adolescents have to find a vocational
self.

4. *A social self:*
   Adolescents have to find a social self, *a clear and differentiated series*
   of roles in the smaller and larger groups of adult society into which they
   are moving.

5. *A philosophic self:*
   Adolescents need to find a philosophic self—*a set of ideas, ideals,*
   principles and interpretations of life which are some sort of guide to
   action in difficult circumstances. This philosophic self may be quite
   rudimentary, of the 'bother you Jack, I'm all right' kind; it may be
   political, religious, social or a highly elaborated amalgam of some or
   all of these; but it is the personal self or identity—the thread of unity
   between the highly other-dependent self-image of the child and the
   elaborated self-consciousness, expanded and intensified emotionally,
   and the autonomy of the fully adult personality. It is the unifying
   principle which brings the other selves into a more or less harmonious
   relation to each other. [22]

It is this quest for new and more adult selves, accompanied by an increase in sensitivity to self, which provides the opportunity for the development of self awareness and self knowledge. If psychologists are
correct in their view that during adolescence young people consciously
seek to distance themselves from their period of childhood, the *educational* opportunity which this time provides for questions such as 'Who
am I?', 'Where am I going?', 'What shall I be?' and 'What is important
to me?' to be rooted in the real and immediate experiences of young
people cannot afford to be neglected by teachers. Wall describes the
benefits of self-awareness which can result from adolescence in the following terms:

> *Fully self-aware persons—(ie, those who are personally auton-*
> *omous)—are transparent to themselves and find their identity in this self*
> *knowledge which renders them able to stand aside from any belonging-*
> *ness-identity they may have. Their security is internal and based on self*
> *understanding and acceptance, not external and dependent upon adopt-*
> *ing and being adopted by a group of any kind. This does not mean that*
> *they necessarily reject group or social norms and loyalties; but that their*
> *obedience to them is critical, rational, voluntary and a matter of re-*
> *newed choice. Such norms and loyalties are not for them a vital source*
> *of personal security; although they are fully accepted, they are rationally*
> *amenable to change.* [23]

That, at least, is the theory. In Chapters Three and Four I will be
examining some of the factors which militate against adolescents

achieving this capacity for discrimination in their personal life styles and attitudes. But Wall is also aware of the difficulties adolescents face. He comments:

> *What usually happens . . . is not so much an increased awareness and a developed identity based on self knowledge, but an enlargement, change in, and reaffirmation of belongingness-identity.*[24]

One of the main reasons why the ideal of what *should* happen in adolescence does not always match the reality of what *does* happen is that we have placed too much stress on adolescence as a *natural* happening in the life of young people and have assumed that we can leave the quest for more adult identity to take place naturally. Wall reminds us that

> *. . . human maturity in the full sense is not achieved by the simple flowering of a natural impulse. Human maturing is largely the product of education and the stimulation it provides; for education, at any level, is a process of conscious shaping and it aims to give a direction to growth. . . . In the absence of an effective shaping process—especially in times when the young are offered a multiplicity of choices—it is not surprising that we witness such mindless conformity to what may appear to be highly stereotyped roles.*[25]

Despite recent curricular initiatives such as TVEI, the Skills for Adult Working Life Project, CPVE, Active Tutorial Work, PSME, TRIST, etc, schools on the whole still provide very little opportunity within either the formal or informal curriculum for young people to engage in reflection on, and re-evaluation and re-interpretation of the self; they have little sense of how they might teach young people to acquire such skills; neither do they generally recognise the essential part self expression plays in helping youngsters come to terms with themselves. Instead, many schools still continue to embrace the notion that such concerns are at worst trendy and at best peripheral, and that the development of the human being is best served by pursuit of cognitive goals. At a time when young people are experiencing the need for more 'subject knowing', some schools appear to double their efforts to flood the curriculum with 'object' knowing.[26]

When we reflect on our own difficulties in reaching any degree of self awareness without prolonged and painful effort, I do not think we should be too critical of young people who mindlessly conform to the norms of their own 'adolescent' culture. Without help, without alternative visions and models, without understanding of how to judge and how to choose, young people will inevitably resolve the 'identity crisis' of adolescence in this way. To conclude this psychological perspective with a final observation by Wall:

Harmony, effectiveness and autonomy at any level can only be reached for any human being if the emotional life, and its deep needs, is rendered articulate and synthesised with a trained cognition. Such a synthesis is of slow growth and is unlikely to be completed by the end of adolescence, however fortunate the individual may have been in childhood and puberty. But schools and colleges must lay the basis of what demands a long period of adult maturation to produce—and this concern must affect and inform the shape of the curriculum and the life of the school as a community.[27]

(iv) Do sociological and psychological accounts of humanisation concur?

Although I have been selective in my use of sources to provide a psychological perspective on humanisation, and brief and incomplete though it is, this account does reinforce, as we would expect, the sociological perspective's emphasis on humanisation resulting from a process of social interaction between human beings. Furthermore, the psychological perspective does give us reason to believe that, despite the powerful influence of the socio-historical context in shaping human beings in terms of what are regarded as normative views of the human, human beings do have a capacity for taking responsibility for the person they wish to become and are not merely passive 'objects' manipulated by social forces. This capacity is seen to be connected with the possession of an ability which is unique to human beings—the ability to be 'self conscious'. It is important that we recognise, however, that the 'self' is socially constructed—as much a product of social interaction as any other 'reality'. What the psychological perspective offers, however, is further insight into the dynamics of social construction related to the self. In Chapter Three we will be looking more closely at what this means and, in later chapters considering its implications for education in general and religious education in particular.

In the meantime, however, we need to give attention to two important questions which arise from our deliberations on the questions 'What does it mean to be human?' and 'Who am I?'.

1. Does the account of how human beings are shaped by their cultural and personal histories allow for the possibility of their discovering and embracing new visions which lie outside these histories?
2. Does the social phenomenologist's view of reality as a social construct provide an adequate account of 'religion' or of a 'religious view of life'?

I see both these questions as being related to the wider one of what place should we give in our description of 'man' and the human condition to 'serendipity'—'the gift of finding valuable or agreeable things not sought for: the happy knack of accidental discovery'.[28]

3. What place for serendipity and transcendence within humanisation?

If human beings are unable to discover and embrace new visions which lie outside their cultural and personal histories, then surely there is little point in education because this is precisely what education is about—helping young people to transcend whatever factors are limiting their growth towards human maturity. An essential task of schools, then, is to enrich children's stocks of personal visions—especially those providing models of the human—and extend their repertoires of belief and value responses beyond those inculcated by their cultural and personal histories. For reasons indicated earlier, one crucial area in which their repertoires will need to be extended will be that of 'faith responses', for, as I have tried to show, all human beings must ultimately live by and through faith. This will involve providing children and young people with opportunities to explore the faith responses of men and women and the dilemmas of the human condition which prompt such responses. It will involve encouraging them to try to relate whatever insights they may obtain from this to their own situations—to their own human condition—so that they can be used creatively in the process of acquiring a series of identities or selves unified by a general concept of who one is and by what standards one is prepared to live.

To do this successfully young people will need to be taught the skills of reflecting upon, re-evaluating and re-interpreting the self. I suggest that they will acquire these skills most easily within contexts which they find naturally engaging, namely their everyday acts, feelings and experiences. It is to these—their feelings and experiences—that they must give meaning, for it will be from these that, ultimately, they will be able to give meaning to everything else. Sam Keen puts the same point like this:

> Our starting point must be individual biography and history. If I am to discover the holy, it must be in my biography and not in the history of Israel. If there is a principle which gives unity and meaning to history it must be something I touch, feel and experience . . . Is there anything on the native ground of my experience—my biography, my history—which testifies to the reality of the holy? . . . Is there anything in my experience which gives it unity, depth, dignity, meaning and value—which makes graceful freedom possible? If we can discover such a principle at the

foundation of personal identity, we have every right to use the ancient language of the holy, and, therefore, to mark out a domain for theological exploration.[29]

Keen's comments about experience 'testifying to the reality of the holy' and seeking 'a principle at the foundation of personal identity' are relevant to my second question—whether the social phenomenologist's view of reality as a social construct provides an adequate account of 'religion'. I would imagine that no religious believer could ever think so and remain a believer. For example, I think the following words of David Edwards, Dean of Southwark, present a perspective which most Christians would share: they also add a new dimension, a religious one, to our earlier discussion of what it means to be human.

Being saved is basically living from, by and to God and not meaning or believing or doing any particular set of things. Because God has committed Himself to history in the particularities in which men are and become human, there always will be particular things to believe, mean and do. But salvation is none of these things, for salvation is God giving Himself to men so that they may be human. Thus salvation is always beyond words and meaning.[30]

I think the sentence '. . . . salvation is always beyond words and meaning' provides us with the key to answering our question about religion. It warns us of the danger of limiting 'reality' to that which we label 'real' and of confusing the 'reality' which we construct with the 'reality' to which our 'human-made' categories of religious meaning can only point. Such categories (which we will be considering in some detail in the next chapter) are subject to the same processes of social construction as any other form of human knowledge; they are social constructs whose value, significance and meaning depend upon the 'plausibility structure' within which they are located. If the 'plausibility structure' is equated here with the 'community of faith' (although such an equation is to over-simplify a complex sociological phenomenon), we can recognise how changes in that structure (such as have occurred in the Roman Catholic Church since Vatican II) necessitate the renegotiation of the meanings of the categories by which the faith is understood.

But the process of negotiating new meanings for religious categories and concepts is not a free for all. Rather, it is informed by the desire to make them into more effective ways of speaking of the realities that lie behind them—realities which, I have suggested, are not 'created' by human beings, not subject to any one cultural form, and not adequately defined by, or confined within, 'human-made' categories of understanding. We might follow Harvey Cox in using the word 'signal' to refer to that aspect of religion which is, in his words, 'coded, systematised, controlled and distributed by specialists'.[31] If there is a 'form of knowledge' which we could call 'religious' we might expect its inner logic and coherence to depend on the use of such signals, but we would also have to recognise their inadequacy in defining the reality to which they point. We could, however, speak of such coding as carrying, for members of a faith community, 'signals of transcendence' within a religion—signals which both disclose and authenticate that truth which religious categories and concepts seek to articulate. The term 'signals of transcendence' has a particular meaning in Peter Berger's work, and as I believe this may have some useful application within our understanding of religious education it is appropriate that we should give some attention to what he has to say. It will also give us an opportunity to see how Berger brings religion within the social construction of reality thesis.

(i) Signals of transcendence

In his book *A Rumour of Angels*, Berger presents the view that 'traditional religious beliefs (by which he means, essentially, Christian beliefs) have become empty of meaning not only in large sections of the general public but even among many people who, with whatever motives, continue to belong to a church.'[32] He suggests that commentators on the contemporary situation of religion are largely agreed that the fundamental religious assumption that 'there is another reality' is defunct and that 'the supernatural has departed from the modern world.'[33] With the disappearance of these categories by which religious people have traditionally sought to give life an overarching sense of meaning (plus the decline of institutional religious power through the process of secularisation), human consciousness itself has been 'secularised'. Berger is interested 'to delineate some facets of the situation in which thinking about religion must take place today'. (In this he shares in concerns which must also be those of the religious educator.) He adds, however: 'I am concerned with the religious questions themselves, on the level of truth rather than timeliness.' While one must be sensitive to one's socio-historical starting-point, it is possible, he argues, 'to liberate oneself to a considerable degree from the taken-for-granted assumptions of one's time.'[34] Thus he sets himself to examine 'the alleged demise of the supernatural'.

As a basis for his examination he adopts a number of premises; we need only concern ourselves with two of these—those relating to the concept of religion as a human projection, and to the concept of the social relativity of knowledge. (We should note, of course, that Berger's premises can be subjected to criticism and his conclusions may therefore be thought contentious.) Concerning the first, Berger writes:

I would like . . . to suggest that the entire view of religion as a human product or projection may once again be inverted, and that in such an inversion lies a viable theological method in response to the challenge of sociology. If I am right in this, what could be in the making here is a gigantic joke on Feuerbach.[35]

The reference to Feuerbach needs explaining. Feuerbach regarded religion as a gigantic projection of man's own being, that is, as essentially man writ large. He therefore proposed reducing theology to anthropology, that is, explaining religion in terms of its underlying human reality. He took over Hegel's notion of dialectics, 'a "conversation" between consciousness and whatever is outside consciousness', but instead of seeing religion providing the context for a 'conversation' between man and God, interpreted it as a context for a 'conversation' between man and man's own products. Thus instead of religion being a dialogue between man and superhuman reality, religion became a sort of human monologue.[36] Like Feuerbach, Berger takes anthropology as his starting point for devising a theological method of exploration, but he 'inverts' Feuerbach's projection theory as follows:

If the religious projections of man correspond to a reality that is superhuman and supernatural, then it seems logical to look for traces of this reality in the projector (ie, man) himself. This is not to suggest an empirical theology—that would be logically impossible—but rather a theology of very high empirical sensitivity that seeks to correlate its propositions with what can be empirically known.[37]

As, in Chapter One of this book, we have already considered the concept of knowledge as being socially related and therefore socially relative, we do not need to dwell on it here. We should, however, note that the theological approach which Berger is proposing to use derives from this premise about the nature of knowledge and that:

This most emphatically does not mean a search for religious phenomena that will somehow manifest themselves as different from human projections. Nothing is immune to the relativisation of socio-historical analysis. Whatever else these phenomena may be, they will also be human projections, products of human history, social constructions undertaken by human beings. The meta-empirical cannot be conceived as a kind of enclave within the empirical world, any more, incidentally, than freedom can be conceived as a hole in the fabric of causality. The theological decision will have to be that 'in, with and under' the immense array of human projections, there are indicators of a reality that is truly 'other' and that the religious imagination of man ultimately reflects.[38]

Before going further we should note Berger's use of the terms 'inductive faith' and 'deductive faith'. By 'inductive faith' he means 'a religious process of thought that begins with facts of human experience' and by 'deductive faith' he means a process of religious thought which 'begins with certain assumptions (notably assumptions about divine revelation) that cannot be tested by experience.' Thus 'inductive faith moves from human experience to statements about God, deductive faith from statements about God to interpretations of human experience.'[39]

We come now to a consideration of Berger's suggestion 'that theological thought seek out what might be called *signals of transcendence* within the empirically given human situation', and that 'there are *prototypical human gestures* that may constitute such signals.'[40] By 'signals of transcendence' Berger means 'phenomena that are to be found within the domain of our "natural" reality but that appear to point beyond that reality'. Thus he uses the term 'transcendence' literally to mean transcending the normal, everyday world. By 'prototypical gestures' he means 'certain reiterated acts and experiences that appear to express essential aspects of man's being, of the human animal as such'. He then proceeds to give five examples of prototypical human gestures, each of which constitutes a signal of transcendence and each of which provides what he calls an 'argument' for proceeding from 'the faith that is rooted in experience to the act of faith that transcends the empirical sphere . . .'.[40] These are: *the argument from order, the argument from play, the argument from hope, the argument from damnation* and *the argument from humour.* He stresses that he is not providing an exhaustive or exclusive list of human gestures that may be seen as signals of transcendence.[41] In order to illustrate Berger's theological method, we will look briefly at two of these—the argument from order and the argument from damnation.

(a) The argument from order

Berger follows Voegelin in identifying man's 'propensity for order'.

> *Any historical society is an order, a protective structure of meaning, erected in the face of chaos. Within this order the life of the group as well as the life of the individual makes sense. Deprived of such order, both group and individual are threatened with the most fundamental terror, the terror of chaos that Emile Durkheim called* anomie *(literally, a state of being 'order-less').*[42]

But human faith in order is related to man's fundamental trust in reality. This faith is experienced not only in the history of societies and civilisation, but, as we saw earlier in this chapter, in the life of each individual, for 'there can be no maturation without the presence of this

103

faith at the outset of the socialisation process'.[43] Berger argues, therefore, that 'man's propensity for order is grounded in a faith or trust that, ultimately, reality is "in order", "all right", "as it should be" . . .'. But he also points out that 'there is no empirical method by which this faith can be tested. To assent to it is itself an act of faith'. There is, however, the possibility of proceeding from this faith which is rooted in experience to an act of faith which transcends what can be proven empirically. The protypical human gesture or, in this case, *'ordering gesture'*, which Berger sees as signalling a reality which transcends ordinary, everyday experience, is the gesture by which a mother reassures her anxious child when he wakes alone in the night after a nightmare. When the mother says 'Don't be afraid—everything is in order, everything is all right', she is engaging in one of the most routine experiences of life which does not depend upon any religious preconceptions. But, argues Berger, '. . this common scene raises a far from ordinary question which immediately introduces a religious dimension: *is the mother lying to the child?'*. He comments:

> *The answer, in the most profound sense, can be 'no' only if there is some truth in the religious interpretation of human existence. Conversely, if the 'natural' is the only reality there is, the mother is lying to her child— lying out of love, to be sure, and obviously* not *lying to the extent that her reassurance is grounded in the fact of this love—but, in the final analysis, lying all the same. Why? Because the reassurance, transcending the immediately present two individuals and their situation, implies a statement about reality as such.*[44]

Berger's argument now moves to a consideration of what constitutes 'the basic formula of maternal and parental reassurance'. It is not merely that the role of the parent is to 'represent the order of this or that society but *order* as such, the underlying order of the universe that it makes sense to trust'. When the mother says *'everything* is all right' she is using a formula 'that can, without in any way violating it, be translated into a statement of cosmic scope—"Have trust in being" . . .' Berger comments:

> *The argument from ordering is metaphysical rather than ethical. To restate it: in the observable human propensity to order reality there is an intrinsic impulse to give cosmic scope to this order, an impulse that implies not only that human order in some way corresponds to an order that transcends it, but that this transcendent order is of such a character that man can trust himself and his destiny to it. . . . Every parent (or, at any rate, every parent who loves his child) takes upon himself the representation of a universe that is ultimately in order and ultimately*

trustworthy. This representation can be justified only within a religious (strictly speaking a supernatural) frame of reference. In this frame of reference the natural world within which we are born, love, and die is not the only world, but only the foreground of another world in which love is not annihilated in death, and which, therefore, the trust in the power of love to banish chaos is justified. Thus man's ordering propensity implies a transcendent order, and each ordering gesture is a signal of this transcendence.[45]

(b) The argument from damnation

Berger's choice of an argument from damnation is particularly interesting, not least because of all traditional religious concepts that of damnation is probably most obviously focused in the notion of the supernatural and most difficult to integrate within a liberal theology. He points out that it is the *negative form* of an argument from *justice*. It refers to 'experiences in which our sense of what is humanly permissible is so fundamentally outraged that the only adequate response to the offence as well as to the offender seems to be a curse of supernatural dimensions'.[46] As an illustration of this experience he refers to the trials of Nazi war criminals, and of Eichmann in particular. He is not concerned with how Eichmann is to be explained or dealt with, but rather with 'the character and intention of our condemnation of Eichmann'.[47] He comments:

> *There are certain deeds that cry out to heaven. These deeds are not only an outrage to our moral sense, they seem to violate a fundamental awareness of the constitution of our humanity. In this way, these deeds are not only evil, but* monstrously *evil. And it is this monstrosity that seems to compel even people normally and professionally given to such perspectives to suspend relativisations. It is one thing to say that moralities are socio-historical products, which are relative in time and space. It is quite another thing to say that therefore the deeds of an Eichmann can be viewed with scientific detachment as simply an instance of one such morality—and thus ultimately, can be considered a matter of taste.*[48]

The relativising framework within which a scientific or psychological judgment might be made about Eichmann is inadequate to this situation; absolute condemnation is required. It is in the 'impossibility' of any other judgment that Berger finds the signal of transcendence. He sees it manifested in two steps. First, because our condemnation is absolute and final the condemnation is given the status of a necessary and absolute truth—and yet this truth, 'while empirically given in our situation as men, cannot be empirically demonstrated to be either necessary or universal'. Thus 'either we deny that there is here anything that can be called truth—a choice that would make us deny what we experience most profoundly as our own being; or we must look beyond the realm of our "natural" experience for a validation of our certainty'. Second, no human punishment is 'enough' in the case of deeds as monstrous as these. Berger puts it thus:

> These are deeds that demand not only condemnation, but damnation in the full religious meaning of the word—that is, the doer not only puts himself outside the community of men; he also separates himself from a moral order that transcends the human community, and thus invokes a retribution that is more than human.[49]

Berger provides a further illustration of this argument from damnation by citing two pictures which came out of the war in Vietnam. Both pictures display prototypical gestures: the anguish in the face of a woman against whose head a solider holds a rifle, and the anguish in the face of a man carrying his dead daughter in his arms after a massacre. He argues that both gesture and countergesture imply transcendence and that both point to an ultimate, religious context in human experience. He explains his view as follows:

> Just as religion vindicates the gesture of protective reassurance, even when it is performed in the face of death, so it also vindicates the ultimate condemnation of the countergesture of inhumanity, precisely because religion provides a context for damnation. Hope and damnation are two aspects of the same, encompassing vindication.[50]

(c) Discovering signals of transcendence in religious traditions

Although Berger does 'confront the traditions' with the theological method which we have been considering, he is clearly less comfortable when applying 'inductive faith' to explicit religious phenomena. I do not necessarily wish to stay within the line of his argument at this point because that would mean making further excursions into sociology to explain the concepts of 'alienation' and 'false consciousness' which Berger uses to interpret experiences of the numinous and 'otherness' as 'alienated projections'. But something of the difficulties his position entails when it is related to, for example, religious experience, may be discerned in the following quotation from his earlier book, The Sacred Canopy, which was published in England under the title The Social Reality of Religion.

> If one grants the fundamental religious assumptions that an other reality somehow impinges or borders upon the empirical world, then these

features of the sacred will be dignified with the status of genuine 'experience'. Needless to say, this assumption cannot be made within a sociological or any other scientific frame of reference. In other words, the ultimate epistemological status of these reports of religious men will have to be rigorously bracketed. 'Other worlds' are not empirically available for the purposes of scientific analysis. Or, more accurately, they are only available as meaning-enclaves within this world, the world of human experience in nature and history. As such, they must be analysed as are all other human meanings, that is, as elements of the socially constructed world.[51]

It is here, then, that doubts about the adequacy of the social phenomenologist's account of religion arise and I summarise the characteristically perceptive observations of Ninian Smart, namely: that it is 'reductionist'; that many objects which enter into religious beliefs and interactions are not human products; that the theory of projection is not invoked to explain, for example, existentialism's way of dealing with an objectively indifferent universe; that our present picture of the world has been determined by the inner methods of science in interplay with the outer facts of the universe, and could Feuerbach with much plausibility have introduced the theory of projection to account for Newtonian physics?[52]

More generally, however, I think Berger's theological method does offer helpful ways of approaching the study of explicitly religious phenomenon within our present, pluralist situation, and is especially pertinent to the need for religious concepts to become relativised in order to bring about a relationship between education and religion. For example, he stresses that the historical dimension of all human experience must be taken into account theologically. He contends that 'if each age is seen in its "immediacy to God", each age must be carefully looked at for whatever signals of transcendence might be uniquely its own'.[53] He says the same of each religion—'The traditions, *all* traditions must be confronted in search of whatever signals of transcendence may have been sedimented in them.' He argues that 'in any empirical frame of reference, transcendence must appear as a projection of man. Therefore, if transcendence is to be spoken of *as* transcendence, the empirical frame of reference must be left behind'. The application of the inductive (as opposed to the deductive) method means confronting religious phenomena with the questions:

What is being said here? What is the human experience out of which these statements come? *And then:* To what extent, and in what way, may we see here genuine discoveries of transcendent truth?

In Chapter Six I hope to show how questions like these as well as the method which Berger applies to elucidate religious meaning through 'signals of transcendence' have an application within religious education.

Chapter Three

The social construction of reality and of human consciousness

Introduction

In this chapter I intend to extend my earlier consideration of the thesis that reality is socially constructed by focusing on some of the different factors within the human social world which combine to produce human consciousness. My interest in doing this arises from my view that any educational rationale for religious education that purports to show that the study of religions can contribute to pupils' personal development should be informed by an understanding of those processes by which human beings come to hold beliefs and values and should address itself to those everyday realities which constitute the pupils' 'life-world'. As we noted in Chapter One, an educational process which isolates 'academic knowledge' or 'truth' from the social 'life-world' of the pupils does not assist them in valuing that world or reappraising its value but expects them to abandon it for an alternative social 'life-world'. Or, as Richard Pring puts it, 'the pupil's own viewpoint, his own construction of reality, needs to be respected, even though it does not fit those viewpoints, those categories "legitimated" by the school'.[1]

Difficult and complex though it may be, we need to be clear about what we are referring to when we speak of human 'consciousness'. Jaynes suggests that:

> Consciousness is an especially complex metaphorical construction, which, once attained, provides a framework for interpreting our remembered past, our anticipated future, and the world around us.[2]

Crook comments:

> The consciousness we experience is most usually derived from complex processing of information from the senses and elaborately categorised to make a consistent 'picture' against which fresh information can be

sorted and 'understood'. Interaction with the environment is a complex transaction between biological structure and the energy flows of the world 'out there' mediated by the categories we impose upon raw experiencing. In social life we build personal 'constructs' and use them to create consistent patterns of relating with others . . . . . The 'I' and the 'me' are likewise structures excerpted and narratised from experience. These are not the immutable basis of our world but rather the constructs we create to produce a stable world of subject and object within which we act.[3]

If we accept this definition, consciousness may be understood as an 'interior analogue of the exterior world' by which human beings do not just interpret their experience, but 're-present' their experience to themselves. When we perceive something, such as a person engaged in religious worship, we do not register the action as it is understood by the worshipper, but as *we* understand it. In other words, we reinterpret what we see by reference to whatever 'structures of consciousness' we have acquired through our interactions with our social world. We may begin to contemplate these structures (ie, observe, as it were, our own observation) by asking such questions as 'How do I see this action?' and 'Why do I see it as I do?'. Generally, however, we accept that 'how we see things' is 'how things are'; we function on the basis that there is 'a taken-for-granted' world which we share with others. While, of course, this in a sense has to be true, in another sense all individual consciousnesses are unique. But individual consciousnesses are formed within a culture and are contingent upon its construction of reality. Thus the history of human consciousnesses is the history of human social life and 'the consciousnesses of one epoch may differ as greatly from those of another as do the construed worlds of a polar Eskimo and a city dweller in New York'.[4]

With these observations in mind we turn to examine some of the different factors within the social world of our modern, plural society which combine to produce contemporary 'consciousness'.

The following diagram (Figure Two) purports to represent how human beings respond to *Human Givens* and seek to interpret and understand *Shared Human Experience* (especially the 'ultimate' questions which they discern within it) within a cultural framework consisting of *Myths* which reflect and influence that society's response to *Core Values* and, similarly, reflect and influence the way in which *Substantive Religious Categories* of meaning are interpreted within *Traditional Belief Systems*. The central circle, labelled '*Moral, Religious and Spiritual Consciousness* indicates how moral, religious and spiritual meaning which arises from this process and forms part of the cultural history into which each human being is born, impinges upon and contributes to the construction of human consciousness. The relationship between all the meaning-making 'components' of the social world may be described as a dialectical one; their mutual interactions being indicated by the arrows in the diagram. I should add that the diagram greatly over-simplifies the thesis, especially in so far as only those components which have a direct bearing on the development of religious, moral and spiritual consciousness are represented. In the previous chapter I gave attention to *Human Givens*: now I would like to consider each of the other six components but with the discussion of *Moral, Religious and Spiritual Consciousness* deferred until Chapters Four and Five.

Figure Two: Reality and human consciousness as social constructs.

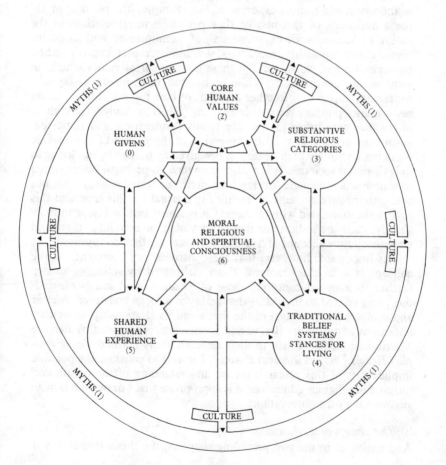

1. The mythic framework

The mythic frame of reference for contemporary societies in the Western world is highly complex, comprising a multiplicity of 'myths', often at variance with each other. As a working definition we can take 'myth' in this context to be any account of the world and human experience which enables order and meaning to be imposed upon it. Thus we may speak of myths being generated by, for example, politics, economics, science, technology, philosophy and, of course, religion. Within each of these categories of myth, in a manner reminiscent of 'Russian dolls', exist many more myths, derived in some way from the category in which they are contained but providing their own distinctive accounts of the world and human experience. For example, 'the political myth' has a multitude of variants, be they particular interpretations of the nature of 'democracy', of 'socialism', of 'communism' and so on, or myths about nationality, race, class, sex, human rights, animals rights, conservation and work, etc. All these myths express values which, in some sense, are utopian. While each myth may appear to be self-contained, impervious to other accounts of how the world is or should be, it is also 'porous', constantly evolving (if it is to survive) through its interaction with other myths. My totally symmetrical and static diagram thus gives a very false impression of the nature of this mythic framework within which 'reality' is perceived by human beings living in today's plural societies. It is a diagram which is, perhaps, better suited to a time when a single 'overarching myth' provided society with but one authoritative account of 'reality'. It is usual for this time and this myth to be associated with medieval Christianity, but, as I hope to show shortly, there are indications that the day of an 'overarching' myth and an authoritative account of 'reality' has not altogether disappeared.

It is important, however, that these introductory comments on the concept of a 'mythic framework' are elaborated by reference to two further sociological concepts, those of *'secularisation'* and *'modernisation'*, and related to the thesis that reality is a social construct. A clear and sympathetic portrayal of the thesis and its relationship to secularisation, as advanced by Berger and Luckmann, is provided by Bernice Martin and Ronald Pluck in their research study entitled *Young People's Beliefs*.[5] As, in the next chapter, I intend to consider the possible implications of this research for an understanding of the nature and purpose of religious education, it is appropriate that I draw on it now to augment my own observations.

(i) The concept of secularisation
As I indicated in the two preceding chapters, the thesis that reality is

socially constructed takes as its premise (or, as I would prefer to say, starts with the 'given') that 'all men must make sense of the world: they cannot live by meaninglessness and chaos, so pragmatically the human enterprise must always be a process of imposing ordered meaning on the flux of perception and experience'.[6] Martin and Pluck comment:

In most pre-modern societies religious institutions were crucial participants in this creation of meaning. They provided the specialist personnel to explicate and integrate meaning systems on behalf of the ordinary citizen. Moreover they linked the human order of meaning to a sacred, extra-terrestial order so that the human 'nomos' (ie, meaning system) was integrated with a 'sacred cosmos'—'God's in his heaven/All's right with the world'. But human life constantly throws up marginal situations and experiences—confrontations with loss, mortality, injustice and the like—which threaten ordered meaning and face men with the spectre of chaotic meaninglessness. Thus 'nomos' activity may be expected to cluster around these 'marginal' situations—death, loss, changes of status, personal and social crises, etc.

None of this alters in its fundamentals in the modern world except through the impact of differentiation, fragmentation *and* privatisation. *The role of the official bodies, and especially churches and states, in providing and effectively purveying ready-made 'nomoi' (ie, meanings) to the population is greatly reduced because they lose their monopoly in conditions of pluralist competition. Meaning-systems moreover are not mere intellectual exercises but must be* lived *collectively; constant interaction with other people who perceive and interpret reality in the same way as oneself is necessary if one's 'nomos' or 'sacred cosmos' is to be automatically effective in imbuing one's everyday experiences with meaning. But modern societies have largely dissolved these supportive systems or 'plausibility structures', and among them the churches. This happens when the individual in his multiple and fragmented role exists partly inside and partly at a tangent to so many institutions and associations that no one of them addresses itself to 'meaning' throughout the whole range of life experience, but only to snatches and fragments. So in the end the individual is in a certain sense alone with the task of making sense of the world and his own place in it out of scraps and oddments culled here and there in his differentiated life and contacts.*[7]

There are certain points in this account that Martin and Pluck draw attention to as a consequence of their research findings:

First, the attribution of meaning is a pragmatic activity: it is only partly intellectual and it may well be that articulated intellectual coherence is only occasionally a feature of 'nomos' construction.[8]

It is their view that coherent intellectual articulation of meaning may lie almost completely with the specialists—moral theologians and philosophers. They suggest that the nearest ordinary folk may get to intellectualisation of a meaning system is when they 'unexpectedly confront the marginal experience—bereavement, divorce, a child's rebellion, etc'. Even here 'they may only ponder one or two of the items in their meaning system and leave the rest alone'. But their major point is that:

> . . . so long as people have group support, or conventional, shared assumptions to make sense of their world, they seem to tolerate without noticing them all sorts of hiatuses and contradictions. They behave in fact as if life were underpinned by beliefs but they do not work them out into coherent verbalised philosophies. In short, system, if by that we mean a logically coherent pattern, may be exactly the wrong word to use of the phenomenon: it is more like a patchwork quilt or much-mended net than like a system. And it operates most of the time as an implicit attribution of 'sense' to the way things are in the world, and only seldom orders itself into formal propositions about what things 'mean' and why. Even when something approaching formal propositions has a part to play, it may not take the form of a consistent single system of meaning.[9]

Martin and Pluck illustrate how pragmatism and glaring inconsistency are hidden by the piecemeal application of whichever ready-made saying fits the particular case, by the several responses that enable misfortune to be made sense of, namely:

> 'God works in a mysterious way',
> or 'Be sure your sins will find you out',
> or 'Bad luck comes in threes',
> or 'It was just my turn',
> or 'Life was never meant to be easy'.

The second point which they draw attention to in the Berger and Luckmann account is the suggestion that:

> one of the corollaries of specialisation and privatisation in modern societies is a tendency for the sacred, cosmic reference to be found redundant and for meaning systems to become this worldly . . .[10]

Finally they make reference to Berger's suggestion that:

> . . . one of the important ways in which the individual copes with uncertainty and fragmentisation and his isolation from primary community is to anchor his meaning system to an underlying concept of a personal 'life plan', which then becomes a source of identity. He envisages himself at the centre of his meaning system and arranges most other perceptions and experiences by virtue of their relevance or irrelevance to the life plan. He perceives himself as selecting from available influences

and activities to create his own on-going identity in a rather open-ended and permanently unfinished fashion. So along with the concept of the privately created person goes a privatised 'nomos', religion or belief system.[11]

Clearly Martin and Pluck give close attention to the Berger and Luckmann thesis because of the striking way in which it provides an explanation for what they discovered about young people's beliefs. (I will be indicating in the next chapter what they discovered). They stress, however, that all they can argue for is 'the *plausibility* of the Berger and Luckmann case'.[12] I share their view. It is apparent, however, that the effects of secularisation upon contemporary Western societies are considerably extended not only by the fact of *pluralism* but by the *institutionalisation* of pluralism, and it is certainly conceivable, as Berger and Luckmann contend, that these factors can combine to promote a markedly different form of human 'consciousness'. For example, in a pluralist society, because alternative perspectives on meaning are available and similarly institutionalised, it is possible for a consciousness to be created which is characterised by open-mindedness and individuality and for these characteristics to be seen as the desirable and necessary agents of choice and of personal belief. But an attendant danger in such a situation is an unrealistic expectation that individuals possess the necessary capacity for taking responsibility for personal meaning-making. Apprehension about this may increase as we turn to consider the effects of 'modernisation' upon human consciousness, especially its contribution to the creation of what I will call 'secular consciousness'. I cannot hope to do justice to the many complexities of 'modernity' but I can hope to show why any consideration of the relationship of religious education to personal development must take account of it. Once again I will take the work of Peter Berger as a basis for understanding it.

(ii) The concept of modernisation

In his book *Facing Upto Modernity*, Berger, commenting on Marion Levy's definition of modernisation as 'the ratio of inanimate to animate sources of power', writes:

'This is not an altogether satisfactory definition, but useful in pointing to the core of the phenomenon, namely, the transformation of the world brought about by the technological innovations of the last few centuries, first in Europe and then with increasing rapidity all over the world. This transformation has had economic, social and political dimensions, all immense in scope. It has also brought on a revolution on the level of human consciousness, fundamentally uprooting beliefs, values and even the emotional texture of life. A transformation of such vastness could not

have taken place without profound anguish, first of all material (due to the exploitation and oppression that have accompanied modernisation virtually everywhere), but also cultural and psychological.[13]

Berger points to the *institutional* processes on which modernity rests— 'the capitalist market, the bureaucratised state (as well as the numerous non-state bureaucracies of more recent origin), the technologised economy (as well as the domination by technology of non-economic sectors of society), the large city with its heterogeneous agglomeration of people, and the media of mass communication'.[14]

But whereas it is possible to define and discuss modernisation in terms of institutional processes, 'such analysis . . . misses a crucial dimension, the dimension of consciousness'.[15] In other words, modernisation creates a specific social situation which is conducive to a particular type of consciousness by which individuals give meaning to the ordinary events and encounters of their lives. What is the nature of that consciousness and how is it created?

Following Max Weber, Berger identifies *primary and secondary carriers* of modernisation, each also being carriers of 'constellations of consciousness'.

The primary carriers are those processes and institutions that are directly concerned with technological production. The secondary carriers are processes and institutions that are not themselves concerned with such production but that serve as transmitting agencies for the consciousness derived from this source. The institutions of mass education and mass communication generally may be seen as the most important of these secondary carriers. Through school curricula, motion pictures and television, advertising of all sorts, and so on, the population is continuously bombarded with ideas, imagery and models of conduct that are intrinsically connected with technological production.[16]

In his analysis of technological production and consciousness, Berger considers how knowledge is organised. Specific knowledge, such as may be necessary for the worker to perform his (*sic*) part in a 'sequence of production', coheres within a vast body of scientific and technological knowledge which, although present and taken for granted by the worker, is not available to him. He merely participates in the enterprise of technological production in modern society. 'In this way the impressive edifice of modern science and technology *in toto* looms on the horizon of every activity of technological production and in the consciousness of every worker.'[17] Because this view has decisively influenced the present shape of technological society, it has also influenced the consciousness of all its members. This is also true of all the other characteristics of technological production, such as its *mechanis-*

ticity (the actions of the individual worker have a machine-like function), its *componentiality* (reality is ordered in terms of components which are apprehended and manipulated as atomistic units), the *interdependence of components and their sequences* (components are continuously interdependent in a rational, controllable and predictable way), and the *separability of means and ends* (regardless of whether the worker involved in the production approves or even knows about its intended ends—a car or a nuclear weapon—he is able to perform the actions that are technologically necessary to bring it about). The actual meaning of the production process is inevitably long-range, each unit within it deriving its complete meaning from the whole; typically, however, the worker may have no such view so his own experience is apprehended by him as incomplete.

Berger argues that these characteristics have far-reaching implications for the manner in which different sectors of his own life are represented in the consciousness of the worker. 'Segregated constellations of consciousness' are established, each referring to specific social and institutional sectors of the individual's life. But there are carry-over effects between these constellations of consciousness, so that, for example, the 'cognitive style' characteristic of technological knowledge and production might be carried over into the manner in which the individual looks at politics, the education of his children, relationships with his family and other human beings. Concerning the latter Berger notes that technological production brings with it *anonymous social relations* and that the production process necessitates 'human engineering', that is, the technological management of social relations. This also extends to the individual through *self-anonymisation*. He may find either that his identity as 'worker' is 'less real' than his identity as private person or a family man, or that he actually prefers the very anonymity of his work situation to the non-anonymous relations of private life. Furthermore, without any opportunity to relate his work to the complete product, 'there is a constant threat in the situation of meaninglessness, disidentification and experiences of anomie' and this may shape his consciousness within other social contexts.

Berger concludes his analysis with the following comment:

In so-called developed or advanced industrial societies, in which technological production provides the economic foundation of society as a whole, these carry-over effects are massive. Everyday life in just about every one of its sectors is ongoingly bombarded, not only with material objects and processes derived from technological production but with clusters of consciousness originating with the latter. Thus many of the above-named themes serve as contributions to an overarching symbolic universe peculiar to modernity. It is especially important to understand

117

this, since the majority of the population is never directly in technological production. For better of for worse, it is not necessary to be engaged in technological work in order to think technologically.[18]

In a recent paper,[19] John Hull addresses the issue of 'secular consciousness' by focusing on the way in which the mass societies of today are created by what Alvin Gouldner calls the 'consciousness-creating industries'. Communications and information revolutions of recent times provide the means of changing the world and of bringing about the utopian goal of a technologised economy which is the ideological dream of capitalism. A 'technological consciousness' is thus created whereby 'the consumerism of late capitalism feeds upon itself in the belief that in the products of modern technology all happiness is available now, provided you can afford to buy everything'. The effect of this is social inactivity, 'since meanings are sought in private life and in leisure pursuits, and people are stimulated only by acquisitiveness'. Following Gouldner, Hull draws a parallel between the technological consciousness which is produced by modern communications and the mass media industries and 'religious consciousness' created by the traditional forms of religious faith. Both guide people in what they should feel as well as in what they should think. But the parallel is not an exact one, for what characterises the consciousness of members of the consumer society is the absence of the transcendent and a lack of joy and hope. Hull writes:

Just because so much unhappiness and human want continues to exist in the midst of the plenty provided by technology, many people feel a sense of passivity and hopelessness. The technological promise is fulfilled, and the future holds only more and more of the same kind of thing. Even as it satisfies the needs which it creates, technology builds up a drab hopelessness because it leaves no further horizon. This hopelessness is rooted in faith in the adequacy of technology as a source of meaning for human life, and may thus be thought of as an anti-religious feature of the consumer society.

(iii) Modernity and 'secular consciousness'

Although technology may be the means by which capitalism 'captures' consciousness, what I have called 'secular consciousness' is not merely a product of capitalism, but of 'modernity' itself. We might try and identify a number of characteristics of modernity which are especially influential in this respect. Firstly, modernity imposes a number of 'abstract structures', notably those given with technology and bureaucracy, which progressively weaken individuality and inhibit personal initiative and choice. For example, bureaucracies, whether state or private, operate through powerful but 'faceless' (and, therefore, 'alienating') structures which appear to 'process' people like technological components. Anonymity applies to both the civil servants 'serving' the 'public' and the 'public' they 'serve'. Human beings often experience a sense of powerlessness and frustration in the face of such bureaucracies and, although some may protest, many acquiesce to the inevitability of their lives being controlled by 'them'. The same situation obtains in politics. Although accession to political power in a democracy is achieved through the very concrete means of the ballot box, the voters' initial sense of being able to use it to have some control over their lives quickly disappears after the election. Then the 'political machine' develops a momentum and will of its own and the rhetoric of politicians moves 'political debate' into a sphere of abstraction which, despite assurances to the contrary, never seems to connect with the concrete realities of everyday life in the way their supporters envisaged when they registered their votes.

This illustrates a further characteristic of modernity which perpetuates 'abstraction', namely the extension of what we might call 'specialised professionalism' to all areas of human life. 'Technological knowledge' (like 'bureaucratic knowledge') is, by nature, specialised knowledge, and although 'user friendly' features can be built into it, the role of the user, whether in the home, the office or the factory, is essentially passive. The users of technology (and that means everyone) are conscious of a vast network of specialised knowledge lying behind even the simplest product, not only in order to produce it but also to maintain it. When things go wrong, specialist help is essential and the passive role of the user is reinforced. Although it has always been the case that 'specialist services' have been available in communities (ranging from plumbing and motor engineering to medical and social services), in the past most of these have been called upon only intermittently; they have only rarely occupied the central arena of people's lives except in times of crisis. Increasingly today technological and bureaucratic services are occupying the middle ground of many people's lives. Take, for example, the way in which at least three million families in Britain survive only because of the permanent intervention of the Department of Health and Security. There is no more passive role than being 'unemployed' and the recipient of unemployment 'benefits'. But equally, whether employed or unemployed, people are increasingly subject to planning whatever fragments of their lives remain their own within structures imposed by a process of decision-making from which they are effectively excluded.

We might ask, therefore, what are the fundamental 'values' which inform modernisation and which, consequently, become the 'normative values' which shape 'secular consciousness'? Undoubtedly, fundamental to modernity are 'economic' values. Modernity trades on the belief that the creation of wealth is not only the necessary foundation for a successful nation but for the 'good life' itself. National and personal well-being thus turns on the strength of the pound against the dollar, on economic 'growth', on the 'level' of inflation, on returns from overseas investment and so on. As we have already noted, the 'technological society' is a consumer society. In order to consume you have to have wealth, but the consumer label applies to everyone in society, whether rich or poor. The pressure to orientate one's life around acquiring wealth in order to acquire the 'good life' is, therefore, immense. This places an intolerable burden on the vast majority of the population, but more so on those who occupy the lower socio-economic levels. It is little wonder that so many people fall victim to the many facilities that now exist for 'credit'—indeed, 'credit services' represent a major national and international industry wholly given over to the maintenance of consumerism. It is not difficult to see how such a situation generates a consciousness which raises the value of materialism above all other values and subordinates people to an endless quest for the unattainable—for in the end modernity, as John Hull indicates, can hold out nothing but more of the same.

What I have been attempting to describe here is one of the dominant 'myths' which provides the frame of reference for modern Western society. It is a 'myth' which influences the consciousness of all people in contemporary society, not merely those who, in some special sense, are committed to its maintenance. That means that the other myths with which it competes are invariably brought within its sphere of influence, even though they may be fundamentally opposed to the concept of order and meaning which it advocates. The nature of the relationship which exists between competing myths is complex, but something of the dynamic which this entails is indicated by Jurgen Habermas in his book, *Legitimation Crisis*. There he points out that the modern combination of powerful state bureaucracies and multi-national corporations cannot generate significant meanings for people's lives. These can only be found in the traditional, value-laden and spiritual ways of life. Thus one of the dilemmas of late capitalism is that society needs these traditional cultures in order to give meaning to life and to lure people into co-operation with the economic structures, and yet at the same time it is these traditional cultures of spirituality which are marginalised and silenced by the contemporary combination of bureaucracy, industry and the consciousness creating media. The marginalisation of religious and spiritual values within the taken-for-granted life of modern societies also means, of course, that religious and spiritual perspectives on meaning are marginalised or even removed from human consciousness. While it would be unrealistic to imagine that education can resolve this dilemma, it is not unrealistic to hope that education should seek to address itself to the situation that creates it. In this, religious education must be shown to make some special contribution.

2. Core human values

Setting aside, for a moment, the issue of conflict between the values of late capitalism and those of the traditional cultures of spirituality, let us now consider whether it is possible to identify a core or cluster of 'human values' which, like the 'human givens' we identified in Chapter Two, are in some sense implicit within the human condition. If this could be shown to be the case we might then argue that *how* a society responded to or interpreted such values would provide its recognisable identity and contribute to its sense of cultural continuity.

In Chapter Two I suggested that a *causal* relationship exists between what human beings believe and what human beings become. I further suggested that human beings are constrained by the human 'givens' of *interdependence, freedom,* and *responsibility* (as previously defined) to formulate *beliefs* about human nature and the nature of human interdependence, freedom and responsibility. The formulation of such beliefs, however, inevitably involves making *moral* judgments about how human beings *ought* to be, including forming estimates of the desirable qualities and characteristics of being human. It is not surprising, however, to find that the human 'givens' carry with them certain inevitable consequences for human beings and that these are influential, if not decisive, in prescribing, in a very general way, what is to be valued, but not necessarily why or how. In this sense we can say that certain values—*core-values*—are implicit within the 'givens' of the human situation and act as kinds of 'value-imperatives'. For the sake of illustration we might include the following values within this category:

(a) The value of order, purpose and meaning;
(b) The value of human life and of human beings;
(c) The value of a just society;
(d) The value of the individual's right to self-fulfilment;
(e) The value of ethical endeavour and the necessity of exercising moral responsibility;
(f) The value of commitment to interpersonal relationships and to the notions of 'family' and 'community';
(g) The value of human spirituality and the desirability of spiritual development.

But, as it may be seen, these values are very general; they demand to be interpreted and only then are they able to issue in what might be called 'codes of belief and conduct'. How they are interpreted will depend upon the particular beliefs about the human which are brought to bear upon them, but, at the same time, particular beliefs about the human are a product of core values needing to be interpreted. Another characteristic of core values is, I suggest, that they both unite and divide human beings. They unite human beings in so far as they are values which, like the 'givens', cannot be ignored and demand to be interpreted. They divide human beings in so far as they give rise to alternative interpretations which, in turn, issue in alternative codes of belief and conduct. It is when these values are interpreted and made specific within particular codes of belief and conduct which a society considers to be 'normative' that they exercise a profound influence on the nature of human consciousness and, consequently, upon what human beings become.

Two points emerge from this type of analysis. Firstly, the analysis suggests that there are core values of a very general kind which transcend cultural boundaries and which—in so far as they prescribe, again in a very general way, what human beings have to value—are necessary to any society's identity and continuity. But the analysis also suggests that any society's identity or sense of cultural continuity lies in the *specific* interpretations that it gives to core values and in the *specific* codes of belief and conduct which arise from them. Here we encounter the highly complex problems presented by modern, secular, plural and 'multi-faith' societies. Although it is, I believe, possible to identify core values (as I have defined them), we have to recognise that within such societies these values are interpreted, and so made specific, in *diverse* ways, each issuing in their own distinctive codes of belief and conduct. Furthermore, although some of these interpretations result in highly systematised and coherent codes of belief and conduct (and I am thinking here, for example, of some of the traditional belief systems of religion, such as Islam), others provide a greater degree of flexibility for alternative understandings to occur within their own interpretations (eg, Christianity). In addition, a secular, plural society enables individuals to live a 'chameleon-like' existence in so far as they can move easily between the 'systems' and take on different interpretations of core values in proportion to their social and cultural mobility. The effect of this may be the development of a 'kind of believing' which is highly privatised and relativistic and, at the same time, incoherent.

The point I wish to stress in making these observations is that the nature of the shaping process by which human beings are 'humanised' (and the function of belief and believing within it) is the same, whether they encounter beliefs through a highly structured belief system issuing in a very rigid code of beliefs and conduct, or though a more flexible system allowing for variations of interpretation, or through a variety of competing 'systems' between which they move quite haphazardly. The pervading influence of modernity, which we considered in the previous section, must also be taken into account as a major factor in the shaping process for it, too, offers, if only by implication, a specific interpretation of core values which issues in a distinctive code of belief and conduct. In all these cases, the form of the 'human' that individuals take (and, consequently, what they regard as 'normative') corresponds to the beliefs about the human that they encounter, or to use psychological and sociological terminology, whatever model of the human their consciousness admits. The problem which is peculiar to the so-called 'open' society is that individuals can exist, as it were, in the 'cracks' between the systems and consequently experience (and, therefore, be shaped by) ambiguous, partially-defined impressions of the human and be only minimally exposed to core values in any precise form. Another feature of modern societies is the multiplicity of social roles individuals play; thus there is pressure on individuals to adopt (both consciously and unconsciously) different beliefs and values within the context of each of their many and varied roles. I will be giving closer attention to this in the next chapter, but here we may note that this is likely to be a contributory factor to the creation of 'pluralised' consciousnesses.

The task of identifying a secular, plural, multi-faith society's recognisable identity and sense of cultural continuity through its *specific* interpretations of core values is, then, a daunting one. Some have proposed that we should seek to identify a *consensus* of values (by which, in the terms of my own definition, I assume they mean a consensus of specific interpretations of core values)—a sort of eclectic common denominator of values among competing standpoints. I am very dubious about the value of such an approach. For example, it is not consistent with the way in which individuals *encounter* values in their lived experience (ie, values are not merely encountered intellectually but have to be lived through if they are to constitute or be constituted within their consciousness); neither can a *consensus* of values purport to represent social reality, for they have no 'purchasing power' in the transactions of everyday living. I believe that a more satisfactory approach is the one that I am suggesting, namely identifying the very general values which give rise to interpretations and then exploring the specific values as *interpretations* of them. Some indication of the process I envisage may be given by looking a little more closely at the seven core values I proposed earlier.

(a) The value of order, purpose and meaning

All human societies eschew chaos, anarchy and strife. 'Anomie' is always seen in negative terms. The same is true of the human person: we look for 'wholeness' not 'illness'; 'integration' not 'disintegration';

'harmony' not 'discord'. Even the most negative philosophies—such as Nihilism—are preoccupied with questions about meaning and purpose. In the population at large one detects a basic optimism about the universe—that there is order and purpose and that there is the possibility of this being understood—and a basic optimism that human societies can be created which sustain and further human well-being. Already, in making these brief observations, we can recognise why core values unite and divide human beings. Although human beings are united in their recognition of the *value* of order, purpose and meaning, they are divided in the way in which they interpret and understand it. The value itself is a source of conflict and yet it is a value which cannot be ignored. I suggest that this is a basic characteristic of all *core* values.

(b) *The value of human life and of human beings*

We attribute to human life a value higher than anything else in the created order. We aspire to imbue it with dignity, mystery, uniqueness and sancitity and we are affronted and offended by acts and situations which cheapen and degrade it. The value of human life is surely one of the core values of any human society. It is one of the civilising necessities for any society to safeguard; it is a value that cannot be ignored. Yet here again we see how the value itself is a source of conflict. There are competing interpretations of what it means in practice for human life and its preservation to be more highly prized than anything else, just as there are competing reasons for holding that it should be so prized. There are competing beliefs about what may constitute extenuating circumstances when human life is not preserved, and, of course, competing beliefs about the purpose of human life itself and the value or worth of the individual. Ironically such interpretations have led human beings to go to war in order to preserve this value.

I would like to take the following four values as a 'cluster' of values arising from the human 'givens' of interdependence, freedom and responsibility, and comment briefly on them together, viz:

(c) The value of a just society;
(d) The value of the individual's right to self-fulfilment;
(e) The value of ethical endeavour and the necessity of exercising moral responsibility;
(f) The value of commitment to inter-personal relationships and to the notions of 'family' and 'community'.

Like all other core values, this cluster of values both unites and divides human beings. What *meanings* are we to give to 'justice', 'self-fulfilment', 'ethical endeavour', 'moral responsibility', 'inter-personal relationships', 'family' and 'community'? Contrast, for example, the likely interpretations given to 'justice' by management and workers in an industrial context; the interpretations of pupils and teachers in a school context; the interpretations of blacks and whites in the context of South Africa. The conflict in interpretations is matched by the conflict in views about how such an ideal is to be achieved—and that is true of the other values in the cluster. That is why I insist that the core values of a society are not a *consensus* of specific values but a number of general values or 'value-imperatives' which are inevitable and which give rise to alternative interpretations and alternative ethical judgments which are more specific (and therefore controversial) and which may ultimately be expressed in particular codes of belief and conduct. It is in committing oneself to a specific interpretation and coming under its moral constraint that the individual and the group is shaped in a particular form of the human.

Finally I would like to give rather more detailed consideration to:

(g) *The value of human spirituality and the desirability of spiritual development*

Some will be inclined to question why it is necessary to introduce so controversial a concept as human spirituality and its development as a *core* human value. In reply I suggest that although the use of the term 'spiritual' in this context has obvious difficulties because of its traditional association with religion, the concepts of human spirituality and spiritual development can be given wider and more general meanings than those which religions place upon them.[20] In speaking of human spirituality, therefore, I am referring to a human capacity for a certain type of awareness—often called 'spiritual awareness'—which may be stimulated by religious consciousness but which is not contingent upon it. Similarly, in speaking of spiritual development I am not speaking of *religious* development, which is but one way in which an understanding of human spirituality may be fostered and given shape and direction, but of the activation of the human capacity for self-transcendence and movement towards a state of consciousness in which the limitations of human finite identity are challenged by the exercise of the creative imagination.

The highest and most noble aspirations of which human beings are capable—love, forgiveness, compassion, self-sacrifice, hope, joy, trust, and so on; their sense of being personally touched and helpless before intense beauty, pain, tradition or genuine greatness; their search for meaning and their yearning for personal wholeness and integration; their willingness to commit themselves to an ideal in the face of impossible odds, etc—all witness to the hierarchy of human needs exceeding the material. (Indeed, it is often the experience of human beings that material success once attained turns to ashes in the mouth, unable to satisfy their spiritual hunger.) They also witness to the need to account for this capacity of human beings to heighten their consciousness above the level of finite knowing prescribed by an empirical and positivist approach to knowledge and experience.

Although it is the privilege of the few to attain to a highly developed state of sustained spiritual awareness, equivalent, in religious terms, to that of attaining true Buddhahood, entering nirvana or nibbana, or perfecting the imitation of Christ, the view that all human beings are endowed at birth with a capacity for spiritual awareness cannot be lightly dismissed. For example, such a view might be supported by drawing a parallel between the human capacity for spiritual awareness and other human capacities, such as the human capacity to acquire consciousness and use of language. Noam Chomsky has put forward the view that human beings are endowed at birth with a 'linguistic competence' which allows them to draw on a deep linguistic structure which is common to all human beings.[21] Might it be argued that human beings are similarly endowed with a 'spiritual competence'? That human beings can aspire to achieve higher states of consciousness through which they 'intuit' what they call 'ultimate' values could, of course, be attributed to their being endowed with a general capacity to learn or a 'competence' for learning. But this does not preclude the need to posit that human beings are endowed with a 'spiritual competence'; it merely incorporates this competence within the wider competence for learning that human beings possess.

While it is possible for the development of spiritual awareness to be understood as a form of human learning which shares some of the characteristics of cognition, such as the exercise of reason and imagination, and which involves responding to feelings, it is not possible to equate this capacity merely with the human capacity to reason or respond to emotion. What makes the development of spiritual awareness a distinctive form of human learning and consciousness (and so establishes 'the spiritual' as an irreducible component of human being) is that it challenges the adequacy of that understanding which is solely a product of exercising the intellect or responding to the emotions and provides an alternative understanding of human experience which is the product of neither of these. It is the irreducibility of 'the spiritual' to any of the other categories by which human experience can be classified or interpreted—such as 'the intellectual', 'the emotional', 'the physical', 'the social', 'the moral', and so on—that strengthens the view that human beings are endowed with 'spiritual competence', in the Chomskian sense, and supports the claim that human spirituality and its development is something to be valued and desired.

It is also worth noting that despite the considerable difficulties that arise when attempting to provide an adequate account of the aetiology of human spirituality or give the concept a universally accepted meaning, it is impossible to conceive of a human society which is able to ignore the fact of human spirituality and deny its ultimate significance in estimating what it means to be human. Even those societies which attempt to suppress particular forms of spirituality, such as the religious, find it necessary to provide an alternative locus or medium in and through which this very powerful human phenomenon can be channelled or expressed and 'the spiritual' known. While such societies may try to harness the natural aspirations which stem from human spirituality to certain temporal, ideological goals and so influence the shape of human development in particular directions, it is a common characteristic of human spirituality that it breaks out from such impositions. Indeed one might say that it is because human beings are endowed with a spiritual capacity that they can and do strive beyond whatever limits are placed upon them. Human spirituality is not annihilated by its suppression but stimulated by it. 'Dissidents' are invariably men and women with heightened spiritual awareness who reaffirm the priority of human spirituality in understanding what it means to be human and point to the desirability of 'spiritual values' in comparison with those which are a denial of them.

(i) Are core values spiritual values?

Human spirituality as something to be valued typifies, therefore, the characteristics of core values. It cannot be ignored; it demands to be interpreted, and it unites and divides human beings. Human experience is, I believe, considerably enriched by the variety of interpretations—religious and humanistic—which constitute the responses of human beings to this value. But a society's response to the value of human spirituality through the interpretations which it places upon it is an important factor—perhaps *the* important factor—in determining that society's recognisable identity and sense of cultural continuity. In like manner, how a society responds to this value influences the shape and direction of spiritual development among its members. Neglect of 'the spiritual' at the societal level invariably leads to an impoverishment of the spiritual sensitivities and consciousnesses of its people.[22]

There is a sense, however, in which the value of human spirituality differs from the other core values I have suggested. If we take seriously the view that human beings are endowed with a spiritual capacity for self-transcendence through which they may 'intuit' certain 'ultimate' values which, by definition, have the status of 'ultimacy' and do not need to be legitimated by reference to criteria beyond themselves, then it follows that the human capacity to discern core values and to recognise the need 'to value' is a consequence of possessing a spiritual capacity. In other words, human spirituality is not merely a core value among others but the source of the human capacity 'to value'. Without the capacity for spiritual awareness, therefore, human beings would be unable to recognise that the 'givens' of the human situation carry 'value imperatives' and that their response to these determine who and what they become. Thus, the view that all human beings are endowed with 'spiritual competence' is an obvious corollary to the view that all human beings must enter the 'arena of faith responses' and ultimately live by faith.

A further point may be added. If, as I suggest, 'core values' are implicit within the 'givens' of the human situation and carry 'value imperatives', could it not be said that the 'givens' also possess a 'spiritual' nature of their own? There is the view (usually referred to as 'essentialism') that every object has its own 'inner nature' or 'essence', including human beings, the world and the cosmos. (We see this view worked out in religious terms in primal religions where every object is understood as being animated by its own 'spirit'.) Human beings do not, of course, stand outside the human situation, they both define it and are defined by it. In this sense they do not merely have a capacity to generate 'spiritual awareness' but rather are able to recognise and respond to that which is, as it were, already present in themselves, in other human beings, in the world, and so on. In an important sense, therefore, to speak of the 'givens' of the human situation is to speak of the 'essence' of that situation, of that which could not be otherwise. The word 'spiritual' may be used in this connection, signalling that which is 'essential' to human 'givens'. It is because the 'inner nature' of human 'givens' is 'spiritual' that they carry 'value-imperatives'. I suggest, therefore, that 'core values' may justifiably be seen as *spiritual* values'. They are, however, still subject to the need to be interpreted and such interpretations may be diverse.

One way in which they may be interpreted is by bringing them into a relationship with what I have called 'substantive religious categories'. This is not to impose an alien set of concepts upon human 'givens' and core values, for these religious categories, I suggest, are actually derived from them. In other words, 'substantive religious categories' are in essence categories which interpret and express the 'spiritual' nature of human 'givens' and core values. It would be odd if this were not so, for in such a situation the 'substantive religious categories' would not necessarily address the need, for example, to interpret core values, but could focus upon some altogether different concern. This would have the effect of severing the necessary link between religion and human 'givens' and creating a system of belief which had no immediate connection with, or relevance to the human situation. Moreover it would mean that religion would, at best, have but a tenuous relationship to the spiritual. But although it may be necessary for substantive religious categories to have a direct relationship with human 'givens' and core values, it does not necessarily follow that human 'givens' and core values *must* be interpreted by such categories. Other ways of interpreting 'core-values' may, legitimately, shun 'substantive religious categories' and use categories drawn, for example, from ethics and aesthetics. My interest, however, is in considering the necessary link between core values and religion, and, more particularly, the interpretation of core values within traditional belief systems. It is to this that we now need to turn.

3. Substantive religious categories

It is generally recognised that the identification of 'key' concepts of religion and their specific interpretation within particular religions is an essential pre-requisite to curriculum decision-making in religious education, mainly as a means of providing a criterion for the selection of content. Other criteria—such as the capacities, interests, experiences and questions of the pupils themselves—do, of course, need to be placed alongside this criterion. Additionally, I suggest, we should bear in mind the necessary relationship of *Substantive Religious Categories* to *Core Values* and recognise that this relationship may have important educational implications. For example, while it is simplistic to argue that Christianity must be taught in order to preserve the cultural values of our society, it is not unreasonable to believe that the study of Christianity can help pupils become aware of its shaping influence on our society's cultural values, both in the past and in the present, and can provide the context within which they can explore 'Christian values' as specific interpretations of 'core values'. For this to be effective, however, both the selection and the treatment of content will need to be decided upon with this objective in mind. A desirable learning outcome would thus be one in which pupils would appreciate how the Christian interpretation of human experience has contributed to our society's sense of identity and cultural continuity and how their own development as human beings continues to be influenced by an essentially Christian interpretation of core values, including human spirituality, even though the religious reference point has largely disappeared.

But the task of identifying the key concepts of religion is made particularly difficult by the fact that there are no generally agreed substantive categories which apply to all religions. In European languages the use of words like 'God', 'Soul', 'Creation', 'Providence', 'Salvation', and so on, simply reflects the history of these terms in Graeco-Roman and Judaeo-Christian cultures. In non-European languages these theological terms have to be translated into words whose history is very different, and even then there may not be direct correspondence between either meaning or usage. The following analysis of 'substantive religious categories' draws upon religious concepts within the European cultural tradition and is offered only as illustration of a possible approach to this task.[23]

Substantive religious categories	Secondary or derivative concepts
1. Providence	—destiny, guidance, creation;
2. The Sacred	—holiness, eternity, divinity, heaven, supernatural;
3. Law	—commandment, will, judgment, righteousness, goodness;
4. Soul	—spirit, conscience, obligation, sin;
5. Discipleship	—conversion, initiation, vocation, obedience, martyrdom;
6. Priesthood	—chosen people, laity, community of faith, people of God;
7. Revelation	—prophecy, vision, miracle, salvation;
8. Worship	—purification, sacrifice, thanksgiving, atonement.

4. Traditional belief systems or stances for living

Substantive religious categories and their derivative concepts may be seen as symbolic expressions of a religious framework within which *Shared Human Experience* may be interpreted. As they stand, however, they are very general categories which, like *Core Values*, are in need of specific interpretation. It is for this reason that the diagram (Figure Two) distinguishes between *Substantive Religious Categories* and *Traditional Belief Systems*. It is through their incorporation within traditional belief systems such as Christianity, Judaism and Islam, for example, that the substantive religious categories and their derivative concepts acquire more precise meanings, as does the religious framework within which they cohere. Each traditional belief system thus offers a *distinctive* religious framework within which *Shared Human Experience* and *Core Values* may be interpreted, and the more distinctive (or 'unique') the framework the more controversial it becomes. In other words, each traditional belief system provides its own *Mythic Framework* within which *Shared Human Experience* and *Core Values* are to be understood, and this understanding is mediated through *particular* interpretations of *Substantive Religious Categories*.

It should be noted that the diagram links *Traditional Belief Systems* with *Stances for Living*. Some would regard these terms as interchangeable and equally appropriate to describe a commitment to reflecting and acting upon a view of humanity that (a) can be expressed in and through a developed and coherent system of key-concepts and principles, (b) is communicated through distinctive forms of human behaviour, and (c) provides a basis or stance for living (ie, what I have previously called 'a code of belief and conduct'). The circle labelled *Traditional Belief Systems or Stances for Living* thus signifies the phenomena of 'faith' as expressed in and through both religious and non-religious (or 'naturalistic') systems of belief.[24] Others would consider the term *Stances for Living* is less appropriate when applied to a religious faith, such as Christianity or Islam, than it is when applied to naturalistic faiths such as Humanism, Marxism and Atheistic Existentialism.

But returning to substantive religious categories, I have already indicated my view that these are categories which interpret and express the 'spiritual' nature of human 'givens' and core human values, and indeed are derived from them. This can now be seen more clearly if I realign my examples of core values with the examples of substantive religious categories, viz:

Core Values	Substantive Religious Categories
1. The value of order, meaning and purpose	—Providence
2. The value of human life/human beings	—The Sacred
3. The value of a just society	—Law
4. The value of the individual's right to self-fulfilment	—Soul
5. The value of ethical endeavour and the necessity of exercising moral responsibility	—Discipleship
6. The value of commitment to inter-personal relationships and to the notions of 'family' and 'community'	—Priesthood/Community of faith
7. The value of human spirituality and the desirability of spiritual development	—Revelation/Worship

Although it is not my intention in this chapter to relate my comments on each of the areas represented in the diagram to religious education itself, the above discussion does provide an opportunity for making what I think is an important point about the contribution of religious education to an understanding of values. It is worth recalling the following comment by Her Majesty's Inspectorate:

> *Religious Education also makes a distinctive contribution to the curriculum in directing attention to the religious understanding of human life and to central values (many of them derived from religion) which society seeks to uphold and transmit. In this consideration of religion and values, the intention is to help pupils to understand the nature of religious questions and religious affirmations, and to develop a personal and intellectual integrity in dealing with the profoundest aspects of their own experience now and in adult life.*[25]

Religious education thus shares a concern for exploring core values with many other subjects in the curriculum—the arts and literature, the human sciences, the physical sciences, and so on. What is distinctive about religious education's concern is to help pupils to explore such values *within the context of a religious view of life*—hence the importance of considering the relationship of values to substantive religious categories and their interpretation within traditional belief systems. This point is often lost sight of, especially within integrated 'personal, social and moral education' courses. The contribution of religious education to the exploration of such topics as war and peace, gambling, corporal and capital punishment, sex, marriage, work, leisure, law and order, advertising and the mass media, the family, conservation, personal relationships etc, is in considering them from a religious perspective. Comments one hears from pupils often appear to indicate that this perspective has been excluded and that what religious education teachers actually do is indistinguishable from what teachers of social studies do. This could reflect a failure of nerve on the part of the religious education teacher who might feel, though erroneously, that the introduction of a religious perspective constitutes 'confessionalism'. This is clearly a nonsense. Examples of how values and topics may be interpreted within a religious framework of understanding are given in Part Two of this book.

5. Shared human experience

We now need to give some attention to that area represented by the circle labelled *Shared Human Experience*. As the title implies, this circle represents the *total* arena of everyday human existence—the arena in which human beings experience love and hate, acceptance and rejection, care and neglect, cruelty and kindness, violence and compassion, meaninglessness and purpose. It is also, as a consequence, the arena in which they seek to give meaning to all their diverse experiences and do so by reference to whatever meaning systems (or what Schutz calls 'finite provinces of meaning') are available to them through their cultural history. We should note, however, that these meaning systems have arisen from human reflection on 'shared human experience' and are human responses to the questions and dilemmas posed by the human condition.

An essential element in this process of making meaning is that of *differentiating* between experiences and *categorising* them by means of different classes of propositions. How a culture has differentiated between experiences and categorised them is built into its language. To learn to speak and use the language of one's culture is, therefore, to be initiated into a way of structuring one's own experience and imposing meaning upon it. B L Whorf expresses this point as follows:

> *The world is . . . a kaleidoscopic flux of impressions which has to be organised by our minds—and this means largely by the linguistic systems in our minds. We cut nature up, organise it into concepts and ascribe significances as we do, largely because we are parties to an agreement to organise it in this way—an agreement that holds throughout our speech community and is codified in the patterns of our language. The agreement is, of course, an implicit and unstated one, but its terms are absolutely obligatory. No individual is free to describe nature with absolute impartiality but is constrained to certain modes of interpretation even while he thinks himself most free.[26]*

R S Peters concurs with this view when he says:

> *It is a grave error to regard the learning of a language as a purely instrumental matter, as a tool in the service of purposes, standards, feelings and beliefs. For in a language is distilled a view of the world which is constituted by them. In learning a language the individual is initiated into a public inheritance which his parents and teachers are inviting him to share.[27]*

Another way of putting the same point is to say that *language structures consciousness*; thus our perception of *Shared Human Experience* is always within a structure of meaning which is part of ourselves; we can never encounter it, as it were, 'in the raw'.

The structure of meaning which language imposes upon experience also allows for its further differentiation and categorisation in terms of what Hirst calls 'forms of knowledge' and Phenix calls 'realms of meaning'. It is the arena of *Shared Human Experience* which provides the common ground or data for all such categories. As we saw in Chapter One, Peters, Hirst and Dearden emphasise the importance of education being concerned to initiate pupils into an understanding of the forms of knowledge because they see these to be the fundamental categories of all truth-seeking activities, and it is through engagement with them that 'mind' is constituted. One could also say that it is through engagement with such forms that they become part of human consciousness—indeed, that human consciousness is *structured* by means of these categories of meaning. We, however, are primarily interested in those categories of meaning which are called moral, religious and spiritual. Here, however, we encounter a number of problems.

(i) Problems with 'the spiritual'

Whereas it may be possible to distinguish (as Hirst does) between 'the moral' and 'the religious' as different forms of human awareness, or between 'ethics' and 'religion' as different forms of human knowledge, how is 'the spiritual' to be distinguished? In what sense is it possible to invest something with 'spiritual' meaning as distinct from 'moral' or 'religious' meaning? What is the 'form' or 'structure' of the spiritual? What are its central concepts? What are its means of verification? What is its mode of expression? The odd thing about the spiritual is that it defies this type of classification; it is not possible to identify fundamental, ultimate or categoreal concepts of the spiritual as one can identify those of religion and morality. And yet human beings continue to speak of 'spiritual meaning'. Of course, if the spiritual is linked with the religious it can then be articulated (and thus made into a specific category of meaning) through the categoreal concepts of religion. Without doubt, the traditional religions of the world are not only the greatest repositories of human experience of the spiritual, they have been the most obvious means by which 'spiritual meaning' and 'spiritual values' have been sustained and expressed within human societies and the 'spiritual consciousness' of human beings shaped and developed. Here, however, 'spiritual consciousness' is indistinguishable from 'religious consciousness' and yet, as I argued earlier in this chapter, spiritual consciousness is not contingent upon religious consciousness; if anything it is the reverse.

I raise these difficulties because they are especially pertinent to our consideration of the contribution of religious education to personal development. If, as our earlier analysis of secularisation and modernisation suggests, the traditional means by which human spirituality has been articulated—religion—has been muted if not silenced, then both the religious and spiritual consciousnesses of human beings are being impaired, possibly to the point of their becoming vestigial. Thus, in our modern, pluralist societies, not only does the dominance of 'secular consciousness' mean the demise of religious consciousness but it may also mean the diminution if not the demise of 'spiritual consciousness' —that which is unique to human beings. If we believe this represents a step which can only lead to the 'dehumanisation' of human beings, it is imperative that we seek to restore the spiritual within human consciousness. The issue is how to do it.

It seems to me that we have a number of options. The first would be to seek to restore 'spiritual consciousness' within society by restoring the place of religion within public and private life. Although some commentators are given to identifying trends which indicate a resurgence of interest in religion, I am not persuaded that this is a viable option. The second would be to focus our attention on the contribution education can make, in the words of the HMI Working Paper, *Curriculum 11–16*, to introducing pupils during the period of compulsory schooling to certain essential 'areas of experience', one of which it defines as 'the spiritual'.[28] This option would appear to have greater possibilities; and yet, as we have seen, the notion is fraught with difficulties. In omitting 'the religious' from among its seven 'areas of experience' the compilers of the HMI Working Paper appear to concur with the view that 'the spiritual' is a category which is inclusive of religion but not exclusively religious.[29] Thus it admits to the need for all school subjects to contribute in introducing pupils to the spiritual area of experience, including religious education. Because of the traditional association of the spiritual with the religious, and in the absence of clear, alternative means by which the spiritual can be articulated, we might interpret this suggestion as indicating that the task of religious education is to develop the pupil's 'religious consciousness' and thereby put him or her, as it were, in touch with 'spiritual meaning' and 'spiritual values'. But we need to consider carefully what this means.

(ii) The implications of 'secular' and 'religious' consciousness for our understanding of the concerns of religious education

Certainly it is common to hear religious educators bemoaning the fact that the majority of our pupils are 'secularised' and that this presents a major obstacle to the task of helping them to 'understand religion' or appreciate 'religious meaning'. This may well be the case; but implicit in this view is the belief that religious education is concerned with combatting secular consciousness and reasserting the viability if not the necessity of religious belief as a more desirable perspective from which to view life and give it meaning. On this view religious education *is* seen as promoting 'religious consciousness' not just 'consciousness of religion' or awareness of religious interpretations of life. It seems to me that such a view, unless subject to careful qualification, comes close to making religious education an instrument of religious ideology. Certainly the view as it is expressed here does not appear to differentiate adequately between the value of religious faith *to* personal development and the value of studying religion *for* personal development. If by 'religious consciousness' we mean an internalised framework of religious meaning within which the individual *consistently* re-presents his or her total experience to him or herself, then I do not think there can be any doubt that such consciousness can only be created and sustained within the context of a community of religious faith through its common life and language. In other words, the attainment of 'religious consciousness', as I have defined it, is dependent upon all the ingredients of religious nurture being present in the life of the individual; it cannot be a product solely of studying religions. 'Religious consciousness' in this sense is indistinguishable from 'religious faith' and clearly the promotion of this cannot be the intention of religious education.

But we may assume that we can speak of *degrees* of 'religious consciousness'. If, for example, we continue to equate 'religious consciousness' with 'religious faith' then we can recognise that among adherents to all religions there will be those who have more developed religious consciousnesses than others. If this were not so we would be unable to distinguish between, for example, those deserving of the title of 'saint' or 'guru' and those who constitute the majority of religious adherents. Being able to make such a distinction is only possible if we admit to there being different degrees of religious consciousness. While it may be the mark of *developed* religious consciousness that it pervades all the meaning-making activities in which the religious adherent engages, this cannot be the mark of religious consciousness itself, for there are many religious believers for whom their religious faith is of great personal significance but does not consistently pervade all their meaning-making activities. For the latter their religious consciousness is coexistent with other forms of consciousness and its application partial rather than total. In similar manner we can speak of *degrees* of religious understanding, that of the theologian being, one trusts, of a different degree from that of the layperson.

If these *degrees* of religious consciousness and understanding may be distinguished among the members of religious faiths, can they also be distinguished among those who are not members of those faiths but are members of a society in which those faiths are represented? Can we speak of such people as having 'religious consciousness'? Probably not if we apply the term in its strongest sense; but it would be difficult to argue that persons outside the religious faith communities do not possess any degree of religious consciousness, for their consciousnesses are a product of a society in which religious meaning is present even if it has ceased to be all-pervading. We might, of course, distinguish between being 'conscious of religion' and having 'religious consciousness', but surely these are different points on a continuum and it is extremely difficult to identify when and how the former passes into the latter. In seeking to enable pupils to become more conscious of religion, religious beliefs and values and a religious interpretation of life, religious education may be seen as contributing to a process which enhances the religious consciousness of pupils even though it is not its intention to bring it to a form which is indistinguishable from religious faith. Similarly, if one of our concerns is to help pupils to have some understanding of religion, then that must involve assisting them towards some understanding of the 'religious consciousness' of adherents. Through the use of phenomenological method we seek to help pupils to place themselves within contexts in which alternative perspectives from their own operate. In studying Jewish, Hindu, Muslim, Sikh and Christian family life, for example, we encourage them to imagine what it would be like to be Jewish, Hindu, Muslim, Sikh and Christian and how these different ways of thinking about life affect life in the family. In so doing, we not only enable them to be conscious of religion and conscious of the way in which religious beliefs affect those who hold them, we also encourage them to be conscious of their own family life and of those beliefs and values which affect them. Promoting this kind of understanding and awareness through the study of religion cannot but serve to enhance the religious consciousness of the pupil, even though, from the point of view of the religious adherent, this might fall far short of that which is fully deserving of the term. In so far as it enhances the religious consciousness of the pupil, it also contributes to his or her awareness of 'spiritual meaning' and 'spiritual values'.

But, although there may be exceptions, what I observe of religious education is often little more than the amassing of information about different religious traditions—'multi-fact' religious education. The intention to investigate religion from the 'inside', from the 'point of view of the religious adherent', so that something of its meaning and significance can emerge, may have some educational point and purpose but all too often such investigations only serve to make religion even more remote from the life of the pupils. One might excuse the proliferation of 'facts' if they contributed to a greater appreciation of the 'spiritual vision' which informs them, but much that commonly passes for religious education is peculiarly devoid of interest in spirituality and one can excuse pupils for equating religion with 'things that you are supposed to do'. I do not believe, therefore, that the type of religious education which is currently regarded as 'normative' is likely to introduce pupils to 'the spiritual' area of *Shared Human Experience* in a way which enables them to recognise it as part of their own experience. In this respect, for the majority of our pupils, the spiritual is no more a part of their everyday realities than is religion. What this means, of course, is that they have no means of questioning the taken-for-granted assumptions and values of their 'secularised' consciousness; these are their 'norms' against which any other response to questions of meaning are judged. Ironically, however, the absence of alternative values to those into which they are conditioned by modernity means that questions of meaning become marginalised. Contemporary consciousness, depleted by the absence of the spiritual and the religious, is not a consciousness which could be said to be self-critical. It is this which both highlights the absence of the spiritual and the religious in modern society and provides the clue to how we might identify not only the concerns of religious education but the concerns which should inform the teaching of all subjects in the school curriculum and education itself. But it is not my intention to attempt to pursue this task at this point. Rather I wish to consider whether *Shared Human Experience* can be utilised as a source of insight into moral, religious and spiritual meaning even though in our contemporary society the taken-for-granted assumptions about life may be largely unsympathetic to such perspectives.

(iii) Problems with approaches from 'Ultimate Questions'

Because they normally start from the premise that there is no dichotomy between religious experience and ordinary experience, the *experiential* and *existential* approaches to religious education developed in the late Sixties and early Seventies place considerable stress on children being encouraged to deepen their awareness of everyday experience (ie, of *Shared Human Experience*) as a way of encountering both the 'raw material' from which religious concepts are made and the 'ultimate questions' to which religions address themselves. These approaches thus assume that an understanding of *religious* meaning can arise from the questions which are promoted by reflection on ordinary, everyday experience—questions such as 'Who am I?', 'How am I related to others?', 'Why is there suffering?', 'Is death the end?', and so on. Questions like these are seen to be capable of generating such understanding because of their status as 'ultimate questions'.

While there may be considerable value in such explorations for the growth of sensitivity to human questions and human dilemmas, it is important that we recognise that reflecting on 'ultimate' questions does not necessarily bring us to an awareness of 'religious' meaning. Certainly religions do address themselves to what might be called life's 'inescapable' questions. but religions also raise 'ultimate' questions of their own. For example, all religions address themselves to the question of the meaning of life and to the problem of suffering and death, and in this sense could be seen as offering 'answers' to such questions as 'Does life have a purpose?' and 'Why do human beings suffer and die?'. But neither of these questions is an 'ultimate' question for religious believers in the sense that it may be for those who do not hold religious beliefs. For religious believers, 'ultimate' questions arise from setting their belief in the purposeful activity of an omnipotent and omniscient God within the context of the vagaries and scandals to which human life is constantly subjected. In other words, it is the assurance that there *is* meaning which presents religious believers with 'ultimate' questions, not the question *whether* there is meaning. For example, it is their belief in the goodness and power of God which makes the pain and evil in the world puzzling. It is their belief in the justice of God and in the moral seriousness of human actions which makes it seem intolerable that death should be the end. Such 'ultimate' questions are clearly 'religious' questions, arising from a religious understanding of human experience. That understanding requires *Shared Human Experience* to be viewed from the perspective of 'divine ultimacy'.

But contemporary use of the word 'ultimate', especially when qualifying 'questions', is not restricted to equating 'ultimacy' with the divine—although there are grounds for believing that the concept of 'divine ultimacy' continues to influence the form and nature of these questions.[30] For example, 'ultimate' is often used of questions to which answers are not available. But what if answers did become available? Would this mean that as each answer was found, 'ultimacy' was reduced, so that when, eventually, all answers were found, 'ultimacy' disappeared and asking 'ultimate' questions became redundant? Placing human questions within this perspective of ultimacy is not the same as placing them within a perspective of 'divine ultimacy'. As the purposes of God become known, religious believers do not believe God is reduced, for that would make 'divine ultimacy' and 'divine omniscience' contingent upon the state of human ignorance. Religious believers do not conceive of their quest for understanding 'emptying' divine ultimacy of meaning, but of bringing them into the presence of divine meaning. If the perspective of 'ultimacy' within which an 'ultimate' question is framed is not that of 'divine ultimacy', it is difficult to see how it can promote an understanding of 'religious' meaning.

A similar situation arises from using 'ultimate' to designate those questions which individuals believe to be personally significant— questions such as 'What is my ultimate purpose in life?', 'What are my ultimate concerns?', 'What concerns me ultimately as a human being?', 'Who am I?', 'What ought I to do?', and so on. These are not questions to which there are no answers; indeed it is the range and variety of answers which are possible that creates the dilemma. Here, then, the perspective of 'ultimacy' is personal and to be equated with whatever the individual decides is 'ultimate'. Of course reference may be made to what others have decided to confer 'ultimacy' upon, but in the end it is the individual who is the arbiter of 'ultimacy'. This means that it would be extremely difficult for a critique of our own or another person's 'ultimate' concerns to be attempted. By what criteria would we decide that the choices made were worthy of being called 'ultimate'? If I say my ultimate purpose in life is to grow prize marrows, on what grounds can this be either contested or approved? While we should not, of course, dismiss questions which cause us to reflect on our priorities as unworthy of being designated 'ultimate', if personalising an 'ultimate' question also means personalising 'ultimacy', we find ourselves in a considerable dilemma when we speak of 'shared' human experience. While religious meaning, like any other form of meaning, needs to be personalised (which also means that it is relativised), all religious claims derive from a view of reality which is not contingent upon what individuals happen to call 'real'. If the concept of 'ultimacy' as well as the 'ultimate' question is relativised, it is difficult to see how this can contribute to an understanding of religious meaning.

(iv) The critical function of 'ultimate questions' and of religious education

Brief and incomplete as these comments are, they indicate something of the difficulty of using 'ultimate' questions as a means of bringing a 'religious' perspective to bear on *Shared Human Experience* and of promoting 'religious consciousness'. However, some value can be salvaged from the competing senses of meaning to which these questions are subject. Whatever perspective of 'ultimacy' is envisaged, the effect of asking such questions is to 'overload' our meaning system. In other words, asking 'ultimate' questions pushes our meaning-making strategies to their limits and places our taken-for-granted conception of reality under threat. Faced with this situation we can either ignore the question (by saying, for example, that it is meaningless) or we can seek to absorb the question within our meaning-system by 'reconstructing' our concept of reality in such a way as to encompass it. But one of the distinctive features of an 'ultimate' question (which, perhaps, contributes to its status of 'ultimacy' however we may define it) is that it persistently resists our attempts to absorb it into the relativising constructions we use to create personal and public meaning. Either the question 'Why?' still applies to our response or we are confronted by a variant on the original question. 'Ultimate' questions, therefore, *problematise* our conceptions of meaning, including religious meaning. They perform the critical function of turning our attention on what we know as well as on what we don't know, on what we believe as well as on what we don't believe, on what we value as well as on what we don't value. In short, 'ultimate' questions are 'consciousness-expanding' questions; they cause us to reflect on why we see things as we do and encourage us to set our own understanding against other ways of understanding. In so far as they promote awareness of our own consciousness, they may be regarded as being 'self-disclosing' questions which may then lead us to re-construct our consciousness to accommodate alternative forms of consciousness, including, of course, religious consciousness. If they do this, 'ultimate' questions must have educational value. The question is, how to bring them within the educational process.

I suggest that we should consider how far it is possible for education to stimulate pupils to look critically at their *own* beliefs and values as a basis for the formulation of their *own* 'ultimate' questions about meaning. I see such a process as being as educationally valuable to pupils who hold religious beliefs as to those who do not. Firstly, the process is concerned with encouraging pupils to explore the taken-for-granted assumptions of their own 'life-worlds' as a first step towards the development of what I will call 'critical consciousness' and 'self-awareness'. I see this as an essential prerequisite to the development of moral, religious and spiritual awareness. Secondly, by encouraging religions to be studied in such a way as to juxtapose their 'content' with the 'content' of the pupils' life-worlds, the process does not merely fulfil the intention of informing pupils about religious beliefs and values but also that of helping pupils to *use* religious beliefs and values as instruments for the critical evaluation of their own beliefs and values. While this will involve pupils in learning *about* religion, it will also involve them in learning *from* religion about themselves. The advantage of juxtaposing the study of religion with the life-worlds of the pupils is that it enables pupils not only to become critically conscious of their own cultural histories but also of their own personal histories; it thus contributes to their capacities to become consciously involved in their own personal development or to be 'autobiographical'.

It should be noted that this conception of how religious education might contribute to the 'humanisation' of pupils stems from the recognition that *all* young people, whether or not they are practising members of a religious faith community, have their *own* beliefs and values which, consciously or otherwise, exert a considerable influence on their way of looking at the world, their adoption of particular life-styles and, most important of all, their development as human beings. In discussing the centrality of beliefs and values to human development in Chapter Two, I made the following observation:

We should note, too, that the 'culture' into which we are born is a repository of other people's 'acts of faith' both from the past and the present. We are 'humanised' as receptors of those beliefs and values ('civilising values') which a society has come to embrace as important and necessary to human life and its fulfilment within the context of community. This means that the individual, from the time of birth onwards, lives within the 'arena of faith responses' but does so unconsciously. Thus the individual, in seeking to choose between beliefs, does not do so in vacuo but draws upon and so makes conscious the beliefs and values by which he or she has been formed. (p88)

Our discussion of those factors in the social world which combine to produce human consciousness has, I believe, contributed to the further elucidation of some of the important features of the process of humanisation I described in Chapter Two. What this account lacks, however, is reference to the concrete realities which constitute the everyday experiences of our pupils and a clear indication of what forms adolescent 'life-worlds' take in a plural society. It is to a consideration of these that we now turn.

Chapter Four

Adolescent life-worlds in a plural society

Introduction

From a number of studies on adolescents and adolescence,[1] I have selected two sociological studies as being particularly relevant to our interests of becoming better informed about the concrete realities which constitute the everyday experiences of young people, and learning something of the beliefs and values which inform and shape their outlooks. These are Tom Kitwood's research into *Adolescent Values In An Advanced Industrial Society*, which was published in 1980,[2] and the piece of research into *Young People's Beliefs* commissioned by the Church of England Board of Education and undertaken by Bernice Martin and Ronald Pluck in 1977[3]—the study to which I referred in Chapter Three.

More recently, however, the Swedish National Youth Council have published nine reports on 'commercial youth culture'; and in 1983 an English translation of their final report, written by Benny Henriksson, was published with the title *Not For Sale*.[4] This latter piece of research has contributed a particularly interesting analysis of the effects of 'modernity' on adolescent consciousness and, although based on Swedish society, offers insights into the 'life-worlds' of young people which are, I believe, relevant to an understanding of youth in any modern, technological society. It is from this report that I would like first to extract data; and then from the other two mentioned above. By including fairly extensive quotations from these works, I hope both to communicate something of the distinctive 'picture' of adolescent life in modern societies which each piece of research portrays and to bring these important research findings to the attention of religious education teachers as being particularly pertinent to their concerns. Following the extracts, I will offer some reflections on the possible application of these findings to a way of understanding how the development of critical consciousness and self-awareness enhances young people's sensitivities to issues of a moral, religious and spiritual kind.

1. Research into adolescent values

(i) Not for Sale: Young People In Society

In the preface to the English edition of this book, Brian Ashley writes:

> This book is concerned to highlight the social and economic situation of young people. It presents a very clear picture of the critical position of youth in the grip of a modern commercial system which holds the consumer as a helpless prisoner within trends and fashions. The search for profit dictates the policy decisions of that system, and the welfare and development of a generation of youth is, in the opinion of the author, being surrendered to the satisfaction of material needs which are themselves created by the system which supplies the ready-made answers.[5]

We have already looked at the characteristics of modernisation; what we now need to know is how it has affected the consciousness of youth. The report's findings point to the following outcomes of modernisation:

(a) **Children and adolescents are cut off from productive paid work.**
> There is no place for them in the entire work for the common welfare. Instead they are left to their own devices in an environment with a surplus of people of their own age. Their potential is not being used—in the housing area they only get in the way. . . . They are not given responsibility for others, they don't do work that is necessary for other people. They are held in an extended hiatus between childhood and adulthood. They have landed in a vacuum of leisure which waits only to be filled.[6]

(b) **Children and adolescents lack contact with adults.**
> Youth surveys show that children are often materially satisfied but socially starved. Often a pet, or the dream of owning one's own pet, compensates for the lack of social contacts . . . . . . when asked which of the things they possess is their favourite, they nearly always mention an adult with whom they have a social relationship—grandmother, grandfather, brother, cousin or an animal. Interviews with young people show the picture of a society where the adult generation, to an increasing extent, chooses to live without children. This too reinforces the vacuum.[7]

(c) **Children are not happy without the limits which emerge from natural co-operation between the generations.**
Satisfaction is only possible where desires and needs are limited.[8]

(d) **Adolescents have little faith in the future and are increasingly self-absorbed.**
In a situation in which people do not believe that they can change their lives or the conditions of their lives, they have persuaded themselves instead that it is self-realisation which is significant. Those who do not believe society has any future consider it better to live for the moment, not for ancestors or descendants. Withdrawal into the cult of one's own personality stems from . . . our culture-bureaucracy, therapeutic ideologies, the rationalisations of our inner lives, separations, changes in family life, patterns of specialisation and consumer culture, increased unemployment, adolescent vulnerability etc.[9]

(e) **Adolescents are onlookers not participants.**
Although a society may claim to have been striving for the recognition of such ideals as equality, equal values, fellowship, security, responsibility, progress and a purpose in life, many adolescents daily experience the opposite of these ideals. . . . They withdraw into passivity or they devote all their energies to their close group and use their time and attention in acquiring possessions. It becomes a substitute for human involvement.[10]

(f) **Adolescents today get paid for work that would previously have been part of the home's production and work.**
They negotiate for as much as they can get for these jobs so that they can buy consumer goods, which are a 'must'. The new 'child jobs' and wages are. . . . an example of how the market's laws about everything having to be valued in money terms are eating deep into the family's private life and reaching an ever younger age group.[11]

(g) **Children and adolescents are taught and trained to be consumers:**
(See f above) but only 4% of the sample said that what they bought was more important than socialising with friends or having contact with people or pets.[12]

(h) **Children and adolescents are formed by commercial youth culture which has become an ever increasing source of values.**
Several conditions must prevail if this artificially created culture is to work as a formational force in society. The principal training of young people must take place within their own peer group, and parents and other adults must have abandoned, more or less, their

attempts at influence. In this way the culture industry's products affect every single individual, not so much directly, as by way of the peer group. Increasingly it is the peer group which has come to help an adolescent to choose and, to some extent, also interpret the symbols and values with which he associates himself. The sources may vary, but without doubt one of the most important is the market's youth products. Parents and other adults accept, to an increasing degree, the values created for and by adolescents. In practice it means that parents and other adults more or less accept that adolescents and commercial youth culture have taken over the doctrinal role themselves. It even seems that many parents are themselves being indoctrinated by the adolescents. . . Themes which recur frequently in the products of commercial youth culture are sexual prejudices, sex and eroticism, violence, fear and excitement. Commercial youth culture continually prescribes consumption as an antidote to the difficulties of everyday life.[13]

(i) **Adolescents look for identification within their group of friends and/or in commercial youth culture.**
Normally society and adults afford the opportunities for positive identification which strengthens the ego. If there are not people to identify with, or if adults do not help the child (see b above), the worse the individual's self-awareness becomes and the easier the identification with the products of mass culture. . . . Many adolescents identify themselves by quickly changing their models, without going through any real identification. Something that is easy to identify oneself with, or easy to plagiarise, is also attractive. Identification that requires preparation or reflection is less so. Life becomes constantly transient, while commercial youth culture, which, in ever accelerating tempo, has specialised in selling new lifestyles, makes new conquests. Life-styles and ideals become throwaway articles, just like consumer goods. . . . To stimulate sales, the market has developed a world of pretence, a world full of promises—a material-aesthetic *world. This industry of experiences and consciousness overwhelms young people with its products including the electronic sensuousness and vehement emotions of video and sound recordings. They encroach upon the formation of ideals and values. . . They appeal to the young consumer's irrationality and idleness. . . Because the market is supported by a quick turn over of goods, the utility value of the products decreases. The system encourages waste of economic and human resources. Thus commercialism's 'negative effects' deal not just with youth leisure, but have long-term consequences for young people's future*

and for the kind of society and view of humanity they will take over.[14]

(j) **Children and adolescents are sold values through marketing and advertising.**
Many advertisements are aimed directly at children and adolescents. A lot of it is 'nag advertising', ie, its purpose is to make the child pressure its parents into buying some article or other. Concepts, ideas, values, qualities and emotions are consistently linked with certain products by being transferred from a person or an object to those products. eg, In Sweden, crispbread is linked with people who represent certain values; Bjorn Borg's association with the product implies that it is linked with such qualities as strength, fitness, clean living, sensuality and winning. . . Through advertisements the more inaccessible (but highly desired) emotions and states of mind—love, wealth, happiness, etc,—are linked with something accessible, ie, the product. The idea is given that these emotions can be attained by buying the product. . . Finally, the product becomes the emotion, a surrogate for love, happiness, excitement. If the product can create emotions or become an emotion, it becomes more than just a symbol—it actually becomes one with the emotion. If 'Pepsi' opens the door to love, the product becomes a kind of currency with which one can buy love and happiness.[15]

(k) **Adolescents do not accept unreservedly the ideology of commercial culture.**
An active choice is being made the whole time. Teenagers, especially those who belong to a certain sub-culture, extract from the commercial life-styles certain types of clothes, music etc, and adapt them to fit the key values in their own group identity. The varying life-styles are thus not completely absorbed, but on the contrary, adolescents have filtered, reinterpreted and adapted them. What we see of a sub-culture's style is a refashioning of different symbols from their normal social context, and of commercialised symbols into a new, complex whole with its own specific characteristics.[16]

(l) **Adolescents have an enormous creative drive of their own which helps them to withstand the forces trying to exploit them.**
In our conversations and interviews with children and adolescents, they expressed a robust life-force and awareness. Even those with a difficult upbringing and whose life is dominated by the mass media's values and life styles, show a great ability to resist and form their own ideas.[17]

147

The authors of this extensive report conclude as follows:

We have tried to explain which forces militate against individual creative work. Our analysis deals with the grave structural problems in our society and the market's method of exploiting them. We have tried to understand the attractions of commercial youth culture, how it fills a vacuum, plays on the child's need for fantasy, emotions and experiences. The most challenging thing about our analysis is that society does not seem to want to avail itself of the child's unutilised awareness and resources, but seems, if anything, afraid of them.[18]

(ii) *Disclosures to a Stranger: Adolescent Values in an Advanced Industrial Society*

Kitwood sought to design an 'ideographic' method of enquiring into adolescent values which was 'anchored in the realities of adolescent life' and which 'might elicit a person's repertoire of value constructs and explore the ways in which they are used'.[19] The method involved identifying a number of 'situations' which had 'at least potentially, a relevance to aspects of what is commonly considered to be the domain of values'.[20] The fifteen 'situations' which Kitwood eventually used were:

1. *When there was a misunderstanding between you and someone else;*
2. *When you got on really well with people;*
3. *When you had to make an important decision;*
4. *When you discovered something new about yourself;*
5. *When you felt angry, annoyed and resentful;*
6. *When you did what was expected of you;*
7. *When your life changed direction in some way;*
8. *When you felt that you had done something well;*
9. *When you were right on your own, with hardly anyone taking your side;*
10. *When you 'got away with it', or were not found out;*
11. *When you made a serious mistake;*
12. *When you felt afterwards that you had done right;*
13. *When you were disappointed with yourself;*
14. *When you had a serious clash or disagreement with another person;*
15. *When you began to take seriously something that had not mattered much to you before.[21]*

These 'situations' were used as the basis of 'face-to-face' interviews with 153 adolescents, aged between fourteen and twenty, equally divided between the sexes and between urban and rural backgrounds, and representative of a threefold class division. Kitwood reports that no adverse comments were made by interviewees after their interview and that the following appraisal by a boy of eighteen is characteristic of their reactions:

> *I think that this is about the first time I've sort of sat down and discussed myself. I've sat down and discussed other people, but I've never sort of sat down and discussed myself because nobody's really been interested in me as a person. I, er, they just sort of take you for granted that way, and that's it. That's the sort of start and finish of the sort of thing. Never at school, you know, I never even had a discussion about myself at school. I'm not pulling my school to pieces. I know it sounds like I am, but I'm not. We used to talk about other people but never about yourself, you know. Nobody ever sort of stopped to say, "Well, why don't we talk about you for a change?". We'd talk about somebody else. It were always about, well, "What, what do you think about so and so and so and so?"; "Write an essay on so and so". It were never "Write an essay on yourself", like.[22]*

As an additional check on reactions to the interview, a short questionnaire was sent to seventeen boys and girls afterwards. One 'older' girl replied:

> *Apart from being helpful to the researchers, I feel, and can only really say for myself, that it was very helpful for me. It was a very good opportunity to talk about what's important to you or just about you to a completely objective person which, I think, is a constructive thing to do in the sense that it helps self-awareness. . . .[23]*

Kitwood noted that certain themes were emphasised more than had been anticipated (ie, domesticity, relationships, reputations, personal achievement and affiliation with the adult world); and others less than had been anticipated (ie, television programmes and pop music, 'the search for meaning', sexuality, and 'the search for identity'). The omission of the four latter themes was considered 'noteworthy for any attempt to understand the place of values in adolescent life' and Kitwood offers a number of comments upon them.

Television did receive the occasional brief reference, but only as 'the immediate precipitant of a family quarrel, or as an occupation to fill in time when there was nothing much else to do. There was virtually no indication, however, of boys and girls attributing learning, growth of understanding, interest, concern or satisfaction to its influence.' When *pop music* was mentioned it was because a person was actively involved 'in doing, making, creating, organising or meeting, rather than passively listening or responding'. Pop music was, however, considered 'as a valid topic of conversation, as a basis for friendship groups and for rivalry between them, or as a ground for meeting with other people'. Kitwood concludes:

Thus both television and pop music generally seemed to form part of the 'background noise' against which more dramatic episodes were enacted. For most adolescents they appear to have become pervasive but not outstandingly significant parts of the taken-for-granted world, in much the same way that the British Empire or the harvest festival were in the youth of their grandparents.[24]

Concerning the 'significant absence' of the *search for meaning*, Kitwood comments:

Adolescence is sometimes portrayed, particularly by writers in the psychoanalytic tradition, as a period when some persons will show an intense interest in the affairs of the intellect, an eager search for a philosophy by which to live, and for ideals in the light of which to strive for a better world. That kind of image is not confirmed by this research. Much more striking was a general lack of concern about or involvement in ideas as such, even among those who were academically very successful. For example, with item 15 ideas as such account for a mere 8 out of 103 categorised choices concerned with 'taking something seriously'. This general picture is reinforced in the way attitudes to school were presented . . . Throughout the whole range of social class covered there was hardly any indication of commitment to school as a source of significant learning, or of concern with truth and understanding as these are academically viewed.

Three types of exception to this picture must be mentioned, though they do not modify it greatly. A few participants made reference to politics as an area of concern, the main emphasis being on socialist thinking. Some also spoke about their religious involvement; of those who expressed an active commitment, it was mainly a way of living and relating to persons, rather than fundamental issues of truth, that apparently attracted them. There were also a few boys who had a well developed knowledge either in practical mechanics or electronics, arising from their leisure-time pursuits . . . The picture of widespread apathy about the more 'pure' academic realm is scarcely qualified by such instances.[25]

Concerning the 'significant absence' of references to *sexuality*, Kitwood does not think this can be accounted for by the view that active sexual behaviour has become so much a part of the taken-for-granted world of adolescents that it does not need to be spoken about. On the contrary, he suggests that 'there is some ground for thinking that many younger adolescents do not have the social skill to form intimate relationships with the opposite sex. . .', although he concedes that 'sexuality is a domain of life too personal for some to discuss with a stranger'.[26]

Finally, the 'significant absence' of a *search for identity* causes Kitwood to comment that there is little evidence to support the idea that this is a major feature of adolescence. He adds:

> There were indications that some wished to adopt a distinctive personal style in specific contexts; that, however, is a very different matter from developing an inner integration.[27]

The interviews produced such a wealth of data that the author restricted himself to a detailed analysis of values that emerged from a consideration of four themes: relationships in the home, social life among peers, experiences of formal and informal work, and the development of the self-image. Here we can only pick out a few indications of what values Kitwood found to be significant to adolescents as they were revealed through the many individual 'situation descriptions' his book contains. Something of the danger of merely 'listing' values as 'entities' may be seen from his observation that:

> . . . it is possible for a boy or girl to have as many sets of values as the groups in which he or she participates, and without necessarily noticing that these are mutually inconsistent. In the light of this the idea of making simple measurements among those of this age, to determine the constituents of a 'personal value system', is virtually meaningless. Insight will be gained, rather, by looking at the values that are associated with particular kinds of group activity.[28]

The family is the primary group of which adolescents are members and this is 'a pervasive and sometimes relatively featureless part of the taken-for-granted world'.[29] But it is only one of the many social-life worlds occupied by adolescents and between which they move either with ease or with considerable difficulty and tension.

> From the adolescent's point of view, home often, therefore, acquires an ambivalent character. On the one hand it is valued as a place of physical provision and (in many cases) of relative stability; a continued loyalty is definitely fitting. On the other hand, some degree of independence from it must be achieved. Adolescence is thus a period of moving away from parents, both physically and psychologically. There are clear values relating to this transition.[30]

What Kitwood points to is the way in which each social environment, especially the family, provides a context in which adolescents engage in 'a prolonged, unstructured and highly informal course of "sensitivity training" which neither they nor many of the adults who are involved in them recognise as such'.[31] Complying with certain values, such as cooperating with parents, giving practical help in the home, responding to parental expectations, is thus indicative of the adolescent's growing recognition of what is necessary to the development of interpersonal relationships, and of his or her progress in acquiring the foundations of social skills. The values with which adolescents comply, therefore, are not so much their 'own' but are embedded in the social life-worlds themselves. Kitwood points out that out of a total of seventy-four categorised choices there were only eleven cases of a boy or girl 'standing alone' for a value at the level of action. He suggests that the probable inference is that a person much below the age of sixteen is unlikely to hold values in an individual way. The following comment from a boy of eighteen reinforces this view:

We had our own values that you get in a group. It's the way you do things, and the way you react to people, and it's your relationships—that are the values you build up. And I think the people you're with, and the different relationships you build, give you different values. So—I mean, at the time I, I probably had quite a few changing values then, because I was changing groups, and sort of going from group to group . . . But, um, your values do change, I think, with, with the different people.[32]

Kitwood's analysis of values related to specific contexts leads him to conclude that, generally, the level of abstraction at which values are consciously held is low and that there are indications that most boys and girls do not make clear or extensive correlations between their actions in separate social life-worlds. He points out, however, that the problem of being a member of a group with shared values is that one also has to be able to sustain a sense of being a person distinct from the others, viz:

Whenever a major decision is consciously made, and something of its long-term implications are realised, 'self-values' are involved. For the question 'What shall I do?' subjectively appears to entail such questions as 'Who am I?' and 'What kind of person do I wish to be or to become?'[33]

He thus gives attention to 'self-values' and the issue of how the larger question of personal identity is related to adolescence. He suggests that questions about self-values must be asked in dynamic rather than static terms and any methodology for identifying the process by which they are developed must assume the person to be perceptive, active and reflective. He poses the question:

What types of circumstances in everyday life might a person face, and as a necessary part of solving the problems which they present believe that it is necessary to choose to be one kind of person rather than another?[34]

He suggests that such circumstances occur when the individual 'severs social bonds'. He expresses his view as follows:

This is the kind that involves the relinquishing of some activity, the cutting off of previous associations, the resolution to dispense with some existing means of support. The emphasis here is often negatively on breaking, rather than positively on commitment. For many of the circumstances in which adolescents find themselves are not created by their own deliberate action, but are part of the ready-made world in which they found themselves; and it is often the case that involvement in social life or the development of particular interests is gradual, unmarked by any one decisive step. To break away, however, means a definite choice; a movement from the known to the unknown. It involves risk, perhaps requiring a person to rely upon inner resources rather than social support; and it is logically possible only in the light of reflection of what a person wishes to be or to become. [35]

In concluding this summary of this important piece of research, we should note Kitwood's rejection of the common stereotypes of 'adolescence':

The participants in this inquiry did not show much resemblance to the adolescent of the popular stereotype: they were not mindless consumers, practitioners of violence and sensuality, rebels against authority, degenerate, feckless or lazy. The feature that emerges most strongly . . . is the way in which so many adolescents are concerned to be effective interpreters and performers in the social environments that are personally significant to them. The apparent conservatism, shown particularly in attitudes towards locality, sex roles, employment and the family, may be viewed as a temporary cognitive necessity, facilitating the mapping of immediate relationships . . . Similarly, such fundamental values as freedom and justice are generally encountered during adolescence only in relation to highly specific issues; it is rare to find a person correlating such experiences in different social life-worlds, or making abstractions towards more general principles or ideals, because there are more urgent issues to be faced. [36]

(iii) Young People's Beliefs: an exploratory study of the views and behavioural patterns of young people related to their beliefs

Martin and Pluck began their work by seeking to determine what factors in a young person's life contributed to or detracted from the possibility of Christian belief. They interviewed 100 young people aged between thirteen and twenty-four from a range of social backgrounds and from urban and rural areas. In the course of analysing the material provided by the interviews it became clear that the notion of 'belief' was very difficult to define. They comment: 'One way of using the term relates to the acceptance of dogmatic propositions which fit a coherent system. In that sense one might conclude from the findings that these young people do not believe'.[37] They found that only two out of the hundred young people interviewed were attached to any kind of religious movement and these were both recent converts to a Christian sect. All the rest 'tread the wobbly and doubtful line which separates agnosticism from some vague and woolly version of Christianity'.[38] Typical comments from interviewees were:

Well, I suppose there might be something in it, and then again there might not.[39]
At about 12 or 14 years old religion just wore off.[40]
It's just part of growing up. You get beyond that stage.[41]

On the basis of the responses gathered by this research study, young people are, apparently, completely indifferent to traditional religious beliefs. They are not necessarily anti-religious or overtly hostile to religion but just indifferent about it and entirely dismissive of its social relevance. If this is the case, what then *are* their beliefs? What *do* young people believe in? What *do* they see as socially relevant? To what *are* they committed? What follows summarises some of the findings of this research project:

The first point is the virtual absence of interviewees who had a clearly defined, consistent, and verbalised pattern of beliefs. . . . among the vast majority of the sample there was clear evidence that for purposes of their normal life they had never so far required an articulated and systematised account of their 'belief' in order to cope with existence.[42]
More surprising almost than the absence of traditional church commitment is the non-appearance of items of the counter-cultural value-system. It is true that there is some weight given to sincerity over hypocrisy and a widespread belief that institutions, especially religious ones, are irrelevant to life. There is too a strong emphasis on the private and individual nature of belief . . . But ecology, communities, oriental mysticism, anti-bourgeois existentialism are nowhere to be seen . . . There is, though, acceptance of moderate hedonism as a normal and legitimate end in life; nothing is wrong unless it has an obvious victim, you'd be a fool not to get the best experience you can for yourself in life, and it's perfectly all right, and nobody else's business if you sleep with your girl/boy friend. The protestant work ethic as a driving force for work and self-denial is undoubtedly in very bad shape among our sample. Nor is anyone here replacing it by anything reminiscent of a spiritual quest. Our respondents live on a much less effervescent, much more mundane and pragmatic plane than any of that. When they are asked what matters to them in life, they are mostly at a loss for a reply. For themselves they want a good job and happiness and the things about

which they *wax spontaneously eloquent are sex, marriage, clothes, their own plans for the future and their own images of their personal identity.*[43]

It cannot be too strongly stressed that a universal individualism was found in the approach of these young people. What you believe is essentially private, it is your own affair, you have the right to believe anything you like. The corollary of this individualism is a strong dislike of having other people's beliefs pushed on you. . . Going along with this individualism and privacy of belief is an equally strong and universal insistence on one's own open-mindedness. 'I like to keep an open mind' must have been repeated as often as 'What you believe is your own affair'.[44]

There is a total absence of any drive to intellectual consistency either in the belief pattern itself or between belief and behaviour. . . This inconsistency relates to two further widespread features of the respondent's beliefs. First, childhood belief is breached with incredible ease on the basis of a simplistic scientism. . . What takes over is a vocabulary and ambience of empirical science. . . The scientific vocabulary asks for 'facts' and 'proof', and seeks to reduce all the stories of conventional religion to scientific formulae. But it can encompass without so much as a blink of the eye ghosts and poltergeists. . . exorcism, superstition, belief in luck and fate, the use of horoscopes, the reading of tea-leaves, the efficacy of crosses and Bibles against hauntings. And time and time again it is 'open-minded' to the point of credulity about Martian spaceships as the 'true' 'scientific' source of early religious beliefs. In short, any sort of idea, however fantastic, will be given house room if it can be dressed up in a scientific, or more accurately perhaps, a 'science fiction' garb. The second notable feature of the internal incoherence of belief is that while it can tolerate any degree of inconsistency it seems very intolerant of uncertainty. What causes unease is not an overall lack of consistency in a system but detailed factual lacunae. To the question, 'What would make you believe?' the typical answer is 'More facts'. . .[45]*

2. The research findings applied to an understanding of the moral, religious and spiritual consciousness of adolescents

(i) The relationship between critical consciousness and self-knowledge

The most striking feature of the findings of all three pieces of research is their confirmation that children and young people (like adults) today have pluralised consciousnesses. As we have seen, pluralism and relativity are the products of modernity and it is not at all surprising that this 'outer pluralism is matched by an inner pluralism'. John Hull expresses this as follows:

> *The pluralisation of society is mirrored in the pluralisation of consciousness. We are not so much unified persons facing many realities as disunified persons containing many realities.*[46]

It is by reference to the pluralism of consciousness that we can begin to offer some explanation of the reason why, as Kitwood shows, 'it is possible for a boy or girl to have as many sets of values as the groups in which he or she participates, and without necessarily noticing that these are mutually inconsistent'.[47] Similarly it offers a way of accounting for 'the virtual absence of interviewees who had a clearly defined, consistent, and verbalised pattern of beliefs' among the young people with whom Martin and Pluck talked. One way in which sociologists address this phenomenon is by reference to 'role theory'. We all perform multiple roles in our life, each having its own perceived expectations. Certain 'values' are built into these expectations and in so far as we fulfil them we may be said to 'have values'. These roles, however, are situated in different social life-worlds (eg, the home, the school, the place of work, the place of leisure and recreation, the faith community, etc), and so separate may these various worlds be that we fail to connect them. Thus our 'values' are not really our own but 'values-in-roles', and these may be mutally contradictory. We may only become overtly conscious of the contradictory nature of such values when we consciously or otherwise apply values from one role within a context requiring the values of another. So, for example, the 'values-in-role' of being a double-glazing salesman are likely to be contradictory of the 'values-in-role' of being a husband, parent or friend; and to attempt to apply them in the latter role contexts is to place one's personal relationships in jeopardy. This situation arises from the fact that the background stock of knowledge which is taken for granted in one social world will not be the same as that stock of knowledge which is the common property of people in another social world. Given these different situations, how, if at all, are different meanings to be evaluated? Who is to say that one set of values is, in some sense, superior to another? Who is to say that one's values should not be contradictory?

One of the difficulties of using 'role-theory' to account for our having pluralised consciousnesses is that it appears to deny the possibility of our having an enduring 'self' which enables us to be, as it were, more than the sum of the different roles we play in our different social worlds. But just as the thesis that reality is a social construct cannot admit to there being enclaves of meaning which are not subject to social construction, so role-theory cannot admit to the notion of the self being anything but a product of the roles we play. In other words, the problem is not merely that moving within these different worlds of meaning and value requires us to adopt different meanings and values as we do so; it is that these worlds are moving within us; their meanings are part of our consciousness. Our 'self' is thus a 'social' self formed by the same social processes by which all reality is constructed. However, it is because the self *is* a product of social interactions—a *social* product—that we can have some influence upon it. Not only can we become aware of our own 'consciousness'—ie, aware of those frames of reference into which we have been socialised and which provide multiple perspectives on meaning—we can also become 'self-conscious'—ie, aware of that personal identity which has emerged, and continues to emerge as a consequence of our individual interactions with others within the particular circumstances of our life. I suggest that what I have called 'critical consciousness' combines both of these forms of consciousness and issues in *self-awareness and self-knowledge*. Moral, religious and spiritual awareness may thus be seen as both arising from critical consciousness and contributing to it. Let us examine this suggestion more closely.

In Chapter Two I spent some time looking at the notion of 'identity', first by speaking of the 'belongingness-identity' of childhood and then by referring to adolescence as a natural opportunity for reflection on, and re-evaluation and re-interpretation of the self. I quoted Wall's observation that:

Fully self-aware persons (ie, those who are personally autonomous) are transparent to themselves and find their identity in this self-knowledge which renders them able to stand aside from any belongingness-identity they may have. Their security is internal and based on self-understanding and acceptance, not external and dependent upon adopting and being adopted by a group of any kind. This does not mean that they necessarily reject group or social norms and loyalties; but that their obedience to them is critical, rational, voluntary and a matter of renewed choice. Such norms and loyalties are not for them a vital source of personal security; although they are fully accepted, they are rationally amenable to change.[48]

The process of becoming 'self-aware' (which culminates in 'self-knowledge') involves our becoming *conscious* of those beliefs and values which have shaped us as a person, and more particularly, have formed our identity. This will involve, of course, our becoming conscious of those 'values-in-role' which we embrace in our different social life-worlds. A necessary concomitant of being conscious of these is the necessity to appraise them and to exercise a conscious choice between them and between other beliefs and values which may be available to us. Through this process we do not only begin to identify 'self-values' (as defined by Kitwood) we reflect on, re-evaluate and re-interpret our 'self' and thus become actively involved in its shaping and development. Undoubtedly we are speaking here of a complex process, and psychological literature offers us many different models by which it may be charted and understood.[49] Without making any other claims than that it is another possible model, the process may be conceived of as having six stages and being cyclic: viz:

Figure Three: Stages of self-awareness in the growth of self-knowledge

The different segments of the circle represent different stages of awareness in the growth of self-knowledge. Each stage is characterised by its own dominant questions which prompt the need for personal response and personal decision. (I will be suggesting what some of these questions are in Chapter Six.) It is tempting to see each stage within a hierarchy, but more important is the recognition of the cyclic nature of the process itself. Just as in the once familiar curriculum development models using a circle where evaluation leads to a redefining of aims,[50] so here evaluation leads to a redefining of self-identity in a process which is life-long. The model suggests that the first three stages of awareness in the growth of self-knowledge are: being aware of how one sees 'oneself' to be (the cognised or known self: *self-identity*); how one feels about, or values oneself (*self-acceptance*); and how one has become oneself or become the person one is (*self-illumination*). Beyond these stages lie three more—referred to as *self-ideal*, *self-adjustment* and *self-evaluation*—which promote the conscious reconstruction of self in which one explores the possibilities of an ideal-self, considers how one might adjust one's self to such an ideal, and finally reflects on the new identity which has emerged from the process—a process which will repeat itself again and again throughout life.

(ii) The relationship between self-knowledge and religious, moral and spiritual awareness.

But in what sense does this process relate to the development of moral, religious and spiritual awareness? I suggest that the relationship between moral, religious and spiritual awareness and self-awareness is a symbiotic one, ie, they are mutually informing and sustaining. Early in Chapter Two, when we were considering the question 'Who am I?', I suggested that 'in trying to know myself in order to answer this question, I encounter the mystery of my being'. I further suggested that each of us is groping for some understanding of ourselves—self-understanding—but that we only have glimpses of this at odd moments when we become 'self-conscious'. If we were to attempt to follow up such glimpses by consciously engaging in a sustained effort to formulate systematically a more adequate or coherent account of who we are, then, I suggest, we would find ourselves involved in the sort of reflective and evaluative process to which I have been referring. In so doing we would be focusing on our own subjectivity, interiority or spirituality.

In Chapter One I drew attention to Phenix's identification of a realm of meaning which he calls 'Synnoetics' and his view that synnoetic meanings are *subjective* and give rise to *personal knowledge*. He sees such knowledge as consisting of *intersubjective* awareness and *intrasubjective* awareness and holds that this is largely a product of social experience, not of instruction. I suggest that the process I have been identifying relates to the development of synnoetic meaning, and that although Phenix is undoubtedly correct in attributing its development to social experience, it does not necessarily follow that this precludes the possibility of the formal curriculum also contributing to its development. Indeed, I suggest that if we are to speak realistically of education contributing to the personal development of pupils, it is essential that the formal curriculum becomes a stimulus for each pupil to develop synnoetic meaning or self-knowledge. In Chapter Six I will be arguing that *all* school subjects have a responsibility to contribute to pupils' development of this kind of personal knowledge, not just religious education; but here I am concerned with attempting to justify my view that there is an especially close relationship between the development of self-knowledge and the development of religious, moral and spiritual awareness. We can consider this relationship from a number of angles.

While it is necessary to conceive of ethics and religion as 'finite provinces of meaning' or 'systems of belief and conduct' which offer *impersonal* modes of understanding into which we may try to 'fit' our personal, interior experiences, what 'ethics' and 'religion' enable us to order and articulate is something which is already there—in us. I refer here to our inherent human tendency to preserve and affirm our existence, to seek order and purpose in our lives, to find worth and value in ourselves, to seek personal fulfilment in what we do and in what we are, etc, and to do so through holding beliefs by an act of faith. Those fundamental human experiences to which religion and ethics address themselves are not, as it were, set apart from us, but are part of us. For example, we are able to incorporate the religious concept of 'transcendence' into our thinking because we already have an experience of 'transcendence' in our personal experience; indeed, the very process of experiencing ourselves is that we are 'more than the sum of our separate parts' and that our identity is not adequately defined by the terms and references by which we are publicly known (eg, by reference to one or other of our roles). But equally it is because there are impersonal, public systems of meaning which articulate and define what we perceive personally that we can become aware of our own experiences; my sense of needing to transcend the limitations of a finite identity is dependent on my identity being conceived of as finite; my sense of being more than the roles I play is dependent on roles being ascribed to me, and so on.

In the previous chapter I argued that the view that all human beings are endowed at birth with a capacity for 'spiritual' awareness cannot be lightly dismissed. Now I want to link this capacity with the human capacity for self-awareness. In speaking of this type of awareness as *personal, intersubjective* and *intrasubjective* we are, I suggest, coming as close as we are able to come to defining the *locus* of the human capacity for *spiritual* awareness. I draw back from identifying them as the same, but there can be no doubt that all human understanding of spirituality, including that understanding provided by the great religions of the world, links spiritual development with the growth of self-awareness. In other words, implicit in all conceptions of the religious and spiritual quest is the notion that it involves our response to the question 'Who am I?', even if, as in Buddhism, that response must involve the annihilation of 'I'. That response cannot be made apart from becoming involved in the process of growing in self-knowledge. Characteristically, each religion not only prescribes a *model of the human* but also the means by which it can be realised in the life of the individual. Thus implicit in each religion's understanding of the religious or spiritual quest is its understanding of the meaning and end of personal development and of the different stages of self-awareness which contribute to it. I suggest that such stages will bear a resemblance to those identified in the model which I have put forward. We should note, however, that considerable differences will exist between the viewpoints of the different religions about the meaning and end of personal development and the means by which this is to be promoted.

What follows from these observations? If, as I have argued, the relationship between religious, moral and spiritual awareness and self-awareness is a symbiotic one, it follows that any process which results in our becoming critically conscious of the beliefs and values that have shaped us enhances our capacity for religious, moral and spiritual awareness. It should be noted that it is our *capacity for* religious, moral and spiritual awareness which is enhanced by this process; the process of becoming self-aware does not, for example, give us an *understanding* of religious meaning, nor does it, in itself, promote 'religious consciousness'. For an understanding of religious meaning to occur it is necessary for the process to involve reflection on explicitly religious values as interpreted within specifically religious frameworks of belief such as are provided by *Traditional Belief Systems*. Furthermore, if by 'religious consciousness' we mean, as I suggested in the last chapter, 'an internalised framework of religious meaning within which the individual consistently re-presents his or her total experience to him or herself', then we are speaking of something which is difficult to distinguish from 'religious faith' and which is dependent upon more than knowledge of religion. The process with which we are concerned is, therefore, one which *sensitises* us to the significance and function of beliefs and believing within human development; it does not purport to induct us into different kinds of belief, nor does it seek to be prescriptive of what kinds of belief are in some sense preferable to others. However, insofar as one of the outcomes of being critically conscious of our beliefs and values is the recognition that we become what we believe, the process does cause us to confront (largely through questions) issues which are fundamental to the human condition and to personal identity. In Chapter One I tried to show how the question 'Who am I?' presents in personalised form that question which Kant posits as the central question of human philosophising—'What is man?'. I also indicated how this question is related to all other questions—that, for instance, it encompasses metaphysical questions ('What can I know?'), ethical questions ('What ought I to do?') and religious questions ('What may I hope?'). Insofar, therefore, as we are confronted by the question 'Who am I?', we are confronted by the necessity of entering the arena of faith responses.

We are now in a position to relate these observations to the situation of adolescents having pluralised consciousnesses and multiple social life-worlds. Firstly, young people, like all human beings, cannot escape the necessity of holding beliefs by an act of faith. As we have seen, all human beings are born into other people's 'acts of faith' and are humanised in accordance with whatever beliefs a culture regards as 'normative'. From our discussion of the social construction of consciousness in Chapter Three, we are now able to see why human beings become what they believe; the beliefs into which they are born shape their consciousness. But, as we have seen, human beings also possess a capacity to choose consciously between beliefs and act in accordance with the beliefs they choose. In order to do so, however, they must reconstruct their socially-constructed consciousnesses; they must extend or expand them to accommodate new and alternative perspectives of meaning not previously available to them. To some extent the pluralisation of consciousness to which human beings are subject in our contemporary society may assist them in this process. Relativity is a fact of social life and a fact of human consciousness.

Although I have been careful to avoid equating the development of self-awareness with the development of religious awareness, I hope I have succeeded in showing that the human capacity for self-awareness is integral to the attainment of moral, religious and spiritual awareness. Indeed, unless 'the religious', 'the moral' and 'the spiritual' as impersonal, finite provinces of human meaning can be incorporated within our own personal, subjective and interior worlds of meaning, their capacity to enable us to order and articulate our self-understanding as well as to reflect on it, evaluate it and re-interpret it will not be made available to us. In reflecting on questions which focus our attention on our own self-identity we are, I suggest, focusing on that dimension of human experience within which moral, religious and spiritual awareness develops and which, in turn, issues in the development of moral, religious and spiritual consciousness. We can illustrate this by reference to the four 'situation descriptions' which Kitwood numbered 4, 7, 13 and 15: viz:

4. *When you discovered something new about yourself;*
7. *When your life changed direction in some way;*
13. *When you were disappointed with yourself;*
15. *When you began to take seriously something that had not mattered much to you before.*

All four questions invite reflection on situations in which some form of evaluation and re-interpretation of self is involved and prompt answers which draw on synnoetic meaning. We need to consider, however, what, in young people's lives, can act as a stimulus for such reflection and what frameworks of reference are available to them within which they can begin to interpret their experiences. The questions given above were posed by researchers; they are questions which required interviewees to confront their own experiences and discern some pattern of meaning within them which they alone could find. It was the interviewer's questions which caused these young people to be critically conscious, and it was their participation in a piece of research which gave them both the reason and the motivation for taking such questions seriously. We might consider, therefore, if, without such external stimulus, young people are normally inclined towards such reflection and evaluation.

Certainly, particular events—especially tragic ones—which occur in the lives of human beings may have the effect of promoting such reflection, and under such circumstances their actions may be 'self-disclosing'. But for most human beings these events occur too infrequently to act as a sort of pedagogical device which teaches them to be reflective and evaluative as a normal and necessary aspect of being themselves. Besides, such events when they occur are normally so charged with emotion that it is only when the dilemmas they present have in some sense been resolved that reflection upon them ceases to be painful and threatening. But reflection of this sort requires the event, situation or circumstance to be placed within some framework of meaning if it is to be interpreted. Kitwood's research gives some grounds for believing young people attach particular significance to 'getting on well with people' and that reflection on self is often a consequence of either success or failure in this respect. This suggests that one framework of reference which is available to young people is what they understand to be successful social performance; thus they interpret their experiences by reference to the expectations they have of their own and other people's social behaviour—that of their parents, peers, significant adults, heroes (fictional or otherwise) and so on.

(iii) The relationship between education, religious education and self-knowledge, and moral, religious and spiritual awareness

But as we saw earlier, a particular feature of living in our contemporary, plural society is that young people inhabit a plurality of life-worlds, each with their own values and expectations of how individuals should behave within them. While this conflict of values and expectations may in itself act as a stimulus for personal reflection and evaluation, resolution of such conflict in terms of identifying and becoming committed to particular values (such resolution being taken as indicative of human development) requires individuals to formulate criteria against which to evaluate a plurality of values. It is here that formal education may fulfil its objective of extending the repertoire of young people's responses to belief and value beyond those inculcated by family, peer group, sub-culture and the consciousness-creating industries of our contemporary society, by providing them with an understanding of the diversity of

163

beliefs and values which is a feature of human meaning-making activities and encouraging them to explore the implications that making a commitment to particular beliefs and values may have for the direction in which human beings develop.

While all curriculum subjects may have a contribution to make towards promoting such understanding, the particular responsibility of religious education is, I suggest, twofold. Firstly it is to acquaint pupils with the diversity of *religious* beliefs and values and to consider the effect of the religious adherent's commitment to particular religious beliefs in terms of his or her understanding of self, others, the world, and so on. Secondly it is to offer young people a means of evaluating a plurality of values—religious or otherwise—by setting them within particular frameworks of religious meaning. Thus religious values are to be seen as being both part of the plurality of values which contribute to pluralised consciousness, and yet they are also understood to be one of the means by which a pluralised consciousness may be unified. Relating this to the four questions given earlier, this means that through the study of religions pupils are given an opportunity not only of reflecting upon and evaluating their responses to such questions by reference to religious beliefs and values, but also of discerning such questions as a result of studying religions. In so far as the process encourages them, for the sake of evaluation, to place their own experiences within a religious framework of reference, it also permits the possibility of their discerning a religious or spiritual dimension within their own experience of self. It is in providing pupils with an opportunity to consider this possibility and its implications for how they define themselves that religious education may be said to contribute to the development of their moral, religious and spiritual consciousness.

In other words, the study of religions can be seen to connect with the process of promoting critical self-consciousness in two different but related ways. Firstly, reflection on *Shared Human Experience*, especially on the dilemmas and questions which arise in one's personal life (resulting, for example, from the death of a near one, the loss of status in a group, the failure of a personal relationship, and so on), leads to reflection on self, on the beliefs one holds about oneself, on what one values and on what one fears, etc. Such reflection constitutes the means by which one becomes self-aware, which, I have argued, is as close as we are able to come to defining the locus of the human capacity for spiritual awareness. Developing young people's capacities to become self-aware thus increases their capacity for moral, religious and spiritual awareness; it does not, however, give them an understanding of religious meaning, nor does it give them religious consciousness. The latter is dependent upon their studying religions and being encouraged to relate their knowledge of religious concepts, religious questions, religious symbols and religious language, etc, to their understanding of self and to use these in the interpretation of their experiences. Thus the value of studying religions is not merely to be found in the understanding of religious meaning that it promotes, but in what understanding religious meaning contributes to the pupil's understanding of self. Secondly, the study of religions provides both the occasion and the stimulus for young people to become aware of the centrality of beliefs and believing in human meaning-making activities. Thus studying religions provides the context within which issues of belief and value can be raised and explored in such a way as to be illuminative of the situations and circumstances in which young people find themselves. Indeed, although it may often be possible to draw directly on the experiences, questions, beliefs and values of the pupils themselves as the starting-point for work in religious education, there are, as we shall see in the next chapter, particular difficulties with regarding these as, in some sense, lesson content or part of the subject's field of enquiry. Consequently the phenomenological focus which is a natural and necessary part of any attempt to study religions in the classroom provides the obvious context within which reference to, and exploration of the pupils' own beliefs and values should take place.

(iv) Spirituality within materialism?: a postscript

A careful study of the research reports cited earlier indicates the tension many young people experience between seeking personal meaning and personal identity through identification with the trends, fashions and goals of 'a consumer world', and dismissing this world as unable to meet these needs. This tension, I suggest, arises from the basic conflict which exists between 'material' and 'spiritual' values in a culture—a conflict which is replicated in the life-worlds and consciousnesses of its members. It is significant, however, that young people who are materially satisfied should dream of owning their own pet and rate social relationships more highly than any of their possessions. It is significant that, cut off from meaningful contact with adults and made to be onlookers rather than participants, they should look for personal and social worth in their relationships with each other. It is significant that interviewees who at school had never been asked to talk about themselves, should be appreciative of the opportunity that participating in a research project gave them to do so. Although many adolescents are prepared to accept the 'ready-made' answers provided by the 'consciousness-creating industries', their attachment to them is rarely through personal commitment to the values they represent but merely a consequence of social conditioning. Intuitively they recognise such values to be hollow; but, ironically, they live in a society which seems to make few efforts to place alternative ones before them which might enable them to choose for themselves.

Despite all the pressures against their becoming developed, young people do, then, have incipient moral and spiritual consciousnesses, and they do have beliefs and values to which they are attached with varying degrees of commitment. But what of their 'religious consciousness'? At one level, any child or young person living in a society in which there are many manifestations of religious beliefs and values cannot fail to have some embryonic religious consciousness. But most young people are woefully ignorant about religion, have many misconceptions about it and, according to Martin and Pluck, believe it to be both socially and personally irrelevant. While it may be possible, through religious education, to help young people clear up some of their misconceptions about it, salvaging its relevance is far more difficult. If, however, it can be shown that the study of religions is able to make a contribution to helping young people achieve critical consciousness and self-knowledge by providing the context within which they can examine and explore their *own* beliefs and values, then it is possible that in addition to clearing up some of their misconceptions about religion, it could contribute to the development of their 'religious consciousness'. For this to be achieved, however, we may have to accept that helping children and young people to learn *about* religion is insufficient. What we have to do is to help them to learn *from* religion about themselves.

But it may be objected that throughout this chapter I have assumed that all young people inhabit a plurality of life-worlds, and that all have pluralised *secularised* consciousnesses, even though there are many pupils in our schools who are practising members of faith communities. Consequently it might be thought that my attempts to locate the development of moral, religious and spiritual consciousness within a process which focuses on the development of self-awareness are largely irrelevant and even harmful to those pupils who may be said to have religious faith. While I do not share this view, the issue of the 'religious' child in state school religious education is an important one, and it is to a consideration of this that I now turn.

Chapter Five

Moral, religious and spiritual consciousness

Introduction

In the last chapter I suggested that in reflecting on questions which focus our attention on our own self-identity we are focusing on that dimension of human experience within which moral, religious and spiritual awareness develops and which, in turn, issues in the development of moral, religious and spiritual consciousness. I also suggested that our human development is contingent upon our becoming aware of our own consciousness—ie, aware of those frames of reference into which we have been socialised which provide our perspectives for viewing the world and giving it meaning—and also becoming self-conscious—ie, aware of our own self or selfhood as providing us with a unique and evolving identity indistinguishable from our 'person' or what we call 'me'. I further suggested that moral, religious and spiritual consciousness both arises from such awareness and contributes to it. I now want to explore further the nature and characteristics of moral, religious and spiritual consciousness.

From our earlier discussions we can recognise that moral, religious and spiritual consciousness is a component of human consciousness which has the capacity to become all-embracing in terms of human meaning-making. Hence I defined 'religious consciousness' as 'an internalised framework of religious meaning within which the individual *consistently* represents his or her *total* experience to him or herself'. We could say, therefore, that just as 'religion' is a 'synoptic realm of meaning' which includes all other realms of meaning, so 'religious consciousness' is a synoptic form of consciousness which includes all other forms of human consciousness. Because 'moral consciousness' and 'spiritual consciousness' also have the capacity to become all-embracing, we may take as a working definition of 'moral, religious and spiritual consciousness' (as represented by the central circle (6) of the diagram labelled Figure Two in Chapter Three) that component of our consciousness which alerts us to the value-imperatives implicit within human 'givens' (ie, core values), places before us the possibility of a self-transcendent reference point for the interpretation of our total experience, and discloses the necessity of our entering the arena of faith-responses as a condition of personal meaning-making.

I indicated towards the end of the last chapter what contribution I believe religious education is able to make towards helping young people—all young people—to develop their moral, religious and spiritual consciousness. In terms of the working definition of this given above, that contribution consists of (a) enhancing their awareness of, and sensitivity towards core human values and their interpretation within specific cultural traditions; (b) encouraging them to evaluate their own experiences by reference to interpretations which place the source of 'ultimate meaning' outside and beyond the self; (c) enabling them to recognise the necessity of holding beliefs and values by an act of faith; and (d), recognising the influence which holding these beliefs and values exerts upon who and what they become. While emphasising the importance of studying *Traditional Belief Systems* for the purpose of enabling pupils not only to evaluate their own responses to their experiences but also to discern important questions within them, I have stressed the centrality of critical self-awareness, especially of one's own beliefs and values, as the basis for the development of moral, religious and spiritual consciousness. While this may be an appropriate assumption with regard to young people who have little if any attachment to a religious faith, a question which follows from it is whether such an assumption is equally appropriate in the case of those pupils who have religious faith and are practising members of a community of faith. In other words, if the 'religious' child already possesses a developed religious consciousness, the emphasis I am proposing could be seen as being largely irrelevant to his or her needs; or, given that the 'religious' child already has an all-embracing meaning system within which issues of personal belief, value and identity have been resolved, causing him or her to evaluate this within the context of a plurality of beliefs, many of which will be in conflict with his or her own, could be seen as impairing the essentially unitive function of the child's own religious faith.

It is important, therefore, to give some attention to the possible implications that the presence of the 'religious' child in religious education lessons has for our understanding of the subject. In order to relate the issues which arise from this to those factors which I have identified as influential in determining a rationale for religious education within the context of our modern, plural, multi-faith society, I intend to take this opportunity of commenting at length on some recent suggestions made respectively by Daniel Hardy and David Hay which, if adopted, could each lead to a re-conceptualisation of religious education.

1. Moral, religious and spiritual consciousness derived from the child's religious faith

One may legitimately speak of the 'moral, religious and spiritual consciousness' of a child who has been nurtured within a particular religious faith and is a participating member of a community of faith as being derived from their personal religious faith. In other words, their religious faith provides the perspective from which they are alerted to the value-imperatives implicit within human 'givens', provides a self-transcendent reference point for the interpretation of their total experience, and prompts them to recognise the necessity of entering the arena of faith responses as a condition of personal meaning-making. At the same time their religious faith provides the means by which this consciousness is not only articulated and shaped (through religious categories of meaning) but actually made known to the child. Thus such a child's perception of 'ultimate' questions will be informed by that understanding of religious meaning which is integral to his or her consciousness.

When developing a curriculum for religious education we are, however, sometimes inclined to overlook the important fact that pupils may already have a religious faith which is meaningful to them and which provides them with a way of looking at the world and interpreting their experiences. Certainly in the case of many pupils attending schools in the inner-ring areas of our cities, to study religions is to study those living faiths which inform their daily lives and which are the source of their personal identities. For these pupils to explore their own faith is to explore their own life-world and religious consciousness and to reaffirm the meaning that their religious faith gives to their everyday acts and experiences. While it cannot be part of the intention of religious education to nurture pupils in a particular faith, the fact remains that many pupils find their understanding of their own faith is enriched and deepened by it. The *Birmingham Agreed Syllabus* of 1975,[1] for example, makes provision for pupils to choose to study their own faith in the secondary school by offering them a choice of religion for detailed study in addition to Christianity and a non-religious stance for living. Thus Muslim pupils can choose to study their own faith—as may Sikhs, Jews, Hindus and Christians. We may note, too, that *The Agreed Syllabus of the Inner London Education Authority* of 1984[2] states an aim for religious education which recognises that the knowledge and understanding of religious insights, beliefs and practices which pupils gain from their study may enable them 'to continue in' their own beliefs.

That there is value in providing pupils with such an opportunity for learning more about their own religion is not, however, the point I wish to emphasise. My interest is in considering what educational potential the religiously plural classroom has and whether the presence of religious pupils should influence the nature and purpose of religious education. In Chapter One we gave some thought to the thorny issue of the perspective from which the study of religions might proceed. There I expressed the view that 'it would seem perfectly logical that a study of ideologies and religions should proceed from a perspective which is consistent with the dominant ideological assumptions of the majority of the pupils'. I then identified this perspective as 'a secular point of view'. While not wishing to demur from this statement, I do, however, recognise that the presence of large numbers of practising members of different faiths in the classroom may enable the teacher to offer an experience of studying religions which is rather different from that which is likely to be the norm, for example, in the outer-ring classroom where religious pluralism may be very much less in evidence. Because of its relevance to curriculum decision-making and because it challenges some of the normally unexamined assumptions of recent agreed syllabuses, I would like to consider this point further.

(i) *The implications of religious pluralism for religious education: the views of Daniel Hardy*

In an important contribution to the debate about the implications of religious pluralism for religious education, Daniel Hardy raises a number of interesting questions. He comments:

> We have been trying to safeguard the truth and dissimilarity (or uniqueness) of the truth in religious traditions. There is then the question of the 'locality' of this truth. For example, when given a class whose members are drawn from various religious traditions, do we talk about the traditions as though they existed somewhere else than in the class—as true for 'them' ('those people over there') rather than true for some of 'us'? In other words, do we place the truth 'somewhere else' than where we are, at a distance from us?[3]

Hardy's main concern in this article is to challenge the suppositions of the phenomenological approach which he sees as forming 'a kind of critical orthodoxy which produces a certain view of the religions but also, in doing so, domesticates them.' He is interested in teaching religious traditions in such a way as to enable pupils to become 'open to' and able to 'share in' the 'truth' in each religious tradition without the method of study prejudging it for them. His view requires pupils to approach the religious traditions 'through reason and practice and personal contact'. He comments:

> The practice of religion in this case is the establishing of real communication between religious traditions as mediations of truth, as carried on by the shared activity of students and teachers—in all the dimensions in which the traditions do operate. . . . A great deal happens when such communication is begun. Far from threatening the individual freedom of the student, this real communication involves a careful and rational listening to his position and to him as a person; and his effort to communicate his position causes him reflectively to become critical about it, and about himself as a person. If the listening is as it should be—and the teacher particularly must ensure that it grows towards this—it will give new dignity and integrity to the particular student, while at the same time enhancing his life in and representation of the truth in which he participates. In other words, it aids him to participate in the truth so far as it (the truth) enables him to do so—and not simply to stay in a neutral position and imagine what the religious tradition does for 'those' people somewhere else. This is precisely to assist the student's quest for meaning.[4]

(ii) Religious education as participation in 'the giving of meaning' and in 'open communication'

It is important to recognise that Hardy is not merely suggesting the use of a device which may improve student participation or motivation. In a more recent paper he makes it clear that he is advocating a radical shift away from 'the supposition that education is centrally concerned with objective knowledge of the kind supposed to exist in the natural sciences'.[5] He expresses strong opposition to 'the use of descriptive techniques and language which cause the one approaching the religions, stories, behaviour and so on to adopt the position of a relatively passive observer who "receives" the meaning which has been declared in the religions, stories, behaviour'. His view is that if 'he or she has this meaning done *for* him or her, and the meaning comes to him or her as "given", and as a "claim" which he (or she) can simply assimilate as information of an objective sort', then 'the meaning remains "alien" in its objectivity even when he or she assimilates it'. What is crucial for Hardy is that students *'participate'* in this meaning, and he sees this happening 'primarily through the *giving* of meaning, not by *being given* meaning, and by giving meaning in a way appropriate to that to which meaning is given; and through that giving we appropriate ourselves'.[6]

Hardy gives considerable importance to the notion of what he calls 'self-extension and self-appropriation' as essential characteristics of 'meaning-finding'. I am not sure what connection he envisages between 'meaning-giving' and 'meaning-finding', but I hazard the guess that 'meaning-finding' relates to one's discernment of what he calls 'the presence of an all-embracing meaning' (ie, presumably, as disclosed by, in and through a religious tradition), and 'meaning-giving' relates to the impingement of this all-embracing meaning upon the process whereby the meaning of one's own experience and therefore of oneself is achieved. For this to take place 'acts of meaning which history has selected as anticipating the fullest truth' (such as those, presumably, which religions affirm and which are normally taught 'descriptively' in religious education) have to be assented to 'by being open to them in respect and trust, prepared to search them and understand them'. In assenting to these acts of meaning, *'we give them* meaning' by 'our expansion of them in our own individual and social experience. . . Furthermore, such assent in expansion actively makes the past *present*; and so there is no disjunction between past and present'.[7]

Hardy presupposes that 'meaning' which is found and self-appropriated is part of 'higher and wider notions of meaning'. While admitting it is possible to avoid the premise that there is 'an all embracing meaning' by 'declaring it sufficient to establish the meaning of something in itself—by reference only to the area of concern at the moment, and without wider considerations',[8] he argues that 'the very process of meaning-establishment will show what notion of an all-embracing meaning may be present in that process'. He sees the notion of there being 'an all embracing meaning' (which some will call the 'Divine Word') as 'the notion which is central' to religious education, and that it is this notion which religious educators must defend. He writes:

It seems to me that the defence for religious educators lies precisely in providing for the establishment of meaning which gives the possibility for self-appropriation which shows the presence of an all-embracing meaning. . . In other words, religious educators can work expansively with meaning and self-appropriation, lifting particular experiences into a more complex pattern of meaning or a wider horizon, and thereby find the presence of an all-embracing meaning which had been present in earlier religious meaning: they can recollect the earlier presence by finding it anew.[9]

In expressing this view, it would appear that Hardy is advocating that any rationale for religious education must derive from theological premises rather than from the premises of 'critical realism'. Indeed, he expresses his opposition to 'a self-generated "educational" rationale for the subject, developed in sharp contradistinction from church or theological rationales'.[10] This view places the study of religions on an entirely different footing from the study of any other 'subject' in the curriculum. In short, Hardy is challenging the rationale for a religious education curriculum which rests upon the 'beliefs' of critical realism with a rationale which rests upon theological 'beliefs'—although one suspects that just as he is opposed to the notion of religions making 'truth claims' he may also be opposed to 'religious truth' being called 'beliefs'. He does not appear to countenance the possibility of the view of 'truth' and 'meaning' that he presents being the object of study without it also providing the assumptions upon which the study is to proceed.

Hardy does not attempt to spell out the implications of his views in practical terms other than to alert us to the dangers of doing religious education in the 'critical realist' or objectifying modes. Without attempting to relate them closely to his work, some practical observations might, however, be made which have some relevance to the foregoing discussion.

(iii) The educational use of 'confessionalism'

Firstly, in a classroom situation in which the majority of pupils possess a consciousness which is predominantly 'religious', there are grounds for religious education seeking, in Hardy's words, 'to foster open communication between truth-tellers in an atmosphere of mutual respect and trust'. Certainly since 1971, when the Schools Council Working Paper Number 36, *Religious Education in Secondary Schools*, was published,[11] the term 'confessional' has been interpreted pejoratively when used in the context of teaching religion in school. While it was appropriate to signal the departure of religious education from its Christianising roots by this term, in the Seventies many teachers had become so wary of falling into its trap that the 'religious heart' of the subject was in danger of becoming atrophied or, at least, buried beneath a curriculum overweighted with the 'externals' of religion. Even now 'multi-faith' religious education can easily become 'multi-fact' religious education. Interestingly enough, pupils, unlike their teachers, are not required to avoid confessionalism; indeed they may not necessarily be conscious of their teachers being required to do so. Most teachers will attest that when children speak of religion (other than of its externals) they speak 'confessionally', that is, as if from within the belief system rather than from outside it. The device of 'bracketing' one's own personal beliefs and values when speaking of one's own religious tradition, so assiduously learned and practised by the teacher, is not practised by pupils. Even those pupils who have no links with organised religion may speak of 'God' in a way which is hardly distinguish-

173

able from those who have. Often it is through such talk, *confessional talk*, that some of the most personally illuminating (and, therefore, educationally beneficial) experiences occur. To be anecdotal, I recall the moment of mutuality which was experienced in a religious education lesson by several Muslim boys and a Christadelphian boy when, through conversation, they discovered that they shared common ground in belief in the Oneness of God. Before that moment it is likely that the Muslims had assumed that all Christians believed in the Trinity, and that the Christadelphian had, probably, seen no possible link between his faith and theirs. Would it be unreasonable to see this experience as an example of the 'giving of meaning' (to use Hardy's term) and of religious education as 'open communication'? Would it be unreasonable to believe that good religious education should actively seek to promote such a learning experience as this?

(iv) Personal faith as a resource for understanding other religious traditions

Secondly, we might consider that pupils who practise a religion and who, consequently, have a developed religious consciousness, possess a rich personal resource upon which they can draw in seeking to understand other religious faiths. A quotation from Simone Weil's book *Waiting on God* may help us to examine this possibility more carefully. She writes:

> *The comparison of religions is only possible, in some measure, through the miraculous virtue of sympathy. We can know men to a certain extent if at the same time as we observe them from outside we manage by sympathy to transport our soul into theirs for a time. In the same way the study of different religions does not lead to a real knowledge of them unless we transport ourselves for a time by faith to the very centre of whichever one we are studying. Here moreover this word 'faith' is used in its strongest sense.*
>
> *This scarcely ever happens, for some have no faith, and others have faith exclusively in one religion and only bestow upon the others the sort of attention we give to strangely shaped shells. There are others again who think they are capable of impartiality because they only have a vague religiosity which they can turn indifferently in any direction, whereas on the contrary, we must have given all our attention, all our faith, all our love to a particular religion in order to think of any other religion with the high degree of attention, faith and love which is proper to it.*[12]

The opening sentence of this quotation reflects the era from which it comes; Simone Weil died in 1943 and this work was published posthumously in 1951. Although 'comparative religion' still holds an important place in the study of religions, it is not a term that matches the concerns and intentions of contemporary religious education, and is best avoided. The basic principle, however, of seeking to ally observation and description with 'empathy' (a word which avoids the sentimental associations that have become attached to 'sympathy') remains the *sine qua non* for beginning to appreciate both the meaning that someone else's religion has in their lives and the 'all-embracing meaning' that flows from it. Certainly one can understand how one's appreciation of this must be, in some important respects, relative to one's appreciation of the meaning of one's own faith.

It would, however, be rather more accurate to say, as Simone Weil implies, that it is the *level of maturity* of one's own faith which determines the extent to which one can empathise with the someone else's faith. We cannot, therefore, ignore the thought that if it is through one's religious faith that order and coherence in one's life is found, and that this is consequent upon one's personal commitment to a 'way of knowing' which is grounded in powerful and, possibly, exclusive concepts of authority which prescribe one's expected conduct, including one's relationship to others who do not hold to the same faith, then there are considerable barriers to be overcome before one can be 'open to' and willing to 'share in' the 'truth' of other religious traditions. This is not the place to attempt a detailed examination of the implications of recent work into stages of faith development, but these studies give grounds for believing that the religious faith of children and early adolescents will reveal those characteristics which James Fowler,[13] for example, suggests are indicative of what he calls Stages 2 ('mythic-literal faith') and 3 ('synthetic-conventional faith')—an identity and outlook sustained through conformity. Even those who persist with religious faith through to late adolescence may successfully shield it from the maturing influence of criticism and so fail to develop to 'individuative-reflective faith' of Stage 4 in which the development of the capacity for recognising the relativity of experience may lead to a willingness to be 'open' to the 'truth' of other religious traditions. Indeed, we should note Fowler's observation that many adults never succeed in constructing their faith in such a way that it becomes 'individuative-reflective', and research undertaken by my students has indicated that, in some religious traditions, for one to move beyond the 'synthetic-conventional faith' of Stage 3 is to place oneself, from the point of view of the particular religious tradition, outside (religious) faith itself. We should also note, however, that Fowler's analysis is based on a sample of approximately 400 subjects confined to America which were 'overwhelmingly white, largely Christian, evenly divided by sex and distributed through the age categories'. Furthermore, his definition of 'faith' as 'a way of constructing or interpreting experience' is likely to lead to a rather different understanding of people's development in this area than if he had taken 'faith' to mean 'adherence to a religious belief system' or, more simply, 'religious belief'.

These reservations apart, Fowler's work, I believe, does raise a number of serious doubts about the applicability of Hardy's concept of 'religious education as open communication' to the school classroom. What might be desirable and theoretically possible with adult persons with mature religious faith may be neither desirable nor theoretically possible with young people with immature religious faith. As teachers who are experienced in teaching religious education in religiously plural classrooms know, young adolescents in particular are given to engaging not in an open sharing of 'truth' but in 'tribalistic' support for their own commitments. It is apparent that some religiously committed pupils are openly hostile to even being expected to study faiths other than their own. These pupils are 'ideologically enclosed'. Whereas we might accept that it is desirable for pupils to become 'open' to the 'truth' in other religious traditions, and that one of the goals of religious education is to bring this about, we clearly cannot expect it to happen in the way Hardy imagines. In short, his 'ends' are admirable but he offers us no 'means' of attaining them. Let me try to be more precise about some of the practical problems which arise from his suggestions.

(v) Some practical problems arising from Hardy's suggestions

Firstly, I have set this discussion in the context of religiously plural classrooms where we may assume that the majority of pupils are practising members of a religion. I have suggested that this is not an unrealistic expectation of classrooms in the inner-ring of our cities. Although the composition of these classrooms may vary from region to region, what we are likely to find is that the majority of pupils are Muslims and Sikhs and/or pupils of Afro-Caribbean origin who belong to traditions, usually gospel or pentecostal, within Christianity. In some cases pupils will come from homes where two different religions are practised, usually through inter-marriage (eg, Irish Catholic/Pakistani Muslim/Afro-Caribbean Rastafarian). At the simplest level, religious education can provide an opportunity for these pupils to 'share' in each other's religions and cultures, mainly through learning about each other's beliefs, practices and customs. But the extent to which pupils will feel able to 'identify' themselves publicly with their own religion as it is studied and offer personal expression of its meaning and value to them will depend on many different factors, eg, their own sense of self-esteem and personal worth, their informal standing or status within the group, the standing or status of their religion and culture in the community, the level of their religious understanding, whether or not their faith is 'exclusive', their ability to express themselves clearly in English, and so on. Very similar factors will also influence the extent to which other pupils will be prepared to listen to them and to appreciate their contribution. The overriding factor in moving the class towards this simple form of 'sharing truth' will be the attitude of the teacher towards the pupils and towards their religions and cultures. An empathetic teacher is essential to the development of empathetic pupils, but even so the process of sharing which is envisaged by Hardy has to grow from very simple beginnings and even by the end of the period of formal schooling is likely to fall considerably short of the model of 'inter-faith dialogue' which, I suspect, informs his suggestions.

Secondly, no legitimate educational process can depend for its efficacy upon the individual contributions of participants. As we have seen, Hardy is unhappy about the assumptions which underlie methods of study being used in contemporary religious education; he sees them as prejudging religions, setting them, for example, in a false relationship to each other. He comments:

> *In the course of this communication, it will become evident—especially as the participants develop in their understanding—that religious traditions manifest very different aspects of truth, and do so very differently. How then are they to be seen in relation to each other: what order emerges between them? The first answer is:* non in advance. *It cannot be said in advance whether all are different and equivalent, or if some are more developed, and if so in what respects, etc. Furthermore, such statements are prejudgments, and ought not to be employed. The spirit of tolerance (or of intolerance) in which they are spoken ought to be manifested (or corrected) in the willingness to hear the other religion in its truth-teller, rather than in a polemic directed toward oneself or toward the other. The right ordering of the religious traditions will emerge from the communication between them; it should not be imported into the communication to form it in advance.*[14]

A central task of the teacher is that of selecting content for study which is best able to bring about the educational intentions of religious education. Note that it is not just the content which brings about such intentions, it is the process of studying the content which does this. Religious educators are concerned to answer the question. What does the *study* of religion contribute to pupils' development?', *not* 'What does *religion* contribute to pupils' development?'. If their concern was with the second question they would be proposing a form of religious education whose efficacy was determined by its capacity to promote religious faith. There are, then, at least three vitally important judgments which the teacher cannot avoid making prior to seeking to engage pupils in the study of religion. These are: the choice of educational aims and objectives, the choice of methods of study, and the choice of content. All three choices will reflect a particular understanding of the nature of religious education and of the contribution to pupils' development that the subject makes.

The efficacy of the study, under these circumstances, is determined by appeal to particular principles and procedures which are deemed to be educational and which are to be applied irrespective of the personal religious commitments of either the teacher or the pupils. While the efficacy of the study is not dependent upon the latter, personal value and belief positions may, of course, be taken into account; not necessarily with the purpose of deepening or sustaining them, but rather with the intention of bringing them within the educational purpose of the study itself. For example, at one level it might be thought educationally desirable (perhaps in terms of increased motivatation and interest) that pupils who have first-hand experience of a religious tradition might 'share' their experience with other pupils in the class, but only, of course, if they are willing to do so. Such contributions would be essentially *illustrative* of the content being studied, not the content itself. At another level, because education involves the application of critical techniques to an area of study (eg, the use of techniques of scriptural criticism), it would be reasonable to assume that such techniques should be applied in a classroom even though individual pupils may find this contrary to their own way of approaching scripture. Whereas this is possible when the object of study is defined independently of the pupil's faith (even though, in practice, the pupil's faith impinges upon the study), this is no longer possible when content and personal faith are not differentiated. Although education is concerned with extending the repertoire of pupils' responses to life beyond those inculcated by their families and cultural and religious upbringing, it does this by indirect rather than direct confrontation and gradually over a period of time. For this to occur it is essential that the teacher provides carefully structured learning experiences which are decided upon *in advance* of lessons. Although these will allow for some interaction to occur of the 'sharing' type between what the child is studying and the child's own faith position, the child's contribution will still be 'illustrative' rather than 'foundational' and will contribute to the achievement of altogether different intentions from the ones Hardy identifies.

We may conclude that although there may be occasions when it is desirable for *educational* purposes to draw on the experiences of the religious child, using the child's religious faith as a personal resource for promoting understanding of other faiths or, as Hardy suggests, using pupils as 'truth-tellers', is not without its pitfalls. Certainly the child's faith provides an obvious perspective from which the world is viewed and meanings are given to self and others, but the educational enterprise cannot restrict itself to the exploration of the present understanding of pupils—that is but its starting point. In the religiously plural classroom it is essential that, for example, new understanding is developed of the secular, post-religious mentality which is as much a part of pluralism as the presence of many religions. For most pupils with an Asian background such a mentality is in conflict with a religious understanding of life and a denial of it, and the Muslim community in particular view it as a threat to their cultural and religious values. For them there can be no bridges built between the two, and as a consequence creative relationships between their own and other cultures are very difficult to achieve. And yet contributing to a process by which this may become less difficult must be one of the main objectives of religious education in particular and education in general. I think it is inevitable, therefore, that good religious education, while attributing worth to the pupils' own religious commitments, must encourage pupils to be critical of them by setting before them alternative perspectives, both religious and secular. What provides the common thread between such perspectives may be, as Hardy contends, that they 'manifest very different aspects of truth, and do so very differently'; but equally the common thread can more easily be identified as the 'ultimate questions' which are variously addressed from different religious and secular standpoints. Encouraging pupils to explore such questions first from their own religious standpoints and then from the standpoints of others seems to me to be not only a way of identifying distinctively 'religious questions' and exploring religious and naturalistic perspectives on meaning (so raising the issue of which is 'truth'?) but of also initiating pupils into the process of 'interfaith dialogue' through which their own religious commitments may become more mature and their own moral, religious and spiritual consciousness may be expanded and developed.

2. Moral, religious and spiritual consciousness derived from the child's religious experience

One may also speak of the 'moral, religious and spiritual consciousness' of a child who has had a 'religious' experience as being derived from that experience. For such children we may assume that this experience would provide the context within which they are alerted in some respect to the value-imperatives implicit within human 'givens', become aware of a self-transcendent reference point for the interpretation of their total experience, and recognise the necessity of entering the arena of faith responses as a condition of personal meaning-making. We may also assume that the experience would be 'self-disclosing' of their own moral, religious and spiritual consciousness and considerably influential in its development. Their perception of 'ultimate' questions from within this perspective would, therefore, be informed by their own personal religious experience.

(i) What is a 'religious' experience?

Here, however, we encounter a problem of language, because to speak of children having 'religious experiences' is still, perhaps, to conjure up a picture of children as young St Bernadettes having visions of the Blessed Virgin Mary in grottos. This is not the impression that those who have an interest in religious experience wish to convey. Perhaps 'an experience which results in a sense of spiritual awareness' comes nearer to what they have in mind; and others have spoken of 'transcendental experience', 'unitive experience' and 'moments of truth'. Those who are familiar with the work of Sir Alistair Hardy, Michael Paffard, Edward Robinson and David Hay will already know something of the difficulties of finding an appropriate term which encompasses the range of meanings which may be given to the phenomenon with which we are concerned. Though I cannot follow Robinson in believing such experiences are 'really something quite ordinary, commonplace if you like',[15] I do accept that they are sufficiently widespread as to be worthy of careful consideration.

Michael Paffard defines 'transcendental experience' as 'an experience which *must* by implication or description be felt by its recipient to transcend to a marked degree ordinary consciousness, thought, feeling or perception: to be experience 'in another dimension' or 'on another plane'. He describes the characteristics of such experience as: 1, ineffable; 2, transitory; 3, rare; 4, unitive or involving a desire for union or contact; 5, involving the loss of bodily sensation, of being outside the body; 6, being valuable or important (but not necessarily joyful); 7, giving knowledge and insight; 8, giving a sense of timelessness or placelessness; 9, having a divine or supernatural origin; 10, being an exceptionally intense form of aesthetic experience.[16] His research among 264 sixth-formers and university students claiming to have had such experiences led him to identify ten associated feelings: awe (112), joy (105), fear (83), enhancement of perception (47), calm (44), trance (43), pleasure (41), melancholy (28), longing (20), and pain (16). Paffard's writings are full of personal accounts of what the following quotation from Andre Malraux's *The Voices of Silence* points to:

> *Most men would have no idea about painting, sculpture and literature than they have about architecture—were it not that sometimes they have fleeting intimations of that 'something behind everything' on which all religions are founded: when gazing, for example, into the vastness of the*

night, or when they are confronted by a birth, a death, or even a certain face.[17]

A detailed account of both the phenomenon of religious experience and contemporary investigations of it is provided by David Hay in his book *Exploring Inner Space* (1982). Hay refers to the outcome of the National Opinion Poll 'omnibus survey' of approximately 2,000 British adults in 1978 which included the question: 'Have you ever felt as though you were very close to a powerful spiritual force that seemed to lift you out of yourself?'. Thirty-six per cent of the sample said they had at some time been aware of or influenced by such a presence or power. Hay followed up this survey by asking a random sample of 100 postgraduate students at Nottingham University the same question. He found that 65 per cent claimed to have had such an experience.[18] Using a twenty-seven-page questionnarie as the basis for the interview, he then visited a random sample of 172 adults living in Nottingham and collected 124 positive responses, or 72 per cent of the total.[19] Approximately two-thirds of both the Nottingham city adults and the postgraduate student group who claimed to have had such an experience interpreted it as being 'religious'; but as Hay points out, 'the label "religious" continues to be used by many whose interpretations would certainly not be considered as Christian orthodoxy. . .'.[20] Later, he adds: 'The range of experience presented is a good deal wider than that encompassed by a strict definition of "numinous" or "mystical".'[21] He concludes:

> *On the basis of what people have said to us, then, I feel that 'religious experience' is not quite the right term for what we have been describing. It would be more correct to say that it is a type of experience which is commonly given a religious interpretation. For reasons of shorthand I intend to continue to use the word 'religious' while recognising that this is only one way of looking at it.*[22]

But the most extraordinary feature of such experiences, as Edward Robinson's research has shown,[23] is the frequency with which they seem to occur during childhood. Fifteen per cent of the 4,000 adults who 'felt that their lives had in any way been affected by some power beyond themselves' started by going back to events and experiences in their earliest years. For example:

> *The most profound experience of my life came to me when I was very young, between four and five years old.*

> *I just know that the whole of my life has been built on the great truth that was revealed to me then (at the age of six).*

As far back as I can remember I have never had a sense of separation from the spiritual force I now choose to call God.

Such was the frequency of comments like these that Robinson was led to wonder 'if there was not in quite young children capacities for insight and understanding that had been underrated by the developmental psychologists.'[24]

(ii) The educational implications of children having 'religious' experiences

If it is true that some children have such experiences, what are the implications for religious education in schools? In Chapter Three I suggested that one of the core-values is the value of human spirituality and the desirability of spiritual development. Whatever difficulties the phenomenon of religious experience presents in terms of understanding, explaining or classifying it, I think there can be little doubt that for those who have such experiences they represent a heightened sense of 'the spiritual' in themselves and in the world. For some this experience is fleeting, for others it means that they and the world are significantly changed and can never be the same again. In this latter case the experience bears some relationship to the experience of 'religious conversion', but not necessarily conversion to religious faith. I would not, however, wish to suggest that 'spiritual awareness' is necessarily dependent upon 'religious experience' because that would not only restrict the meaning of 'spiritual' but imply that the number of human beings capable of attaining such awareness is limited. 'Spiritual awareness' may be taught, or at least it is susceptible to being developed through teaching. This is not so of religious experience. If in some senses the human capacity for spiritual awareness is seen as being foundational to being 'human'—the source of the human capacity 'to value'—any experience which discloses that capacity or makes it actual in human consciousness makes an important contribution to human development. In this sense, religious experience must be seen in positive terms and some account of it must be taken when considering the nature of an educational enterprise which purports to be concerned with human development. How to take account of it is not an easy question to answer. We can, however, distinguish between taking account of the possibility that some children in religious education classes may already have had 'religious experiences'—which then presents us with the issue of what, if anything, can be done 'with' such experiences in the religious education lesson—and taking account of the possibility that the concept of 'religious experience' has wider relevance to our deliberations about religious education generally and that research findings in this area provide new insights which are applicable to our work with *all* pupils. Taking the latter notion first, how might research findings in religious experience be brought to bear on our understanding of how pupils learn?

(iii) Keeping the spirit of childhood alive through the process of growing up

One approach, initially suggested by Robinson and now being developed by Hay, takes seriously the view that it is in 'childhood' that there exists a peculiar ability to see 'reality' in a way which is quite distinct from adult conceptions of 'reality'. It is appropriate that we should permit this view to be expressed in Robinson's own words:

> *I believe that what I have called 'the original vision' of childhood is no mere imaginative fantasy but a form of knowledge and one that is essential to the development of any mature understanding.*
>
> *I believe that this vision is related to what is often imprecisely described as mystical experience, though the latter phrase may include a great deal more than is commonly experienced in childhood and is anyway too vague and emotive to be useful in this context. I believe that this vision is one that can only properly be understood when studied over a period of time; that it is in fact to be included in the Aristotelian category of 'natural' things which 'move continuously by virtue of a principle inherent in themselves towards a determined goal'.*
>
> *I believe that many of these childhood experiences are self-authenticating: they have in themselves an absolute authority that needs no confirmation or sanction from any other source.*
>
> *I believe that they are also self-authenticating in another sense: they bring to the person who has them an awareness of his true self as an individual, with an identity, freedom and responsibilities of his or her own.*
>
> *I believe that this vision can only be understood, either by the person who has it or by the outside observer, in purposive terms: there seems here no substitute for the old-fashioned word 'destiny'—which however must be clearly distinguished from 'fate'.*
>
> *And I believe finally that this vision and the experiences which are associated with it are essentially religious, and that no understanding, let alone definition, of that word is possible without sympathetic insight into all that is here included in the concept of childhood.*[25]

On this view, 'childhood . . . is not just a chronological period . . . it is an element of the whole person'.[26] One of the tasks of education thus becomes that of 'helping children to keep the spirit of childhood alive through the process of growing up',[27] so keeping them in touch with that dimension of their own experience—variously called the 'spiritual' or 'religious'—which is so easily overlaid and even obliterated by their progressive initiation into more publicly acceptable forms of knowledge. One implication of this view is that education must guard against allowing purely cognitive learning to dominate the curriculum, but integrate this with an equal concern to encourage pupils to reflect upon their own experiences at depth and to become more aware of their feelings as reference-points in the process of finding meaning in their lives. Earlier I referred to this as the development of 'interiority' or 'subjectivity'. In terms of religious education this means that we must question the common assumption that assisting pupils towards an awareness of the religious dimension of life is synonymous with, or dependent upon, informing them of the traditional forms and language of institutional religion. Many of Robinson's and Hay's respondents would be able to identify with the following comments:

> *I feel that all my education was a block and barrier to real religious experience. It gave little help or guidance in 'living' and was always wary of delving into mystery and crossing thesholds. I felt, particularly in adolescence, that my real self was neglected by the educational system and teachers, and that they were ignorant of fundamental truths. An education lacking in wisdom. As a child I longed to break free from the rigid day to day round of lessons which I always felt stifling and often irrelevant.* [28]

> *I think it is true to say that I was, and am, essentially 'religious' in spite of church 'worship' or other forms of organised religion.* [29]

> *I've never been very interested in religion. I suppose religion implies belief, and this was pure experience.* [30]

(iv) Experiential education in religion

In recent years more careful thought has been given to the implications for religious education of these research findings through the work of the *Religious Experience and Education Project* in the School of Education at Nottingham University. Directed by David Hay, this project has evolved a number of exercises in 'experiential learning' which are designed on the one hand to focus on personal, inner experience and thus 'assist young people to explore silence, to centre themselves, to be aware of the here-and-now of their experience, to discover awe and wonder in themselves' and, on the other hand, 'to reflect on these realities in the light of the metaphors and expectations of the (religious) believer'.[31] The belief which underlies this approach is that 'that awareness out of which religion grows is a natural, but often (in our culture) neglected, part of being human'.[32] By using techniques developed within the fields of counselling and 'transpersonal' or 'humanistic' psychology, the project seeks to help pupils to increase awareness, creativity and emotional sensitivity, and so put them in touch with those 'corners of ordinary human experience which are often ignored in our culture, but are of interest and importance to religious people because they are the typical context for their religious experience'. It should be noted that it is emphatically not the intention to attempt to give pupils 'religious experience'; not only would this be unacceptable educationally but all the research evidence into religious experience points to the impossibility of this. Rather the intention is to 'help pupils, through a guided reflection on their personal experience, to gain some knowledge of what it might be (like) to see the world through the eyes of a religious believer'. For example, Hay stresses the importance of helping pupils to appreciate what he calls the day-to-day 'praxis' of the religious person. He explains this as follows:

> By 'praxis' I intend to refer to the ordinary meaning-filled activities that emerge in people's lives as a result of the practical interchanges they have with the environment in which they live. It is, if you like, the commonsense which emerges from grappling with the realities of life as they present themselves in a given culture.
>
> In a highly secular culture such as ours, the relatively unreflective praxis of most people is quite likely to be insensitive or even blind to the religious dimension. As I see it, the task of the R E teacher in this circumstance is both critical and emancipatory. It is to help students to be more profoundly reflective in their praxis, in the light of the alternative set of metaphors, rituals, symbolic acts and the like, which are part and parcel of the praxis of religious people.[33]

(v) Challenging the 'hermeneutics of suspicion' with the 'hermeneutics of faith': the views of David Hay

It would be inappropriate at this time to comment on the present work of the Religious Experience and Education Project, as publication of its report and curricular materials lies in the future. In 1985, however, David Hay contributed an important article to the Special Issue of the British Journal of Religious Education devoted to exploring 'Spirituality across the Curriculum'.[34] In this article, entitled 'Suspicion of the Spiritual: Teaching Religion in a World of Secular Experience', Hay presents a powerful argument for religious education paying attention to the 'hermeneutics of faith'—a term by which Paul Ricoeur refers to the believer's attempt to probe the meaning of an experience of the sacred. He contrasts this with the apparent willingness of modern religious education to pay attention to the 'hermeneutics of suspicion', the legacy of scientific scepticism which causes people to conceive of their experience of the sacred as illusion or the lies of consciousness. Hay's point, which is reminiscent of Newbigin's, which we examined in Chapter One, is that the metaphors used by the European scientific and intellectual community to speak of the world 'act as unintentional indoctrination' and that 'these pictures of reality are often taken by ordinary people to be absolute statements, indeed, true doctrine'. Consequently, '. . . when someone's experience appears to contradict official reality, a kind of cultural brainwashing tends to make them suppress and keep secret that experience, for fear they will be thought stupid or even mad'. Thus Hay accounts for the 'secrecy amounting to a taboo' which characterises the behaviour of those admitting to religious experiences as 'a natural consequence of powerful cultural interpretations which distort or deny what people find to be a genuine and important dimension of their experience'. He concludes:

> If my consciously available experience of reality is mediated via secular metaphors, it is very difficult for me to enter into religion apart from an imperialistic foray to see how the natives live. I may be humane, sympathetic, even concerned that such cultures should survive, but within me is an experiential apartheid which detaches me from the possibility of genuine understanding.[35]

Hay suggests that religious education teachers should respond to this situation in two ways: they should 'honestly present religion for what it claims to be—the response of human beings to what they experience as the sacred'—and 'help pupils to open their personal awareness to those aspects of their experience which are recognised by religious people as the root of religion'.[36] He gives an indication of the nature of the 'exercises' which the project is developing to assist teachers in these two concerns:

> The religious education teacher can respond to this cultural mechanism for stifling awareness by using exercises which invite pupils to examine what happens to their experience when they intentionally vary descriptive metaphors. Such exercises are derived from phenomenological investigation. What happens, for example, if we invite someone to look at a person 'as if' she were a machine? How does that person's experience change when they look at her 'as if' she were a child of God? What is the pupil's experience of looking at the world 'as if' it was purely matter? How does the experience change if it is looked at 'as if' it were pervaded by a spiritual presence? In none of these cases is any absolute statement being made about the truth of the metaphors; the exercise is neither religious nor irreligious. What they are designed to do is assist the pupil to empathise with the believer's way of experiencing reality.[37]

Turning now to the question of our response to the presence of pupils in the class who may already have had 'religious experiences', Hay contends that it is 'well nigh a certainty that in every class above the third form (and in some cases at a much younger age) there will be some pupils who know from their own experience what the religious education teacher is talking about'.[38] He suggests that the role of the religious education teacher is 'to liberate them from the taboos which inhibit them from exploring freely the experiential and cognitive options available. . . The objective is to give permission for, rather than to disclose, personal experience'.[39] Certainly if the fact that these children have had 'religious experiences' means that they are more 'spiritually aware', this is an unexpected bonus for the religious education teacher; but we should note that it does not necessarily follow that such experiences will automatically predispose them to view the study of religion in positive terms. If there are benefits to accrue to the class as a whole from the presence of such children it will probably be through their contribution of an informed critical perspective on religion which is impatient of preoccupation with its 'externals' and dismissive of attempts to equate belief systems with repositories of truth. If there are benefits to accrue to these individual pupils from religious education itself, it will probably be through the opportunity that the study of religions provides for them to seek to integrate these very personal experiences within the wider framework of humanity's experience of the religious and the spiritual. It is important that individuals who may be unsettled and anxious about an experience which seems to mark them out as different or peculiar recognise, through the study of the rich heritage of religious experience and human spirituality, that this is an unnecessary anxiety. The need to be reassured through becoming aware of the similar experiences of others is well illustrated by the following comment from one of Robinson's respondents:

I turned to books increasingly for companionship, searching for expressions of experience similar to my own, both as to the beauty of the natural world, and my own sense of something beyond it, a timeless eternal 'something' behind natural phenomena. . . Early in my teens I discovered Richard Jefferies, Henry Williamson and Traherne, and felt strong comfort from knowing that others—and adults—experienced these strange feelings, which I never mentioned to any person, though I have no idea why not. They seemed too precious and personal—a sort of talisman to be treasured in private.[40]

(vi) Religious education and 'religious' experience: the need for caution

I believe that the work we have been considering indicates how easily academic and professional concerns to establish religious education on a sound educational footing can cause us to lose sight of the need to involve pupils in very much more 'personalised' activities than those which, for example, are commonly associated with a descriptive and critical approach to religious study. While we may honestly believe there is considerable educational benefit to be obtained from involving pupils of all ages in 'expressive' activities such as story and poetry writing, drama, dance and movement, painting and sculpture, and so on, we have considerable difficulty in incorporating such activities within the more formal learning situations which we normally impose when, for example, we expect them to learn about sacred texts, holy books, places of pilgrimage, initiation rites, prayer and worship. At best we achieve a balance between separate 'existential' activities and 'phenomenological' activities and more or less trust that pupils will be able to link insights gained from one to insights gained from the other. What we do not help pupils to achieve is the *integration* of these insights within a single, coherent activity which is mutually illuminating of self and religion. Seeing a correspondence between the 'heartland' of the 'self' and the 'heartland' of religion in experience appears to offer an attractive way of providing for the confluence of existential and phenomenological concerns. There are, however, still issues which remain unresolved within this view, and it is to these which we finally turn.

We have already noted the difficulties presented by the term 'religious experience' and here we can add the further observation that its inherent ambiguity means that any use which is made of it within proposals which lead to the 'reconceptualisation' of religious education can create both confusion among teachers and opposition to the subject. It is essential, therefore, that we are clear about what it is that Hay and others working in this field are proposing. The fundamental issue, it seems to me, is whether or not their proposals derive from certain assumptions about the relationship of 'religious experience' to 'human experience'. For example: whether they see 'human experience' and 'religious experience' as points on a single continuum of experience, or 'religious experience' as a 'dimension' of all human experience, or 'human experience' as a dimension of 'religious experience'. They certainly appear to assume that 'religious experience' is not a *sui-generis* experience which is autonomous of 'human experience'. Each of these assumptions implies a position which, if adopted as the basis for studying religion in the classroom, is open to objections. For example, supporters of a phenomenological approach argue that there is a dichotomy between the sacred and the profane which cannot be bridged by some hermeneutical device, a 'conceptual bridge' or a 'common experience' because if 'religious experience' is a *sui-generis* experience having its own essence and structure, trying to use pupils' own experience as a basis for understanding 'religious experience' is to distort and misrepresent that experience. Alternatively, those who support 'existential' and 'experiential' approaches, in arguing that there is no dichotomy between the sacred and profane and that 'ordinary experience' can be the starting-point of 'religious experience', find themselves giving tacit support to the view that all human experience is essentially religious. This, of course, revives a fierce debate between religious educators which took place in the late Seventies; and it is interesting to note that Surin's attempt to reconcile the experiential and phenomenological approaches led him to conclude that:

> . . . (if) we can place a wider, less religiously chauvinistic, construction on 'experience' (ie, than equating 'experience' with 'Christian experience') and take it to include any form of experience that constitutes a revelation of the numinous . . . then (there) is no reason for rejecting the experiential approach to RE. No good phenomenologist can quibble with this construction, especially since it eschews altogether the idea of conceiving the child's experience in biblical hermeneutical terms. All the child need have is some awareness of the numinous, and surely to be aware of the numinous is to have some experience of it?[41]

The problem of allowing the concept of 'religious experience' to influence one's understanding of the nature, aims and approach of religious education lies in the ambiguity of the term itself which, of course, reflects the ambiguity of the experience to which it points. It would appear from research findings in 'religious experience' that *any* human experience has the potential to be the *locus* for a 'religious' experience and equally for an experience which, though manifesting the characteristics listed by Paffard, may not be termed 'religious'. Similarly, research findings indicate that *anyone* is potentially capable of having a 'religious' experience; they do not, for example, have to be trained in the special arts or techniques of this form of awareness, although, as Hay indicates, certain 'exercises' or methods are available which help 'individuals to focus carefully on personal, inner experience as a means to prepare themselves for deeper religious understanding'.[42] To bring these facts to the attention of pupils—ie, to inform them about the phenomenon as I have described it—is, of course an entirely legitimate educational activity and I would expect it to be a feature of the work of all religious education teachers. Part of the process of informing pupils will, of course, include helping them to *understand* the phenomenon, and an acceptable way of doing this may be to encourage them to relate their own experiences to what they are studying. This might even include giving them exercises to try out to increase their empathy with those who claim to have had such experiences. In similar fashion, turning to the phenomenon of 'religious experience' as it is understood within traditional belief systems, once again it is a legitimate educational activity to inform pupils about such experiences and, in order to increase their *understanding* of what these experiences mean for the religious person, encourage, them, as far as it is possible to do so, to relate these to their own experiences. None of this is new to religious education and it can all be accomplished within the sort of conceptual framework which I proposed in 1973 without changing its educational rationale.[43]

What I have described above is a 'phenomenological approach' to religious experience. We should note that the approach applies equally to *understanding* the phenomenon of 'religious' experience which individual, 'non-religious' people have as well as to *understanding* the phenomenon of 'religious experience' as it occurs within traditional belief systems. In no way is this approach based on certain assumptions which are derived from religious experience itself. For example, while the approach allows pupils to understand that some people believe that 'all human experience is religious' or, conversely, that 'religion is a dimension of all human experience', neither of these assumptions provides the unexamined perspective from which the phenomenon is to be explored: indeed, such beliefs are the object of study. Similarly, we are not seeking to place pupils in a situation or creating in them a state of mind which may be conducive to the occurrence of 'religious experiences', nor are we assuming that the sensitivities of pupils who have not had such experiences are, in some sense, impoverished or undeveloped in comparison with those who have. While we may recognise that there is a need for 'the hermeneutics of suspicion' to be augmented in such a way as to enable pupils to appreciate and understand that there are also 'hermeneutics of faith', this does not mean that 'the hermeneutics of suspicion' are *replaced* in religious education by 'the hermeneutics of faith'. On the contrary, 'the hermeneutics of faith' are examined within the context of 'the hermeneutics of suspicion', for it is only by so doing that we are able to preserve the necessary distinction between educating pupils in an understanding of religion and nurturing them in religious faith.

From these comments it should be apparent that I am unhappy about the direction in which religious education could move, or, more importantly, be thought to be moving, if the notion of 'religious experience' is allowed to occupy a central place in the conceptualisation of the subject itself. As 'developments' which took place in the late Sixties testify, without the restraining influence of a phenomenological focus in religious education it is very easy for 'everything' and 'everyone' to become 'religious'. While it may be possible for Hay to argue that in using 'experiential' exercises he is not seeking to 'catechise' pupils in religious faith but enhance their capacity to understand religion, the fact remains that, except in terms of intention, there is not much difference between what he proposes to do with pupils and what religious adherents may be encouraged to do in order 'to prepare themselves for deeper religious understanding'. Admittedly the nurture of faith has to be specific to a particular faith—it is *Christian* nurture or *Jewish* nurture, or *Sikh* nurture, and so on—but contemporary religious education must take cognisance of the strong objections which non-religious believers, such as Humanists, have to any process which can be seen to 'bias' pupils in favour of religion. While some may find this view difficult to accept when the subject is entitled 'religious education', it does not necessarily follow that the study of religions should proceed on the basis that 'religious' faith is the 'norm' of either faith or belief.[44]

Some observations made recently by Dennis Starkings on the view that 'so-called "religious experience" ought to be regarded as the heart and soul of religion and of religious education' are worthy of reproduction as a conclusion to this section. Starkings writes:

The crux of the problem is that the sensitivities clustering around the idea of the holy—such as the awareness of awe and wonder—not only characterise the distinctively religious experience but (for the believer) go far to authenticate it. If we look further still into religious experiences (into the ecstatic and visionary states, into mystical experience) their power to authenticate the believer's faith is enormous. But authentication, validity, justification are precisely the matters at issue between the religious and the secular frames of mind; and it must be surely admitted that the insights of intense subjectivity are acceptable currency only within the framework of belief. It is entirely appropriate to take note of, to study, the states of mind which go to establish the believer's particular conviction—bearing in mind also that many believers know little or nothing of such states. It is also appropriate to devise classroom activities which might help with the appreciation of such states of mind. What is not appropriate—and there has been some incautious advocacy in this direction—is to regard those states as commendable in themselves. Exercises directly designed to inculcate the senses of love, joy, awe and wonder are valid to the extent that they apply to objects that are lovable, delightful, awesome or wonderful. But precisely because they (in a religious context) authenticate beliefs which are in dispute, we must treat such exercises with great care. We must be careful not to suggest to pupils (or allow them to think) that such experiential adventures into the states which confirm the believer's convictions automatically confirm those convictions for pupils themselves. Whether or not confirmation is appropriate for any individual pupil would have to be judged by the pupil in terms of wider criteria, and to the extent that this occurs we shall be able to stay within the proper orbit of religious education. On any other terms there will be indoctrination.[45]

3. Some concluding observations

In speaking of the moral, religious and spiritual consciousness of the 'religious' child being derived from the child's personal religious faith or personal religious experience, we are speaking of that perspective of meaning from which the child reflects upon his or her experiences of self, others and the world and evaluates alternative perspectives of meaning. In the case of children who hold to a religious faith we may reasonably assume that this perspective of meaning is informed by the beliefs and values mediated through a traditional belief system. In the case of children who have had 'religious' experiences we may reasonably assume that this pespective is informed by their transcendental experiences. In both these cases we may reasonably assume that these respective perspectives of meaning contribute to the child's self-awareness; that the child holds to certain beliefs and values in a *self-conscious* manner. If this were not so, then we could justifiably assume that their attachment to certain beliefs and values was nominal and of little personal significance, or that it was the result of a process of social conditioning operating only at the unconscious level.

But there are certainly grounds for believing that many who profess religious belief *are* only loosely attached to their beliefs; that they do *not* hold to their beliefs in a *self-conscious* manner. What is influential in their lives is not their commitment to particular beliefs and values but the sense of belonging which accrues from being a member of a faith community. Such children and young people could *not* be said to have a critical awareness of self or of their beliefs and values *through their religious faith*, even though they may profess religious faith. Neither could it be said that their religious faith serves to promote critical self-consciousness and so furthers their moral, religious and spiritual consciousness. I make this point not in order to be critical of such children and young people (for, indeed, this may be the norm of childhood and adolescence) but in order to demonstrate why we should not necessarily assume that the 'religious' child is not in need of a religious education which produces critical self-consciousness or that my earlier observations on the importance of assisting young people with *secularised* consciousnesses to develop this do not apply equally to the 'religious' child. For religious faith to perform a unitive function within the life of any human being, it cannot be an enclave of meaning which is only drawn upon within the sheltered confines of a faith community. Such 'religious consciousness' is sorely in need of development through the stimulus provided by the opportunity to evaluate professed beliefs critically in the light of alternative beliefs and values.

Turning finally to the case of the child whose moral, religious and spiritual consciousness may have been shaped by 'religious' experience; although it is very likely that such a child may be exceedingly *self-conscious* about this experience (to the point of telling no-one about it), the task of drawing meaning from it sufficient to inform and sustain his or her daily life so that it becomes a vehicle for the development of self-identity remains after the experience. Thus a 'religious' experience is as much the beginning of the search for meaning as it is the end of it. While the experience may be cherished and reflected upon as some precious and privileged moment, the need remains for its meaning to be unpacked, explored, scrutinised and verified. Far from seeing the critical study of such phenomena as harmful to 'religious' experience, I believe it to be a necessary requisite for its positive evaluation. In other words, if moral, religious and spiritual consciousness shaped by 'religious' experience is to develop so that it, like the experience, is unitive for the individual, it needs to be continually enriched and tempered by a disciplined study of the religious and spiritual experience of humankind. I suggest that the outcome of such study for the individual will be a critical awareness of self and of his or her beliefs, and that this will contribute significantly to the further development of his or her moral, religious and spiritual consciousness. On this basis the study of religions makes a significant contribution to the personal development of both the child who is 'religious' and the child who is not. The presence of 'religious' children in religious education should not, therefore, significantly influence the rationale upon which that study rests. It is to a consideration of such a rationale for religious education that we now, finally, turn.

Chapter Six

The concerns of religious education

Introduction

In this chapter I would like to propose a rationale for religious education which takes into account the many different issues which I have
identified in the previous five chapters as being pertinent to such an
undertaking, namely: the problematical nature of knowledge and of
values; the necessity of human beings holding beliefs by an act of faith
and the shaping influence of beliefs in the formation of human beings
and of individual identities; the effects upon human consciousness of
cultural, ideological and religious pluralism and of secularisation and
modernity; the symbiotic relationship between self-awareness and moral, religious and spiritual awareness and between critical consciousness
and moral, religious and spiritual consciousness; the value-laden nature
of any educational enterprise, including religious education, and so on.
In view of the prominence I have given to the concept of 'humanisation'
in this book, it will come as no surprise that I now wish to suggest that
this concept provides us with the common basis for establishing a relationship between personal development, education and religion.

1. Formulating educational concerns: the relationship between education and religion

(i) The interpretative and humanising concerns of religion and education

In Chapter One, following the discussion of two different conceptions
of religious education, I suggested that what constitutes the problem
in seeking to establish a relationship between religion and education
is that neither can tolerate the conception of a value-free method of
study. Consequently each seeks to impose its values upon the other. It
might be asked, therefore, if this is the case, what is the importance of
attempting to provide a value-free description of humanisation? Is it not

inevitable that both religion and education will be hostile to such a conception; and if so what possible relevance does it have to solving the problem of religion's relationship to education?

What emerges from my analysis of humanisation is that it is a human 'given' that human beings cannot be value-free in their thinking. Thus human beings have no alternative but to formulate beliefs about their nature and the nature of their human experience and to commit themselves to particular beliefs about themselves and their world by an act of faith. Holding beliefs or believing is therefore an essential constituent not only of meaning-making but of humanisation itself. Put another way, the only alternative to belief for the human being is not unbelief but another belief. (Charles Hartshorne expresses a similar view when he says: 'There can be no alternative to alternativeness itself.'[1]) This is why human beings cannot be value-free in their thinking. As we have seen, this fact is recognised by both religion and education, for both contribute to its interpretation. Consequently both contribute to the process of humanisation. It is, I suggest, because religion and education are both *interpretative and humanising* that it is possible to bring them into a relationship with each other. In order to do so, however, it is necessary to identify what it is they interpret—ie, human 'givens' and 'core values'—and describe the process of humanisation to which they contribute.

(ii) The 'functional' concerns of religious education

In my description of humanisation I have stressed the importance of the *function* of beliefs and believing in human development. While it is obvious that the *particular* beliefs human beings hold will be at variance with each other and promote different degrees and directions of 'human development', it is also obvious that these beliefs cannot be at variance in functional terms, ie, they all exert some significant influence on human shaping. They cannot be at variance in another respect, too; they all have functional value in the process by which human beings engage in meaning-making and truth-questing. If this *functional* analysis of beliefs and believing is then related to education, it follows that education is concerned with promoting understanding of the different ways in which human beings engage in meaning-making, and religious education is especially concerned with promoting understanding of the contribution that holding *religious beliefs* makes to this process and recognising the effects that holding particular religious beliefs have upon human development.

An advantage this conception of religious education has over the other two conceptions of religious education which we examined in Chapter One is that in seeking to concentrate upon the interpretative and humanising concerns of religions through focusing upon the function of beliefs and believing within meaning-making, it enables aims to be formulated for religious education which are compatible with the self-understanding of religions but which also contribute to the interpretative and humanising concerns of education. The perspective from which the function of belief and believing may be examined may, of course, be essentially sociological and anthropological, but in so far as the intention is to become more aware of the interior experience or 'life-world' of individuals, especially how individuals (both religious adherents and the pupils themselves) order their interior experience and create personal meanings, the perspective will also be phenomenological.[2]

At one level, therefore, the 'functional' concerns of religious education will be characterised by exploring such questions as: In what manner does this religion (or religious tradition) interpret the core-value that human beings have value? What effect does holding these beliefs have on the way in which its adherents understand themselves and others, order their life-styles, bring up their children, respond to moral issues, and so on? What beliefs does this religion advocate as a basis for interpreting the value human beings attach to order, meaning and purpose?; to justice?; to self-fulfilment?; to ethical endeavour?; to interpersonal relationships?; to human spirituality? What are/have been the effects of such beliefs upon the way of life or culture of a society in which they are regarded as normative? Placed within the context of a plural, multi-faith society, how do the beliefs of this religion differ from those of another religion?

(iii) The 'personal' concerns of religious education

While my analysis of humanisation has given due regard to the influence upon human shaping of those 'normative' beliefs and values which are enshrined within a culture—ie, the human being's *cultural history*—it has also indicated the shaping influence upon each individual of his or her own *personal* history—ie, that which makes each individual different and unique. A consideration of psychological literature has lent support to the view that individual human beings possess a capacity for choosing between beliefs and values and, consequently, for becoming involved in their own shaping. Similarly a consideration of sociological research has indicated that human beings, while subject to the influence of adopting 'values-in-role', also have a capacity to formulate 'self-values' and do so when confronted by situations in which 'it is necessary to choose to be one kind of person rather than another'.[3] Integral to the exercising of this capacity is the attainment of two related types of awareness: awareness of one's own *consciousness* (ie, awareness of those frames of reference into which one has been socialised and which provide multiple perspectives on meaning); and *awareness of self* (ie, awareness of that personal identity which has emerged, and continues to emerge, as a consequence of one's interactions with others, conditioned by whatever beliefs one holds about oneself and others).[4] I have suggested that it is in becoming *self-aware* in this manner that human beings find themselves involved in a reflective and evaluative process which focuses upon their subjectivity, interiority or spirituality and which contributes to their *self-knowledge* and, consequently, to the development of their moral, religious and spiritual consciousness.

This analysis of the internal dynamics of humanisation is, I suggest, not only informative of personal development, it is also informative of both education and religion. Religion, as we have seen, links spiritual awareness with the growth of self-awareness; the deepening of personal faith, through which religious adherents seek to fulfil the spiritual quest, is accompanied by the deepening of awareness of self. As one grows in faith one grows in knowledge of who one is. Education links the attainment of knowledge with the development of the human being; for example, in being initiated into the language of one's culture and into those forms of knowledge or modes of awareness through which a society has interpreted human experience one is enabled to participate in shared meanings and in so doing is humanised (or civilised). But participating in shared meanings does not mean being only a passive recipient of other people's understandings. While it may be possible to conceive of human beings holding knowledge in common and of having experiences in common, what distinguishes one human being from another is the way in which they choose to integrate such knowledge and experience within the fundamentally personal and unique experience of self, and in so doing discover personal meaning. For example, one does not experience others, one experiences self in relation to others. In so far as education and religion seek to assist the individual in the pursuit and discovery of self-knowledge and personal meaning, they fulfil their interpretative functions. For education to proceed upon the narrow basis that 'knowing about' contributes to personal meaning-making and thus to personal development is either to underestimate the complexity of the transactions which take place between 'knowledge' and 'self' in the processes of interaction and integration or to recognise that these are so complex that they lie beyond its scope. Whichever is the case, the result is the provision of no more than what might be called 'the curriculum of hope'—ie, courses of study which it is hoped will contribute to personal and social development. In using the concept of 'humanisation' as a basis for establishing a relationship between education and personal development, the inadequacies of our current conceptions of what sort of learning contributes to personal and social development are quickly exposed. What follows, therefore, represents an attempt to address this problem.

(iv) The 'humanising' concerns of education

A conception of education which can be derived from the analysis of humanisation which I have offered in this book is as follows:

> *Education is a process by, in and through which pupils may begin to explore what it is, and what it means, to be human.*[5]

To describe 'education' as a 'process' is to stress the on-going nature of the enterprise; it is to recognise that it starts at birth and continues until death and takes place within a number of different contexts—the home, the peer-group, the local community, the groups to which we belong, the school, the work place, etc—and operates through a number of different experiences—the childhood experience, the adolescent experience, the work experience, the marriage experience, the parenting experience, the ageing experience, etc. We, however, are primarily concerned with the contribution of 'formal' education in schools to that on-going process. We should note, though, that 'formal' learning in schools—or, as some prefer, 'schooling'—occupies a relatively short period of time within the wider context of 'informal' learning, and that it may well be the case that the school's contribution to an individual's personal development will inevitably be less than the total effect of all these other contexts. In focusing our attention on the contribution that the formal curriculum can make to pupils' personal development, it is essential that we do not lose sight of this continuous process of education within which the school participates and which it serves. There is a necessary relationship between what is provided by the school and what is needed by a young person during formal schooling, immediately afterwards and in the future. What learning is given to pupils during formal schooling must be readily transferred and effectively applied. Injecting theoretical knowledge into pupils without helping them to see how to apply it is a formula for such knowledge to become inert or forgotten, or just carried about like so much verbal lumber.[6]

The notion of education as a lifelong process, and of school assisting pupils to acquire transferable knowledge, skills and attitudes, is also reflected in the use of the words 'begin to explore'. To press pupils to commit themselves to final answers during their period of formal schooling, especially in the moral and religious spheres, is unacceptable educationally. It is also—as we saw in Chapter Two—to deny that human beings have an 'open' future and are in a state of becoming. Two possible criteria for assessing the value of the period of formal schooling, including the value of the formal curriculum, are, therefore, whether it succeeds in setting young people on the way to being receptive to the present and future lessons to be learned from life, and whether it encourages them to be imaginative and creative in their responses to new personal circumstances and experiences in a rapidly changing world. It is salutary to note that both good and bad schools are equally effective in creating a 'curriculum for life' but with very different results.[7] It is also salutary to note that it is really only the recipient who can evaluate, eventually, the worth of the schooling he or she has received.

While our attention in what follows will be given mainly to the formal curriculum, we should keep in mind the considerable influence the 'hidden curriculum' exerts on pupils' learning, especially of attitudes and values. The hidden curriculum consists of all those attitudes and values the school regards as normative and which are tacitly or indirectly taught to pupils because of the way in which the work and life of the school is planned, organised and experienced, not least through the interpersonal relationships between members of staff and between staff and pupils. Social roles, for example, are learnt mainly through the hidden curriculum, as are sex roles, attitudes to class and race and to many other aspects of living. In some schools it is likely that the attitudes and values pupils encounter through the hidden curriculum are in conflict with the professed commitment of the school to an open exploration of civilising values through the formal curriculum. It is not uncommon for religious education teachers, for example, to complain that they are unable to teach effectively in a particular school because the religious and spiritual values they wish to explore sympathetically in their lessons are refuted by the values communicated by the ethos of the school. This may occur when the ethos promotes competitive attitudes rather than co-operative ones; when all pupils are not treated with equal sensitivity, as may be the case when the hidden curriculum supports racist and sexist attitudes; when a rigid system of streaming by academic ability appears to impugn the moral worth of less academic pupils; when there is a ritual of punishment but no ritual of forgiveness or reconciliation, and so on. There is, then, little point in teachers devoting careful thought to devising a formal curriculum intended to further the pupils' personal and social development if equal thought is not given to planning and consciously implementing an ethos in the school which supports and sustains the values encountered through such a curriculum.

We might usefully note at this point that a lack of awareness of the effects of other influences and constraints in schools can also make nonsense of grand curricular designs immaculately conceived in the blinding light of reason. Among these will be the effects of inadequate teaching resources, classroom space and timetable time; interdepartmental territorial disputes, parental and pupil expectations, option choices, external examination syllabuses and, unfortunately, incompetent teachers with a lack of vision and little sense of vocation. Whereas the shape of the formal curriculum may emerge from philosophical debates about the logic and structure of subjects, its effectiveness as the school's most potent means of translating its educational aims into actual achievements will depend on factors altogether more human and mundane. This may be particularly true of a subject like religious education, which still lacks parity of status and esteem in the eyes of teachers and pupils despite the introduction of a considerable number of changes in its formal curriculum over the last decade or so. The importance of gaining entry to the decision-making structures of the school is still greatly underestimated by many religious education teachers. In reality it is often through securing membership of planning committees and working parties (appearing, at first glance, to have very little to do with religious education) rather than through far-reaching revisions of its syllabus, that the educational potential of a subject like religious education can be realised.

(v) The curriculum's common 'humanising' educational concerns

But to return to the conception of education I introduced earlier, as we would expect it is a conception which has implications for the *whole* curriculum. To accept that education is *'a process by, in and through which pupils may begin to explore what it is, and what it means to be human'* is to accept that *all* subjects in the curriculum (maths, science, history, geography, literature and the creative arts as well as religious education) need to be taught in such ways as to further this process and contribute to its concerns. Naturally each subject will have its own concerns appropriate to its own subject matter and those disciplines which are of central importance to it, but teachers of each subject should also attempt to assess how, or in what manner, it is able to make a distinctive contribution to the pupils' 'humanisation' and should seek to do so consciously through its subject matter. I suggest, therefore, that all subjects need to hold a number of 'humanising' educational concerns in common: this would then enable each subject to offer pupils two broad types of insight:

(a) insight into the questions and dilemmas posed by the human condition and the beliefs and values which human beings have adopted in response to these;

(b) insight into whatever aspects of the subject are regarded as necessary to understanding its nature (eg, its key concepts, structure, language/form of communication) or which are thought to be intrinsically worthwhile or worth studying for their own sake.

The ideal would be for a subject to be taught in such a way as to permit insights arising from (b) to promote insights into (a).

Six common 'humanising' educational concerns might be the following:

1. To provide pupils with an opportunity to become aware of the fundamental questions and dilemmas posed by the human condition, especially those which prompt the formulation of normative views (as expressed through beliefs, values and attitudes) of what it means to be 'human';

2. To help pupils acquire the knowledge, skills and attitudes necessary to enable them to participate consciously and critically in the processes by which they and their lives are shaped;

3. To help pupils explore and reflect on those civilising or humanising beliefs, values and attitudes which provide the basis for a society's sense of cultural continuity and its recognisable identity;

4. To assist pupils in the task of clarifying their own beliefs, values and attitudes as a necessary preliminary to taking responsibility for their own life-styles;

5. To contribute to pupils' self-knowledge and the development of their capacities for personal, social, moral and religious decision-making;

6. To enrich pupils' stocks of models of the human, expanding their visions of self, others, the world, life, etc, and extending their repertoires of responses to belief and value beyond those inculcated by family, peer group, subculture, culture, etc.

While I am sure other humanising educational concerns could be added, these are sufficient for illustrative purposes. Let us now ask two questions about religious education:

(a) What distinctive contribution can religious education make to furthering these humanising educational conerns?

(b) What aspects of religious education's subject matter are to be regarded as intrinsically worthwhile or worth studying for their own sake?

There is a problem in responding to these two questions without qualification. It is a problem caused by the fact that by and large few subjects in the curriculum of the secondary school may currently be taught with the intention of promoting both types of insights which we are considering. In seeking to identify religious education's distinctive contribution, are we, therefore, to recognise that these across-the-curriculum concerns are not being met? Or are we to assume that they are? This is a dilemma with far-reaching consequences. For example, if all subjects do share fully in the task of sensitising pupils to human problems, questions and values, then religious education may legitimately concentrate on the exploration of these within an explicitly religious context. If, however, other subjects fail to make this contribution, it may well be necessary for more time in religious education to be devoted to an exploration of those aspects of *Shared Human Experience* which prompt questions of value and belief, leaving, consequently, less time to concentrate on the responses of *Traditional Belief Systems* to such questions. Putting the problem another way, it is a matter of being conscious of the educational irrelevance of exploring *religious responses* to questions pupils do not discern within the context of their total experience and do not feel constrained to ask. Although this may point to the need for religious education teachers to come out of their isolation and set up dialogue with their colleagues teaching other subjects, pupils generally display a depressingly consistent reluctance to relate work done in one subject to work done in another. On the surface these observations might appear to support a policy of integration of subjects, such as bringing religious education within 'Personal, Social and Moral Education' courses or within integrated humanities courses. But, as I will indicate later, such policies often limit the educational value of religious education rather than enhance it.

(vi) The 'humanising' concerns of religious education

But to return to the question of religious education's distinctive contribution to furthering the humanising concerns of education, I suggest that religious education could provide pupils with an opportunity to:

Concern 1. (a) Learn about the nature and demands of those inescapable questions which being human poses, and investigate what it means to make a 'faith response' to such questions; (b) investigate and evaluate those areas of shared human experience which contribute to moral, religious and spiritual awareness and which prompt a religious interpretation of life and/or the adoption of moral perspectives and principles; (c) gain insight into a religious interpretation of life as a distinctive way of responding to questions of meaning and of understanding what it means to be human.

Concern 2. (a) Understand that holding beliefs and values by an act of faith is a necessary condition of all meaning-making activities; (b) consider the relationship between what human beings believe and what they become; (c) recognise and be able to describe the different ways in which they have been, and continue to be, shaped as human beings, especially those which involve the transmission of beliefs, values and attitudes.

202

Concern 3. (a) Consider the relationship between human givens, core human values and religious values; (b) recognise and be able to describe specific interpretations of core human values within particular religions and religious traditions and how these issue in specific codes of belief and conduct; (c) understand the influence of 'normative' religious beliefs and values upon a culture that regards them as such, and upon human development within that culture; (d) reflect on the implications of religious pluralism for a society's sense of cultural continuity and its recognisable identity, and for the religions themselves.

Concerns 4, 5 and 6. (a) Discover that in learning about religion they can also learn about themselves, especially about the influence of their own beliefs and values on their own development as a person; (b) evaluate the claims of religion and a religious interpretation of life by engaging in an open and critical exploration of the interface between what they perceive to be the central teachings of religions and their own questions, feelings, experiences and ideas about life; (c) discover that learning about other people's beliefs and commitments can contribute to their own self-knowledge and the development of their capacities for personal decision-making.

In accepting such concerns as these as legitimate educational concerns for a subject called 'Religious Education' we also need to accept that these concerns provide us with at least one set of criteria for the selection of content, and also have implications for how that content is taught (ie, in a way which fulfils these intentions). Earlier I suggested that the ideal would be for these concerns to be furthered through teaching those aspects of the subject which might be regarded as being important for their own sake. But even only a moment's reflection should convince us that much that is currently taught in religious education is unlikely automatically to promote the sorts of insight we are considering. What we need to search for is that content which is most illuminating of the personally-shaping experiences confronting young people—content which is capable of speaking to them in their own existential situation. While seeking to present religions and religious interpretations of life as authentically and accurately as possible, we must learn to harness this with the needs, experiences and questions of young people themselves, especially those which either arise from their own search for meaning and identity or which are conducive to their recognition of the importance of engaging in such a search. This observation indicates the need to give attention to the *structure* of the religious education curriculum—a structure, I suggest, which should be informed by the process by which human beings make meaning, especially that which issues in self-awareness and self-knowledge and in the formation of personal identity.

At this point I would like to introduce a diagram (Figure Four) which, I hope, will facilitate understanding of the structure of the religious education curriculum which I am about to propose. The diagram serves a number of purposes: it illustrates a *process* of curriculum decision-making in religious education; it indicates criteria for the selection of curriculum content and learning experiences in religious education; it provides an overview of the relationship between learning *about* religion and learning *from* religion; it illustrates the complexity of the problem of designing a curriculum in religious education which contributes to pupils' personal development as well as providing them with information about, and an understanding of religion.

2. Religious education's field of enquiry

We have already considered the relationship between 'Humanising Educational Concerns' and 'The Concerns of Religious Education' (Layer 1 of the diagram); so we can now give attention to what constitutes the 'Field of Enquiry' of the subject (Layer 2 of the diagram).

Clearly, in order to learn about religion one must investigate that part of the 'arena of faith responses' which I have designated *Traditional Belief Systems*, because it is in and through these that religious interpretations of meaning are made explicit in the social world. Equally, however, in order to appreciate the necessary relationship that religious faith responses have to everyday experiences of life, one must also investigate *Shared Human Experience*. One can conceive of the necessary relationship between *Shared Human Experience* and *Traditional Belief Systems* as being evident in two different but related ways. Firstly, through investigating *Shared Human Experience* one can learn to discern the questions and dilemmas to which *Traditional Belief Systems* address themselves. This derives from the view that religious belief systems arise in response to human dilemmas of meaning and value. Secondly, through investigating *Traditional Belief Systems* one can learn to discern how a religious interpretation of *Shared Human Experience* 'problematises' the human condition. This derives from the view that human dilemmas of meaning and value arise when human experience is placed within a framework of meaning which locates the source of reality outside the human condition itself and attributes the status of 'ultimacy' to certain values. A fundamental assumption of this second view is that 'truth' is 'revealed' in some form and that it is the revelation of 'truth' which enables the human condition to be seen as problematic. These

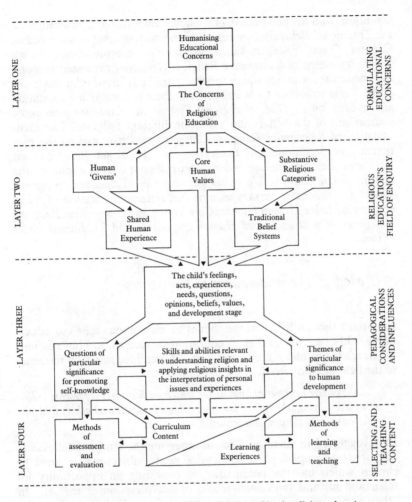

Figure Four: The process of curriculum decision-making in religious education

two views may be seen to parallel Berger's concepts of 'inductive faith' (which moves from human experience to statements about God), and 'deductive faith' (which moves from statements about God to interpretations of human experience).[8]

A similar situation exists with regard to *Core Values*. *Core Values*, as I have defined them, may be discerned *inductively* by reflecting on the 'givens' of the human condition, or *deductively* by viewing the human condition from the perspective of whatever values—'religious values'—the *Traditional Belief Systems* regard as 'normative'. But as we noted in Chapter Three, 'religious values' are specific interpretations of *Core Values* by means of *Substantive Religious Categories* expressed through the particular meanings which these acquire in different religious traditions. Thus to *deduce Core Values* from their particular interpretation and expression in *Traditional Belief Systems* invariably involves some comparison of the beliefs and values of different religions. The identification of *Substantive Religious Categories* which transcend the particular interpretations and expressions of *Traditional Belief Systems* facilitates such comparison and also provides a means of exploring the obvious relationship which exists between *Core Values* and 'religious' values. On this basis we may assume that religious education's field of enquiry includes *Human Givens, Core Values* and *Substantive Religious Categories* as well as *Shared Human Experience* and *Traditional Belief Systems*.

3. Pedagogical considerations and influences

Important though it is that we should be clear about religious education's field of enquiry, religious education's concerns, as I have defined them, cannot be met if the curriculum is determined solely by reference to the field of study itself. As Wall has warned:

> '. . . *the ordered corpus of knowledge which each subject represents will not of itself bring about that understanding of oneself and others which is the basis of a genuine humanism.*'[9]

As I suggested in Chapter Two, in order for the study of religion to contribute to pupils' personal development, subject-matter must be chosen which has the potentiality of providing an opportunity for reflection on, and re-evaluation and re-interpretation of the self. In other words, what is studied (and how it is studied) must have the capacity to prompt young people to ask: 'Who am I?' This is only likely to occur when what is studied is able to mirror the needs, experiences and questions of the adolescents themselves, not just the needs, experiences and questions of teachers or of public examination boards. Thus, instead of merely proceeding with a vague hope that pupils will find the work personally relevant and illuminating, we need actually to construct the curriculum in such a way as to accommodate the questions adolescents are asking and the situations they are experiencing. In this way the curriculum can then help them to discern and define themselves through their own questions. In my discussion of 'Knowledge as

Type B' in Chapter One I referred to Paulo Freire's view of education when he says:

> *It means 're-entering' the world through the 'entering into' of the previous understandings which may have been arrived at naively because reality was not examined as a whole.*[10]

What I am proposing is that as a consequence of young people investigating religious education's field of enquiry, they should be helped to 're-enter' their personal life-words—especially as they impinge upon their self-image and self-identity—so that they are enabled to become critically self-conscious and aware of the need to participate consciously in the re-formulation of self, not in terms of the *other-dependent* (as in childhood), nor in terms of irresponsible and unbridled individuality, but as a unique person in relationship to others.

But 'uniqueness' only has meaning in relation to a person's corporate life. As Wall indicates, growth towards autonomy means increasing critical awareness of oneself as a social being, that is, as a person under the continual pressure of demands and expectations, but making counter-claims of one's own, facing alternative choices and opportunities and yet always being required to be the author of one's own conduct and to answer for it. How one defines oneself is thus related to how one defines oneself in relation to others, and particularly to human groups. Thus, the process of growing in self-knowledge involves continually keeping in focus the interplay which must exist between self and others—between the individual and the family, between the individual and groups within the local community, between the individual and other members of a plural society, even between the individual and the worldwide human community. Personal development is thus inextricably interwoven with social development. To ask 'Who am I?' is also to ask 'Where do I belong?'. Here, I think, we have a useful illustration of the process to which Freire points. Let me explain.

As we have seen, the acquisition of 'belongingness-identity' is essential to children's development; it is the vehicle of their humanisation. It is an identity, however, which they are given, not one that they choose. At adolescence they become conscious of the need for new, more adult identities but there is the danger that these too will be given to them rather than chosen by them. If, however, young people can be helped to gain more insight into what is happening to them, why they feel the need for a different self-image, why new and different self-ideals are attractive to them, why they feel in conflict with themselves and with others (especially those closest to them), then they may become free to make conscious choices—personal choices—of what and who they are. In other words, they may be able to *choose to belong* as a way of expressing their own understanding of themselves. Equally they may choose to belong because they recognise that it is only by belonging that they are able to give sense and meaning to themselves. But belong to what or to whom? The simple answer would be 'to different human groups', but that says very little.

What we are really concerned with here are *ways* of valuing, *ways* of relating, *ways* of acting, *ways* of thinking and believing *within* human groups and *within* human relationships, and, of course, *ways* of thinking and believing *about* human groups and relationships and *about* life as a whole. Helping pupils towards critical self-consciousness means helping them towards some perception of the gap between the real and the ideal in domains hitherto uncritically accepted—the family, the adult world in general, the normative values which are imposed or expressed in schools, the normative values communicated through the consciousness-creating industries, and so on. Assisting pupils to understand *religious ways* of valuing, relating, acting, thinking and believing, not only expands their ways of looking at the world and their place within it, it also provides them with the means of being critical of that world and of themselves because religion problematises the human condition. It is in this manner that religious education can contribute to assisting pupils with the task of clarifying their own beliefs, values and attitudes—itself a necessary preliminary to any form of personal decision-making or the conscious adoption of a life-style, or, indeed, of a stance for living. Harvey Cox puts the point well when he says that in a world in which life-styles are often prepackaged we should seek every opportunity to strengthen young people's capacity to 'roll their own'.

These observations indicate why it is necessary for what I have called 'pedagogical considerations' to be incorporated into the process of curriculum decision-making. It is important, therefore, that I now give specific attention to each of the four areas which Figure Four indicates as comprising Layer 3 of that process.

(i) *The child's feelings, acts, experiences, needs, questions, opinions, beliefs, values and developmental stage*

There is a considerable literature in religious education which advocates the use of children's own experiences as a basis for developing their understanding of religious concepts. Typically one can cite the work of Douglas Hubery, Ronald Goldman, Harold Loukes, John Hull, Jean Holm, and my own attempt to provide a framework for the subject which combines two complementary approaches—the *Existential Approach* and the *Dimensional Approach*—designed to enable pupils to build conceptual bridges between their own experiences and what they recognise to be the central concepts of religion.[11] Generally speaking, however, contemporary thinking about religious education has moved

away from these concerns, largely because those influences which provided the impetus for curriculum change in the Sixties and early Seventies (eg, insights from developmental psychology and child-centred
theories of education) have been superseded by other influences less
sympathetic to such concerns. One such influence is the widespread
acceptance of the view that by applying the principles of phenomenology to the study of religions in schools the subject is given a sound educational basis.

(a) Phenomenology of religion and religious education

While it is clearly the case that phenomenological techniques of investigation have an important contribution to make to the task of studying
religions, the principles of phenomenology, however, do not, and cannot, purport to provide adequate educational grounds for religious
education in schools, nor a sufficient methodology for teaching the subject. Three points may be made in support of this assertion.

Firstly, although religious phenomena can be an object of much fas-
cination for some children and good teaching can stimulate the interest
of others, expecting children and young people to exhibit a sustained
willingness to explore religions 'from the point of view of those who are
adherents' is unrealistic if, at the same time, such exploration does not
also meet their own needs and relate to their own experiences and interests. However rich the subject-matter and however many possibilities exist for it to be studied through different modalities and forms of
expression, ranging from dance to doctrine, if children's interest in religion is to be stimulated and sustained to a point where they are prepared to work hard at acquiring complex skills of enquiry, the study
must also be felt to be relevant to their own situation and able to meet
their own needs. But seeking to make the study of religions relevant
to pupils' needs—although educationally desirable—is, as my next
point indicates, inconsistent with the principles of phenomenological
methods of investigation.

Secondly, phenomenological method discourages observers from
using their own personal experiences or personal values as reference
points for understanding religion. The reasons for this are laudable, but
the phenomenological principle of 'bracketing' one's own questions and
experiences (and any beliefs and values derived from them or informing
them) is in direct conflict with the central principle of all child-related
conceptions of education. Child-related and child-centred educational
theories represent a definite and intentional use of children's immediate
existential situations and experiences to provide a basis for all aspects of
learning. Such experiences are seen as influential factors in the acquisition of concept formation in any area of study. The experiences them-

selves are, therefore, deliberately incorporated into the process of study where, in the early stages of learning, they are seen to provide the main motivating factor in children's attitudes to learning and, at all stages of learning, provide natural reference points against which children set new experiences. Indeed, a fundamental task of the teacher is to assist pupils in the task of accommodating new areas of knowledge within their own 'schemas' (to use Piaget's term) so that, through the adaptive processes of assimilation and accommodation, new knowledge prompts the reconstruction of these existing schemas.

It is salutary in the present climate of 'multi-faith' teaching to re-read the research findings of Goldman which identify the difficulties which pupils below the mental age of fourteen have in grasping formal religious concepts, and the effect this has on their attitudes to religion during the adolescent years.[12] Although his research was confined to assessing the difficulties (and the dangers) of teaching essentially biblical concepts to children, the results are transferable to the difficulties of teaching any religious concepts to pupils in school. But contemporary multi-faith syllabuses require pupils to move between a multiplicity of cultures and faiths, each expressing their own distinctive religious concepts through language and symbols which are unique to them, without, apparently, offering them any assistance in assimilating or accommodating these concepts within their own schemas and so facilitating their conceptualisation of them. It is inevitable in these circumstances that their so-called knowledge of world faiths will often amount to little more than 'verbalisation' and will fall considerably short of the learning outcomes so confidently proclaimed in the aims and objectives of many syllabuses. Without support of the sort of mechanisms Goldman introduced to aid conceptualisation (such as 'Life Themes', or my own 'Depth Themes', 'Symbol and Language Themes' and 'Situation Themes') or some equivalent, pupils can neither be expected to 'understand religion' nor be motivated to do so. In this sense the religious education curriculum must be 'developmental' in so far as its purpose, content and methods should relate to children's needs, experiences and the stage of their conceptual development. Furthermore it should seek to assist children towards succeeding stages in their personal development. It is an unrealistic expectation that a curriculum which is based on the principle that religion should be 'studied for its own sake' can fulfil these educational criteria.

Thirdly, a basic principle of phenomenological investigation is that evaluation of a religious tradition will not be personal but only in terms of the self-understanding of that tradition. Although there are good grounds for discouraging premature judgment of a religious view or belief until such time as it has been adequately understood, any educational process which excludes judgment or criticism as a matter of principle can hardly be said to be extending pupils' capacities for personal decision-making or contributing to their personal knowledge. Those who have argued that religious education consists in encouraging pupils to relate their understanding of religion to their own experiences and *vice-versa* have done so on the grounds that this allows children's perception and understanding of themselves and of religion to undergo continual redefinition, refinement and re-evaluation, and that it is this process which engenders the study with educational value. Not only, therefore, should the religious education curriculum be 'developmental' but it should seek to encourage pupils to make personal evaluations of the truth, significance and value of what they are studying. I will be developing this notion later, but in the meantime some comment on the reasons for incorporating the child's 'opinions, beliefs and values' as a reference point for curriculum decision-making is required.

(b) Phenomenology and education

In the previous section I offered several reasons why certain principles underlying phenomenological approaches to the study of religion are in conflict with educational principles which need to inform the religious education curriculum. But the phenomenology of religion is only one branch of phenomenology—a term which encompasses a wide variety of viewpoints, subject areas and methods. (We encountered alternative conceptions in Chapter One when we considered 'Knowledge as Type B'). While techniques drawn from the phenomenology of religion have a part to play in religious education, there are other branches of phenomenology which also have relevance to an educational enterprise such as religious education, especially, perhaps, the branch linked with existentialism.[13] Phenomenology focuses on the interior experience or 'life-world' of the individual—how he or she perceives the external world and reacts to those perceptions, particularly before attempting to fit these personal experiences into any kind of impersonal or public mode of understanding. Its main concerns are, firstly, to expose certain essential structures of consciousness and to shed light on how these enable the individual to order his or her interior experience and create personal meanings. Secondly, phenomenology is interested in indicating how the individual re-orders these personal meanings in such a way as to accommodate them within public modes of expression, such as academic disciplines, including religion.[14]

There are several ways in which phenomenology has a direct application to education. Firstly, if offers valuable insights, complementary to those which have emerged from developmental psychology, into how pupils learn. In so doing it points to the inadequacy of structuring content only by reference to the inner logic of a subject or discipline (ie, the impersonal or public mode of understanding). It shows that attention must also be given 'to the ways of thinking, the reflective experience and the modes of operating of those who are to learn, for it is this—the rich and complex mental life they already have—which is to be educated'.[15] Here phenomenology lends some support to the 'new directions' movement of sociology which insists that the definitions and categories of knowledge are treated as problematic and that the pupils' own viewpoints are respected. Secondly, it reveals the need for the development of a pedagogy which encourages self-consciousness and an intuitive grasping of the situational elements within which each individual forms personal meanings (ie, how they see things as they do). Such a pedagogy could take a number of directions. The one I am proposing in this book equates self-consciousness with an awareness of personal self or identity and suggests that the religious education curriculum might be used as a means of encouraging pupils to reflect on the shaping properties which beliefs and values have had, and continue to have, on their lives. Such self-consciousness is seen as a necessary prerequisite to their being able to participate consciously and critically in making decisions about the directions in which they are to develop as human beings. Additionally I have suggested that moral, religious and spiritual consciousness both arises from self-consciousness and contributes to it; thus in seeking to promote self-consciousness the religious education curriculum can also be said to contribute to the development of the pupil's moral, religious and spiritual consciousness.

From these observations it should be apparent that recognising that pupils have 'opinions, beliefs and values' is of crucial significance both to the way in which the religious education curriculum is constructed and to the type of interaction the curriculum should seek to promote between the pupils and what they are studying. Generally speaking, while considerable attention has been given, for example, to identifying and describing the processes by which pupils form concepts (ie, Piagetian type investigations into the formation of mathematical, historical, religious concepts), much less is known about how children develop self-concepts and, more particularly, how their self-concepts are influenced and developed through what they are required to study as a part of the curriculum.[16] If, as I have argued throughout this book, human beings become what they believe—that it is the particular structure of their own beliefs and values which determines who and what they become—then it is important not only that pupils become conscious of their own beliefs and values, but also that they are encouraged to evaluate them in the light of alternatives. The issue, however, is how to promote such consciousness through the study of religions.

I have suggested that we understand this as a process whereby insights gained from an exploration of religious education's field of enquiry (ie, *Human Givens, Core Values, Substantive Religious Categories, Shared Human Experience* and *Traditional Belief Systems*) are translated into personal terms. Thus content studied in religious education is not only intended to promote awareness and understanding of religion and religions but also to promote reflection on the part of pupils on the implications that the adoption of a religious view, or a different religious view, would have on their own understanding of self and their subsequent development as a person. What I am proposing is, therefore, that pupils, as a result of their religious education, should not only 'be able to describe what it means to be a Christian / Hindu / Jew / Muslim / Sikh, etc', but that they should also be encouraged to:

Evaluate their understanding of religion in personal terms and evaluate their understanding of self in religious terms (ie, in terms of the religious beliefs they have learned about).

Thus, pupils should 'be able to describe what it would mean *to them* to be a Christian / Hindu / Jew / Muslim / Sikh etc'. We should note that this requirement applies to all pupils, irrespective of whether they are practising members of a religious faith. Thus a Muslim pupil would be encouraged to describe what it would mean to him or her to be a Christian or a Hindu, just as a Christian pupil would be encouraged to describe what it would mean to him or her to be a Muslim, a Jew or a Sikh. The process, of course, is just as applicable to pupils who are not members of a religious faith; and indeed an important variant would be for those who are members of a religious faith to be able to describe what it would mean to them not to have religious faith, or to adopt a naturalistic stance.

Requiring pupils to *apply* their knowledge of the beliefs and values of different religions to an understanding of *themselves* provides an opportunity for them to become more aware of the beliefs and values they currently hold or into which they have been socialised. It is an opportunity, however, which may be missed unless the teacher designs learning situations specifically intended to promote this form of personal learning. The four areas I have identified as constituting 'pedagogical considerations' in relation to curriculum decision-making all have a bearing on this task, as all contribute to facilitating a process whereby pupils can be assisted to *learn from* religion. A fuller discussion of this process will follow but further comments on the significance of 'the child's opinions, beliefs and values' can now be made.

(c) Are the child's opinions, beliefs and values part of religious education's field of enquiry?

Firstly, as we noted in Chapter Two, it is important to distinguish between consciously held beliefs and values and unconsciously assimilated beliefs and values. Human beings do not choose between beliefs *in vacuo* but draw upon and so makes conscious the beliefs and values by which they have been formed. But being confronted by the need to choose between beliefs and values is dependent upon the extent to which human beings recognise their experience as problematic. Earlier in this chapter we considered the view that religions, in locating the source of reality outside the human condition, enable the human condition to be seen as problematic. Although I do not wish to argue that religions have an exclusive claim in doing this, it is not unreasonable to assume that when pupils *learn about* the different ways in which adherents to different religious faiths understand themselves and the world they are confronted by the problematical nature of human experience, including their own. At one level the problem is to do with the diversity of beliefs—how can they all be right? At another level it is to do with what these diverse beliefs have in common—they all challenge the 'taken-for-granted' assumptions that human experience is self-explanatory and self-authenticating; they all point to certain values that have the status of absoluteness or 'ultimacy' over and against the relativity of human constructs. While subtle theological arguments about the nature of reality are likely to elude all but a few pupils, most pupils are able to grasp the essential difference between a religious and a non religious view of life, at least in terms of what people do and believe. They are also likely to have 'opinions' about these—opinions which are expressive of both the beliefs and values which they have assimilated unconsciously and those which they have arrived at more reflectively. The expression of 'opinions' by pupils is an important step towards their conscious examination of personal beliefs and and values; providing for such expression is, therefore, a necessary function of the curriculum. It is also important that learning situations should be devised which facilitate the expression of opinions and encourage pupils to recognise the need for these to be scrutinised and informed by knowledge.

But, it might be argued, if all pupils have beliefs and values these might be seen as actually constituting part of religious education's field of enquiry and be available for investigation in the same manner as the other constituents of that field. If religious education seeks to explore the religious consciousness of human beings (as expressed through their sacred literature, ritual acts, doctrinal beliefs etc), could it not be said that this should also include the religious consciousness of the pupils? While there are some grounds for holding this view, it also presents a number of difficulties. Firstly, there are difficulties in defining what are the pupils' own beliefs and values. As our consideration of relevant research literature has shown, it is not appropriate to speak of young people having coherent 'systems' or even 'patterns' of belief, viz:

The first point is the virtual absence of interviewees who had a clearly defined, consistent, and verbalised pattern of beliefs . . . among the vast majority of the sample there was clear evidence that for purposes of their normal life they had never so far required an articulated and systematised account of their 'belief' in order to cope with existence.[17]

Secondly, as we noted in our discussion of Hardy's views in the previous chapter, in so far as pupils are willing to 'share' their personal beliefs and values with others, the teacher may legitimately draw upon them for illustrative purposes. But the efficacy of the study itself is not dependent upon or determined by the nature of the beliefs and values of either the pupils or the teacher, but rather by the application of certain principles and procedures to the subject's field of enquiry. If this field of enquiry is not differentiated from personal beliefs (even though these beliefs may be compatible with those being studied) then the freedom which permits an educational enquiry to be conducted in a critical manner will of necessity be curtailed, if only out of concern for the susceptibilities of those pupils who are willing to express their beliefs.

Thirdly, irrespective of the beliefs and values held by pupils, the task of religious education is not to *confirm* pupils in their own beliefs but to provide them with an opportunity to *appraise* their own beliefs. This is an inevitable consequence of the subject matter of religious education being drawn from the diverse beliefs of many religious traditions. If the opposite view were held, namely that religious education should seek to confirm pupils in their own beliefs and values (or deepen their present religious commitments), how then could the requirement that pupils study religious traditions other than their own be justified? For what purpose would they engage in this study? In order to satisfy themselves of the superiority of their own beliefs? Similarly, for what reason would pupils who do not hold religious beliefs be required to study religions? To confirm them in their belief that religious beliefs are mistaken? Indubitably a consequence of studying diverse religious traditions will be that some pupils *are* confirmed in their own beliefs (preferably because their studies have assisted them in a more profound appreciation of their own religious tradition); but this outcome must lie beyond the intentions that inform the study as an educational exercise. Placing the pupils' own beliefs and values within the subject's field of enquiry obscures the necessary distinction between a legitimate educational activity which is concerned with clarifying issues of belief and values in a way which is appropriate to the needs of all pupils, and a faith-nurturing activity which is appropriate only to the needs of some of the pupils and which can only be conducted legitimately within the context of the communities of faith.

But despite the difficulties of defining the relationship of the subject matter of religious education and its treatment to the pupils' own beliefs and values and the dangers that might stem from encouraging interaction between them, a religious education curriculum which avoids this cannot be said to be contributing much to pupils' 'religious' education. What religious education (and education in general) seeks to further are pupils' capacities to take responsibility for their own beliefs and values—to 'own' them. (This is not the same as seeking to confirm pupils in their own beliefs; furthering their capacities to 'choose' should not be confused with supporting pupils in the choices they make.) In order to do this, religious education must give pupils the opportunity to acquire skills which enable them to use their understanding of religion in the interpretation of their own personal experiences. This is not to make the pupils 'religious'; rather it is to make available to them a way of understanding their experiences in religious terms, just as other subjects make available to them a way of understanding their experiences in scientific, historical, political and aesthetic terms. Like any form of interpretation which can be applied to human experience, an understanding of religion and an ability to apply it is only acquired through learning by practice. Contemporary curricula in religious education tend to equate learning about religion with the acquisition of knowledge about religions, and although many include the application of religious thinking to human situations, this is normally only explored at the level of generality—ie, religious responses to birth, marriage, family life, death, abortion, war, animal rights, and so on. Although, as we have noted, eliciting the opinions of pupils on religious views can be an important step in moving them towards the conscious examination of personal beliefs and values, unless learning situations are so structured as to require pupils to make connections between religious views and their own, the chances of them acquiring even minimal skills of religious interpretation are exceedingly remote.

(ii) *Skills and abilities relevant to understanding religion and applying religious insights in the interpretation of personal issues and experiences*

We might approach the question of how to assist pupils in the development of skills which are relevant to the interpretation of personal issues and experiences by asking if the study of religion itself promotes such skills. In looking at this question I intend to draw on my earlier work concerned with what I have called the development of 'abilities in pure religion' and the development of 'abilities in applied religion'.[18]

(a) *The development of abilities in pure religion*

If we were to ask 'What is necessary to achieve an understanding of

216

religion and its place and significance in the life of religious adherents?', we would probably include an *understanding* of the key concepts, doctrinal structure, basic tenets, scriptures, traditions, practices and festivals of several religions. Engagement with the content of study would, presumably, promote something like the following abilities:

(1) The ability to identify religious phenomena: eg, religious objects, buildings, writings; religious behaviour and actions; religious language and symbolism; religious questions and issues; religious experiences; religious beliefs; religious perspectives and interpretations.

(2) The ability to describe religious phenomena accurately from the point of view of religious adherents (ie, as expressed through their thoughts, feelings and actions).

(3) The ability to classify observations and descriptions of religious phenomena in terms of a religion's central concepts and doctrinal structure.

(4) The ability to relate the central concepts of a religion and its teaching to the interpretation of human experience.

(5) The ability to distinguish and make a critical evaluation of the truth claims, beliefs and values of a particular religious tradition.

(6) The ability to discern and assess the influence of a particular religion on the way of life of a society (ie, on its cultural values, the life-styles of its members, etc).

Additionally, the study would also, presumably, contribute to the development of more general abilities; viz:

(1) The ability to observe and record, to abstract and analyse information.

(2) The ability to make use of observation, to ask questions, to solve problems and to identify what is relevant to an enquiry.

(3) The ability to pursue a line of enquiry by making connections, thinking logically, recognising what is of importance and knowing how to seek further information.

(4) The ability to make intelligent choices on the basis of evidence of all kinds.

(5) The ability to communicate information, ideas, questions, feelings, effectively in both spoken and written forms.

(6) The ability to appreciate the reason for the existence of different forms of understanding with different investigatory techniques and different estimates of what can be regarded as reliable evidence.

Furthermore, the study would, presumably, promote certain attitudes, some of which would be needed in order to study religion effectively; viz:

(1) Interest in religion and in different ways of looking at life;
(2) Critically open to the claims and experiences of religion and prepared to apply onself imaginatively to their investigation;
(3) Accepting the importance of religion and feeling it to be worthy of further study;
(4) Willing to suspend one's own beliefs in order to enter as fully as possible into the beliefs and values of others and to learn from them;
(5) Committed to furthering one's understanding of life and seeking truth.

What makes the abilities and attitudes I have listed above important is that they are necessary to an *understanding* of religion and religions. The need for pupils to acquire such abilities is determined, therefore, by the view that to study religion is a worthwhile activity in itself. That these abilities are not necessarily transferable outside the study of religion is not seen to invalidate the educational value of the study. This does not, however, mean that an understanding of religion is not transferable outside the confines of the study. For example, it would be difficult to develop an understanding of many aspects of life in a society without an understanding of the religion (or religions) which has shaped, and continues to shape its culture. Great literary and artistic works, moral and political values, legal and institutional systems owe much to religion, and an adequate understanding of these and of history could not be achieved without some understanding of the influence of religion upon them. Similarly, an understanding of religion is of significance to our understanding of people—to our understanding of what Hirst calls 'our own and other people's minds'. And in so far as we have been shaped by a culture which has been influenced by religious values, understanding religion also enables us to understand ourselves. But while we may recognise that an understanding of religion has an application outside the confines of the study itself, how can we help pupils to see this and, more importantly, how can we help them to engage in that application? In other words, how can we help pupils to develop 'abilities in applied religion'?

(b) The development of abilities in applied religion

In looking at this question we need to distinguish between identifying abilities which are necessary in the application of *religious knowledge* to other areas of study—such as using an understanding of Christian

218

eucharistic theology to aid an understanding of reformation history, or of Christian symbolism to aid an appreciation of the literary works of Shakespeare or the paintings of El Greco, or of Muslim and Jewish beliefs to aid an appreciation of contemporary conflicts in the Middle East—and identifying abilities which are necessary in the application of *religious insights* to an understanding of personal issues and experiences. My intention is to concentrate on the latter as being more obviously in line with the concerns of this exploratory study and to offer some thoughts on the possible application to this task of Berger's conception of 'signals of transcendence', which we considered in Chapter Two.

Contained within the beliefs, teachings and practices of the religions of the world are the great recurrent themes of human experience—the search for truth, goodness, harmony and wholeness; the quest for meaning and purpose; the conflict between good and evil, freedom and responsibility, the physical and the spiritual, faith and doubt; the problem of evil, pain, suffering and death; the capacity of human beings for love and hate, for kindness and cruelty, for hope and despair, for joy and sadness, for holiness and depravity, and so on. These themes are eternal; they encapsulate the essence of all human experience; to be human is to encounter these 'themes of life'. How they are encountered, become part of individual consciousness and are responded to will, of course, differ for each individual. But if education is a process by, in and through which pupils may begin to explore what it is, and what it means, to be human, it is axiomatic that the religious education curriculum will provide a context for the systematic exploration of these themes. Such a study will, I suggest, have a two-fold function: it will seek to explore the themes from a religious perspective, and it will seek to encourage pupils to discern the themes within their own experience and to use religious insights in their interpretation.

Berger's methodology for 'discovering signals of transcendence' both in religious traditions and in the normal experiences of the everyday world has, I believe, relevance to the task of identifying 'abilities in applied religion'. Let us first consider the application of his inductive method to the religious traditions. The questions he suggests we can use to confront religious phenomena are:

1. What is being said here?
2. What is the human experience out of which these statements come?
3. To what extent, and in what way, may we see here genuine discoveries of transcendent truth?

Let us apply these questions to two particular instances provided by Jewish and Christian sacred literature: (i) the statement recorded in

219

Genesis 1:27 and (ii) the parable of the labourers in the vineyard as recorded in Matthew 20:1–16.

(i) In Genesis 1:27 we find the following statement:

So God created man in his own image, in the image of God he created him.

Berger's first question might be answered by examining the theology which underpins the book of Genesis—in other words, by promoting 'abilities in pure religion'. This would enable us to be aware of the tradition's 'self-understanding' of the passage, ie, how the writers of the Bible understood it and how it has been interpreted in the life of the faith community for whom it is sacred scripture. Such understanding might then inform our own understanding of the passage—what we make of it: what we understand it to be saying, ie, that human beings possess the nearest likeness there is to what God is like; that human beings possess divine qualities; that human beings are powerful and capable of great achievements; and so on.

In answer to Berger's second question, we might talk of those qualities we experience in human beings which could be called 'divine'—qualities of caring, giving, loving, protecting, forgiving, and so on; we might also consider ways in which human beings are powerful and exercise their power, are capable of great achievements, and what these achievements are. In so doing we would probably find ourselves having to differentiate between the power human beings have for good and the power they have for evil; between the creative and destructive powers of human beings; between their achievements which enhance the quality of human life and those that diminish or impoverish it. We might 'personalise' our response by considering if we have 'divine' qualities ourselves, if we are powerful and, if so, how we use our power, if we have achieved something and how we would judge the worth of what we have achieved, and so on.

In answer to Berger's third question, we might formulate some view of what human beings *ought* to be like and why they should be like this; we might consider how they might become like this; we might consider what prevents them from becoming so; we might reflect on the gap between the ideal and the everyday reality and ask why this is so. Finally we might consider how it is that human beings do have a capacity for discerning ideals; that, despite their continual failure to achieve what they think human beings ought to be, they do have a sense of what *'ought to be'*. Might it be said, then, that human 'being' participates in 'divine' or 'ultimate' being?; that the 'essence' or inner nature of human 'being' is one with that of the universe and of God, and that that essence is what human beings call 'spiritual'? Is not this 'transcendent truth' to be discerned within our human experience, and is it not to this that the statement in Genesis points?

(ii) The parable of the vineyard tells how the owner of a vineyard hired some labourers at the beginning of the day and they agreed to work all day for one denarius. The owner, however, set on more labourers throughout the day telling them that 'whatever is right I will give you'. At the end of the day all the labourers, including those who had worked only an hour, received one denarius. Those who had worked all day long protested but were told by the owner:

> *Friend, I am doing you no wrong; did you not agree with me for a denarius? Take what belongs to you, and go; I choose to give to this last as I give to you. Am I not allowed to do what I choose with what belongs to me? Or do you begrudge my generosity?*

Again, we might respond to Berger's first question by acquainting ourselves with the exegeses of this parable (and its use by Matthew) offered by New Testament scholars. This would constitute promoting 'abilities in pure religion'. We might then, however, try to formulate our own understanding of the parable; that, for example, it indicates that we are free to do with our own money as we please; that wealthy individuals have greater freedom than poorer people to do as they like; that the 'management', typically, does not respect the rights of the worker; that workers should seek solidarity in order to prevent exploitation by the management; that without negotiated wage settlements between management and unions, individuals will always seek to take advantage, be they management or workers, and so on.

In answer to Berger's second question, we might talk about our experiences and our knowledge of other people's experiences of employment; consider the responsibilities of employer to employee and *vice-versa*; discuss the meaning of 'fair', 'right' and 'rights' and how such meanings are arrived at; share our experiences of people we consider to be 'generous' and how they show their 'generosity' (through giving time, attention, sympathy, assistance etc) and ask why they are like this. We might then consider if there are any principles to which we might appeal in deciding upon what is 'just' and how 'justice' can be achieved in human life and experience (eg, although the owner was generous to some labourers was he 'just' to all?).

Berger's third question might prompt us to consider what it means to be human. For example, a typical response to the situation depicted in the parable would be that 'it's only human to want as much as you can get' or that 'those who protested were only human to do so'. If a signal of transcendence has been 'sedimented' (to use Berger's word) in this parable, it is to do with the paradox that human beings experience about their 'humanness'—that it permits them to glimpse or intuit the ideal but also prevents them from achieving it. (In this respect it is the same signal as the one sedimented in St Paul's statement, 'I can will what is right, but I cannot do it. For I do not do the good I want, but the evil I do not want is what I do.' Romans 7:18–19). To be 'human' in this parable is to fall short of the Christian ideal of what it means to be human; it is to obscure the 'image of God' of which the human is an expression; to use 'human' standards of conduct is to limit oneself to being less than human. While human beings may use the 'it's only human to . . .' argument to normatise their values, they do so in the knowledge that such values fall short of what *ought to be*. The 'transcendent truth' to which this parable points confirms and articulates what human beings can discern in their own experience. Both generate 'signals of transcendence'.

Applying the inductive method to human experience is the reverse of the process of applying the inductive method to the religious traditions. The method consists of recognising 'signals of transcendence' in one's own experiences (in what Berger calls 'natural' reality) and trying to articulate the meaning they have for an understanding of 'ultimate' reality. That meaning may or may not be expressed in terms derived from the language and symbols of the religious traditions. It is important to recognise that giving meaning to one's own experience (what I earlier called developing 'personal meaning') involves employing all one's personal epistemic functions—ie, *intuition, reason, sense experience* and *feelings.* The reasons for this will become apparent as we consider a few examples of experiences in which 'signals of transcendence' may be discerned by human beings, including adolescents, in the contemporary world.

The first example illustrates how a 'signal of transcendence' (which has always been present in human experience) may suddenly be brought to human consciousness on a universal scale. The example is that of 'Band Aid' (and 'Live Aid'). Although the giving of aid to people in distress has always been a familiar enough feature of public and private life in our society, it would, I think, be true to say that through the dedication of Bob Geldof it became a universally discerned 'signal of transcendence' in 1985 and 1986. By employing the immense power of the media, most notably that of television, to show both the need for aid to Africa and the worldwide response to that need, Geldof succeeded in presenting a situation which touched the hearts and souls of millions of people who, under normal circumstances, would have been indifferent to the plight of people in a far away continent even though they were aware of it. But wherein lay the signal? Was it in the starving African children? Was is it in the act of giving which awareness of these children inspired? Just as Berger finds a signal of transcendence in the *'ordering gesture'* by which a mother reassures her anxious child that 'everything is all right', so, through the power of the media, millions of people were able similarly to engage in an 'ordering gesture' which constituted a 'signal of transcendence'. That ordering gesture was to give aid; but, I suggest, it transcended the immediacy and particularity of starving African children and represented an awareness and expression not only of what *ought to be* but what *is*. The conflicting worlds of wealth and poverty, of glamour and unspeakable ugliness, of hope and despair were, momentarily, resolved into one world inhabited by an interdependent humanity. What *'ought to be'* is the oneness of humanity and the absolute obligation upon all human beings to give to other human beings who are in need. But why is this so? Because that oneness and the obligation which stems from it is a reflection of the oneness of God with his creation and of his obligation to it. Obligation is thus binding upon Reality itself—it is in the essence of Being to be like that. Or, as the Christian scriptures express it:

For God so loved the world that he gave his only Son, that whosoever believes in him should not perish but have eternal life. (John 3:16)

That the sensitivities and imaginations of many adolescents have been touched by becoming part of the experience of 'Band/Live Aid' can be witnessed to by many teachers and parents. Whether or not they have been encouraged to use that experience to help them to reflect more deeply upon questions of personal belief and value and upon their commitment to what they intuitively know to be 'ultimate values' cannot be known. Rather more private and personal experiences, however, have the same potential. Take, for example, the adolescent experience of 'love'. We are inclined to smile at the idea of young people experiencing their first 'love affair', of being 'in love' for the first time, but there are few situations which are more engaging and illuminating of the whole self than this experience. Could it not be said that to *feel love* is a 'signal of transcendence'? Love, in the Christian tradition, is '. . . the supreme Christian virtue because it is the being and activity of God himself'.[19] But, it may be objected, the love of God cannot be compared to that of an adolescent; and besides, Christian love is *agapeistic*—it is love for the undeserving or love for the unlovable. Certainly the types of love may not be the same, but what of the intensity of loving? And is it not possible, even in the first flushes of adolescent romance, that young people may be only too aware that love must grow, be deepened, be transformed, be perfected if it is to survive? Do they not also have the experience of loving or being loved by others with whom they are not romantically involved? What is it about love that it can be said to 'make the world go round'? Surely, of all human experiences, feeling love, being in love, giving and receiving love, making love, etc, must be seen to express an essential aspect of human 'being'?

Does not the experience of human love, then, provide a powerful argument for the existence of a transcendent order of reality in which love is perfected? Does it not also suggest that human love, despite all its imperfections, is a reflection of an ultimate, unfailing Love?

Conversely, the human experience of the *loss* of love, of rejection, of separation, of being alienated from others, of being unloved and unwanted, etc, can also be a 'signal of transcendence'. The 'agony aunts' of popular tabloids—today's 'gurus of love'—devote most of their columns to giving assurance to those who have been 'unlucky in love' that, with patience, love will find them. The 'Problems Page' of adolescent magazines testifies to the tragic state of young people who are lonely, in conflict with parents, unable to make friends, suffering from fears that they are unattractive, unable to see any value in themselves. Unhappily such people are victims of a society in which the meaning of love has become trivialised. But although being successful in love may have been reduced to being a performance indicator of one's social competence or a sign of one's physical attractiveness, all human beings have a sense of what love *'ought to be'*, of the life-transforming power that resides in loving and being loved, and of the human needs that it meets. It is ironic that something so important should be so neglected in the curriculum. Is it so unrealistic to believe that an understanding of the human experience of 'divine love' which is enshrined in so many of the religious traditions cannot be of some value in helping young people to explore and refine their own understanding of love as they experience it and search for it?

In this section I have tried, albeit briefly, to apply Berger's methodology to the task of considering how young people can develop 'abilities in applied religion' which will enable them to apply religious insights to an understanding and interpretation of personal issues and experiences. Inevitably my illustrations have been limited to but a few examples of the many teachings, beliefs and practices of the religious traditions and the everyday experiences of young people which could be explored in this manner. Although it may well be possible to identify specific skills which are necessary to this process, what I have proposed is that the application of the inductive method itself constitutes a skill of interpretation. Seeking to accommodate the teaching of this skill within the religious education curriculum will thus have important implications for the choice of curriculum content and how it is studied.

(c) *Evaluating religious beliefs and values*

It is important that we recognise, however, the crucial role that *evaluating* religious beliefs and values plays in any process directed towards encouraging pupils to use religious insights in the interpretation of their own experiences. Earlier I suggested that we should encourage pupils to *'evaluate their understanding of religion in personal terms and evaluate their understanding of self in religious terms'*. We now need to give closer attention to this notion and consider what is involved in this process. We can do this by further elaboration of the distinction between *learning about* and *learning from* religion.

When I speak of pupils *learning about* religion I am referring to what the pupils learn about the beliefs, teachings and practices of the great religious traditions of the world. I am also referring to what pupils learn about the nature and demands of ultimate questions, about the nature of a 'faith' response to ultimate questions, about the normative views of the human condition and what it means to be human as expressed in and through *Traditional Belief Systems* or *Stances for Living* of a naturalistic kind, about the discernment and interpretation of *Core Values*, about the shaping influence of religious beliefs and values on cultural and personal histories, and so on. This type of learning might be said to be initiating pupils into 'an impersonal or public mode of understanding' or, to use Witkin's term, promoting 'Object Knowing'.

When I speak of pupils *learning from* religion I am referring to what pupils learn from their studies in religion about themselves—about discerning ultimate questions and 'signals of transcendence' in their own experience and considering how they might respond to them, about discerning *Core Values* and learning to interpret them, about recognising the shaping influence of their own beliefs and values on their development as persons, about the unavoidability of their holding beliefs and values and making faith responses, about the possibility of their being able to discern a spiritual dimension in their own experience, about the need for them to take responsibility for their own decision-making, especially in matters of personal belief and conduct, and so on. This type of learning might be said to result in self-awareness and personal knowledge, or, to use Witkin's term, 'Subject Knowing'.

The process of *learning from* religion (or 'developing abilities in applied religion') involves, I suggest, engaging in two different though related types of evaluation. The first type of evaluation—which I will call 'Impersonal Evaluation'—involves being able to distinguish and make critical evaluations of the truth claims, beliefs and practices of different religious traditions and of religion itself. Although various writers imply that assisting pupils to make such evaluations should be one of the concerns of religious education—and its inclusion in the National Criteria for the GCSE in Religious Studies endorses this view[20]—identifying suitable criteria for this purpose is fraught with difficulties and considerable work still remains to be done before this important aspect of religious education is placed on a sound educational footing. Clearly, though, 'Impersonal Evaluation' of religions and religion requires alternative interpretations, differing from an adherent's understanding of his or her faith, to be applied to the phenomenon. These would include psychological and sociological interpretations of forces influencing religious beliefs and activities, and philosophical considerations of the difficulties presented by religious language and the nature of religious belief. Additionally, the beliefs of one religious tradition could be evaluated by reference to those of another religious tradition, or, of course, by reference to those of a non-religious or naturalistic stance.

While 'Impersonal Evaluation' of this kind might be seen as contributing to the pupils' 'Object Knowing', its relevance to any form of truth questing ensures that it also has a bearing on the second type of evaluation, which I will call 'Personal Evaluation'. This form of evaluation is, however, more directly concerned with promoting self-knowledge or 'Subject Knowing' and involves using such questions as the following to confront the religious traditions:

1. Are these beliefs / values / practices / attitudes, etc, attractive or persuasive to me?
2. Why / Why not?
3. If I adopted such beliefs, etc, what difference would it make to me?—to my personal life, family life, to my relationship to others, to my priorities and goals?
4. What beliefs do I hold which are similar to or different from these?
5. Why do I hold these views? Should I continue to do so? What are the alternatives?
6. Is there anything here which teaches me something about myself?—about what I should regard as important?—about what should matter to me?

In the case of 'Personal Evaluation', what begins as an attempt to confront and evaluate religious beliefs and values becomes a process of self-evaluation. It is at this point that the type of interaction which underlies *learning about* and *learning from* religion permits the pupils' knowledge of religions to become formative in promoting knowledge of self. Once again, however, the curriculum must be so constructed as to facilitate this process. I suggest that this means choosing content and devising learning experiences which are sufficiently engaging at a personal level to promote what I have called 'questions of particular significance in the promotion of self-knowledge'.

(iii) Questions of particular significance in the promotion of self-knowledge

The following questions are illustrative of those that might be derived from a phenomenological analysis of the interior experience or 'life-world' of individuals:

Self-identity: Who am I? Where do I belong?

Self-acceptance: What am I really like? What do I feel about myself? How do others see me? How do I feel about others? How do I act towards others? How do others act towards me? (How would I like them to act towards me?)

In what ways am I like, and different from, others?

Who are the most significant persons in my life?

What is the most important thing that I know?
What is the most important thing that I can do?
What is the most important thing that I need?
What is the most important thing that I believe?
What are my priorities in life? What interests me most? What experiences do I value most? What do I believe/believe in? What are my deepest feelings, questions and convictions? To what do I feel myself committed?

Self-illumination: Why am I like I am? Why am I like this? Why do I feel the way I do about this? Why do I see this in the way that I do? Why do I act towards others like this? Why do I need this? Why do I believe/believe in this? Why do I regard this as being important? Why do I regard this person, or this group, as significant to me? Why do I value this experience? Why did I commit myself to this?
Who are/have been my 'heroes' and 'models'? What do/did they believe in? What views about the world, about life, about themselves and others do/did they hold? Why? Are their views attractive/persuasive to me still? Why? Do these views and beliefs help me to make sense of my life? What can I continue to learn from them? Do I want to be similar to, or different from the adults I know when I become an adult?
What are the most important decisions I have taken so far? What have been their consequences for me and for other people? Would I now make the same decisions? How do I make decisions?
What is the single most important unsettled value or belief issue for me at this moment? Why is this issue important to me?

Self-ideal: What/who shall I be? What is the right thing for me to be/do? What is my purpose? What is my value? Where do I fit

227

into the scheme of things? To what values/beliefs ought I to commit myself? Why do I need to commit myself to anything? What seems to me to be worth dying for? What seems to me to be worth living for? What seems to me to be worth knowing? How do I decide?

What kind of person would I most like to be? How might I become this kind of person? What would this person believe/believe in? How would this person act? Why?

Self-adjustment: Can I change? Should I change? How ought I to change? What do I have to do in order to change? What help do I need in order to change? Where will I find support to help me to change? (NB change = growth)

What will change mean in terms of my view of myself? What will change mean in terms of my relationships with others, especially with my family and friends? What will change mean in terms of my life-style, my ambitions, my attitudes to the future?

Am I prepared to take responsibility for the sort of person I wish to become? Do I have faith in my decisions?

Self-evaluation: How am I doing? How can I judge my progress? How do others respond to me now? How do I feel about myself? Is it worthwhile? Have I learned anything more about myself? Have I learned anything more about others, about life, about what is important in life?

Who am I? Where do I belong?

These questions are, of course, very unlike the sort of questions teachers are used to asking and pupils are used to answering in the classroom. They are personally relevant or 'autobiographical' questions; questions one asks oneself while engaging in *interior dialogue*; questions which enable the individual to monitor the state of their personal knowledge; questions which promote personal knowledge. If, however, they are entirely personal questions, how can the curriculum take account of them? While some of these questions might be posed directly by the teacher, the majority could not and should not be posed in this way. But that does not mean that they should be disregarded; on the contrary, it is, I suggest, the responsibility of teachers to create learning situations which have the explicit intention of promoting this type of personal questioning. There are good precedents for this. The hallmark of good literature is its capacity to engage the reader at a personal level. For example, telling young children a story about a boy called Johnny and his mother can elicit both enjoyment and interior dialogue. If the story is well told and the situation it depicts can be conceived of as being possible within the experience of the children who are listening to it, it is not unreasonable to expect that dialogue to include such questions as, 'Am I like Johnny?', 'Is my mother like Johnny's mother?', 'Are my friends like Johnny's friends?', 'Would I do what Johnny did?', and so on. At the secondary level the use of material portraying people engaged in such reflections can act as a stimulus for interior dialogue of a similar type. Talk in the third person singular is readily translated into first person terms if the subject or situation is seen to have personal relevance. Obviously this underlines the need for both the choice and presentation of content to be influenced and informed by the pupils' feelings, acts, experiences, needs, and questions and directed towards the development of interpretative and evaluative skills such as those which we have been examining in the last section.

But while the successful promotion of 'personal knowledge' through religious education will depend on the skill of the teacher in devising interactional forms of learning experience, the outcome will be considerably influenced—for better or for worse—by the overall structure chosen for the curriculum. For example, contemporary agreed syllabuses of religious education vary in their recommendations regarding structure, but most favour those which are determined by an appeal to the inner logic of religion. For example, while one syllabus advocates studying each major religion in turn, another chooses to organise content by means of typological themes, such as Founders, Festivals, Sacred Places, Holy Books, Pilgrimages, and so on. A popular alternative is the type of thematic treatment based on the religious concept of the *rite of passage* where content from a number of different religions is grouped under headings such as Birth, Initiation, Marriage and Death. Lying behind these thematic approaches is a basic principle of phenomenology of religion—that one moves from the description of the phenomena to the comparison and contrast of common features of different religions in order, eventually, to be able to elucidate the universal essence and structure of religion itself. But the level of understanding of which pupils may be capable means that the study of religion may rarely move beyond the descriptive level, and this raises a query about the value of choosing and structuring content solely by reference to such phenomenological principles. Furthermore, as we have seen, the adoption of such principles as a basis for religious education does not allow the study to comply with basic educational principles, such as using the pupil's experience to assist conceptualisation and ensuring that the concepts to be understood do not require a level of abstract thought which is beyond the present cognitive capacities of the pupils. For these and many other reasons one must express doubt about the educational viability of structuring the curriculum in this manner, especially if the complex forms of interaction which I am suggesting are necessary to the development of 'personal knowledge' are to be achieved. We must ask, therefore, what alternative structures might be more appropriate to our concerns.

(iv) Themes of particular significance to human development

A way of approaching this question is to devise a structure for the religious education curriculum which is informed by the process of humanisation rather than by the inner logic of religion or the principles of phenomenology of religion. This is in line with the view I expressed in Chapter Two that if we are concerned that formal education should contribute to the 'human' development of pupils, it is necessary that what we teach and how we teach it is both informed by the process of humanisation and actually contributes to it. Just as my analysis of humanisation has contributed to my understanding of how religion and education can be brought into a relationship with each other, has led me to identify what I have called the 'interpretative', 'humanising', 'functional' and 'personal' concerns of religious education, and has provided the basis for the interactive process of 'learning about' and 'learning from' religion, so now it can be used to suggest a structure for the religious education curriculum.

In my analysis of humanisation I have tried to show how the beliefs that human beings hold (both consciously and unconsciously) have a 'shaping' influence on their personal development. But we should note that the word 'development' in itself offers no sense of direction for the process of humanisation. Personal 'development' can only be judged to be taking place if it is in the direction of a precisely stated 'goal'.[21] Of course, one of the functions of belief is to define such a goal; thus, to hold certain beliefs means that one is, at least theoretically, developing in the direction of a goal. Similarly, when we speak of certain beliefs and values being enshrined within a culture, what we mean is that to be born into that culture is to be shaped by its beliefs and values in the direction of certain goals. Thus individual 'development' might then be judged by (a) whether one accepts and lives by those beliefs and values which a society regards as normative and which are enshrined within its culture, and (b) whether one fulfils in one's own development the 'model of the human' which that society regards as normative.

I suggest that within this process whereby individuals, through the beliefs they hold, may be said to be 'developing' in the direction of particular goals, it is possible to identify a number of experiences which are especially formative in shaping them in the direction of these goals.

These experiences, like *Human Givens* and *Core Values*, transcend cultural boundaries and particular belief systems, indeed they could be classed as further examples of human 'givens'. For illustrative purposes we can include the following experiences:

1. The experience of group membership (eg, family, peer group, ethnic group, nationality, religion, etc).
2. The experience of sharing in regular celebrations and affirmations of the values of a group's own traditions.
3. The experience of perceiving through different forms of communication—verbal and non-verbal—a group's common core of values and beliefs and of communicating these to others in the group and to those outside it.
4. The experience of identifying with human models embodying those virtues and moral attitudes which are consistent with a group's normative goals of personal development and expressive of a group's normative beliefs and values.
5. The experience of regular exposure to a group's consistent beliefs about the nature of human beings and of the world (ie, to its ideological perspective).

We can now attempt to relate this analysis of experiences which are fundamental to human shaping to the task of devising a structure for the religious education curriculum. Firstly, we may reasonably assume that the pupils' own development is influenced by their own exposure to these experiences. Secondly, we may reasonably assume that the religious development of adherents to religions is influenced by their exposure to these experiences. Thirdly, we may reasonably assume that by using these experiences as a basis for structuring the religious education curriculum we can accommodate both the concerns of the subject as they relate to the needs of the pupils and the concerns of the subject as they relate to the demands of understanding religion and religions. In doing so we can preserve the integrity of the relationship between education and religion which is based on their both being interpretative and humanising in their concerns.

The five experiences provide five 'themes' within which an infinite variety of content—secular and religious—may be incorporated and explored. A range of nomenclature can be used for these themes, but the following titles are expressive of the central 'organising concept' of each theme:

1. Growing together
2. Celebrating together
3. Learning together
4. Acting together
5. Believing together

The addition of the word 'together' stresses that human development occurs within the context of human interdependence, and that each of the themes provides for the exploration of a different aspect of what it means to be human and what it means to belong. Indeed, if there is a single overarching theme which can be derived from these five fundamental human experiences it is 'Belonging together'.

While the five themes are based on five experiences which transcend cultural boundaries and particular belief systems, how individuals are shaped by these experiences is through the *particularity* of these experiences. Exploring the *particularity* of the experiences, especially that which stems from being a member of a religious faith, enables pupils not only to learn about religious beliefs and values but, at the same time, to discern the shaping influence of particular religious beliefs and values on the development of human beings towards a clearly defined goal. What is significant here is that the pupils' own development is influenced by the shaping influence of those beliefs and values to which they are themselves exposed through the *particularity* of their own experiences. Learning to discern these and to evaluate them as a result of exploring the *particularity* of other people's experiences is to develop their capacities for critical self-consciousness, self-knowledge and self-awareness—the keystones of their own personal development.

The opportunity for pupils to explore the *particularity* of the experiences which shape the development of religious adherents (and which, in so doing, shape their moral, religious and spiritual consciousnesses) is provided by incorporating content from a religious tradition within the themes, viz:

1. Christians growing together
2. Christians celebrating together
3. Christians learning together
4. Christians acting together
5. Christians believing together

Or, equally, by incorporating content from different religious traditions within the themes, viz:

1. Christians / Muslims / Jews growing together
2. Sikhs / Hindus / Christians celebrating together
3. Christians / Muslims / Jews learning together
4. Jews / Hindus / Sikhs acting together
5. Christians / Muslims / Hindus believing together

If some of the nomenclature seems cumbersome and some of the religious traditions appear to fit rather uncomfortably within specific themes, it is because I am deliberately, at this point, seeking to establish the principle that the religious education curriculum should be organised by reference to these fundamental human experiences rather than by reference to explicitly religious concepts or typologies which are outside the experience of many of the pupils. The curriculum examples which follow in this chapter and in Part Two of this book should indicate that this principle does allow for considerable flexibility in application and does not, of course, preclude explicitly religious concepts and typologies from being explored from within each of the themes.

4. Selecting and teaching content and evaluating pupils' learning in religious education

We come now to a consideration of Layer 4 of my diagram representing the process of curriculum decision-making. The first task is to consider how we might select curriculum content and devise learning experiences which will allow pupils to investigate religious education's field of enquiry in such a way as to enable them to *learn about* and *learn from religion*.

(i) Selecting curriculum content

The pedagogical considerations we have already discussed provide an 'educational mesh' through which content drawn from religious education's field of enquiry needs to be passed before it can be used to further the educational concerns of the subject. Applying the 'mesh' enables us to identify that content which is most directly applicable to the educational concerns of the subject. In other words, the religious education *curriculum* does not comprise *all* the beliefs, teachings and practices of *all* the *Traditional Belief Systems*, or *all* the *Substantive Religious Categories*, or *all* the many experiences which constitute *Shared Human Experience*, or *all Human Givens* and *Core Values*. It comprises only a selection from each of these, namely those beliefs, teachings, practices, categories, experiences, givens and values which are the most appropriate for pupils to study in order that the educational aims of the subject are achieved.

In recent times there has been a marked tendency for agreed syllabuses of religious education to draw back from applying *educational* criteria in the selection of content and, instead, to identify content only by reference to what adherents to a faith regard as essential to understanding it. The same has been true of many recent textbooks written for use by pupils in religious education. The compilers' neglect of the educational needs of pupils, including their need for assistance in concept formation, is symptomatic of their mistaken belief that to be educational means to make available to pupils the same understanding of a faith that religious adherents possess but to do so in a manner which is not confessional. The effect of such syllabii and textbooks has been to increase the amount of religious content in the curriculum and to reinforce the view that successful teaching means 'covering' as much of this content as possible within the limited time available to the subject. Furthermore it has reinforced the use of 'methods' of teaching which hardly qualify to be called either 'methods' or 'teaching'. (I am thinking here of the prevalence of the throughly unsatisfactory practice of teachers distributing 'information sheets' or 'work sheets' on aspects of religious belief and practice to pupils, 'explaining' them by reading the sheets aloud with comments, and then requiring pupils to complete a series of questions which test only their capacities for factual recall or for identifying and copying out a word, sentence or passage given on the sheet.)

While it is important that decisions about what religious content to include in the curriculum are *informed* by a knowledge of what religious adherents regard as essential, educational judgements about the suitability or appropriateness of studying that content *as a means of achieving the subject's educational goals* must take precedence. It does not follow that what is 'essential' to religious adherents in terms of their needs and interests (or to how they 'understand' their religious faith) is the same as what is 'essential' to the needs and interests of pupils or to those of an educational enterprise. This is so even if we limit the concerns of religious education to *learning about* religions. Here what is 'essential' to the religious educator is the identification of an 'essential minimum' of fundamental or key concepts in each religion which pupils need to understand in order to become informed about what Christians, Hindus, Jews, Muslims, Sikhs, etc, believe. Identifying an 'essential minimum' of concepts then enables content which is most illuminative of these concepts to be distinguished from content which is not. It also enables both concepts and illuminative content to be ordered sequentially so that they may more easily be understood by pupils within the limitations imposed by their own experiences and developmental stages. Furthermore, by promoting an understanding of fundamental or key concepts rather than a random collection of unrelated facts, pupils are better able to *apply* their understanding of religion in such ways as we considered earlier in this chapter. The educational principle underlying the procedure which I am proposing is clearly stated by J S Bruner in the following words:

The more fundamental or basic the idea he has learned, almost by definition, the greater will be its breadth of applicability to new problems . . . what is meant by 'fundamental' in this sense is precisely that an idea has wide as well as powerful applicability. . . . . the school curricula and methods of teaching should be geared to the teaching of fundamental ideas in whatever subject is being taught. . . The first and most obvious problem is how to construct curricula that can be taught by ordinary teachers to ordinary students and that at the same time reflect clearly the basic principles of various fields of inquiry. The problem is twofold: first, how to have the basic subjects rewritten and their teaching methods revamped in such a way that the pervading and powerful ideas and attitudes relating to them are given a central role; second, how to match the levels of these materials to the capacities of students of different abilities at different grades in school.[22]

Bruner is arguing the case for teaching the 'fundamental structure of a subject' rather than an unrelated collection of background information, facts, themes, topics and so on, chosen, perhaps, rather randomly. He offers four general claims that can be made on behalf of the approach that he is advocating:

1. *Understanding fundamentals (ie, central ideas, concepts and principles) makes a subject more comprehensible;*
2. *Unless detail is placed in a structured pattern it is rapidly forgotten;*
3. *Understanding fundamental principles and ideas assists 'transfer of training';*
4. *By constantly re-examining material taught in elementary and secondary schools for its fundamental character, one is able to narrow the gap between 'advanced' knowledge and 'elementary' knowledge.[23]*

Consequently he argues that:

If the hypothesis is true—that any subject can be taught to any child in some honest form—then it should follow that a curriculum ought to be built around the great issues, principles, and values that a society deems worthy of the continual concern of its members.[24]

A curriculum as it develops should re-visit these basic ideas repeatedly, building upon them until the student has grasped the full formal apparatus that goes with them.[25]

Bruner's concept of the 'spiral curriculum'—one 'that turns back on itself at higher levels'—has, I believe, application to the task of selecting content and devising learning experiences in religious education. It offers a way of conceiving of a curriculum which is able to accommodate both the need for pupils to learn about religion and to learn from it. For example, our discussion of the desirability of identifying fundamental or key religious concepts as a basis for selecting content from the different religious traditions is in line with the view that the curriculum should

235

be organised (or sequenced) in such a way as to enable these concepts to be 're-visited'. Thus the curriculum becomes a vehicle for understanding an 'essential minimum' of key religious concepts through a variety of content drawn mainly from *Traditional Belief Systems* but also from *Shared Human Experience* and chosen for its capacity to illuminate these concepts and to 're-present' them in ways which assist pupils' conceptualisation of them. Selected *Human Givens, Core Values* and *Substantive Religious Categories* can also be accommodated within the curriculum in exactly the same manner. Sometimes these will be illuminated and 're-presented' by the same content chosen for its capacity to illuminate and 're-present' key religious concepts and sometimes by content chosen specifically for this purpose from *Shared Human Experience*. Similarly, the great recurrent themes of human experience, and the central questions of belief and value which arise from reflecting on them, can be 're-visited' in the curriculum by the inclusion of contrasting situations and experiences drawn from everyday life which are particularly illuminating of such themes and provocative of such questions. The curriculum can then allow for the exploration of different religious responses to these experiences and questions in a way which builds on previous awarenesses.

One way of identifying an 'essential minimum' of key religious concepts from each of the religions from which content is to be taken is to use the *Core Values* and *Substantive Religious Categories* I identified in Chapter Three as criteria. Obviously there are other ways of doing this, but as the concerns of religious education that I am seeking to further include providing pupils with an opportunity to 'consider the relationship between human givens, core human values and religious values' and 'recognise and be able to describe specific interpretations of core human values within particular religions and religious traditions and how these issue in specific codes of belief and conduct', then using these as criteria is particularly apposite. I have already discussed in Chapter Three the view that there is a necessary relationship between *Core Values* and *Substantive Religious Categories* and sought to demonstrate this. In the chart that follows (Figure Five), I have conflated the eight *Substantive Religious Categories* and the seven *Core Human Values* which I used in Chapter Three for illustrative purposes, to produce eight *Core Values Criteria* for the selection of an 'essential minimum' of key religious concepts from Christianity, Hinduism, Islam, Judaism and Sikhism.

But having identified the 'essential minimum' of fundamental or key religious concepts from each religion which we think pupils should understand, and the recurrent themes of human experience and the central questions of belief and value to which we think they should be sensitised through reflecting on *Shared Human Experience*, the problem

Core Values Criteria	'Essential Minimum' Key Concepts
1. Providential source of order, meaning and purpose in the universe; The Sacred; Source of Revelation and Truth;	
2. Agent or agencies of Revelation; records of Revelation; experience of Revelation/ What is truth?	
3. View of the human;	
4. View of a just society;	
5. Individual self-fulfilment through:	
6. Ethical perspective;	
7. Community of faith/ View of community:	
8. Spiritual values/ Core human values;	

For details of the key religious concepts from these five religions which might be regarded as an 'essential minimum', see Part Two, pages 289–290; 299–300; 311–312; 324–325; 337–338.

Figure Five: Using Core Values and Substantive Religious Categories as criteria for the selection of an 'essential minimum' of key religious concepts from Christianity, Hinduism, Islam, Judaism and Sikhism

remains of how to organise this content within the five themes I have identified so that pupils are enabled to learn from it. The root of the problem is how to ensure that pupils are able to apply what they learn about *Traditional Belief Systems* and *Shared Human Experience* to their own existential situations. In other words, how, in terms of curriculum content and its organisation, do we 'operationalise' the notion of the pupils' study of religions contributing to their self-knowledge and the development of their moral, religious and spiritual consciousness? It is here that insights arising from my analysis of humanisation, especially those pertaining to the nature and influence of the 'social life world', can be linked with the notion of a 'spiral curriculum'.

Earlier in this chapter I stressed the view that if studying religions is to contribute to pupils' personal development, subject matter must be chosen which has the potentiality of providing an opportunity for reflection on, and re-evaluation and re-interpretation of the self. I suggested that, as a consequence of young people investigating religious education's field of enquiry, they should be helped to 're-enter' their personal life-worlds *so that they are enabled to become critically self-conscious and aware of the need to participate consciously in the reformulation of self, not in terms of other-dependent (as in childhood) but as a unique person in relationship with others'*. Consequently I stressed the need for young people to increase their critical awareness of themselves as social beings who define themselves in relation to others, and particularly to social groups, and I suggested that *'the process of growing in self-knowledge involves continually keeping in focus the interplay which must exist between self and others—between the individual and the family, between the individual and groups within the local community, between the individual and other members of a plural society, even between the individual and the world-wide human community.'* (p 207)

I now want to suggest that if young people are to derive personal knowledge of this kind from studying religions, the religious education curriculum must enable them to *keep in focus* the interplay between self and others and the contexts within which this takes place. Indeed, I want to suggest that the four 'contexts' I have just identified as the loci of interaction between self and others—*Family, Local Community, Plural Society* and *World-Wide Community*—provide 'organising categories' for subject matter drawn from *Traditional Belief Systems* and *Shared Human Experience*. Furthermore, in so far as they are the fundamental contexts within which human shaping occurs, they also provide a means of structuring this content within the five themes I identified in section 3 (iv) as 'Themes of particular significance to human development'. The effect of using these four 'organising categories' in combination with the five themes is to create a matrix which enables not only key religious concepts and selected givens, core values, substantive religious categories, recurrent themes of human experience and central questions of belief and values to be 'revisited' in the curriculum, but the four 'contexts' within which interaction between self and others takes place also to be 'revisited'.

Although what I am suggesting may appear, from my description, to be inordinately complicated, the following diagrams should indicate that the curriculum structure which emerges is really quite simple and has easy practical application.

Figure Six indicates how the four 'organising categories' can be applied to *Shared Human Experience* and to *Traditional Belief Systems*. The left hand circle labelled *Shared Human Experience* represents the *context* in which all human beings seek to make sense of themselves and the world. This context, through the application of the four 'organising

238

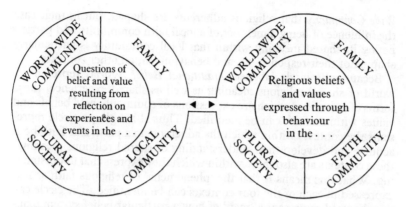

SHARED HUMAN EXPERIENCE   TRADITIONAL BELIEF SYSTEMS

Figure Six: The application of the four organising categories of Family, Local Community, Plural Society and World-Wide Community to Shared Human Experience and Traditional Belief Systems

categories', is sub-divided into four separate but related contexts, in each of which events and experiences may occur which are shaping of the individual, pose ultimate questions about the human condition, and prompt the individual to reflect on central questions of belief and value. Adherents to a religious faith live in exactly the same world as all other human beings—that of *Shared Human Experience*—and their interactions with other human beings occur in the same context as those of other human beings, namely within the contexts of *Family, Local Community, Plural Society* and *World-Wide Community*. Religious adherents, however, *transform* this world by investing it with religious meaning. This meaning extends to the four contexts in which their interactions with each other and other people take place, and it extends to the interactions themselves. In other words, the *behaviour* of religious adherents in the four contexts will be expressive of the particular religious beliefs and values they derive from their religious faith. This means that what constitutes *Shared Human Experience* for the religious adherent is both the world they share with all other human beings and the *shared religious meaning* with which they invest it in common with other members of the same religious faith. Thus the right hand circle labelled *Traditional Belief Systems* does not represent a different world of *Shared Human Experience* from that represented by the left hand circle, but the same world invested with shared religious meaning. Like any other human beings, it is through their interactions with others within the four contexts of *Family, Local Community, Plural Society* and *World-*

239

Wide Community that religious adherents are shaped, but in their case the influence of being a member of a local faith community and participating in shared meaning within that local community is particularly shaping of their responses to, and behaviour in, all other contexts.

Because the circle labelled *Traditional Belief Systems* represents a world of shared religious meaning as well as shared experience, those forms of behaviour which are expressions of commonly held beliefs and values within a faith can be identified. Thus although the circle represents the contexts within which the adherents to a particular faith both acquire and develop their understanding of shared religious meaning, these contexts are also those within which they express that understanding. What this means is that the 'phenomena' of religious faith as it is expressed in each of the four contexts can be identified. The circle can thus be used to present a 'map' of how a particular belief system manifests itself through the behaviour or actions of its adherents within a given social context in a given time and place. Thus a 'map' of how Christian faith may be perceived and manifested from the point of view of Christians living in contemporary English society might be as follows:

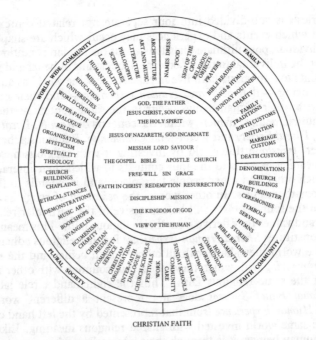

Figure Seven: A Traditional Belief System: Christian Faith as perceived and manifested from the point of view of Christians living in contemporary English society

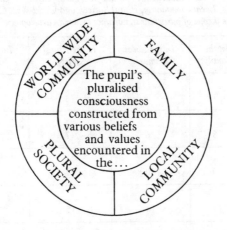

The pupil's pluralised consciousness constructed from various beliefs and values encountered in the…

WORLD-WIDE COMMUNITY

FAMILY

PLURAL SOCIETY

LOCAL COMMUNITY

Figure Eight: The application of the four organising categories of Family, Local Community, Plural Society and World-Wide Community to the personal lives of pupils

Although I have specifically excluded the personal lives of pupils from religious education's field of enquiry, I have stressed that for pupils to *learn from religion* means to develop skills and abilities in applying religious insights to an understanding of their own situations and experiences. The structure of the curriculum, its content and learning experiences should, therefore, be specifically designed to assist pupils in developing these skills and abilities. I suggest that a curriculum which uses the four categories of *Family, Local Community, Plural Society* and *World-Wide Community* as contexts for the exploration of central questions of belief and value and of religious responses to them, offers pupils considerable encouragement and support in transferring insights from their studies to their own situations and in using them to clarify their own beliefs and values. The reason for this is obvious; their own interactions occur within these contexts. Learning to recognise the shaping influence of the different beliefs and values which they themselves encounter through their own involvement in these four contexts is an important step towards their becoming critically conscious and self-aware and, ultimately, responsible for who and what they become. In this sense, using these contexts as 'organising categories' for content is infinitely more appropriate to the educational concerns of religious education than using specifically religious concepts, themes or typologies for this purpose.

Figure Nine: A Spiral Curriculum Matrix formed from the application of the four organising categories of Family, Local Community, Plural Society, and World-Wide Community to the five themes of particular significance to human development

Theme:	In the Family:	In the Local Community:	In the Plural Society:	In the World-Wide Community:
Growing together:	1	2	3	4
Celebrating together:	5	6	7	8
Learning together:	9	10	11	12
Acting together:	13	14	15	16
Believing together:	17	18	19	20

(a) Selecting content from Traditional Belief Systems

The matrix provides for twenty units of content chosen from either *Traditional Belief Systems* or *Shared Human Experience*, or from both. In the case of content chosen from *Traditional Belief Systems*, the matrix allows for this to be taken concurrently from several religious traditions or from a single tradition. Themes can be explored vertically or horizontally. For example, taking Sikhism as the religion from which content is to be chosen, a vertical theme might explore how Sikhs:

—grow together in the family,
—celebrate together in the family,
—learn together in the family,
—act together as a family,
—hold common beliefs with other Sikh families.

A horizontal theme might explore how Sikhs:

—grow together in the family,
—grow together in their local faith community,
—preserve their identity in the plural society while relating to non-Sikhs,
—preserve their unity with other Sikhs in a world-wide context.

An example of an across-the-religions approach with content drawn from Hinduism, Islam and Judaism might be a vertical theme in which the activities of adherents to these different faiths in their local faith communities would be explored with reference to—

- —the social and spiritual support provided by the communities for their members (*growing together*),
- —their forms of worship and how they celebrate their festivals (*celebrating together*),
- —how teaching, as contained within their sacred scriptures, is communicated to members of the communities and how they express this in their daily lives (*learning together*),
- —the views and attitudes of members of the communities to ethical and social issues (*acting together*),
- —the fundamental tenets of each faith as illuminated by the content incorporated within each of the above themes (*believing together*).

A horizontal theme drawing on content from Hinduism, Islam and Judaism might include:

- —how Hindu, Muslim and Jewish families nurture their children in their faith through birth ceremonies, family prayers, stories, observation of special days, food laws, personal example, etc (*learning together in the family*),
- —how Hindu, Muslim and Jewish faith communities instruct adherents in their faith through public worship, ritual and symbolic actions, the architectural features of their places of worship, 'schools' attached to places of worship, the use of sacred and religious literature, the use of religious objects and artefacts, visiting teachers and preachers, initiation ceremonies and festivals, etc (*learning together in the faith community*),
- —how Hindu, Muslim and Jewish people communicate their beliefs to other members of the plural society through wearing distinctive clothes, eating special food, having their own places of worship, following their own cultural and religious customs with regard to courtship and marriage, celebrating festivals, providing services to the community through their shops and businesses, being involved in local politics, etc (*learning together in the plural society*),
- —how the 'religious vision' enshrined within Hinduism, Islam and Judaism has contributed to the spiritual heritage of humankind; eg, the respective contributions of the religions to human civilisation and an understanding of what it means to be human through their moral codes, art, literature, religious teaching, etc (*learning together in the world-wide community*).

Three comments need to be made regarding the selection of content from *Traditional Belief Systems* for inclusion within the matrix. Firstly, content should illuminate those religious concepts which have been pre-selected as the 'essential minimum' in each religion which pupils need to understand in order to be informed about what Christians, Hindus, Jews, Muslims, Sikhs, etc, believe. These concepts will be 're-visited' through the different content explored within each unit of a theme, whether the theme is a vertical or a horizontal one. In the case of a vertical theme, the final unit of each theme (*believing together in the family, local community, plural society, world-wide community*) will allow for those key concepts encountered through the other units of the theme to be examined more directly; the same will be true of *all* the units in the horizontal theme '*believing together*'.

Secondly, although religious concepts invariably acquire a distinctly metaphysical character—as do the belief-systems of which they are a part—it is not their metaphysical character which is the focus of study but the way in which religious adherents understand these concepts, accommodate them within their own religious faith responses, express their beliefs about them personally and corporately through behaviour and action and are, subsequently, shaped by what they believe. Thus, the focus of the study in the curriculum is on the *beliefs* of Christians, Hindus, Jews, Muslims, Sikhs, etc, not on Christianity, Hinduism, Judaism, Islam and Sikhism as metaphysical systems of belief or even as 'religions' which 'constitute in themselves some distinctive entity' separate from those who hold beliefs about them.[26] In this respect the label '*Traditional Belief Systems*' which I have used to distinguish one of the areas of religious education's field of enquiry, misrepresents the content which is drawn from it *when it is included within the curriculum*. For this reason I have chosen to designate the curriculum which draws its content from *Traditional Belief Systems*, '*The Religious Life-World Curriculum*'.

The third observation relates to the outworking in curriculum terms of the view that interactions of self and others take place within four 'contexts' (family, local community, plural society and world-wide community), and that religious adherents invest the world of *Shared Human Experience* with religious meaning which extends to these four contexts in which their interactions take place and to the interactions themselves. In Chapter One I considered the concept of 'ideology' and, following Elias, identified its essential constituents as (a) a world view or world picture of what is happening in human life, (b) central values and goals that are considered desirable in human life, and (c) an image of the process of social change (or of maintaining the *status quo*) and the particular tactics deemed appropriate for achieving this according to the world view, values and goals. I then put forward the view that, in functional terms, a 'religious view of life' is a 'religious ideology' as subject to the influence of conservative, liberal and radical interpretations as a 'political ideology'. Without any doubt, the traditional religious belief systems all possess the essential constituents of an 'ideology'. There are, however, as we would expect, substantial differences between them with regard to each of these constituents, more especially differences in their image of the process of social change necessary for achieving the goals they consider desirable for human life. Although no religion is a static, fixed system of beliefs able to escape the modifying influence of the cumulative experience of its adherents, no religion is likely to be the same as another in how it responds to such influences—positively or negatively. We see this illustrated dramatically in the differing responses of religions (and of the traditions within each religion) to pluralism and modernity.

For some religions and religious traditions, pluralism represents an open possibility for the discovery of a new religious 'self', a deeper religious and moral awareness of humankind's spiritual vocation within the world, a freeing from the chains of religious tribalism.[27] For others, pluralism is to be eschewed and seen only as the vindication of a religious tradition's vocation to be separate, exclusive, the elect through whom humankind's spiritual vocation is preserved and through whom humankind may ultimately be redeemed. What this means in terms of the choice of religious content for inclusion in the matrix is that some religions will have less to offer in some of the units than others, especially in those units exploring the expression of religious faith within the context of the 'Plural Society'. The truth of the matter is that in focusing on the distinctiveness of, for example, dress, food and custom, etc, within a religious tradition, we are not necessarily examining a positive and creative response to religious and cultural pluralism but one which could be seen either as defensive or uncompromising. Thus the interactions of members of different religions within a plural society will be of a different order. While some will seek to interact positively in the pursuit of shared, inter-cultural or trans-cultural values, others will see this as a denial of their responsibility to truth and will draw back into themselves and work towards the strengthening of an exclusivist ideology.

Here again we see why the needs, interests and beliefs of the religious adherent can inform the concerns of religious education but cannot prescribe them. The ideological stance of most religions towards pluralism (even if this is not so of all traditions within all the religions) is antithetical to the ideological stance towards pluralism which is part of a liberal conception of education. Education endorses the values of being sensitive to, and respectful of, other people's views; being tolerant of people who are different from ourselves; being 'open-minded', etc. But these values are not derived from the values of religion, nor are they consistent with the values of religion. Although all religions may teach that human life is to be valued and respected, no religion advocates that, for example, human beings should be 'open-minded' regarding its beliefs. The 'norm of judgment' which religions offer is an understanding of Truth; to be 'open-minded' about that Truth is not to trust it, and that is to reject it. The 'norm of judgment' which secular, liberal education offers children is a commitment to openness. This is also the norm for the teacher. Ninian Smart asserts:

The test of one who is teaching reasonably in a society such as ours is openness, not what his commitments are . . . [28]

The role of contemporary religious education in a plural society cannot be restricted to helping pupils to see religious faiths as they see themselves; it must raise questions about the contribution of religions to the development of a society which is fully deserving of the term 'community'. The religious education teacher should not, therefore, take the absence of positive interaction between a religion and the plural society as an indication that content from another religion would be more appropriate, but as an indication of the need to encourage pupils to ask why this is so. While religious education has a responsibility not to misrepresent the beliefs of those religions which are its object of study, it also has a responsibility to educate pupils in the evaluation of those beliefs. In so doing religious education may, in a small way, make some contribution not only to the development of the pupils' moral, religious and spiritual consciousnesses, but also to the future development of moral, religious and spiritual consciousness in a plural society. What I am echoing here is Wilfred Cantwell-Smith's view that in an age of modernity, human beings must construct their own religious future, and that means that:

Men of different religious communities are going to have to construct jointly and deliberately the kind of world of which men of different religious communities can jointly approve, as well as one in which they can jointly participate. [29]

Part Two of this book contains illustrations of what I have called '*The Religious Life-World Curriculum*' comprising content drawn from Christianity, Hinduism, Islam, Judaism and Sikhism as a consequence of applying the eight *Core Values Criteria* (conflated from *Substantive Religious Categories* and *Core Values*) to each of these religions. Additionally Part Two contains detailed outworkings of the content of this curriculum using the spiral curriculum matrix discussed in this chapter. In all, therefore, my illustrations of the '*The Religious Life-World Curriculum*' consist of 100 units of content, 20 from each religion, with some developed in terms of classroom schemes of work.

(b) Selecting content from Shared Human Experience

In the case of content chosen from *Shared Human Experience*, the matrix allows for the exploration of an infinite variety of experiences, situations and questions in order to sensitise pupils to the great recurrent themes of human experience as well as to *Human Givens, Core Values* and the central questions of belief and value which arise from reflecting upon them. It also allows for the exploration of this content to be related to the pupils' own feelings, acts, experiences, needs and questions in such a way as to encourage the expression of opinions on the part of pupils and reflection on their own beliefs, values and life-styles. Themes incorporating content from *Shared Human Experience*, like those incorporating content from *Traditional Belief Systems*, can be explored either vertically or horizontally. Indeed, an important reason for introducing themes which draw their content from *Shared Human Experience* is to provide a context in which the distinctive responses of religious adherents to central questions of belief and value (explored by means of the same themes but with content chosen from *Traditional Belief Systems*) can be seen to relate to issues and experiences which are those of all human beings, including the pupils.

Thus, one approach would be to use content from *Shared Human Experience* to explore the vertical theme of 'Living in the Family' (ie, *growing together in the family, celebrating together in the family, learning together in the family, acting together in the family, believing together in the family*) as a preparation for exploring the same vertical theme but with content drawn from one, two or three religious traditions. Another would be to follow the same pattern but to do so unit by unit (ie, *growing in the family* followed by *Muslims / Hindus / Sikhs growing in their families; celebrating in the family* followed by *Muslims / Hindus / Sikhs celebrating in their families,* etc, etc). A third approach would be to combine content from *Shared Human Experience* and *Traditional Belief Systems* within each unit of a single vertical theme. Exactly the same possibilities apply to themes which are explored horizontally. Those who are familiar with my earlier advocacy of combining the *Existential Approach* with the *Dimensional Approach* in order to enable pupils to build conceptual bridges between their own experiences and what they recognise to be the central concepts of religion will recognise that what I am now proposing is a variant of this. Indeed, as some of the curriculum units that are included in Part Two indicate, I continue to see value in using these two complementary approaches within the structure I am now advocating.

Thus a typical example of a horizontal theme exploring 'Acting Together' with content drawn from *Shared Human Experience* might be as follows:

1. *Acting together in the family*
   Should a family have 'rules' about what members of that family can and can't do? Who decides on the rules? What sort of rules might they be? Would they need to be written down and put up somewhere in the house? How else might the family know about the rules? What would happen if someone broke the rules? What would happen if the parents were the ones who never kept the rules? Where do rules about human conduct come from? How do you know what is 'good' behaviour and what is 'bad' behaviour?

2. *Acting together in the local community*
   Make a list of all the different groups pupils have chosen to belong to in the local community (eg, sport clubs, uniformed organisations, youth clubs, faith communities, etc). Consider what 'rules' exist within these groups. Do people act differently when they are with members of one group from how they act when they are with members of another group (including their family group)? Imagine a situation when loyalties to one group might conflict with loyalties to another (eg, there is a clash of dates between attending a family celebration and playing for a team in an important match). How might such conflicts be resolved? Consider ways in which being a member of a group changes people? What makes people change?

3. *Acting together in the plural society*
   Make a list of all the things which people living in a plural society share (eg, social, environmental, health, and educational services; access to public amenities, etc), and all the things they have in common (eg, need for a reasonable standard of living, need to be respected by others, need for relationships with others, etc). Consider if everyone in society has equal opportunities for meeting their needs. Is it important that they do? Why? What responsibilities do all members of a society have for each other? Why do they have these responsibilities? How might a society encourage its members to take these responsibilities seriously? What issues currently 'divide' members of our society?

4. *Acting together in the world-wide community*
   Consider the same sort of issues raised above but within a world-wide context. What responsibilities, for example, do richer nations have for the welfare of poorer nations? Compare and contrast the effects of self-interest in the family and upon members of the family, with the effects of self-interest in the nation and upon members of the nation (and *vice-versa*). What issues currently divide nations and influence how they respond to each other's needs?

Examples of vertical themes with content drawn from *Shared Human Experience* are given in Part Two. The exploration of content drawn from *Shared Human Experience*, however, takes place within what I have called *'The Adolescent Life-World Curriculum'* which parallels *'The Religious Life-World Curriculum'* in so far as it also uses the eight *Core Values Criteria* that resulted from conflating *Core Values* and *Substantive Religious Categories* but this time used for identifying 'Ultimate Questions' and 'Belief/Value Issues' arising from reflecting on *Shared Human Experience*. Detailed outworkings of 20 units of content of *'The Adolescent Life-World Curriculum'*, using the spiral curriculum matrix, are provided in Part Two—these having relevance to work undertaken in any of the five religions included within *'The Religious Life-World Curriculum'*.

(c) The connections between *Shared Human Experience* and *'The Adolescent Life-World Curriculum'*

In Chapter Three (section 5 (iv)) I suggested that 'ultimate questions' which arise from reflection on *Shared Human Experience* problematise our conceptions of meaning and perform the critical function of turning our attention on what we known as well as on what we don't know, on what we believe as well as on what we don't believe, on what we value as well as on what we don't value. In this respect I suggested that 'ultimate questions' are 'consciousness-expanding' and 'self-disclosing' questions. Subsequently I have suggested that an important outcome of studying religions is the stimulus this provides for pupils to look critically at their own beliefs and values as a basis for formulating their own 'ultimate questions' about personal meaning. In order for this to occur, however, it is essential that the curriculum encourages religions to be studied in such a way as to juxtapose their 'content' with the 'content' of the pupils' own life-worlds. In this book I have used the notion of *learning from* religion to encompass this kind of learning and to designate a methodology which is essentially evaluative. (I discussed this in some detail earlier in this chapter in section 3 (ii)(c), pages 224–226). As the term 'learning from religion' implies, this methodology has particular application to *'The Religious Life-World Curriculum'*.

Although I have taken pains to indicate why the beliefs and values of the pupils cannot be regarded as 'curriculum content' or part of religious education's field of enquiry, this does not mean that the design of the curriculum should not be informed by any reference to the pupils' life-worlds. On the contrary, if studying religions is to stimulate the sort of personal interaction between the pupil and what he or she is studying that issues in self-knowledge, it is vital that the curriculum is designed to facilitate this kind of learning. (It is in their neglect of this

249

that many contemporary curricula and syllabii in religious education are educationally deficient). In the case of studying religions—as we saw in our discussion of Hardy's views in Chapter Five—there are particular dangers in *not* differentiating between the beliefs and values which constitute the 'content' of those religions and the beliefs and values of the pupils themselves. In the case of exploring *Shared Human Experience*, these dangers no longer exist. By definition, to explore 'shared' human experience is to explore that which all human beings share or have in common. While it is certainly possible for the great recurrent themes enshrined within *Shared Human Experience* and the 'ultimate questions' which they raise for human beings to be explored 'impersonally'—ie, 'What is "man?"' rather than 'Who am I?'—it would be unnecessarily perverse to insist upon this if the learning outcome of such exploration is intended to be the development of 'self-knowledge'. Besides, if, as I have argued, the curriculum should relate to the pupils' own feelings, acts, experiences, needs and questions in such a way as to encourage the expression of opinions on the part of pupils and reflection on their own beliefs and values, placing the exploration of *Shared Human Experience* within the context of their own life-worlds is an obvious way of facilitating this.

What emerges from these deliberations, therefore, is a religious education curriculum made up of two distinct but intersecting curricula, viz: *'The Religious Life-World Curriculum'* and *'The Adolescent Life-World Curriculum'*. There are several different ways in which these may be related to each other. For example, the exploration of content from each curriculum can proceed in parallel—thus a unit of work drawn from 'The Religious Life-World Curriculum' can be paralleled by a unit of work from 'The Adolescent Life-World Curriculum'; alternatively a unit of work from 'The Adolescent Life-World Curriculum' can be undertaken as preparatory to a unit of work from 'The Religious Life-World Curriculum', and *vice-versa*. Whatever the ways chosen, the points at which interaction between the two curricula will be most obvious will be when the methodology of *learning from* religion is actively pursued in terms of personal evaluation of the beliefs and values encountered in the course of study. In Part Two I have provided a number of examples of how this might issue in practice.

(ii) Devising learning experiences

As the diagram given as Figure Four indicates, there is a very close relationship between devising learning situations and choosing methods of teaching. It is, however, essential that learning situations are determined first by reference to the intention with which certain content is to be introduced (ie, because of its value in illuminating certain religious concepts, promoting sensitivity to central issues of belief and value, encouraging pupils to reflect on their own experience, and so on), and second by reference to their capacity to promote the sort of interactive learning that is characteristic of what I have called *learning about* and *learning from* religion. While I accept that a 'method of teaching' is implicit in the latter, 'methods' of teaching, in popular parlance, relate to the use of particular devices—such as showing a video, initiating a role-play, using an artefact, encouraging pupils to work in groups to produce a component of, for example, a collage or a class newspaper— to promote learning. In my view, the decision to employ one or more of these 'devices' must follow from these prior considerations, namely because the 'devices' are then used as the particularly appropriate means of promoting effective learning of this type.

A difficulty of discussing how to devise learning situations arises from the fact that each learning situation is specific to the intentions that underlie the introduction and exploration of a given piece of content. For this reason I intend, at this point, to refer only to certain general principles which should inform decisions about learning situations and rely on the examples given in Part Two of this book to show how these might issue in practice. The few illustrations I have already offered of possible 'content' for themes may have given the impression that I am limiting learning situations to teachers asking questions and initiating discussion of their own questions. This is far from my intention and reflects only the limitations that are placed upon illustration in a book concerned with detailed consideration of a subject's theoretical underpinning. For example, a learning situation appropriate to the theme exploring 'Acting together', given earlier in section 4 (i)(b), would be the use of a number of short 'case-studies' of families in which the issues of 'rules' and relationships were presented through different situations. Some of these situations could be provided through the use of 'cartoon-style' stories from popular teenage magazines, short playlets (including dramatised incidents taken from television and radio broadcasts to schools), extracts from novels (including those depicting family life in other eras and cultures), and even by reference to happenings in popular television 'soap operas' such as *Coronation Street*, *East Enders* and *Dallas*. Additionally, the subject lends itself to exploration through role-play and/or the creation of fictitious families each facing particular issues which expose them to reflection on questions about family and societal values. Through the use of such 'devices' one would seek to engage pupils imaginatively in situations which would encourage them to raise their own questions and express their own opinions about such values.

The following general principles might be used to guide choices made about learning situations:

1. When dealing with explicitly religious content, seek to balance a study of (a) the external forms and inner logic of religion with (b) a study of the different ways in which religious adherents make their religion personally significant (ie, a study of the individual's 'religious life-world'). This will involve achieving a balance between:

(a)	(b)
Objectivity	Subjectivity
Formal knowledge	Personal knowledge
Impersonal past	Personal past
Cultural history	Personal history
Community values	Personal values
'Signals'	'Testimony'

2. Recognise the value of ensuring that content drawn from the religions is illustrative of the different 'dimensions' of religion: ie, experiential, ritual, mythological, social, ethical and doctrinal.

3. Ensure that the exploration of content both from *Shared Human Experience* and *Traditional Belief Systems* encourages pupils to employ their intuition, reason, sense experience and feelings in the pursuit of understanding, not just their intellects.

4. Encourage pupils to *ask* questions *about* the content they are studying rather than to *answer* questions *on* the content.

5. Employ a variety of learning situations and recognise the importance of varying the pace of learning by frequent changes of activity.

(iii) Evaluating pupils' learning

There has always been controversy attached to the evaluation of pupils' learning in religious education. For example, in the early days of the CSE, much of this arose from examination boards using assessment procedures which failed to distinguish between testing the pupils' knowledge of religion and their ability to give essentially 'Christian' answers to 'Christian' questions. With the advent of the GCSE and the introduction of national criteria for testing Knowledge, Understanding and Evaluation ('KUE') such a situation no longer obtains. In this short section, however, I do not intend to replicate what is available elsewhere[30] but to consider briefly the implications the view of religious education I have set out in this chapter has for the evaluation of pupils' learning, especially the evaluation of what they *learn from* religion. It will be apparent from what follows that, like the evaluation of religious belief itself, a considerable amount of work remains to be done before an adequate procedure for testing learning in this subject is devised.

The view of religious education that I am presenting does not preclude the use of 'objective testing' procedures to evaluate what pupils *learn about* religion. It is important, however, that such tests that are used for this purpose take account of the wider concerns I have identified for the subject. Within the area of learning characterised by the term 'learning about' I have included an awareness of fundamental questions of belief and value common to all human beings, understanding of the shaping influence of belief and value on human development, recognition of the necessity of making 'faith responses' as a component of human meaning-making, appreciation of *Human Givens* and *Core Values* and their relationship, and an understanding of the interpretative processes to which these are subjected (and through which they are expressed) so that they issue in specific codes of belief and conduct. Additionally, I have included a knowledge of the particular beliefs and values which are enshrined within *Traditional Belief Systems* and an understanding of the shaping influence that these, and the practices derived from them, exert on the way in which religious adherents respond to *Shared Human Experience* and give it meaning. I am under no illusion that what I am proposing is demanding of both pupils and teachers—but that would be true of any educational enterprise which seeks to promote *understanding* rather than merely provide information.

But the view of religious education I am presenting goes beyond promoting understanding of what is listed above; it seeks to promote *self-understanding*. Certainly it harnesses the development of *personal knowledge* with the development of *impersonal* or *formal knowledge* and in so doing it appears to concur with assumptions that have long been held by educationists, namely that *personal development* occurs as a result of being initiated into *public* modes of understanding and awareness. But it also goes beyond these assumptions. It seeks to build into the process of initiating pupils into public forms of understanding, learning strategies which are designed to create forms of interaction between the pupils and what they are studying which deliberately relate the content of study to the development of their self-understanding. If developing what I have called 'abilities in pure religion' is demanding, developing 'abilities in applied religion' is even more so. But without the latter, of what value is the former?

While I am sympathetic to a view often expressed by religious education teachers, that the effects of good religious education may only be seen very much later in a person's life, I must be sceptical of its assumption that this precludes the evaluation of what a pupil is learning from religion while he or she is at school. One can certainly test the abilities (or otherwise) of pupils to apply their understanding of religious beliefs and values to everyday issues and experiences. All this involves is devising situations which present a human dilemma and asking pupils to use their knowledge of the teachings of different religions to indicate possible courses of action. Some of the tests Kohlberg has used to assess moral judgment are readily adapted to this purpose. But this, of course, does not necessarily show that pupils consciously apply religious insights to an understanding of those personal situations in their everyday lives through which they are confronted by the need to choose.

If there is a way forward—and it is applicable to evaluating both what pupils *learn about* and *learn from* religion—it may be found in the use of 'profiling' in religious education. Although 'profiling' has been in use in schools for some time, there is little evidence yet of its widespread use in religious education. The use of pupil profiles does not, of course, take the place of objective testing but provides a most valuable picture of many other facets of the pupils' learning than that which can be tested by this means. The profile also, for example, can extend to the pupils' behaviour in class, their responses to specific situations and circumstances arising in class, their initiation of discussion with the teacher, and so on. Particularly valuable to the evaluation of the pupils' learning in religious education is the profile which accommodates the pupils' own written or spoken comments about the work they are undertaking and their response to it. Such comments often provide clear indication of what pupils have found personally illuminating and helpful—and, of course, what they have not.

It is because 'profiling' allows for the regular assessment of the *individual* pupil's progress that it is especially relevant to the evaluation of the development of abilities in applied religion and of self-understanding. By its very nature, the development of self-knowledge is unique to each individual. Although all good teachers constantly monitor the development of their pupils from the many cues that are provided through conversation, behaviour and work, unless they are using a profile it is rare for these cues to be brought together into a more elaborate and comprehensive evaluation. Additionally, if religious education is to further the sort of concerns I have been discussing in this chapter, it is crucial that effective means are found which enable teachers to assess the effectiveness of their teaching. Again I suggest that 'profiling' has considerable benefits in this respect.

Conclusion

In this chapter I have presented an educational rationale and curriculum proposals for religious education which, I believe, enable the study of religions to conform to educational principles and contribute to the pupil's personal development while preserving the integrity of those religions which are its object of study. In doing so I have attempted to address the two questions Peters has raised about the need for criteria to determine that someone is developing as a person as well as academically, and how these two different forms of development relate to each other. Additionally, I hope I have provided teachers of religious education with grounds for arguing that their subject has an important contribution to make to the personal, social and moral education of young people, and for assessing the value or otherwise of religious education becoming part of a wider curriculum enterprise with this as its goal.

Following a brief Postscript in which I consider two particular issues which arise from this rationale, Part Two of this book is devoted entirely to illustrations of religious education curricula which are the outcome of applying the process of curriculum decision-making discussed in this chapter. The following diagram (Figure Ten, overleaf) provides a summary of this process and indicates how 'personal learning outcomes' are related to the religious education curriculum and how the curriculum is related to religious education's field of enquiry.

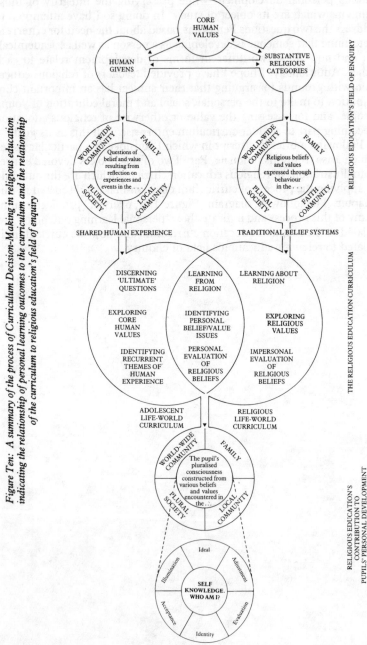

Figure Ten: A summary of the process of Curriculum Decision-Making in religious education indicating the relationship of personal learning outcomes to the curriculum and the relationship of the curriculum to religious education's field of enquiry

CORE HUMAN VALUES

HUMAN GIVENS

SUBSTANTIVE RELIGIOUS CATEGORIES

WORLD-WIDE COMMUNITY

FAMILY

Questions of belief and value resulting from reflection on experiences and events in the . . .

PLURAL SOCIETY

LOCAL COMMUNITY

WORLD-WIDE COMMUNITY

FAMILY

Religious beliefs and values expressed through behaviour in the . . .

PLURAL SOCIETY

FAITH COMMUNITY

RELIGIOUS EDUCATION'S FIELD OF ENQUIRY

SHARED HUMAN EXPERIENCE

TRADITIONAL BELIEF SYSTEMS

DISCERNING 'ULTIMATE' QUESTIONS

LEARNING FROM RELIGION

LEARNING ABOUT RELIGION

EXPLORING CORE HUMAN VALUES

IDENTIFYING PERSONAL BELIEF/VALUE ISSUES

EXPLORING RELIGIOUS VALUES

IDENTIFYING RECURRENT THEMES OF HUMAN EXPERIENCE

PERSONAL EVALUATION OF RELIGIOUS BELIEFS

IMPERSONAL EVALUATION OF RELIGIOUS BELIEFS

THE RELIGIOUS EDUCATION CURRICULUM

ADOLESCENT LIFE-WORLD CURRICULUM

RELIGIOUS LIFE-WORLD CURRICULUM

WORLD-WIDE COMMUNITY

FAMILY

The pupil's pluralised consciousness constructed from various beliefs and values encountered in the . . .

PLURAL SOCIETY

LOCAL COMMUNITY

RELIGIOUS EDUCATION'S CONTRIBUTION TO PUPILS' PERSONAL DEVELOPMENT

Ideal

Adjustment

Illumination

SELF KNOWLEDGE. WHO AM I?

Evaluation

Acceptance

Identity

PERSONAL LEARNING OUTCOMES

Postscript

1. The relationship of religion to education: why not a theological rationale?

The framework for curriculum planning and development in religious education which I have presented in the last chapter is, of course, rooted in the theoretical rationale I have been exploring throughout this book—namely, one derived from an application of the theory that reality and human consciousness are socially constructed to an understanding of the process of humanisation and the contribution beliefs and believing make to that process. Consistent with my view, which I expressed in Chapter One, that we should examine the value assumptions underpinning our understanding of education and the curriculum, I now stress that this theoretical rationale reflects the *ideological framework* within which I have tried to bring my views of *Knowledge, Values* and *The Child* into a dialectical relationship which permits them to be mutually informing and, I hope, provides a coherent basis for the conceptions of education and of religious education that I have presented. Any alternative conceptions of education and religious education which may be offered by those who are not convinced by the theoretical rationale which I have suggested for enabling the study of religions to contribute to the personal development of pupils, will, of course, be equally expressive of alternative ideological frameworks and alternative value assumptions. In other words, there is no possibility of a rationale for religious education being proposed which is ideology and value-free.

But, it may be objected, if this is the case, why have I not chosen to propose a *theological* rationale for religious education rather than a humanistic one? Is not a theological rationale not only sufficient but necessary in the case of 'religious' education? It is certainly the case that I have devoted less attention to 'theology' in this book than to the disciplines of education, but there are good reasons for this. I will attempt to summarise these, although I recognise that to do justice to this important issue would require a much fuller answer than what follows.[1]

First of all we need to be clear about what is at issue. The problem is put succinctly by Hull when he distinguishes five kinds of possible connections between theology (in his case, 'Christian' theology) and education:

1. *Theology might be both necessary and sufficient for an understanding of education.*

2. *Theology might provide a necessary but not a sufficient understanding of education. Theology might, in this case, need assistance from philosophy or psychology.*

3. *Theology might provide a sufficient but not a necessary understanding of education. Other belief systems, including non-religious ones, might also be able to offer sufficient accounts of education.*

4. *Theology might provide a possible and legitimate understanding of education, but one which is neither sufficient nor necessary.*

5. *Theology might be impossible and illegitimate as a way of understanding education. It would have no contribution to offer.*[2]

Here Hull is considering the problem of the connection between theology and educational theory; and clearly how the problem is resolved will be reflected in the sort of educational rationale that is proposed for religious education, and also for the rest of the curriculum. Let me now attempt to pose the problem in a different way.

Despite their title, 'religious' educators are essentially 'secular' educators concerned with the educational value of studying religion and religions. They are 'secular' educators in so far as the educational principles which govern their activities are, in the first instance, those governing the activities of all educators, irrespective of their subject disciplines. This is the case even if theological insights have been used, alongside insights from disciplines such as philosophy, sociology, psychology, etc, in identifying these activities. Such principles relate to the manner in which subject disciplines, including religion, should be investigated—in a manner which assists the development of cognitive perspective or rationality, promotes understanding of the structure and procedures of the disciplines, recognises the integrity, autonomy and voluntariness of the pupil, and so on. Like all secular educators, therefore, religious educators engage in education as their *first-order activity*; their prime commitment is to the achievement of educational goals by way of a process which conforms to general educational principles.

This means that irrespective of whatever *intrinsic* worth may be claimed for religion by religious adherents, religious educators are concerned with religion's *instrumental* worth—with the contribution which the *study* of religion can make to the achievement of educational goals. Thus, in order to provide *education in religion* religious educators are constrained to offer an estimate of religion which is compatible with their commitment to education as their *first-order activity*.[3] Such an estimate may be that religion is a 'form of knowledge', a 'social phenomenon', a 'belief system' or a 'stance for living'. This estimate is invariably different from, and at variance with, the estimate religious adherents have of their own religion because their *first-order activity* is to acknowledge the Truth expressed through their religion and to seek a deeper knowledge of Truth by increasing their awareness of God and their own dependence upon Him. Theologians attempt to explicate the Truth as revealed in a religion and to relate it to the human world of experience. This is the *first-order activity* of theologians.

If, then, we seek to bring education and religion together in some form of relationship, what are the possible combinations open to us? Firstly, we can subordinate the educational enterprise to the religious one by saying that the *first-order activity* of religious educators is not to engage in education in religion but, for example, to increase pupils' awareness and knowledge of the will of Allah as revealed in the Qur'an. The fact that I have specified a particular religion is significant. All religious nurture is specific to a particular religion: it is *Christian* nurture, *Jewish* nurture or nurture in *Islam*. So subordinating the educational enterprise to a religious one also means restricting the enterprise to one faith because children cannot be nurtured in more than one faith.

A second combination which is open to us is really only an extension of the first. We can subordinate the disciplines of education (ie, philosophy, history, sociology, psychology, etc,) to the discipline of theology. The history of Western thought is full of examples of what might be called 'Christian imperialism', which stems from the belief that all human knowledge is incomplete, partial and even in error until it is grounded in the Truth of the Christian revelation.[4] (Islam offers a parallel view in relation to the Truth of Allah's revelation.) On this view, none of the disciplines is autonomous; all must accommodate themselves or be accommodated to the Christian revelation. If we apply this view to the curriculum we are required to argue that none of the school subjects is complete without being grounded in the Christian interpretation of human experience. (We should note that this is a different view from that which leads to the argument that the curriculum is incomplete without the inclusion of the opportunity to study religion.) The products of such a view might be 'Christian Geography', 'Christian Social Studies', 'Christian Chemistry', which is clearly a nonsense, although the equivalent view in Islam is one which is seriously held by Muslims. Alternatively, as was the case as recently as the 1960s, the curriculum could be saved, at best from incompleteness, and at worst from heresy, by casting religious education in the role of the provider of a Christian interpretation of experience. In seeking to subordinate religious education to Christian or Islamic theology we should, therefore, logically, do the same to all other subjects, and, of course, to education itself. Is this really an acceptable view of the nature and purpose of education and religious education in our contemporary society?

The third combination is one in which theology is understood as offering, alongside the other disciplines of education, its own particular perspective on the concept of education but not providing the only way of understanding that concept nor providing the only basis for it. This means including the 'theology of education' among the other disciplines of education. This is a very different proposition from allowing theology to act imperialistically; it is to recognise that theological concepts (like, for example, 'transcendence') have value when placed alongside philosophical, psychological and sociological concepts in assisting us with the task of explicating the nature and purpose of education, just as they have value in assisting us with the task of explicating 'human nature' and the nature of the human condition.

The picture which emerges from this third way of combining theology and education is one in which theology may contribute *to* an understanding of education and the human condition (and may even contribute *an* understanding of these) but it cannot prescribe *on its own* how education and the human condition are to be understood. (In terms of Hull's five kinds of possible relations it points to the feasibility of numbers 2, 3 and 4.) It follows, therefore, that we cannot choose a *theological* rationale for religious education claiming that it alone legitimises religious education's place in the curriculum and still claim that religious educators engage in *education in religion* as their *first-order activity*. To do this would remove religious education from the educational enterprise and the rest of the curriculum and place it within the context of the religious enterprise directed towards nurture in a specific faith.

While theology, therefore, cannot provide a *sufficient* understanding of religious education, in the rationale I have proposed in this book, it does make a *necessary* contribution in providing for the elucidation of *Substantive Religious Categories* which permit the differentiation of 'religious beliefs' and 'religious values' within human beliefs and values. In this respect theology contributes to the rationale alongside other disciplines, and by combining them through what are seen to be their common 'interpretative' and 'humanising' concerns, the integrity of both is preserved, thus enabling religious educators to enagage in education in religion as their *first-order activity*. It would, however, be possible and legitimate for theology to provide the rationale I have offered with a *theological underpinning*—although this would be neither necessary to the rationale nor sufficient for it. For example, Christian theology might offer such an underpinning by providing an 'Incarnational Theology of Humanisation'. It is, perhaps, worth noting that Lehmann, the Christian theologian, speaks of the Incarnation as *'the humanisation of God for the sake of the humanisation of man'*.[5] Other 'theologies of humanisation' are implicit in non-Christian religions: indeed, as I hope I have shown, all religions provide a view of the human and a vision of the goal to which human beings should aspire. In this sense their disagreement is likely to be less with the concept than with its implications for how human beings should respond to it. The development of such theological underpinnings, although unnecessary for religious education's educational legitimation, would, perhaps, enable religious adherents, including teachers, who are disconcerted by the humanistic character of the rationale I have put forward, to be confident that the basis it provides for studying their religion does not assail its integrity.

2. The relationship of 'RE' to 'PSME': what of the present and the future?

There is a growing practice of introducing courses in the upper years of the secondary school (ie, years four and five) which are designed to promote pupils' personal and social development. There is no universal pattern for such courses, the terms 'Personal and Social Education' ('PSE') or 'Personal, Social and Moral Education' ('PSME') being used to designate an area which includes, for example, careers education, citizenship, community studies, religious studies, consumer education, education for parenthood and family life, health education, industrial education and work experience, mass media and leisure, moral education, political education, the social impact of science and technology, economic education, social and life skills, information technology, microelectronic education, and study skills. Such courses, usually of 'modular' design, are primarily concerned with the application of knowledge and are, therefore, 'skill-centred'.

This development has resulted in a number of outcomes, most of which are unfavourable to religious education. For example, although a new breed of 'specialist' teachers of PSME is slowly emerging, my own observation of schools leads me to the view that this new 'subject' draws on teachers of many different subjects who generally offer their services (or whose services are offered) for a few periods a week. The arrangement has many similarities with the situation so familiar in religious education where odd bits of the curriculum are 'farmed out' (to use a popular, teacher's expression) to anyone who is willing and available to 'teach' them. Where this differs from religious education is in the number of periods given to PSME—a whole morning or afternoon, or four periods a week, not being unknown as a time allocation—whereas, traditionally, 'general' religious education has rarely been given more than one single period per week. The effect of this policy is to draw religious education within the PSME structure, and this is even more obviously the case when only one or two periods a week are allocated to PSME— these periods, almost invariably, being achieved by discontinuing 'general' religious education in the fourth and fifth years. The effect of this policy is actually to make religious education teachers into teachers of PSME, because if religious education is removed from the fourth and fifth-form curriculum, what is the religious education teacher to teach? Furthermore, the effect is also to reduce the need for religious education teachers. For example, if they are not used within PSME courses in these years (indicating, therefore, that, where this is the case, PSME does not include the study of religious beliefs and values), they have more time available to teach lower school religious education, thus obviating the need for the appointment, perhaps, of a second or third specialist teacher of religious education. Certainly there are clear indications that in schools where PSME courses have been established, there is a tendency not to replace second or third religious education teachers when they leave.

From these brief observations it should be apparent that the coming of PSME has meant the demise of religious education in the upper years of many secondary schools. Indeed, it is not uncommon to encounter the view among teachers and in the media that 'RE' has been replaced by 'PSME'. This is, in fact, literally the case in many schools where PSME has not only taken over RE's time allocation but has replaced religious education with courses which provide no opportunity for the exploration of religious issues or even of matters to which an understanding of religion has any relevance. The situation in schools is now beginning to be paralleled in some local education authorities where advisers in PSME are being appointed who have no specialist expertise in religious education but who are being required to include religious education within their advisory role. None of these 'developments' can be seen as having anything but a deleterious effect on religious education—on its status as a curriculum subject, on its efficacy within the curriculum, and as a viable subject in which teachers may specialise and through which they may look forward to a worthwhile professional career.

It is, I think, important that we set these observations against the background out of which these developments have occurred. Although there will be notable exceptions, 'general' religious education in the fourth and fifth years has rarely been an unqualified success.[6] With every good will and intention, religious education teachers have been prone to 'sell out' their subject themselves—usually in the cause of 'relevancy'. Thus we have witnessed the practice of devoting much of the religious education time in these years to vague 'discussion' usually of such issues as 'personal relationships', sex, drugs, violence, etc—literally the 'problem-centred' curriculum—often without any direct reference to religion or religious beliefs and values. Such courses have been devised with the personal and social education of pupils in mind, and in all but name they have approximated to what is now included within PSME. What this practice has indicated is our confusion about the educational relevance of the study of religions. We have recognised that religious education *should* make a contribution to pupils' personal, social and moral development but we have, intuitively perhaps, also recognised that teaching about religions seems to fail to connect with this concern. Rather than pursue the issue carefully we have all too often taken the easy way out—by abandoning the 'R' in 'RE' and aligning ourselves uneasily with social education. We really have no strong grounds on which to protest if new developments have now merely regularised or formalised what we have been doing under a different title—and not doing as well as it is now being done in PSME.

So what of the future? In this book I have tried to show that the study of religions has a very important contribution to make to pupils' personal, social and moral education and to suggest how this contribution can be realised through the formal curriculum. Throughout, however, I have been looking at this contribution from the point of view of religious education being a separate curriculum subject, having its own time allocation throughout the secondary school. An important feature of my analysis is its recognition that developing 'abilities in applied religion' is dependent upon pupils also developing 'abilities in pure religion'. For pupils to be helped to acquire both types of abilities it is essential that they continue with the study of religions throughout the entire span of their secondary education: indeed it is when they begin to mature and become more reflective in their late teens that the process of *learning from* religion is best able to function as a powerful means of contributing to young people's conscious involvement in personal decision-making. To relegate this to a mere module in a PSME course (granted by grace and favour) is to limit the educational potential of the study of religions to a point where it can have only minimal effect upon pupils' personal, social and moral development, and even less on their religious and spiritual development. But, while pressing strongly for the retention of religious education's separate identity, we can also seek to influence the nature, content and approach of PSME courses. If, as appears to be the case, religious education teachers are being expected to contribute to such courses, we should take every opportunity to initiate debate about the value-assumptions that underlie these courses, especially those which seem to imply that the study of 'content' is subservient to 'process', that the development of the pupils' 'self-esteem' is paramount (irrespective of the unexamined values and beliefs which underlie it), that 'teachers' should not 'teach' or prescribe content for study but establish 'contracts' with their pupils to undertake self-directed or 'active' learning in areas of their own choosing, and so on.

As I have indicated, the rationale for religious education that I have tried to set out in this book has application to the curriculum as a whole. Education for humanisation recognises that 'mind' must finally be understood as a product of initiation into public traditions and academic disciplines and allows the disciplines, including 'religion', to occupy a central place in the curriculum. But education for humanisation does not permit understanding the inner logic of the disciplines to be the only criterion by which the development of the individual (or the person) is determined and assessed. Subject specialists have a wider responsibility to their pupils than to teach them subjects; they are also required to teach them to understand *why* those subjects are important and *how* they enable individuals to perceive their own experiences differently. It is in enabling pupils to reconstruct their present perceptions of the world, of themselves and of others—by the application of the different perspectives offered by the aesthetic, the ethical, the scientific, the historical, the spiritual, etc—that each subject may claim to make a distinctive contribution to their education. In this book I have tried to show how religious education enables them to do this through the study of religions. It is the responsibility of others to show how this can be done through the other subjects of the curriculum. Given such an analysis, I believe we would be in a better position to devise a total curriculum in which each subject is able to take responsibility for a defined area in the pupils' development and to build on the work of others in doing so. It would also, I believe, enable a more informed and constructive approach to be adopted towards issues of integration, not least in identifying those elements which should be regarded as the essential constituents of any course which purports to further pupils' personal, social and moral education.

PART TWO

Curriculum illustrations

Curriculum
illustrations

Introduction

What follows are not prescriptions for the religious education curriculum but illustrations of possible curriculum outcomes when the process of curriculum decision-making presented in Part One is applied in religious education. Although I have stressed the importance of using a structure which facilitates both *learning about* and *learning from* the religions which are the objects of study, the structure I have proposed allows for considerable flexibility in practice—as, I hope, the following illustrations will indicate. But first I would like to anticipate a number of questions which anyone wishing to use my proposals may ask.

(a) For what age-range are the proposals intended?

Although the conception of religious education I have presented in this book has implications for how the subject might be taught in primary schools, my main concern has been with the 'adolescent life-world' and with the contribution religious education can make in assisting young people towards a conscious involvement in the investigation and appraisal of their own beliefs and values. I believe, however, that the structure for religious education which I have proposed, including the Spiral Curriculum Matrix, offers a viable means of organising the religious education curriculum throughout the secondary school, that is for pupils from eleven to sixteen.

(b) How does the Spiral Curriculum Matrix provide a structure for five years' work?

The structure offers a 'mix and match' approach to curriculum content.

It is important that this potential is fully exploited in its use. Here again is Figure Nine showing the Matrix:

Figure Nine: A Spiral Curriculum Matrix formed from the application of the four organising categories of Family, Local Community, Plural Society, and World-Wide Community to the five themes of particular significance to human development

Theme:	In the Family:	In the Local Community:	In the Plural Society:	In the World-Wide Community:
Growing together:	1	2	3	4
Celebrating together:	5	6	7	8
Learning together:	9	10	11	12
Acting together:	13	14	15	16
Believing together:	17	18	19	20

It would be possible to envisage each of the *horizontal* themes (ie, five themes each with four units of work) providing the structure for one year's work in religious education: theme one (*growing together*) being used with first-year pupils, theme two (*celebrating together*), with second-year pupils, and so on right up to the fifth year, with theme five (*believing together*) completing the final four units of the matrix. Within such a pattern, content for all the units could be drawn from the 'Adolescent Life-World Curriculum' and the 'Religious Life-World Curriculum' in any combination thought to be appropriate (ie, the 'mix and match' principle).

Similarly, and probably better related to the different levels of maturity represented among first and fifth-year pupils, it would be possible to envisage the first four units of work of each of the *vertical* themes providing the structure for one year's work in religious education from years one to four: theme one for first-year pupils would comprise, therefore, units 1, 5, 9 and 13; theme two for second-year pupils would comprise units 2, 6, 10 and 14, and so on; with the work for year five being provided by the *horizontal* theme, *believing together*, namely units 17, 18, 19 and 20. It is important that these latter units are normally left until the upper secondary school because they focus on the theological ideas which inform the beliefs and practices encountered in the earlier units. However, although this should invariably be the case with these units, it does not follow, for example, that units 1–4 or 2–8 are only suited to younger pupils: any unit may be used with older pupils in any combination.

In the case of using the fifth *horizontal* theme (*believing together*) to explore content drawn from *Traditional Belief Systems*, it is preferable to substitute an alternative means of organising content than that provided by the four organising categories of *Family, Faith Community, Plural Society* and *World-Wide Community*. Although these continue to be the loci in which corporate beliefs are expressed and shaped, the main concern of this theme—that of assisting pupils in identifying and understanding those theological ideas which are distinctive of a particular religious tradition—is better served by using organising categories more obviously attuned to theological than sociological concepts. Such categories also facilitate the comparison of 'comparables' in each of the religious traditions. Thus, in the curriculum examples that follow, I have used as organising categories for units 17, 18, 19 and 20 of 'The Religious Life-World Curriculum' the following categories:

Unit 17: *Christians / Muslims / Sikhs, etc, believing together about God*;

Unit 18: *Christians / Muslims / Sikhs, etc, believing together about revelation*;

Unit 19: *Christians / Muslims / Sikhs, etc, believing together about the world, human society and the Church / Ummah / Panth, etc*;

Unit 20: *Christians / Muslims / Sikhs, etc, believing together about human spiritually and the goals of human spiritual development.*

(c) How do you combine content from 'The Adolescent Life-World Curriculum' with content from 'The Religious Life-World Curriculum'?

Again, the matrix allows for considerable flexibility. Work drawn from 'The Adolescent Life-World Curriculum' for, say, Unit 1, can be undertaken either before or after work drawn from 'The Religious Life-World Curriculum'. It might also be introduced immediately after pupils have *learned about*, for example, *Hindus growing together in the family*, and contribute, therefore, to the process of *learning from* Hindu family life. Alternatively, work on a number of units from 'The Adolescent Life-World Curriculum' could precede work on the same units but with content drawn from 'The Religious Life-World Curriculum'. Teachers using the matrix should feel free to experiment with any combination of the two curricula and to learn from their experience of doing so. What is important, however, is that both curricula are used in ways which are complementary.

(d) Will pupils get bored with working within a limited number of themes?

The matrix and its component themes and the distinction between 'The Adolescent Life-World Curriculum' and 'The Religious Life-World Curriculum' are entirely for the guidance of the teacher in making selections of curriculum content. I have used the nomenclature of *'Growing together in the family'*, *'Learning together in the plural society'*, etc, etc, only in order to reinforce the importance of content being structured to facilitate learning which encompasses personal development. It is not intended, therefore, that this nomenclature should be used in the classroom. For example, in an extended illustration of work from Unit 1 given later, although the content is used to explore the theme *'Growing together in the family'* with particular reference to birth customs, I have entitled the unit of work *'What do you think of babies?'* Although pupils may be conscious of 'the family' as a recurrent motif within their work, or of 'the faith community', or 'the plural society', etc, the actual titles given to the units in the classroom should not be restricted to those used in the matrix. The same is true of horizontal themes. Although an important function of these themes is to highlight the effect of certain fundamental human experiences upon human development, the titles for classroom work do not need to incorporate the nomenclature I have given to these experiences. There may, however, be some advantage in pupils being introduced to the distinction between *learning about* and *learning from* religions. In the illustrations I have deliberately used this distinction to indicate a change in the perspective from which the study of religions takes place—ie, from knowledge and understanding of the religions to the evaluation and application of that knowledge and understanding in terms of one's own personal beliefs and values.

(e) How does the use of this matrix relate (i) to GCSE, and (ii) to PSME courses into which religious education has been integrated?

(i) I believe my curriculum proposals are entirely consistent with the demands of GCSE Religious Studies. As indicated above, *learning about* and *learning from* religion, encompasses Knowledge, Understanding, and Evaluation. Furthermore, the actual content which I have drawn from the *Traditional Belief Systems* largely corresponds with that which is prescribed by most examining boards. Thus, pupils who, in years one to three, have studied work from units 1–12 of the matrix are in a particularly advantageous position to benefit from work on the content prescribed for the GCSE. Furthermore, the content I have suggested for horizontal theme four, *Acting together*, parallels much of the content prescribed by GCSE courses which explore the ethical stances of the world's religions, just as the content I have suggested for horizontal theme five, *Believing together*, explores the fundamental beliefs which are central to an understanding of any of the religions GCSE prescribes for study. So often, however, the educational potential of this content for the pupils' personal development has been overlooked. I have tried to show that it is possible for a serious study of religions to encompass a wider understanding of learning than many examination boards permit.

(ii) Although, as I indicated in the Postscript to Part One of this book, integrated PSME courses can undermine the educational potential of the study of religion, the matrix does offer one solution to this problem. It provides an overarching structure for PSME courses as well as for religious education. Although there must be exceptions, I have been surprised at the lack of structure which many contemporary PSME courses display and by the reluctance of those who are committed to them to articulate with any clarity the conceptual basis upon which these courses rest. Indeed, I am prepared to say that many of the courses I have had an opportunity to examine have amounted to little more than a 'ragbag' of unrelated fragments of social and personal learning, with a marked absence of the moral, the religious and the spiritual. The four organising categories which I have used for the matrix—*The Family, The Local Community, The Plural Society* and *the World-Wide Community*—provide, it seems to me, the obvious contexts within which any forms of personal, social, moral and religious learning can take place. That these contexts are equally fitting to the personal, social, moral *and the religious* education of pupils is an important factor in their providing a workable framework for a PSME course in which religious education is a contributory subject. Furthermore, the concept of education for humanisation which I have developed in this book provides, in my view, a far more compelling rationale for PSME than the ill-conceived and vague notions which underlie many of the current PSME syllabii which, in my experience, fail to address the central problem of 'core' or 'community' and 'personal' values. It is my hope, therefore, that this exploratory study may have some benefit in providing religious education teachers with a basis from which they can influence contemporary developments in PSME and, at the same time, strengthen their position in those circumstances where they are facing a situation of integration.

1. Devising an Adolescent Life-World Curriculum

(i) Using the Core Values Criteria to identify 'Ultimate Questions' which can arise from reflecting upon Shared Human Experience.

Shared Human Experience

Core Values Criteria	'Ultimate Questions' arising from reflecting upon Shared Human Experience
1. Source of order, meaning and purpose in the universe?	Is there order, meaning and purpose? Was it created or did it happen by chance? If it was created, by whom or what and for what purpose? Can we assess the evidence for and against creation or chance? What constitutes 'evidence' for one view or the other?
2. What is truth?	How do we know that something is true? Is it possible for there to be different 'kinds of truth'? How might we test them? To what use might we put them? Are some 'truths' more important than others? What are they? Where do these 'truths' come from? How do we find out about them? Whom do we expect to tell us the truth? From whom or what can we learn truth? What truth or truths can we learn from history? What truth or truths can we learn from other people, past and present? What are the most important questions to which people seek answers? Why are these important questions? Are there some questions for which there will never be answers? Why do people continue to search for answers to them?

3. View of the human:	Are human beings of more value than animals? Why? What is the value of a human being? Are all human beings to be valued equally? Why/Why not? Who is to judge the value of each human being? Are human beings good or evil? What do we mean by a 'good' person? Are some people more evil than good? Are they responsible for being like they are? Does it matter if a person is good or evil? Why/Why not? Can people change? Can people be made to change? Should they? What does it mean to be 'human'?
4. View of a just society:	What do we gain and lose from being members of a society? Do we gain more than we lose? Who decides what a society is like? Who decides what values are important in a society? What values are important? What if individuals disagree with these values? What rights do individuals have to be different from others in a society? Should everyone have the same rights whether they agree or disagree? What about people who are mentally sick or infirm?
5. Individual self-fulfilment:	'It's my life and I can do with it whatever I like': is this true? Are there any beliefs which all human beings hold in common—that they all agree on? What is a 'worthwhile' life? Can everyone achieve a 'worthwhile' life? Why do some people suffer more than others? Does human pain and suffering have any meaning or value?

6. Ethical perspective:	How do people decide what is 'right' and what is 'wrong'? Where do morals and laws come from? What is the point of trying to do what is 'right'? Is 'virtue its own reward'? Why/Why not?
7. View of community:	What is a 'community'? How does it differ from a 'society'? Can anyone be a member of a community, irrespective of sex, ethnic origin, class, age, etc? What is the value to the individual of being a member of a local community? Are there disadvantages of being a member? Should people always be loyal to their community? Do they have obligations to their community that they don't have to people outside it?
8. Core human values:	Are there values which all human beings think are important? What are they? How did these values come about? How do you justify a value?

(ii) *Using the Core Values Criteria to identify 'Belief/Value Issues' within the pupils' life-worlds which relate to the recurrent themes of human experience and the 'Ultimate Questions' they can raise.*

Adolescent Life-World

Core Values Criteria	'Belief/Value Issues within adolescents' life-worlds
1. Source of order, meaning and purpose in the universe?	Is there order, meaning and purpose in my life? Should there be? Why/Why not? Should I decide on goals? How do I decide on them?
2. What is truth?	What is 'authoritative' in my life?

274

To whom do I listen? Whom or what do I trust? What persons, experiences or events in my life are influencing me in what I believe about myself, other people, life, etc?

3. View of the human:	Who values me as a human being? Whom do I value? Do I value everyone equally? What sort of person do I regard as 'good'?—as 'evil'? What sort of person do people think I am?
4. View of a just society:	What sort of society do I want? What values are important in a society? What attitudes should I adopt to people who are different from me?
5. Individual self-fulfilment:	What do I think is worthwhile? What makes me happy/ sad/ anxious? Why? What would I like to do? Why? What would I like to become? Why? How might I begin to achieve what I want to be? What is stopping me?
6. Ethical perspective:	How do I know what is 'right' and what is 'wrong'? Does it matter? Why/Why not?
7. View of community:	What is the value of being a member of a community? What does being a member of different groups do for me? Do I have any responsibility to or for others in my community?
8. Core human values:	What values do I personally think are important? Why? Do I hold these values myself?

(iii) *Applying the four organising categories of Family, Local Community, Plural Society and World-Wide Community to Shared Human Experience.*

Figure Eleven: The phenomena of Shared Human Experience

(iv) Applying the Spiral Curriculum Matrix to content drawn from Shared Human Experience which can encourage pupils to identify 'Belief/ Value Issues' in their own life-worlds.

People

Theme:	In the Family:	In the Local Community:	In the Plural Society:	In the World-Wide Community:
Growing together:	1	2	3	4
Celebrating together:	5	6	7	8
Learning together:	9	10	11	12
Acting together:	13	14	15	16
Believing together:	17	18	19	20

(v) Illustrative content of Units with indications of Core Values and Belief/ Value Issues 'visited' in each unit

Unit 1: People growing together in the Family

Core Values and Belief/Value Issues: 1, 2, 3, 5, 6, 8.

Possessions: Make a list of five possessions which each member of your family would want to save in the event of a fire; explain the reasons they might give for the items on their list; compare the views of the class and see which possessions feature most.

The composition of the family: Discuss the advantages and disadvantages of a single-parent family, a 'nuclear' family, an 'extended' family: why is the family the basic unit of human life?

Adults and children: Why do we call adults 'grown ups'? Does it mean that adults do not continue to grow? Find out from the adults you know, how they have grown since they became an adult. What has been the happiest moment in your life so far? Ask as may people as you can this question and make a note of what they say; see how many of the happiest moments had something to do with being with other people.

Imagine you were shipwrecked alone on a desert island: write down what you would miss most: do you think you would have changed much when you eventually returned home?

Being a family: Make a list of all the things a family could do together which would help them to grow together. Invent a family and make up a short script of a conversation they might have during a meal together. Discuss the occasions when members of a family become more conscious of being a family.

Unit 2: *People growing together in the Local Community*

Core Values and Belief/Value Issues: 3, 4, 5, 6, 7, 8.

Belonging to groups: Make two lists of groups that you belong to—the first list, of all the groups you are a member of without having chosen to be (eg, family, class at school, country, sex, etc); the second list, all the groups you have chosen to become a member of. Now say what you think you gain from being a member of all these different groups. Make a pie graph which shows how much time each day you spend in groups. If you had a choice, with which group would you like to spend most time? Why? Imagine you want to start a new group: what would the group be for and whom would you invite to join it? Would you choose people like yourself, or different? What would you expect members of the group to do? Would you have any rules or special ceremonies or customs in the group? Would you have a membership card or ways of telling someone was a member of the group? Where would you hold your meetings? Would you allow adults or members of your family to join the group? Draw a poster (perhaps with an appropriate symbol for your group) advertising it and telling people what it is for.

The individual and the group: Do you think you are the same person when you are alone as you are when you are with other people? Write a short description of yourself (what you look like, what you like and dislike, what you would like to be, etc): now ask a friend of yours to write a description of how he/she sees you—what he/she thinks you are like: see if the two descriptions match: does it matter if they are different?

Unit 3: *People growing together in the Plural Society*

Core Values and Belief/Value Issues: 3, 4, 7, 8.

A place to live: Some families have lived in the same place for generations, other families have moved about a great deal. What are the advantages and disadvantages of staying in the same place or moving about? If you could choose where to live, where (realistically!) might it be? Occasionally people have to move: imagine that you and your family have had to move to a new block of flats: how would you go about making new friends? What do you think of the idea of going to live abroad? What difficulties might you have in making friends then, and how might you try to overcome them?

Local communities in the plural society: What do people who live in a local community have in common? Can you think of any buildings, places or events which help people to meet each other and also help them to become part of the community?

New communities: Some people leave their homes to start new communities. Find out about the 'Pilgrim Fathers' who left Plymouth in 1620 and sailed in The Mayflower to America to start a new community there. Why did they decide to do this? What difficulties did they have to face? When they arrived, one of their leaders, Pastor John Robinson, told the 102 pilgrims: 'We must swear to stand together. If we separate we shall die.' Do you think he was right? Do you think people coming to live in this country should adopt the same view today?

Unit 4: *People growing together in the World-Wide Community*

Core Values and Belief/Value Issues: 3, 4, 6, 7, 8.

The world as a global village: Before radio and television were invented, people had very little idea about what was happening outside their own community and country. Do you think that was a better situation than now, when we can see things as they happen thousands of miles away? Has television changed our attitudes to people in other countries from those that people in this country had, say, a hundred years ago? Does knowing about people (just like knowing someone well) mean that we have greater responsibility towards them? If you had been born in a different country but with the same parents, do you think you would be any different from what you are now?; have a debate on the motion, 'All people are the same, whatever their nationality'.

Unit 5: *People celebrating together in the Family*

Core Values and Belief/Value Issues: 1, 2, 3, 7, 8.

Celebration: What is a 'celebration'? You can have a 'party' any time and it may be a celebration; but a party is not always a celebration: a celebration recalls a special event, marks a special occasion, is an expression of thankfulness for someone or something we regard as important. Make a list of celebrations a family might have as a family and give reasons for them. Why do human beings feel the need to celebrate, to remember, to recall, to 'commemorate'? Is it possible to have a celebration on your own?

Birthdays and anniversaries: Most people celebrate their birthdays: children and young people's birthdays and those of very old people are often seen as more significant than people in middle age: why is this so? What is the meaning of giving people presents and cards? Why do we say 'Congratulations!' and 'Best Wishes'? How do you feel on your birthday? On wedding anniversaries couples often give each other cards and presents, and relatives might also send cards: cartoons sometimes show one of the couple (usually the husband) forgetting it is their wedding anniversary. Do you think it matters if someone forgets it is their wedding anniversary? Role-play two situations—a young couple talking together about their first wedding anniversary and an old couple talking together about their golden wedding anniversary.

To celebrate or not to celebrate: Some people (eg, Jehovah's Witnesses) do not celebrate their birthday. Why is this so? Which of the following events do you think are worth celebrating every year on their anniversary—the day you won £100,000 on the pools; the day you had your first shave (if you are a boy) or went out wearing make-up (if you are a girl); the day you heard you had passed an important examination; the day you left school or started your first job; the day you earned your first wage? If you don't think any of these are worth celebrating, what events are? Do such events always have to be happy ones?

Unit 6: People celebrating together in the Local Community

Core Values and Belief/Value Issues: 1, 2, 3, 4, 7, 8.

Celebrating outside the family: Most clubs, groups, schools, places of work, organisations, etc, have some sort of celebration during the year, eg, a Christmas party, a New Year party. Why do they do this? What benefits do you think result from such celebrations for the organisations and their members?

New Year celebrations: New Year is celebrated in most cultures (though different New Years at different times; eg, the Chinese New Year is celebrated for fourteen days). Why is this so? Is there anything worthwhile in the custom of making 'New Year Resolutions'? Why did this custom develop and why does it continue? Most people who make resolutions break them very quickly. Why bother to make them? Are human beings capable of actually changing the sort of person they are?

The most popular Christian Saint's Day in Britain: February 14, St Valentine's Day (in fact there were two St Valentines, both Christian martyrs of the third century; the custom of choosing a 'Valentine' is more likely to be connected with the pagan festival of Lupercalia that occurred in Rome around the middle of February). There has been a tremendous increase in the sale of Valentine cards and Valentine messages in the local press in recent years. Look at some of the messages sent in the press. Is it just a bit of fun, or does this day perform an important function in people's relationships with the opposite sex?

The local community celebrates: Can you think of an occasion when the whole community celebrate something they have in common? Is it important that such an occasion is found?

Unit 7: People celebrating together in the Plural Society

Core Values and Belief/Value Issues: 3, 4, 7, 8.

Public holidays: Traditional 'Holy Days' in this country have been transformed into 'Bank and Public Holidays' (eg, Christmas Day and Boxing Day; Good Friday and Easter Monday; Ascension Day). Is this a good arrangement? Increasingly shops are open on all of these days except Christmas Day. Should a public holiday be just the same as any other day except that you don't have to go to school or work? Can these days be called a 'celebration'? Do they help to build up a sense of identity in our plural society? Find out about what happens in the USA on July 4 (Independence Day). What is the nearest equivalent that we have of this celebration?

Christmas as a secular celebration: More non-Christians celebrate Christmas than Christians; but what do they celebrate? *'Christmas means more at Woolworths'*—discuss this television advertising slogan. What does it mean? Why was it chosen? Why do people want to find 'meaning' in Christmas? You often hear people say: *'Christmas is for the children'*. Does this mean that its traditional message of peace and goodwill has no point for adults? If you could change Christmas, what would you change it to?

Celebrating other people's religious festivals: Although some members of faiths other than Christianity send Christmas cards, few people in this country other than members of the faiths join in non-Christian celebrations. Why is this so? How might Hindus, Sikhs, Muslims and Jews make it easier for other people in our society to share in their celebrations? Look in the local evening paper on a Friday or Saturday and see if any of these faiths advertise their services like Christians do. Would it help if they did? Would people go to a Divali, Baisakhi, Eid or Pesach festival if they were invited?

Unit 8: People celebrating together in the World-Wide Community

Core Values and Belief/Value Issues: 3, 4, 6, 7, 8.

Our common humanity: Although the form in which they do it may be different, do people the world over celebrate the same things—eg, significant occasions in their personal and family lives, events in their local communities and national communities, the changing patterns of the yearly cycle, etc? Why is it that some countries have more times of festivity and celebration than others (eg, Spain, Italy, South American countries, Mexico)? Is the human impulse to celebrate influenced by temperament and climate? Are we in this country repressed by these factors? Why have we earned ourselves such a bad reputation for our behaviour at football matches? Many festivals are connected with the idea of 'victory'—over evil, over death, over oppression, etc. Is the only victory we can celebrate a win at football?

People and places: Make a list of all the places that you, personally, feel attached to or enjoy being at: eg, home, your grandmother's house, the local park, the city centre (where?), the youth club, the countryside (where?), a museum, the local football stadium, the baths, etc. If you don't feel attached to anywhere, say so. But if you do, try to say why. Now make a list of all the places you would like to go to anywhere in the world; give reasons for your choices. If you could go anywhere but had to give up everything to do so, would you go? Compare your answers with others in the class and see how many people prefer to stay where they are.

Unit 9: People learning together in the Family

Core Values and Belief/Value Issues: 1, 2, 3, 6, 8.

Family names: Why do you have your name? Ask your parents why they chose your first names. See how many in the class have names which someone else (such as their father, grandmother) has or had in their family. If you have such a name, try to work out if you are like the person after whom you were named. Using a dictionary of names, look up the meaning of your name, what language or culture it is derived from, with whom it is associated, etc. Do you think that by being given someone's name you will grow up like them? Do any of your other names remind you about someone who lived before you?

Family traditions: Imagine a situation where someone of your age was coming to live in your family—perhaps your parents had decided to adopt someone who had been orphaned, or perhaps this person was your cousin. How would you help them to fit into the family? What would they need to know in order to become part of the family rather than an outsider? Would there be any rules to observe or could they do as they liked? How would they spend their evenings and weekends? What would your parents expect them to do around the house?

Family stories: Using the stories about their youth which parents are often fond of telling, write a short account of what it would have been like to have been your mother or father at your age.

Unit 10: People learning together in the Local Community

Core Values and Belief/Value Issues: 1–8.

Knowledge and belief: Divide your life into three parts: birth to five, five to ten, ten onwards. See if you can list five important things that you have learnt in each part of your life so far: eg, obviously to walk and talk will come in the first part; but so too might finding out that people die. Compare your answers and now complete this sentence: '*The most important thing that I know is* . . . .'. Now write down the five most important questions that you personally would like answering. How many of these questions can be answered without having to believe something?

Learning from others: Talk about any book you have read (or a TV programme or film) which made a big impression on you. Try to explain why this was so. Now do the same with a person—someone who has influenced you and whom you admire. Try to say what it is about this person that makes him or her different from other people you have met.

Learning at school: Draw up a list of all the subjects you are studying. Imagine you are the teacher; explain to the class why it is important to study each of these subjects; afterwards agree in the class the order of importance of these subjects in helping you to live your life successfully. Consider what 'success' means.

Learning from the community: There was a time when the idea of 'de-schooling' was popular—going out into the community to learn first-hand from people in it rather than sitting at school. Imagine that you were free to do this. Whom would you go to learn from in your local community? What situations might teach you the most valuable lessons for life?

Unit 11: People learning together in the Plural Society

Core Values and Belief/Value Issues: 3, 4, 7, 8.

Learning from other cultures: Imagine you have been invited to organise a multicultural festival intended to introduce people to different cultural traditions represented in British society. The events will include a dinner for the leaders of local communities, ie, Christians, Hindus, Muslims, Jews and Sikhs, together with a number of Afro-Caribbean leaders; an exhibition of crafts, artwork and artefacts; a fashion display; music, singing and dancing; an exhibition of local commercial and industrial enterprises; an introduction to the different languages spoken; visits to local places of worship; and a religious ceremony to mark the end of the festival. Sharing responsibility for these different items among groups in the class, draw up the programme, decide on the menu for the dinner, list and illustrate the exhibits, choose and listen to some music, find out about dancing and dress, compile a chart with examples of different languages in written form, devise an itinerary of visits to local places of worship, and prepare an order of service for the religious ceremony with appropriate readings, hymns and prayers. Be careful not to introduce or do anything which any member of any of the communities might find offensive or contrary to their religious beliefs.

Unit 12: People learning together in the World-Wide Community

Core Values and Belief/Value Issues: 3, 4, 6, 7, 8.

Education for international understanding: How can the different nations of the world come together to share their knowledge and resources in the cause of greater mutual understanding, peace, co-operation, good-will and a better standard of living for those in need? By what principles and values might it be possible to secure this goal?

The Brandt Report of 1980 states: '*We are convinced of the great role education has to play: a better knowledge of international, and not least North-South, affairs will widen our views and foster concern for the fate of* other nations, even distant ones, and for problems of common interest. The Commission feels that schools all over the world should pay more attention to international problems so that young people will see more clearly the dangers they are facing, their own responsibilities and the opportunities of co-operation—globally and regionally as well as within their own neighbourhood.'

Drawing on the interests of staff, arrange a number of seminars on this theme, exploring the issues which divide nations and identifying the areas of common concern.

Unit 13: People acting together in the Family

Core Values and Belief/Value Issues: 2, 3, 5, 6, 8.

Roles in the family: Discuss the advantages and disadvantages of each of the following family structures: (a) patriarchal hierarchy, (b) matriarchal hierarchy, (c) equal division of authority and responsibility between parents, (d) equal rights for all members of the family, including the children; consider alternative patterns of grouping to that of the traditional family (eg, communes) and identify their advantages and disadvantages.

Rules in the family: Imagine that you are a parent of two teenagers and two younger children. Devise a set of rules which you think would encourage everyone to play their part in the family without causing resentments.

Are relatives family? Discuss the responsibilities the family have towards relatives, especially old and infirm ones.

When things go wrong in the family: More than 400 children a day in this country find themselves members of a family split by divorce or separation. Is it too easy (a) to get married, (b) to have children, (c) to get divorced? How might fewer children be made victims of unhappy marriages? How might marriages be made more successful? Find out about the divorce rate among people who have arranged marriages.

Unit 14: People acting together in the Local Community

Core Values and Belief/Value Issues: 2, 3, 5, 6, 7, 8.

Being one of the crowd: If you are a member of group who go out together a lot, write a short description of everyone in your group and see if you can identify those who have most influence in the group (ie, the group's leader(s)). What is it about them that makes them influential? Imagine a situation when they are not there. Would the group be the same? Would you do the same things? Can a group exist without leadership?

It's my life and I can do what I like with it: Is it true that we 'own' our own lives, or are they 'owned' by other people? Consider the different ways in which we are influenced by other people, including, for instance, newspapers, television, the record industry. Listen to the top ten records and jot down what sort of person the different songs are about or what they suggest is important. Do you agree with their views?

Freedom rules: Which is easier, to live your life by following rules and planning your future, or doing things as the mood takes you? Which do you think may enable you to have most control over the sort of person you become?

People serving the community: Through your teacher, invite a number of people such as a district nurse, a police officer, a probation officer, a home help, someone from the Citizens' Advice Bureau, etc, to come and talk to the class about their jobs and what they think is important about what they do. Ask them what they think of the people they are dealing with.

Unit 15: People acting together in the Plural Society

Core Values and Belief/Value Issues: 2, 3, 5, 6, 7, 8.

What is your opinion?—about wealth and poverty, racism, war and peace, defence, human rights, sexism, sexuality, abortion, contraception, euthanasia, gambling, divorce, animals, conservation, materialism/consumerism.

Unit 16: People acting together in the World-Wide Community

Core Values and Belief/Value Issues: 4, 6, 7, 8.

Live Aid: Why did Bob Geldof succeed where politicians had failed? In what other ways might young people take the initiative to deal with the problems in the world which politicans seem unable to solve?

Unit 17: Ultimate questions of Belief and Value: is there a source of meaning, order and purpose in the universe?

Core Values and Belief/Value Issues: 1, 2, 3.

Finding out about what pupils think (some typical pupil responses).

Important experiences which mean a lot to me: Being part of a family; having good friends; being a member of groups; having independence to make my own choices; enjoying sport, recreation and making things; going on holiday; learning something new; meeting people and talking to them; walking in the countryside; giving and receiving presents, etc.

Things I am looking forward to: Leaving school; starting a job; getting a regular boyfriend/girlfriend; having plenty of money to spend on myself; owning a motorbike or a car; having a flat of my own; being able to do what I want; going on holiday with my boyfriend/girlfriend, etc.

Things that worry me: Doing badly in exams at school; having to stand up and say something in public; falling out with people (especially my parents); going up high buildings; being ignored; getting fat; being assaulted; if there is a war, etc.

What I would like people to say about me: That I'm a good mate; that I know how to have a good time; that I'm attractive and dress nicely; that I tell the truth; that I have a nice body; that I'm good at sport; that I'm fair; that I can be trusted, etc.

What I believe: That rapists should go to jail for life—and I mean life; that older people should retire so we can get jobs; that life isn't fair; that God exists; that God does not exist; that religions cause a lot of trouble; that you can be religious without going to church; that there is a devil, etc.

The universe—by chance or design? I don't know and I don't think anyone else does either; what the Bible says is just a myth; I'd like to believe God is looking after us but there's not much evidence of that when you look at what's happening; evolution isn't a matter of chance but choice: some things seem to work out as if they were planned, but then they go wrong, etc.

Unit 18: Ultimate questions of Belief and Value: what is Truth?

Core Values and Belief/Value Issues: 1, 2, 6.

Who can you trust to tell you the truth? Not the newspaper!; your best friend; everyone sees it their way, so you have to decide for yourself; you can prove some things to be true; your parents; you can look things up in an encyclopaedia; little children—before they've learned to tell lies; it depends what you want to know; people often don't know what to believe, etc.

What is true for you? Some things like it is better to be kind than cruel or to love than to hate; 'beauty is truth, truth is beauty'; obvious things like it's raining, but if you mean something you have to believe then there's no proof; true love, etc.

Unit 19: Ultimate questions of Belief and Value: what is right and what is wrong?

Core Values and Belief/Value Issues: 3, 4, 6, 7.

What is right and what is wrong? Doing things which hurt other people is wrong; murder, stealing, rape are wrong; molesting children is wrong; two-timing your boyfriend/girlfriend is wrong; using nuclear weapons is wrong; gambling is wrong; committing adultery is wrong; mugging is wrong; apartheid is wrong, etc.

How do you know what is right and wrong? You learn it from your parents; from the law; it's obvious that you can't go about killing people; sometimes you don't, that's the problem; your conscience tells you, etc.

Where do ideas of what is good and what is bad come from? The Ten Commandments; religion; civilisation; it's a practical thing—everyone has to live together so there have to be rules; laws just develop as we need them, etc.

Are we born good or bad? A bit of both; babies aren't capable of being bad but they soon learn how to be; everyone is both good and bad, it's just a matter of how well you control yourself; some people are so evil they must have the devil in them; it doesn't matter what you do to some people, they will always be criminals; I think everyone has some good in them, they just need the chance to prove it: etc.

Unit 20: Ultimate questions of Belief and Value: what does it mean to be human?

Core Values and Belief/Value Issues: 1–8.

What does it mean to be human? Getting what you can; having weaknesses and giving in to them; being able to think and speak, build things and plan for the future; making mistakes; wanting the best for yourself and for your family, etc.

Can human beings change? If you mean can they be converted, then yes—some people change overnight; everything changes in time, it just happens and you don't notice; you can control yourself if you want;

some people train themselves to do incredible things; human beings don't like change, they prefer to be like they are; some people are born mentally defective and this doesn't change; even saints find it difficult to change, and they try very hard.

2. Devising a Religious Life-World Curriculum

(A) Christianity: a Christian Life-World Curriculum

(i) Using the Core Values Criteria to identify the 'essential minimum' key-concepts from Christianity

Core Values Criteria	'Essential Minimum' Key Concepts
1. Providential source of order, meaning and purpose in the universe; The Sacred; Source of Revelation and Truth;	God, the Father Almighty, Maker of heaven and earth, Jesus Christ his Son, and the Holy Spirit.
2. Agent or agencies of Revelation; records of Revelation; experience of Revelation;	Jesus of Nazareth, Messiah, Lord and Saviour; God Incarnate; The Christian Bible; The Church; The Holy Spirit;
3. View of the human;	Created in the image of God; Possessing free-will; Fallen and sinful; Loved by God; Redeemed by Christ's sacrifice;
4. View of a just society;	Humans reconciled with God; The Kingdom of God; The Mission of God; The Mission of the Church;

5. Individual self-fulfilment through:	The Grace of God; Redemption through Christ's sacrifice; Faith in Jesus Christ; Belief in the Gospel; Resurrection in Christ; Personal discipleship;
6. Ethical perspective;	Following the teaching and example of Christ (discipleship) and the apostles of Christ;
7. Community of faith;	The Church; The People of God; The Bride of Christ;
8. Spiritual values;	The fruit of the Spirit: love, joy, peace, patience, kindness, goodness, faithfulness, gentleness, self-control. 'Whatsoever is true, honourable, just, pure, lovely, gracious, excellent and worthy of praise.'

(ii) *Applying the four organising categories of Family, Faith Community, Plural Society and World-Wide Community to the phenomena of Christian faith.*

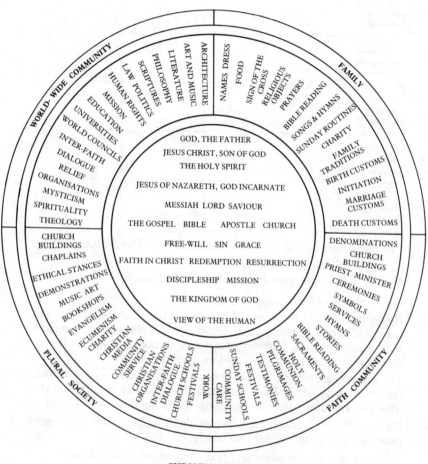

CHRISTIAN FAITH

Figure Twelve: The phenomena of Christian faith

(iii) *Applying the Spiral Curriculum Matrix to content drawn from the phenomena of Christian faith.*

Christians

Theme:	In the Family:	In the Faith Community:	In the Plural Society:	In the World-Wide Community:
Christians growing together:	1	2	3	4
Christians celebrating together:	5	6	7	8
Christians learning together:	9	10	11	12
Christians acting together:	13	14	15	16
Christians believing together:	17	18	19	20

(iv) *Illustrative content of Units with indications of Core Values and Key Concepts 'visited' in each Unit*

Unit 1: Christians growing together in the Family.

Core Values and Key Concepts: 1–8:

Religious objects in the home illustrative of Christian beliefs and practices: eg, cross, crucifix, icon, rosary, palm cross, statues, pictures, holy water (eg, from Lourdes), texts, prayer books, Bible, badges and medals, Christian magazines, posters, records, etc.

The various patterns of Christian family life: eg, actions—grace at meals, family prayers, family Bible readings, giving money to Christian charities, etc; routines—weekday meetings (eg, house group) and Sundays.

Birth customs: christening/baptising/dedicating/naming the baby: thanksgiving by the mother and family. (Or in Unit 5)

Initiation rites: confirmation and first communion. (Or in Unit 5)

Marriage customs: (Or in Unit 5)

Death customs:

Unit 2: Christians growing together in the Faith Community

Core Values and Key Concepts: 2, 4, 6, 7.

The exteriors and interiors of different church buildings: eg, Roman Catholic, Anglican (historic and modern), Nonconformist churches, Quaker Meeting House, Salvation Army Citadel, etc.

Architectural features, furniture and furnishings illustrative of the different emphases within the traditions with regard to Christian belief and practice.

The organisation, use and facilities of church buildings: eg, ritual, social and educational.

The role of the priest, minister, pastor, elders, laity, etc.

What going to church means for Christians.

Unit 3: Christians growing together in the Plural Society

Core Values and Key Concepts: 2, 3, 4, 6, 7, 8.

The different denominations of the Christian Church and some Christian sects; a brief historical survey highlighting their different attitudes to each other and their different responses to cultural pluralism; eg, contrasting views of 'Mission'; differences between 'open' and 'closed' positions, eg, a study of the work of the Church Army, Christadelphian ecclesias, Catholic worker priests, Quakers, Jehovah's Witnesses, etc.

The contribution of Christians to cultural, social and economic life: eg, Christian sponsorship of the arts, neighbourhood schemes concerned with housing, welfare, health, employment, leisure; the involvement of the Church in commerce, industry and financial investment; Christians expressing their faith within secular work; the work of chaplains in hospitals, prisons, industry, etc.

Unit 4: Christians growing together in the World-Wide Community

Core Values and Key Concepts: 1, 2, 4, 6, 7, 8.

Christian ecumenism: The work of the World Council of Churches, Vatican Councils, Anglican Synods, etc.

Centres of Christianity: A study of Rome and Geneva as representing contrasting Christian traditons.

The contribution of Christianity to art, literature and music.

Unit 5: Christians celebrating together in the Family

Core Values and Key Concepts: 1, 2, 3, 5, 8.

Christian family celebrations: eg, birth of baby, confirmation, first communion, wedding or wedding anniversary, etc. (Or in Unit 1)

Family customs associated with Christmas (eg, crib, carol singing, giving presents and sending greeting cards, visits to/from relatives, etc.); Lent (eg, Shrove Tuesday pancakes, giving up something, making a donation to a charity, etc); and Easter (eg, Easter garden, eggs, flowers, greeting cards, etc).

Unit 6: Christians celebrating together in the Faith Community

Core Values and Key Concepts: 1–8.

Different forms of Christian worship: eg, Roman Catholic, Anglican, Eastern Orthodox, Reformed, Pentecostal, Salvation Army, Quaker.

Christian signs and symbols: eg, cross, crucifix, anagrams, liturgical colours, vestments, etc.

Christian Sacraments: Holy Communion in different religious traditions.

Christian Creeds: the Apostles' Creed.

Unit 7: Christians celebrating together in the Plural Society

Core Values and Key Concepts: 1–8.

The Christian liturgical year: Celebration of Christmas, Easter, Ascension and Whitsun.

Local Christian festivals: Commemoration of saints and martyrs (eg, patronal festival of a local church), harvest festivals, industrial festivals.

Christian actions in the local community: eg, well dressing, procession of witness (eg, Holy Week and Corpus Christi processions through the streets), corporate carol and hymn singing in local hospitals, performance of 'mystery plays', Handel's *Messiah*, Stainer's *Crucifixion*, pilgrimages (eg, to Canterbury, Walsingham), etc.

National festivals and occasions (linking Christianity with national life): eg, a royal wedding, Remembrance Day, National Service of Thanksgiving, etc.

Unit 8: Christians celebrating together in the World-Wide Community

Core Values and Key Concepts: 1–8.

Christian celebration in other countries: eg, Holy Week in Spain and Mexico, The Oberammergau Passion Play, celebrating the Assumption of the Blessed Virgin Mary in Brittany, etc.

Places of worldwide Christian pilgrimage: Jerusalem, Lourdes, Canterbury, Rome.

Unit 9: Christians learning together in the Family

Core Values and Key Concepts: 1, 2, 3, 5, 6, 8.

Christians nurturing their children in Christian faith through Bible stories, the lives of the saints, actions (eg, making the sign of the cross), prayers at bedtime, personal example, etc.

Examples of stories and readings from children's Bibles, prayer books and devotional literature; Christian songs and music; Christian videos and records, etc.

Bible-reading schemes for the family and individuals; Christian study groups in the home.

Unit 10: Christians learning together in the Church

Core Values and Key Concepts: 1, 2, 5, 7.

Christian beliefs about God the Father, Jesus Christ and the Holy Spirit as expressed through Scripture, hymns, prayers, the liturgy, actions, sermons, symbols and art forms.

The Christian Scriptures—their origins and transmission.

Key incidents in the life of Jesus; eg, his baptism, healings, relations with the Jewish leaders, Last Supper with his disciples, betrayal, trial, crucifixion, resurrection, ascension.

Christian apostles: a study of Jesus' disciples and of the concept of discipleship.

Unit 11: Christians learning together in the Plural Society

Core Values and Key Concepts: 3, 4, 5, 6, 7, 8.

Christianity and education: eg, the Church's involvement in education; Sunday schools, church schools and colleges, Christian values in education, the concept of 'Christian education', the work of the British and Foreign Schools Society; attitudes of Christians to religious education and morning assembly in state schools.

Christianity and youth: Local and national organisations, eg, youth clubs, uniformed organisations, YMCA, YWCA, MAYC.

Christian community action: eg, the work of the Samaritans and the National Children's Homes; Christian radio and television, etc.

Christianity and other faiths: Contrasting responses, eg, the Christian Mission to Jews, inter-faith dialogue, the work of the British Council of Churches.

Unit 12: Christians learning together in the World-Wide Community

Core Values and Key Concepts: 1–8.

The contribution of Christianity to learning: (a) *historical*: eg, the contribution of Christian monasticism to learning in the Middle Ages; Christian missionary enterprises throughout the ages; the work of the SPCK, SPG, CMS, The British and Foreign Bible Society, and of individuals such as David Livingstone, Albert Schweitzer, etc; (b) *contemporary*: education for liberation/conscientisation—the work of the World Council of Christian Education, the World Student Christian Federation, the All Africa Christian Council, the South-East Asia Christian Council and the Latin American Evangelical Commission on Christian Education; co-operative enterprises between Christians and non-Christians, eg, the influence of Paulo Freire.

Unit 13: Christians acting together in the Family

Core Values and Key Concepts: 2, 3, 5, 6, 8.

The Christian view of marriage and family life: St Paul's teaching on the role of husband and wife and on the relations between parents and children; contemporary Christian teaching on family life.

Stories of Christian family life—past and present.

Unit 14: Christians acting together in the Church

Core Values and Key Concepts: 1, 2, 3, 5, 6, 7.

The Christian view of the human: Beliefs about creation and the fall.

Christian understanding of: salvation, faith and grace.

Spiritual development in the Christian way: Growing in Christian faith through baptism, confession of sins, prayer, worship, taking communion, study and loving one's neighbour.

Christian 'spiritual values': eg, the fruit of the Spirit—love, joy, peace, patience, kindness, goodness, faithfulness, gentleness, self-control.

Unit 15: Christians acting together in the Plural Society

Core Values and Key Concepts: 4, 6, 8.

The attitudes of Christians to contemporary personal, social and moral issues: eg, wealth and poverty, racism, war and peace, defence, human rights, sexism, sexuality, abortion, contraception, euthanasia, gambling, divorce, animals, conservation, materialism/consumerism, etc.

Unit 16: Christians acting together in the World-Wide Community

Core Values and Key Concepts: 1, 4, 6, 8.

Christianity and world development: Rich world/poor world, the concept of human interdependence; Christians and the economic debate.

Christian organisations and aid: The work of Christian Aid, CAFOD, etc.

Christians working for social justice: eg, Christians working for change in the USSR and South Africa; the work and witness of Archbishop Desmond Tutu.

Christians and human dignity: The work of Mother Teresa of Calcutta.

Unit 17: Christians believing together about God

Core Values and Key Concepts: 1, 2.

Christian beliefs about the nature of God: Monotheism combining God's presence and activity in the world ('immanence') with His eternal and infinite reality beyond the world of space and time ('transcendence');

'Three Persons in One Substance'—'The Trinity'—the Father being the Source of all existence ('the God of Abraham, Isaac and Jacob'), the Son the Eternal Object of the Father's love and the Mediator of that love in creation and redemption, and the Holy Ghost (the Spirit of God) the Bond of Union between Father and Son; a doctrine reflecting the distinctive experience of Christians.

Christian beliefs about Jesus of Nazareth: 'Christ/Messiah', 'Saviour', 'Lord', 'God Incarnate'.

Christian beliefs about the Holy Spirit: Distinct from, but consubstantial, coequal and coeternal with, the Father and the Son, and in the fullest sense God.

Unit 18: Christians believing together about revelation

Core Values and Key Concepts: 1, 2, 7.

Through Jesus Christ;

Through the Holy Spirit;

Through the Christian Bible;

Through the Church;

Through personal experience;

Unit 19: Christians believing together about the world, human society and the Church

Core Values and Key Concepts: 4, 6, 7, 8.

The world as God's creation;

The world loved by God;

The reconciliation of the world with God through the Mission of God;

The transformation of human society through the establishment of God's rule or kingship ('The Kingdom of God');

The Church as the People of God and His witness on earth;

Unit 20: Christians believing together about human spirituality and the goals of human spiritual development:

Core Values and Key Concepts: 3, 5, 8.

Christian teaching on the nature of the human person: body, soul/spirit;

Christian teaching about grace;

Christian teaching about human freedom;

Christian teaching about salvation and faith;

Christian eschatology and teaching about the resurrection;

(B) Hinduism: A Hindu Life-World Curriculum

(i) *Using the Core Values to identify the 'essential minimum' key-concepts from Hinduism*

Core Values Criteria	'Essential Minimum' Key Concepts
1. Providential source of order, meaning and purpose in the universe; the Sacred; Source of Revelation and Truth;	Brahman, the Supreme Reality, transcendent but immanent, ever present in the world of particular things and selves; Truth is but one Reality that can be encountered and understood in a variety of forms and ways;
2. Agent or agencies of Revelation; records of Revelation; experience of Revelation;	The Trimurti—Brahma, Vishnu and Shiva; Avatars; In Lord Krishna the impersonal Brahman becomes a personal, loving God; Lord Rama, an avatar of Vishnu, the perfect model of son and husband; The Revealed and Traditional Sacred Scriptures;
3. View of the human;	Human beings are part of the endless cycle of birth, death and rebirth (samsara); Actions in one life determine caste, re-birth or release (law of karma); the goal of human life is release from samsara (moksha);

4. View of a just society;	The world cannot be significantly changed; Human inequalities and fortunes are a product of karma and samsara; striving after Reality is an individual quest and salvation is a personal experience;
5. Individual self-fulfilment through:	Following different paths which lead to moksha; ie, fulfilling the duty of caste (dharma); the ways of knowledge (jnana yoga); action (karma yoga), devotion (bhakti yoga), and meditation (raja yoga); Nirvana—the state of bliss preceding moksha.
6. Ethical perspective;	Fulfilling the duties of caste (dharma); Because all is in Brahman, not taking life (ahimsa)
7. Community of faith;	Fulfilling the duty of caste (dharma)
8. Spiritual values;	Abstaining from taking life, injuring living things, lying, stealing, sensuality, greed; the practice of cleanliness, contentment, self-control, studiousness, awareness of the divine, devotion to God; love, peace, righteous conduct; non-violence, truth, and the attainment of bliss (nirvana).

(ii) *Applying the four organising categories of Family, Faith Community, Plural Society and World-Wide Community to the phenomena of Hindu Faith*

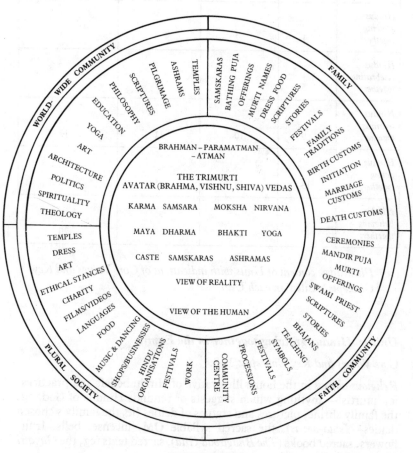

BRAHMAN – PARAMATMAN – ATMAN

THE TRIMURTI
AVATAR (BRAHMA, VISHNU, SHIVA) VEDAS

KARMA SAMSARA   MOKSHA NIRVANA

MAYA DHARMA   BHAKTI   YOGA

CASTE SAMSKARAS   ASHRAMAS

VIEW OF REALITY

VIEW OF THE HUMAN

FAMILY

SAMSKARAS
BATHING PUJA
OFFERINGS
MURTI NAMES
DRESS FOOD
SCRIPTURES
STORIES
FESTIVALS
FAMILY TRADITIONS
BIRTH CUSTOMS
INITIATION
MARRIAGE CUSTOMS
DEATH CUSTOMS

FAITH COMMUNITY

CEREMONIES
MANDIR PUJA
MURTI
OFFERINGS
SWAMI PRIEST
SCRIPTURES
STORIES
BHAJANS
TEACHING
SYMBOLS
FESTIVALS
PROCESSIONS
COMMUNITY CENTRE

PLURAL SOCIETY

TEMPLES
DRESS
ART
ETHICAL STANCES
CHARITY
FILMS/VIDEOS
LANGUAGES
FOOD
MUSIC & DANCING
SHOPS/BUSINESSES
HINDU ORGANISATIONS
FESTIVALS
WORK

WORLD- WIDE COMMUNITY

TEMPLES
ASHRAMS
PILGRIMAGE
SCRIPTURES
PHILOSOPHY
EDUCATION
YOGA
ART
ARCHITECTURE
POLITICS
SPIRITUALITY
THEOLOGY

HINDU FAITH

Figure Thirteen: The phenomena of Hindu Faith

301

*(iii) Applying the Spiral Curriculum Matrix to content drawn from the
phenomena of Hindu Faith*

Hindus

Theme:	In the Family:	In the Faith Community:	In the Plural Society:	In the World-Wide Community:
Hindus growing together:	1	2	3	4
Hindus celebrating together:	5	6	7	8
Hindus learning together:	9	10	11	12
Hindus acting together:	13	14	15	16
Hindus believing together:	17	18	19	20

*(iv) Illustrative content of Units with indications of Core Values and Key
Concepts 'visited' in each Unit*

Unit 1: Hindus growing together in the Family

Core Values and Key Concepts: 1–8:

Religious objects in the home illustrative of Hindu beliefs and practices:
ie, 'murtis'—anything which suggests or reminds Hindus of God: eg,
the family shrine, pictures and statues of deities (ie, the family's chosen
deities—*Ishta-devas*), the sacred syllable OM, incense, bells, fruit,
flowers, sacred books (*The Bhagavad Gita*), sacred texts (eg, the *Gayatri
Mantra*), pictures of famous temples, etc.

The various patterns of Hindu family life: Daily bathing, morning and
evening worship (*puja*), reading sacred scriptures, singing hymns (*bhajanas or kitanas*), family meals, visits to and from relatives, visits to the
temple, feeding animals, etc.

Food, dress and family customs;

'Samskaras'/'sacraments'/rites of passage: (ie, preparing a person for the next phase of their life; 16 samskaras from cradle to grave);

Birth customs: Name-giving (*namadheya*); (or in Unit 5)

Initiation rites: The sacred thread ceremony (*upanayana*), a second birth for boys of the first three castes around the age of seven or later; (or in Unit 5)

Marriage customs: (or in Unit 5)

Death customs:

Unit 2: Hindus growing together in the Faith Community

Core Values and Key Concepts: 2, 5, 6, 7, 8.

The interior of a Hindu temple (mandir): The central shrine (within the inner sanctuary—the *garbha-griha*) with an image of the god to whom the temple is dedicated (eg, Krishna, Rama, Shiva), the canopy over the shrine, other shrines to gods and goddesses who are attendants of the principal god of the temple (eg, Durga, Ganesha, Hanuman, etc), offerings before the shrines, pictures of gods, bells, incense, vermilion powder, flowers, lights, etc.

The organisation, use and facilities of the temple: eg, ritual, social, cultural, educational.

The role of the priest, secretary, members of the temple committee.

What going to the temple means for Hindus: The importance of having the 'darsana' of the deity—vision, spiritual uplift, awareness—and of receiving 'prasada' (an apple or sweet)—the symbolic grace of the Lord.

Unit 3: Hindus growing together in the Plural Society

Core Values and Key Concepts: 2, 3, 4, 6, 7, 8.

Three main Hindu traditions: Vaishnavism—the worship of Vishnu and his incarnations (*avatars*); Shaivism—the worship of Shiva; Shaktism—the worship of the goddess Kali/Durga/Parvati.

The variety of Hindu communities in Britain: Differences of ethnicity, language, culture and settlement patterns; eg, Gujarati groups from East Africa and Punjabi groups from India each speaking different languages, eating different foods and dressing differently; temples established by different groups and reflecting common ethnic or caste identity; eg, Gujurati 'jati' groups and Punjabi 'khatri' groups.

The contribution of Hindus to cultural, social and economic life; the persistence of traditional roles; professional and commercial enterprises, etc.

Unit 4: *Hindus growing together in the World-Wide Community*

Core Values and Key Concepts: 1, 2, 3, 4, 6, 7, 8.

Hinduism—the world's oldest living religion: Famous Hindu temples; eg, Badrinath (Shiva), Divarka (Krishna), Jagannath (Vishnu), Rameswaram (Rama); the art forms of Hinduism, eg, dance (eg, Kathikali dancers who perform the Hindu Epics), sculpture, wood-carving, etc.

Unit 5: *Hindus celebring together in the Family*

Core Values and Key Concepts: 1, 2, 3, 5, 7, 8.

Hindu family celebrations: eg, birth of a baby, the first hair-cutting, good fortune, a visit from a guru or relatives from India, a marriage or wedding anniversary, etc (or in Unit 1).

Puja in the home: Invocation of the deity (*avahana*), invitation to a seat (*asana*), washing of feet (*padya*), adoration through offering flowers (*pushpa*), burning incense (*dhupa*), waving lights (*dipa*), and consecration of food (*naivedya*).

Arti in the home: Waving the flame of a lamp before the murti in a clockwise direction and then receiving the blessing of the Lord by holding one's hands over the flame and touching one's eyes and forehead.

Hindus preparing the home for Lakshmi at the festival of Divali: Cleaning, preparing sweets, making lanterns and deva lamps, rangoli patterns, giving cards and presents, settling accounts, new clothes.

The story of Rama and Sita as told to Hindu children.

Unit 6: *Hindus celebrating together in the Faith Community*

Core Values and Key Concepts: 1–8.

Temple puja: Six categories of ritual performance: obeisance (*pranama*), purification (*shuddhi*), petitioning (*prarthana*), praise (*bhajana*), offering (*upachara*), sharing sacred food (*prasada*).

Arti (aratrika), hymn singing (bhajanas), special ceremonies (eg, vrat katha);

Some gods and goodesses of popular devotion: Shiva, Rama, Krishna, Durga, Kali, Sita, Radha, Ganesha;

Hindu iconography: recognising the gods by their dress, what they are holding, and who accompanies them; eg, Rama (a bow, accompanied by Sita, Lakshmana, Hanuman); Krishna (blue appearance, a flute, accompanied by Radha, *gopis*, etc); Shiva, (many different representations: eg, tangled hair, a third eye, blue throat, cobra round his neck, a trident, dancing, holding a drum and flame, riding Nandi, a bull; Shiva in the form of the phallus (*linga*) etc); Durga, (riding a tiger, carrying a trident); Durga as Kali (dark blue or black, necklace of skulls and severed heads, dancing on the lifeless body of Shiva, etc).

Reading the stories which explain the iconography.

Unit 7: Hindus celebrating together in the Plural Society

Core Values and Key Concepts: 1–8.

The major festivals which unite Hindus: Diwali, Holi, Mahasivaratri, Ramnavami, Janamashtami, Navaratri, Dasera.

Stories behind the festivals;

Festivals as an expression of the yearly cycle of nature and of work: Celebrations reflecting a local group's ethnic roots and traditions: eg, the worship of Vishnu in the form of Balaji.

Cultural festivals and exhibitions: Indian dancing and costume.

Local and national Hindu organisations: eg, the Vedic Society, Hindu Religious and Cultural Society, the National Council of Hindu Temples (UK), the Hindu Swayam Sevak Sangh (Hindu Self-Help Union), etc.

Local and national newspapers reflecting Hindu life and culture.

Unit 8: Hindus celebrating together in the World-Wide Community

Core Values and Key Concepts: 1–8.

Celebrating Hindu festivals in India: eg, Ratha-yatra of Jagannatha, Dussehra (Kali) in Bengal.

Places of worldwide Hindu pilgrimage: eg, Varanasi (Benares), Allahabad (Prayaga), Hardwar, Rishikesh, Khaligat in Calcutta, Vrindavan, Mathura, etc. The Hindu's craving for religious experience; desire to visit places associated with the life of the gods, eg, Krishna in Vrindavan. The Kumbha Mela Festival at Allahabad—attracting thousands of pilgrims to bathe in the confluence of the Ganges and Jumna.

Unit 9: *Hindus learning together in the Family*

Core Values and Key Concepts: 1, 2, 3, 5, 6, 8.

Fables told to young children in Hindu homes; eg, fables from the Panchatantra.

Popular stories from the Puranas;

The Bhagavad-Gita: the story of Arjuna and Lord Krishna.

The traditional four stages (ashramas) of life: 1, student; 2, householder and parent; 3, 'forest-dweller'; 4, holy man (*sanyasin*).

The goals of stages 1 and 2: Pleasure (*kama*); usefulness/wealth/success (*artha*); duty to family, caste and community (*dharma*);

The goals of stages 3 and 4: 'moksha'—release from the round of births (*samsara*) by abandoning all earthly ties.

Unit 10: *Hindus learning together in the Faith Community*

Core Values and Key Concepts: 1, 2, 5, 6, 7, 8.

The Hindu Scriptures: Teachings of the Vedas (the way of action), the Upanishads (the way of knowledge), and the Epics (*Mahabharata* and *Ramayana*) (the way of devotion).

The concepts of: 'Brahman—Paramatman—Atman'; The Trimurti—Brahma, Vishnu and Shiva; 'avatara'.

The aspects of Shiva;

The avatars of Vishnu.

Unit 11: *Hindus learning together in the Plural Society*

Core Values and Key Concepts: 3, 4, 5, 6, 7, 8.

Safeguarding Hindu culture and ideals in the plural society: The importance of transmitting cultural norms to young people born in the UK and subject to non-Hindu influences;

Hinduism and education: eg, the provision, by the temples, of supplementary schools and classes for Hindu children in evenings and weekends; learning Hindi or Punjabi; religious and moral teaching; youth groups, women's groups, dance/music instruction, advice on social matters; the attitudes of Hindu parents to state school education and to religious education in state schools.

Hinduism and other faiths: The 'open' attitude of Hindus to other religious traditions.

The religious development of Hinduism in pluralist Britain: The influence of sectarian movements within Hinduism: eg, the Sathya Sai Baba Fellowship, the Swaminaryan Hindu Mission, the International Society for Krishna Consciousness (ISKON, the Hare Krishna Movement), the Divine Light Mission, etc.

Unit 12: *Hindus learning together in the World-Wide Community*

Core Values and Key Concepts: 1–8.

Hindu Philosophy: The Sankhya System (dualistic and atheistic); the Vedanta System (non-dualism; all but Brahman is illusion (*maya*)); the Yoga System.

The influence of Hindu philosophy and theology on Western culture: Meditation and yoga, the cult of the guru, influence on music and art (pop and classical), Theosophical Society, Anthroposophy, Rudolf Steiner, Christian *ashrams*, etc.

Unit 13: *Hindus acting together in the Family*

Core Values and Key Concepts: 3, 4, 5, 6, 7, 8.

The concept of religious duty: 'Dharma'; fulfilling the *dharma* of 'caste': *Brahmins* (priests, religious teachers), *Kshatriyas* (rulers and soldiers), *Vaishyas* (merchants and farmers), *Shudras* (workers) (plus many subdivisions of caste).

The concept of 'twice-born': 'Dvija'—the first three castes.

The concept of human nature having three qualities or 'guna':—*satva* (a balanced outlook), *rajas* (self-assertive), *tamas* (evil qualities dominating); the importance of balance.

The influence of caste identity on family behaviour, outlook and occupation; preserving traditions of purity especially when eating; marriage within the caste; friendships within the caste.

Unit 14: Hindus acting together in the Faith Community

Core Values and Key Concepts: 1, 2, 3, 5, 6, 7.

The Hindu view of the human: Part of the endless cycle of birth, death and rebirth (*samsara*), the goal of life being release from this cycle and absorption of one's soul (*atman*) with the World Soul (*Paramatman— Brahman*).

The concepts of 'karma', 'samsara', 'moksha', 'nirvana'.

The four paths to salvation:
1. The way of knowledge (*jnana yoga*)
2. The way of action (*karma yoga*)
3. The way of devotion (*bhakti yoga*)
4. The way of meditation (*raja yoga*);

Spiritual development in the Hindu way: as prescribed by the four paths; common characteristics include: abstention from taking life (*ahimsa*), injury, lying, stealing, sensuality, greed: practice of cleanliness, contentment, self-control, studiousness, awareness of the divine, devotion to God.

Hindu 'spiritual values': Love, peace, righteous conduct, non-violence, truth (ie, the five basic values of Sathya Sai Baba).

Unit 15: Hindus acting together in the Plural Society

Core Values and Key Concepts: 4, 6, 8.

The attitudes of Hindus to contemporary personal, social and moral issues: eg, wealth and poverty, racism, war and peace, defence, human rights, sexism, sexuality, abortion, contraception, euthanasia, gambling divorce, animals, conservation, materialism/consumerism, etc.

Unit 16: Hindus acting together in the World-Wide Community

Core Values and Key Concepts: 3, 4, 6, 8.

The lives, work and influence of some great Hindu teachers and leaders: eg,

Ramakrishna, Swami Vivekananda, Rabindranath Tagore, Mohandas (Mahatma) Gandhi, Sarvepalli Radhakrishnan.

Some Hindu saints and gurus: Sahajananda Swami (later 'Swaminarayan'), Sathya Sai Baba, Jalaram Bapa, Sri Chinmoy, etc.

Unit 17: *Hindus believing together about God*

Core Values and Key Concepts: 1, 2.

Hindu beliefs about Brahman: The Supreme Reality, transcendent but immanent, ever present in the world of particular things and selves. Truth is but One Reality that can be encountered and understood in a variety of forms and ways.

Hindu beliefs about the Trimurti—Brahma, Vishnu and Shiva: Whereas Brahman is an impersonal principle and of neuter gender, Brahma is personal and masculine. Brahma is also the all-inclusive deity and the name for the one deity behind all the many names of gods within Hinduism. He does not receive worship. He is the balance between Vishnu (representing existence, light, concentration, preservation, etc) and Shiva (representing annihilation, darkness, dispersion, destruction, etc), both of whom receive worship.

Hindu beliefs about 'avatars': In Lord Krishna the impersonal Brahman becomes a personal, loving God. In Lord Rama the impersonal Brahman appears as the model son and husband.

The syllable 'OM' is a transcendental sound vibration representing the aspect of the all-pervading energy of the Absolute Truth.

Unit 18: *Hindus believing together about revelation*

Core Values and Key Concepts: 1, 2.

The Revealed Scriptures of Hinduism: The Vedas (*veda* means knowledge)—know as 'Shruti'—given directly from God, viz:
The Rig Veda, The Sama Veda, The Yajur Veda, The Arthava Veda (collectively known as 'Samhitas').

Commentaries on the Samhitas: The Brahmanas, Aranyakas, Upanishads (traditionally 108).

The Traditional Scriptures: The Ramayana and *The Mahabharata* (Epics) and the *Puranas* (known as 'Smriti'—the work of men). *The Bhagavad-Gita* is part of *The Mahabharata*.

Vishnu—the central god of the Traditional Scriptures who becomes incarnate to protect and sustain life. The ten avatars of Vishnu, including Rama and Krishna, are described in the *Puranas*.

Hindu belief in the presence of God in His Deity manifestation in home and temple so providing the devotee with an opportunity of rendering direct service to him.

Hindus go before the Deity to take 'darshan' of the Lord.

Unit 19: Hindus believing together about the world and human society

Core Values and Key Concepts: 4, 6, 7, 8.

Hindu beliefs about the world: The world has no beginning and no end. The world cannot be significantly altered.

Hindu beliefs about 'maya': Those who are ignorant of Supreme Reality fail to recognise the divine unity behind what appears to be a differentiated universe; they also perceive themselves to be a separate, individual self. Through attachment to the material world they reinforce this illusion and are unaware of their duty (*dharma*) to their eternal soul (*atman*).

Hindu beliefs about caste: Human inequalities and fortunes are a product of *karma* and *samsara*; the caste system (which is not a religious concept) reflects one's inheritance of *karma* at birth which is a product of one's actions in a previous existence.

Unit 20: Hindus believing together about human spirituality and the goals of human spiritual development

Core Values and Key Concepts: 3, 5, 8.

Hindu beliefs about the transmigration of souls: Beliefs about *atman, karma, samsara, moksha, nirvana*.

Hindu beliefs about 'samskaras' and 'ashramas' and the four paths to salvation.

Hindu beliefs about 'dharma': Universal, divine law with cosmic, moral, ritual and social applications. What Westerners call 'Hinduism', Hindus call 'Sanatana dharma'—eternal dharma/law.

(C) Islam: A Muslim Life-World Curriculum

(i) Using the Core Values Criteria to identify the 'essential minimum' key-concepts from Islam

Core Values Criteria	'Essential Minimum' Key Concepts
1. Providential source of order, meaning and purpose in the universe; The Sacred; Source of Revelation and Truth;	Allah, The One and Only God, the Compassionate, the Merciful, Master of the Day of Judgment (The Oneness of Allah—Tauhid);
2. Agent or agencies of Revelation; records of Revelation; experience of Revelation;	The Holy Qur'an—the Universal and Final Revelation of Allah; The Prophet Muhammad (p.b.u.h)—the Seal of Allah's Prophets; The Hadith; The Sunnah;
3. View of the human;	Created by Allah from clots of blood; Utterly dependent upon Allah ('ubudiyat—'abd = slave);
4. View of a just society;	The Muslim Way of Life (Shari'ah—which includes observing The Five Pillars of Faith) Fulfilling the teaching of the Holy Qur'an, the Hadith and the Sunnah;
5. Individual self-fulfilment through:	Submission to the Will of Allah (sujud—muslim); Earnest striving (jihad): faith (iman); constant consciousness of Allah (taqwa); The Divine Decree of Allah (Qada wa qadar—what Allah has decreed); Being freed from enslavement to anything or anyone but Allah.

6. Ethical perspective;	The Muslim Way of Life (Shari'ah—which includes observing The Five Pillars of Faith)
7. Community of faith;	The Ummah—The Collectivity and Brotherhood of Islam;
8. Spiritual values;	Honesty, truthfulness, discipline, humility, modesty, brotherliness, generosity, caring for the needy, hard work and the love of knowledge.

(ii) *Applying the four organising categories of Family, Faith Community, Plural Society and World-Wide Community to the phenomena of Islamic Faith.*

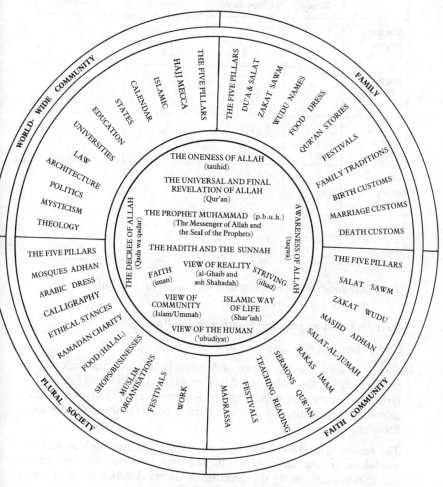

Figure Fourteen: The phenomena of Islamic Faith

(iii) *Applying the Spiral Curriculum Matrix to content drawn from the phenomena of Islamic Faith.*

Muslims

Theme:	In the Family:	In the Faith Community:	In the Plural Society:	In the World-Wide Community:
Muslims growing together:	1	2	3	4
Muslims celebrating together:	5	6	7	8
Muslims learning together:	9	10	11	12
Muslims acting together:	13	14	15	16
Muslims believing together:	17	18	19	20

(iv) *Illustrative content of Units with indications of Core Values and Key Concepts 'visited' in each Unit*

Unit 1: Muslims growing together in the Family

Core Values and Key Concepts: 1–8:

Objects in the home illustrative of Muslim beliefs and practices: eg, an embroidery of the Name of Allah or of *Allahu akbar* (*God is Most Great*), a prayer mat depicting the Ka'aba, prayer beads, an Islamic calendar, 'Eid cards, the Qur'an, Islamic prayerbooks and devotional literature, etc.

The pattern of Muslim family life: eg, saying the *Bismillah ar-Rahman ar-Raheem* (*In the name of God, the Merciful, the Compassionate*) before any undertaking, using the greeting *Assalamu Alaikum* (*Peace be with you*) and the response *Wa Alaikumus Salam* (*And peace be with you, too*); reciting takbirs (ie, *Allahu Akbar—God is Most Great*) and making the Declaration of Faith (First Pillar of Faith)—The Muslim Creed called the *Kalimah or Shahadah—Ashaduan la ilaha illa Allah wa ashaduanna*

Muhammadan Rasool Allah (*I bear witness that there is no deity except God and I bear witness that Muhammad is the Messenger of God*); ablutions (*wudu*) followed by prayer (*salat*—Second Pillar of Faith) five times a day; reciting the Qur'an, engaging in personal devotions (*du'a*) using, perhaps, prayer beads to bring to mind the Ninety-Nine Beautiful Names of Allah.

Food, dress and family customs;

Birth customs: saying the *Adhan* (*the call to prayer*) into the baby's right ear and the *Iqamah* into the baby's left ear; the *Tahneek* ceremony, the *Aqeeqah* ceremony; naming the baby; the *Khitan* ceremony.

Marriage customs; the marriage contract (*Aqd Nikah*)

Death customs;

Unit 2: Muslims growing together in the Faith Community

Core Values and Key Concepts: 2, 4, 5, 6, 7.

The exterior and interior of the mosque (*masjid—place of prostration*): eg, the *minaret, mihrab* (showing the *qiblah*—the direction of the Ka'aba—South East in England), *minbar* (pulpit); facilities for ablution (*wudu*), examples of calligraphy or arabesque, etc.

The organisation, use and facilities of the mosque: eg, ritual, social, cultural, educational.

The role of the imam (*leader*) *and the officials of the mosque.*

What going to the mosque means for Muslims.

Unit 3: Muslims growing together in the Plural Society

Core Values and Key Concepts: 2, 3, 4, 6, 7, 8.

Two main Muslim traditions: The 'Sunnis'—the orthodox or traditional who accept the central core of practice and doctrine as developed from 'The Sunnah' (the practice/example and precept of the Prophet Muhammad (p.b.u.h) and The 'Shi'ites'—dissenters ('the partisans of Ali' and his two sons, Al-Hasan and Al-Husain). Shi'as subdivided; eg, 'Twelver Shi'ism' (ie, twelve Imams after the Prophet, starting with Ali—the state religion of Iran) and Isma'ilis.

Difference of ethnicity, language, culture and settlement patterns among Muslims in Britain: ie, from Pakistan and Bengal; West Africa;

Malaysia, Turkey, Cyprus, the Arab countries; East Africa and the Caribbean. Local mosques and their communities reflecting this ethnic and cultural diversity.

The attitudes of Muslims to pluralism and secular values;

The contribution of Muslims to cultural, social and economic life: professional and commercial enterprises.

Unit 4: Muslims growing together in the World-Wide Community

Core Values and Key Concepts: 1–8.

Islam—the world's fastest growing living religion: Famous mosques: eg, the Great Mosque at Mecca, the Mosque of Muhammad (p.b.u.h) at Medina, the Great Mosque at Damascus, the Dome of the Rock in Jerusalem, the Blue Mosque in Cairo, the Blue Mosque at Isfahan in Iran.

The Islamic contribution to art and architecture: Calligraphy and arabesque; pottery.

Unit 5: Muslims celebrating together in the Family

Core Values and Key Concepts: 1–8.

'Salat' in the home: The five times for prayer (Second Pillar of Faith): daybreak (*fajr*), midday (*zuhr*), afternoon ('*asr*), evening (*maghrib*), night ('*isha*). Ablution (*wudu*).

Muslim family celebrations: Birth and marriage customs (or in Unit 1), visits from relatives, birthdays.

Fasting and feasting in the home: fasting during the month of Ramadan (sawm—Third Pillar of Faith); the fast determined by the onset of dawn and dusk; charts showing this to the nearest minute (in Birmingham on 1st June, 1984, fasting started at 2.48am and ended at 9.23pm); preparing food at night and going to bed early; rising before dawn to eat the *sehri* meal; exchanging greetings, *Asalam alaikum*; the call (*adhan*) to *fajr* prayer; *salat*; returning to bed or reading the Qur'an; no food or drink during daylight hours; abstention from pleasures; *adhans* announce sunset and a snack of dates, samosas, pakoras and water is traditionally taken before the *maghrib* prayer; substantial evening meal before '*isha* prayer and early bedtime; donations to charity—*zakat-ul-fitr*—equivalent to one good meal for each member of the family.

The Eid festivals in the home: *Eid-ul-Fitr*—'the festival of fast break-ing'—also called the Small Festival (*Eid-ul-Sagheer*); first day of the month of *Shawwal*; three days of festivity; special food, new clothes, presents and cards; night of Eid traditionally spent in meditation and prayer with families going to the mosque for the festival prayer (*salat-ul-fitr*) about an hour after sunset; renewal of their pledge to the faith and to the Muslim community. *Eid-ul-Adha*—'the festival of sacrifice'—also called the Great Festival (*Eid-ul-Kabeer*); tenth day of the twelfth month, *Dhul-Hijirah*; four days of festivity; The Day of Sacrifice during the pilgrimage to Mecca but also observed at home and in the community; animal sacrificed and portion of meat given to poor; visiting relatives and exchanging greetings and gifts.

Unit 6: *Muslims celebrating together in the Faith Community*

Core Values and Key Concepts: 1–8.

Attending the mosque for Yaum ul-Jum'a—The Day of Assembly (Friday): Friday the day of obligatory (*fard*) congregational prayer (*salat-al-Jum'a*); (NB *not* a Sabbath; Muslims can work before and after prayer); the two *adhans* (calls to prayer); the sermon (*khutbah*) given by the *imam*; ablutions (*wudu*); prostrations (*rakas*).

Unit 7: *Muslims celebrating together in the Plural Society*

Core Values and Key Concepts: 1–8.

The Islamic Calendar;

Fasting (sawm): The fast of Ramadan: congregational aspects and its impact on secular community life;

Festivals according to Sunnah: *Eid-ul-Fitr*: *Eid-ul-Adha*: congregational aspects and their impact on secular community life: eg, the lighting up of the mosque, booths, stalls and fairs, etc.

Celebrations of historical occasions: The Day of Hijrah (the Emigration of the Prophet from Mecca to Medina), the Birthday of the Prophet (*Meelad-ul-Nabi*), the Night of Power (*Lailat-ul-Qadr*), the Night Jour-ney and the Ascension (*Lailat-ul-Isra wal Mi'raj*), the Night of Forgive-ness (*Lailat-ul-Bara'h*), Muharram (Shi'ite Muslims commemorate the death of Hussain and his little son).

Unit 8: Muslims celebrating together in the World-Wide Community

Core Values and Key Concepts: 1–8.

Pilgrimage (Hajj) to Mecca (Fifth Pillar of Faith): The ritual of *hajj*; Day of Arafat; Festival of Sacrifice (*Eid-ul-Adha*).

The Ka'aba and the Great Mosque at Mecca (al-masjid-al-Haraim).

Unit 9: Muslims learning together in the Family

Core Values and Key Concepts: 1, 2, 3, 5, 6, 8.

Stories told to children in Muslim homes: eg, *Stories of the Prophets of Islam*—selections from the Qur'an by Abdul Rahaman Rukaini (Macmillan Educational, 1986): *From Adam to Hud, Salih and Ibrahim, Ismail and Ya'qub, Yusuf, Musa, Daud, Sulaiman and Ayub, Yunus, Yahya and 'Isa, The early life of Muhammad, Muhammad in Makkah, Muhammad the Bearer of Islam* (p.b.u.h).

Nurturing children in Islam through: prayer, study, charity and hospitality, celebration, personal example.

Unit 10: Muslims learning together in the Faith Community

Core Values and Key Concepts: 1, 2, 3.

The Qur'an: How the Word of Allah was received by the Prophet Muhammad (p.b.u.h) and subsequently written down; the arrangement of its content into 114 *surahs*. Examples: Surah 1 (*Al-Fateha*), Surah 112 (*The Unity Surah*), Surah 110 (*The Surah of Help*), Surah 103 (*The Surah of Time*).

The Qur'an's teaching about The Six Articles of Faith:
1. Allah; (Surahs 2, 24, 93, 112)
2. The Angels of Allah;
3. The Revealed Scriptures of Allah;
4. The Prophets of Allah;
5. The Day of Judgment and The Hereafter;
6. The Divine Decree (*Qada wa qadar—the measure of what Allah ordains*).

The Hadith (Traditions): The uninspired record of inspired sayings of the Prophet Muhammad (p.b.u.h): ie, what he did (*Sunnatu 'l-fi'l*), what he enjoined (*Sunnatu 'l-qaul*) what was done in his presence which he did not forbid (*Sunnatu 'l-taqrir*). The customs, practice and example of the Prophet Muhammad (p.b.u.h) are called *The Sunnah*.

Unit 11: Muslims learning together in the Plural Society

Core Values and Key Concepts: 3, 4, 6, 7, 8.

Safeguarding Islamic culture and ideals in the plural society: The importance given to transmitting Islamic cultural norms to young people born in the UK and subject to non-Muslim influences and values.

Islamic education: its nature and purpose; provision of instruction in The Qur'an, Arabic, the Muslim Way of Life (*Shari'ah*), Islamic history, mother tongue, etc, in Qur'an schools attached to mosques (*madrassas*); the attendance of Muslim children and young people at the *madrassa*; local organisations for Muslim youth, women and girls' groups, cultural centres etc; the attitudes of Muslim parents to state education and to religious education in state schools; the case for voluntary aided Muslim schools.

Islam and other faiths: The traditional attitudes of Muslims to Jews and Christians (*Ahlu 'l-Kitab—People of the Book*); attitudes to secularism.

The religious development of Islam in pluralist Britain: The involvement of Muslims in inter-faith dialogue (eg, the work of the Centre for the Study of Islam and Muslim-Christian Relations, Selly Oak Colleges, Birmingham); the work of the Islamic UK Mission, etc.

Unit 12: Muslims learning together in the World-Wide Community

Core Values and Key Concepts: 1–8.

The Islamic contribution to learning: eg, mathematics, astronomy, medicine, navigation and geography, horticulure, metallurgy, engineering, physics, chemistry, law, theology.

Unit 13: Muslims acting together in the Family

Core Values and Key Concepts: 3, 4, 5, 6, 7, 8.

The Muslim family as the basis of Islamic social order: Marriage and the roles of husband and wife: equal but different roles; the leadership and supportive role of the husband; his maintenance of his wife, daughters and female relatives; the ideals of mutual respect, kindness, love, companionship, faithfulness and harmonious interaction, etc; parent-child relations: the importance of the parents' example of submission to Allah and conscious practice of Islamic teachings; the responsibilities of children to be obedient, respectful and considerate; the willing acceptance of responsibility for parents in their old age; relations with relatives: close family ties; responsibilities for support and welfare, including providing money.

Unit 14: Muslims acting together in the Faith Community

Core Values and Key Concepts: 2, 3, 5, 7, 8.

The Islamic view of the human: This life only a very small part of a Reality so vast that the human mind can only conceive of it in a limited manner; not the final stage of existence; human beings a unique creation of Allah possessing an outward aspect (the physical body) and an inward aspect (the mind, emotions and soul); uniqueness consisting in humans being endowed with freedom of choice and judgment between right and wrong, capacities for thinking, feeling, acting, and possessing an immortal soul which lives on after the death of the physical body; the importance of achieving harmony and balance within the personality; Islam not distinguishing between 'religious', 'spiritual' and 'social' matters—a whole way of life for the whole person; the need to be in harmony with divine Reality.

Spiritual development in the Muslim Way: The development of God-consciousness (*taqwa*) and faith (*iman*); living the Muslim Way of Life (*Shar'iah*).

Muslim 'spiritual' values: Honesty, truthfulness, discipline, humility, modesty, brotherliness, generosity, caring for the needy, hard work and the love of knowledge.

The Prophet Muhammad (p.b.u.h) as the supreme example of the Muslim.

Unit 15: Muslims acting together in the Plural Society

Core Values and Key Concepts: 4, 6, 8.

Alms-giving (zakat)(Fourth Pillar of Faith): All wealth belongs to Allah and is good; Islam permits the gathering of wealth by moral means but places an obligation on Muslims to share it with others; *zakat*—obligatory contribution of one-fortieth of one's wealth to Islam; 'purifies' the remainder of one's wealth and also 'purifies' the heart; promotes the concept of brotherhood; the wealthy have a duty to the poor; the poor are assured that others will not see them suffer; *sadaqah*—voluntary charity.

The Islamic concept of earnest striving (jihad).

The Islamic concepts of what is permitted (*halal*), what is prohibited (*haram*) what is obligatory (*fard*) illustrated by reference to food, dress, violence, animals, alcohol, sexual relationships, divorce, gambling/usury, entertainment, possessions, etc.

The Islamic prohibition of idolatry: the sin of *shirk*.

The application of Islamic teaching to contemporary personal, social and moral issues: eg, wealth and poverty, racism, war and peace, defence, human rights, sexism, sexuality, abortion, contraception, euthanasia, conservation, materialism/consumerism.

Unit 16: Muslims acting together in the World-Wide Community

Core Values and Key Concepts: 3, 4, 6, 7, 8.

The influence of Islam on contemporary world politics: eg, issues in the Middle East; Iran and Iraq; relationships between the West and the Arab world.

Unit 17: Muslims believing together about God

Core Values and Key Concepts: 1, 2.

Muslim beliefs about the nature of Allah:
'He is God, the One, the Self-Sufficient. He begets not nor is He begotten, and there is none like Him.' (The Holy Qur'an 112:1–4)
'To Him belongs the dominion of the heavens and the earth. It is He who gives life and death, and He has power over all things. He is the First and Last, the Evident and the Immanent, and He has full knowledge of all things. It is He Who created the heavens and the earth in six days (stages or eons).' (The Holy Qur'an 57:1–6)
Allah has no body nor form, no physical attributes or characteristics; He is The One who gives such attributes and characteristics to his creatures while He does not share in them in the slightest degree.
He alone is Divine and no other creature can share in His Divinity. ie, *'He knows the Unseen (al-Ghaib) and the Evident (ash-Shahadah). He is the Merciful, the Mercy-Giver. God is He than Whom there is no other deity—the Sovereign, the Holy One, the Source of Peace, the Guardian of Faith, the Preserver of Safety, the Mighty, the Irresistible, the Supreme'* (The Holy Qur'an 59:22–24)
The term *Tauhid* is used to express the Unity of Allah, which is the great fundamental basis of Islam.

Muslim beliefs about Allah's concern for human life: Allah is *The Reality* and His existence has absolute relevance and meaning for every single human being since it is solely in relation to Him that they exist, live and return to Him. Allah is always active and concerned and creatively involved with every single part of His creation. Allah not only creates but sustains, directs and guides human life; He gives human beings the direction necessary for living their lives in such a manner as will ensure their everlasting good in the Life-to-Come.

Unit 18: *Muslims believing together about revelation*

Core Values and Key Concepts: 1, 2.

Muslim beliefs about Reality: Two realms of existence; *The Hidden* or *Unseen (al-Ghaib)*—not accessible to human sense or intellect; *The Evident* or *Witnessed (ash-Shahadah)*—visible and perceptible but only a very small and insignificant part of the totality. There are many *evidences* of Unseen Reality; eg, the physical universe, human beings, especially their spiritual feelings and aspirations, dreams and premonitions. Most important evidences: revelation of Unseen Reality through angels (eg, Gabriel—*Jibreel* in Arabic), through revealed scriptures (the Torah (*Taurat*), the Psalms (*Zaboor*), the Gospel (*Injeel*), through the messengers or prophets (eg, Abraham, Moses, Jesus), finally through the Prophet Muhammad (p.b.u.h) and The Holy Qur'an.

Muslim beliefs about the Holy Qur'an: The Universal and Final Revelation of Allah.

Muslim beliefs about the Prophet Muhammad (p.b.u.h): The Last Messenger of Allah and the Seal of Allah's Prophets.

Muslim beliefs about the Hadith and The Sunnah: The second source of guidance in Islam after the Qur'an.

Unit 19: *Muslims believing together about the world, human society and the Ummah*

Core Values and Key Concepts: 4, 6, 7, 8.

Muslim beliefs about the creation of the world: ie, according to the Traditions (*Mishkat, 24:1*) Allah created the world on Saturday, the hills on Sunday, the trees on Monday, all unpleasant things on Tuesday, the light on Wednesday, the beasts on Thursday, and Adam after the time of afternoon prayers on Friday.

Muslim beliefs about human society: 'Islam' is said to be the religion of all the prophets from Abraham. viz: *'SAY: We believe in God and in what hath been sent down to Abraham, and Ishmael, and Isaac, and Jacob, and the Tribes, and in what was given to Moses, and Jesus and the Prophets from their Lord. We make no difference between them, and to Him are we resigned (ie, Muslims). Whoso desireth any other religion than Islam, that religion shall never be accepted by Him, and in the next world he shall be lost.' (The Holy Qur'an 3: 78–79)*. Thus Muslims, Jews and Christians are *Ahlu 'l-Kitab—People of the Book*—who are accepted by God. Human society must be ordered in accordance with the revelation of God. The Muslim Way of Life (*The Shari'ah*)—the law derived from the Qur'an and the Hadith—is the most complete expression of that revelation.

Muslim beliefs about the Ummah: *Ummah* means a people, a nation, a sect; eg, *Ummatu Ibrahim*—the people of Abraham (Jews): *Ummatu 'Isa*—the people of Jesus (Christians); *Ummatu Muhammad*—the people of Muhammad (Muslims). These are communities of faith living in accordance with God's revelation. Issues of belief and practice arising within Islam are resolved by *ijma'*—the consensus of believers.

Unit 20: *Muslims believing together about human spirituality and the goals of human spiritual development*

Core Values and Key Concepts: 3, 5, 8.

Muslim beliefs about the nature of the human person: Allah created human beings with body, mind, emotions and soul, each element having its role and function, its needs and its rights to satisfaction. In order to bring about the harmony which God intends among them, each individual must exercise the power of his/her will and govern them according to the laws which God has laid down for his/her well-being, thus achieving synthesis, integration and balance within the personality. This is why Islam concerns itself not merely with 'religious' or 'spiritual' matters but with all aspects of human life.

Muslim beliefs about human freedom: Human beings have free will but God asks them to use this freedom of choice voluntarily and deliberately to choose what God wants for them rather than submit (or be enslaved) to their own random, conflicting desires. God has the absolute right to human obedience but He permits human beings to choose to be obedient. Anything which claims human obedience other than God is enslavement to that thing; to be the slave of God (the *'abd* of Allah) is to be freed from such enslavements.

Muslim beliefs about The Divine Decree of Allah (Qada wa qadar): Since the entire scheme or plan of creation is under the direction and control of Allah, nothing can take place without His ordaining it, nor is there such a thing as a random, chance event. Thus all suffering is purposeful; all the events of human life are purposeful. The task of the individual is to strive (*jihad*), to fill his/her mind with consciousness of God (*taqwa*), to have faith (*iman*), and not to sit back and let things take their course. A human being does not know and cannot know wherein his/her destiny lies, and until he/she has exhausted all possible means and what is inevitable occurs, he/she cannot be said to have encountered that destiny.

Muslim beliefs in the Hereafter: ie: belief in the Day of Judgment, bodily resurrection, Heaven and Hell. A Muslim, knowing that God alone controls life and death, tries to do such deeds as will merit the pleasure of Allah and His mercy and grace. No Muslim is guaranteed Paradise.

(D) *Judaism: a Jewish Life-World Curriculum*

(i) *Using the Core Values Criteria to identify the 'essential minimum' key-concepts from Judaism*

Core Values Criteria	'Essential Minimum' Key Concepts
1. Providential source of order, meaning and purpose in the universe; The Sacred; Source of Revelation and Truth;	Y H W H: the One, True, Everlasting God, Creator and Lord of the Universe: the God of Abraham, Isaac, and Jacob: the One whose name is too holy to be written or pronounced.
2. Agent or agencies of Revelation; records of Revelation; experience of Revelation;	Torah; Patriarchs; Prophets; History; Nature;
3. View of the human;	Created by God; Fallen and sinful; Loved by God; Having free will;

4. View of a just society;	All humans reconciled with God; The Community of Israel (Kelel Yisra'el) keeping the Torah (and, therefore, the Covenant); The Kingdom of Heaven; The Messianic Age;
5. Individual self-fulfilment through:	The Community of Israel (Kelel Yisra'el); Learning and keeping God's Commandments (Torah, Talmud); Righteousness; Holiness; Good works;
6. Ethical perspective;	Following the teaching of the Torah and Talmud; Duty to love one's neighbour as oneself (Golden Rule); Duty to promote social justice; Duty to cherish and serve others; Duty to be righteous, moral and holy;
7. Community of faith;	The Community of Israel (Kelel Yisra'el); A Light to all Nations (The Mission of the Community of Israel); The People of the Covenant; A Holy Nation;
8. Spiritual values;	universal brotherhood, social justice, peace; the obligation to be holy, moral, 'righteous', and to perfect one's relationship with God and with other human beings; repentance and remorse for sin: renewed effort to fulfil the commandments of God; seeking truth; rejoicing in God's Law and in His creation; blessing God for all (good and bad) that happens; living life to the full.

(ii) Applying the four organising categories of Family, Faith Community, Plural Society and World-Wide Community to the phenomena of Jewish Faith.

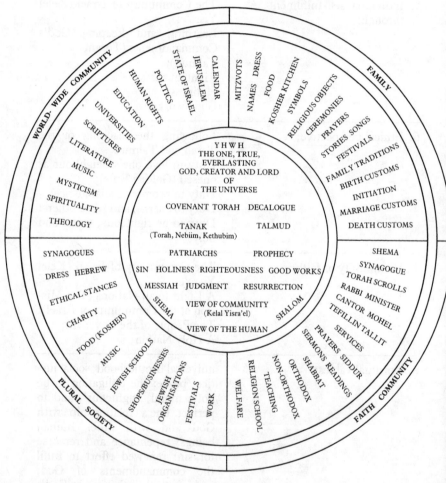

JEWISH FAITH

Figure Fifteen: The phenomena of Jewish Faith

(iii) Applying the Spiral Curriculum Matrix to content drawn from the phenomena of Jewish faith.

Jews

Theme:	In the Family:	In the Faith Community:	In the Plural Society:	In the World-Wide Community:
Jews growing together:	1	2	3	4
Jews celebrating together:	5	6	7	8
Jews learning together:	9	10	11	12
Jews acting together:	13	14	15	16
Jews believing together:	17	18	19	20

(iv) Illustrative content of Units with indications of Core Values and Key Concepts 'visited' in each Unit

Unit 1: Jews growing together in the Family

Core Values and Key Concepts: 1–8:

Religious objects in the home illustrative of Jewish beliefs and practices: eg, mezuzah, Sabbath candlesticks and candles, Havdalah candle, Yahrzeit and Yom Kippur candles, Chanukah candelabrum and candles, spice box, seder dish, kiddush cup, challah cover, tefillin (ie, phylacteries), tallit, yarmulka (kippah or skull cap), greeting cards, mementoes of Israel, Hebrew Bible, prayer books, religious literature, etc.

The various patterns of Jewish family life: eg, actions—saying blessings at mealtimes and at many other times during the day, family prayers, wearing tefillin, etc; routines—preparing kosher meals, the three obligatory meals of *Shabbat* (*the Jewish Sabbath*), visits to the synagogue, entertaining relatives and friends, etc.

Food, dress and family customs: The *Kosher* kitchen; ritual baths (*mikveh*); family names.

Birth customs: *Brit Milah/Brit Banot* (Covenant of circumcision).

Initiation rites: Becoming *Bar/Bat Mitzvah* (*Son/Daughter of the Commandment*) at thirteen years: ie, responsible for the *Mitzvot*—fulfilling your own obligations as a Jew; father traditionally says the blessing, '*Blessed be He who has freed me from this responsibility for my son's behaviour*'; shown by being called up to read the *Torah*.

Marriage customs: engagement customs (*Erusin*) eg, the giving of a *Tallit* and *Kittel* to the groom by the bride; the wedding (*Nissuin*); the contract (*Ketubah*), the groom (*Chatan*) places the veil on the bride (*Kallah*), they stand under the canopy (*Chuppah*), the *Ketubah* is read, seven blessings (*Sheva Brachot*) are said, the groom smashes a glass and everyone says '*Mazal Tov*'.

Death customs: *The Shema*—the last words spoken; wearing a ribbon as a sign of mourning; members of the community perform the *Mitzvah* and prepare the body for burial; three prayers at the funeral, eg, the *Kaddish*; a meal including an egg (the symbol of life); *Shiva*—seven days when the family 'sit'; *Sheloshim*—thirty days during which normal life is resumed but no festivities; *Shanah*—eleven months when the *Kaddish* is said daily; tombstone unveiled on the anniversary of the death.

Unit 2: Jews growing together in the Faith Community

Core Values and Key Concepts: 2, 4, 6, 7.

The interior of the synagogue (*Beth-Ha-Knesset—House of Meeting*): eg, the holy Ark (*Aron Hakodesh*), the Ten Commandments, the Star of David (*Magen David*), the curtain (*a Parochet*), the eternal/perpetual light (*Ner Tamid*), the seven branched candelabrum (*Menorah*), the platform (*bimah*), etc.
The Torah scrolls, the mantle, breastplate, bells (*rimmonim*), crowns, etc. Stained glass windows: symbols and historical events depicted; no human images.

The organisation, uses and facilities of the synagogue: eg, ritual, social, cultural, educational.

The role of the Rabbi, Minister and other officials.

What going to the synagogue means for Jews.

Unit 3: *Jews growing together in the Plural Society*

Core Values and Key Concepts: 2, 3, 4, 6, 7, 8.

Orthodox and Non-Orthodox Traditions of Judaism: Orthodox = Orthodox and Ultra-Orthodox, eg, Hasidic Jews; Non-Orthodox = Reform, Conservative and Liberal Judaism.

The pattern of Jewish migration to Britain: eg, immigrants from Eastern Europe in the early twentieth century and after the Second World War; subsequently from Asia and the Middle East.

The attitudes of Jews to pluralism and secular values: 'religious' and 'non-religious' Jews.

The contribution of Jews to cultural, social and economic life: traditional professional and commercial enterprises.

Unit 4: *Jews growing together in the World-Wide Community*

Core Values and Key Concepts: 1–8.

The Jews as international people living in every part of the world; their adaptation of different cultures to the Jewish way of life; eg, *Sephardim* Jews in Spain, Holland, Italy, Greece, Turkey, Yugoslavia and North Africa; *Ashkenazim* Jews in France, Germany, Poland, Austria, Hungary and Russia; *Falasha* Jews from Ethiopia; their different languages, eg, Ashkenazim speak *Yiddish*, Sephardim speak *Ladino*, Falashas have their own language.

Jewish alternatives to traditional family life: The *Chavurah*—recreating the extended family through friendship groups who may or may not live communally; the *Kibbutz*—a co-operative agricultural or industrial group working together in Israel on national land; children living separately from their parents but spending time with them after the work day and on the Sabbath (*Shabbat*).

Unit 5: *Jews celebrating together in the Family*

Core Values and Key Concepts: 1–8.

Jews celebrating Shabbat in the home: Buying food, wine and candles during the week for the Friday night (Sabbath eve) meal; preparing the table—a white tablecloth, Shabbat candles, Kiddush cups and wine, *Challah* (special loaf of twisted and braided white bread) with a *Challah* cover, flowers, a book of Shabbat blessings and songs; giving *Tzedakah* (money for the poor) before lighting the Shabbat candles (*Hadlakat Nerot*), father blessing the children (*Birkat Habanim*), the *Kiddush* (blessing over the wine), the *Hamotzi* (blessing the Challah loaf), *Shabbat Oneg*—singing, storytelling and conversation between courses—the blessing after the meal (*Birkat Hamazon*), wishing everyone *Shabbat Shalom*—a peaceful Shabbat. The observance of Sabbath is a *Mitzvah* (obligation) and reminds Jews that God made it possible for the world to be. It also reminds them that they are one with all Jewish people, past and present. The eating of three meals is a requirement for Shabbat, ie, between the beginning and the end of the Sabbath, each with their accompanying *Kiddush* over a cup of wine, and a sung Grace after each. Some Jews also attend the synagogue on Friday evening and Saturday morning and study in the afternoon; Sabbath ends with the *Havdalah* ceremony in the home to show the difference between the holiness of the Sabbath and weekdays; a blessing is said over wine and a lighted candle (also twisted and braided) and a spice box is blessed (representing the sweetness of the Sabbath).

Jews celebrating festivals in the home: Pesach (Passover Seder), Succot (Tabernacles) and Channukah.

Unit 6: *Jews celebrating together in the Faith Community*

Core Values and Key Concepts: 1–8.

Jews worshipping in the synagogue: The synagogue is a House of Prayer, a House of Study, and a House of Meeting; three set times for prayer in the synagogue each day; the central importance of the Jewish Prayer Book (*Siddur—order or arrangement, from Seder Tefillot*): the common order of the services: viz:

1. *Morning Service (Shaharit)*: blessings and Psalms, the *Shema*, the *Amidah* (eighteen benedictions said silently), reading of the *Torah* (Mondays, Thursdays, Sabbaths, festivals), *Musaf* (additional benedictions on Sabbaths and Festivals), *Alaynu* (a prayer proclaiming God's Kingship), *Kaddish* (mourners' prayer), closing hymn.
2. *Afternoon Service (Minhah)*: *Ashray (a Psalm)*, the *Amidah*, Supplications, *Alaynu*, *Kaddish*.
3. *Evening Service (Ma'ariv)*: Psalms, the *Shema*, the *Amidah*, *Alaynu*, *Kaddish*.

Tefillin and Tallit: worn by males; *tefillin* is from *tefillah* = prayer: each box containing four passages from the *Torah* (Exodus 13, 1–10, 11–16; Deuteronomy 6, 4–9, and 11, 13–21); *tallit*, worn for its *Tzitzit* (fringes) which the *Shema* requires Jews to *look at* so that they are reminded to do all God's commandments; worn only at the morning service.

Being called up to read the Torah: Three men are called up on Mondays and Thursdays (first a *Cohen*, then a *Levi*, then an *Israel*; five *Israels* read on the Sabbath); each touch the first word with his *Tallit* and makes a benediction; it is a considerable honour to be called up.

Women in the synagogue: the women's gallery in Orthodox and Ultra-Orthodox synagogues; women Rabbis permitted in Reformed Judaism.

Unit 7: *Jews celebrating together in the Plural Society*

Core Values and Key Concepts: 1–8.

The Jewish Calendar;

Festivals: The celebration of Purim and Simchat Torah.

Jewish High Holy Days (Days of Awe): Rosh Hashanan (New Year), Aseret Yemey Teshuvah (the Ten Days of Penitence), Yom Kippur (Day of Atonement).

Unit 8: *Jews celebrating together in the World-Wide Community*

Core Values and Key Concepts: 1–8.

Pilgrimage to Jerusalem: The significance of the Western Wall; Jews journeying to Jerusalem for the 'pilgrim festivals' of ancient times, ie, Passover (*Pesach*), Pentecost (*Shavu'ot*), Tabernacles (*Succot*); 'Seder Night'—a pilgrimage in the mind for Jews the world over; 'Next Year in Jerusalem Rebuilt!'.

The observance of Tisha B'Av: The commemoration of the destruction of the first and second Temples;

The celebration of Yom-ha-Atzmaut: The establishment of the State of Israel.

Unit 9: *Jews learning together in the Family*

Core Values and Key Concepts: 1–8.

The Jewish home as an agent of religious education: Nurturing children in Jewish identity and faith through participating in religious practices in the home; studying the Torah and reading stories from the Hebrew Bible; living by the commandments; performing good deeds in the community; celebrating the festivals and observing the High Holy Days; learning from older members of the family.

Unit 10: Jews learning together in the Faith Community

Core Values and Key Concepts: 1, 2, 5, 6, 7, 8.

The Jewish Scriptures: The *Torah* (Law), the *Nebiim* (Prophets), and the *Kethubim* (Writings) = *Tanak* or *TNK* (*not* the Old Testament);

The Torah: 'the five books of Moses'; three important stages: the giving of the Ten Commandments to Moses; discovery of the Scrolls of the Law by King Josiah in 621 BCE during the redecoration of the Temple; the experience of the Exile after 586 BCE and the part played by the Scrolls of the Law in preserving Jewish identity.

Teaching about God and His relationship to the Hebrew People; the concepts of 'covenant' (*berit*) and 'ethical monotheism'.

The Ten Commandments (Decalogue) and the 613 Biblical Laws;

The Shema: Deuteronomy 4: 4–9; 11: 31–32; Numbers 15: 37–41.

The Thirteen Fundamental Principles of the Jewish Faith (Maimonides' Commentary on the Mishnah): the existence of the Creator; the unity of God; the denial that God has a body; God's pre-existence; God the only One to be worshipped; prophets; Moses the father of all prophets; the Torah is from heaven; nothing to be added to or taken from the Torah; God has knowledge of all human deeds; God rewards those who obey the commands of the Torah and punishes those who do not; a Messiah will come; the resurrection of the righteous. '*When all these principles are held as certain by a man and his faith in them is firm, then he belongs to the Community of Israel (Kelal Yisra'el).*

The Attributes of God: eg, merciful, gracious, endlessly patient, loving and true, showing mercy to thousands, forgiving iniquity, transgression and sin, and acquitting.

The Talmud: Two parts: *The Mishnah* and *The Gemara*.

Unit 11: *Jews learning together in the Plural Society*

Core Values and Key Concepts: 3, 4, 5, 6, 7, 8.

Safeguarding Jewish culture, identity and ideals in the plural society: The importance given to transmitting Jewish cultural norms to young people subject to non-Jewish influences and values.

Jewish education: Its nature and purpose; 'Religion School' in the synagogue; Hebrew; Jewish primary and secondary education; the attitudes of Jewish parents to state education and to religious education in state schools.

Jewish organisations: The Board of Deputies of British Jews; the Jewish Welfare Board; the Jewish Education Bureau.

Judaism and other faiths: Attitudes of Orthodox and Non-Orthodox traditions to other religions, cultures and to proselytes.

The Jewish experience of anti-semitism.

Unit 12: *Jews learning together in the World-Wide Community*

Core Values and Key Concepts: 1–8.

The Jewish contribution to scholarship and learning: eg, Maimonides, Spinoza, Einstein, Freud, Marx.

Some notable contemporary Jews: Yehudi Menuhin, Leonard Bernstein, Sir Keith Joseph, Leon Britton, Barbra Streisand.

Unit 13: *Jews acting together in the Family*

Core Values and Key Concepts: 3, 4, 5, 6, 7, 8.

The family as the basis of Jewish life: Some *mizvot* which relate to Jewish families: to honour parents (*Kibud Av v'Aym*), to establish a home where love and peace are valued (*Sh'lom Bayit*), to have respect for the elderly and for their wisdom and advice (*Leviticus 19: 32; Job 12: 12*), to do kind deeds for others (*G'milut Chesed*), to contribute help or money for others (*Tzedakah*), to marry (*Genesis 2: 18, 22–24*), to have children (*Genesis 1: 28*), to visit the sick (*Bikur Cholim*), to establish regular worship patterns with the family (*T'filah-Avodah*), to engage in study of the Jewish faith (*Talmud Torah*).

Unit 14: *Jews acting together in the Faith Community*

Core Values and Key Concepts: 2, 3, 5, 7, 8.

The Jewish view of the human: Created by God in the divine image with an immortal soul; since the body houses the immortal soul it must not be desecrated or defiled; because all human beings share this divine relationship they are brothers; their relationship with God also imposes ethical obligations upon them; human beings partake of God's holy presence through observing God's moral and ethical commandments; God's gift of the Torah to the Jews means that they are even more obligated to learn the divine commandments and apply them to life; human beings are bound by the limitations of their mortality (the doctrine of the fall) and thus God regards them with understanding and compassion; they have a duty to be grateful to God and praise Him whether in circumstances of joy or sorrow, in prosperity or in adversity; as children of God human beings are endowed with moral freedom and are active co-workers with God in fulfilling His divine purpose and will.

Spiritual development in the Jewish Way: Through prayer, study, observing God's commandments and fulfilling *mizvots*, including good deeds.

Jewish 'spiritual' values: Peace, social justice, the obligation to be holy, moral, 'righteous', and to perfect one's relationship with God and with other human beings; repentance and remorse for sin; renewed effort to fulfil the commandments of God; seeking truth; rejoicing in God's Law and in His creation; blessing God for all (good and bad) that happens; living life to the full.

Unit 15: *Jews acting together in the Plural Society*

Core Values and Key Concepts: 4, 6, 8.

The duty of Jews to protect the environment: The Jewish regard for nature and the natural world; consciousness of the sun and moon, the seasons, seasonal fruits, etc. Planting trees (eg, *Rosh Hashanah la-Ilanot*—New Year for Trees).

The duty of Jews to promote social justice: The application of Jewish teachings to the economic order, to industry and commerce, and to national and international affairs; justice to all, irrespective of race, sect, class is the inalienable right and the inescapable obligation of all; the state and organised government exist in order to further these ends.

The duty of Jews to ensure the survival of the Jewish people so that they can fulfil the task for which God has chosen them.

The application of Jewish teaching to contemporary personal, social and moral issues: eg, wealth and poverty, racism, war and peace, defence, human rights, sexism, sexuality, abortion, contraception, euthanasia, conservation, materialism/consumerism.

Unit 16: Jews acting together in the World-Wide Community

Core Values and Key Concepts: 3, 4, 6, 7, 8.

The Jewish experience of the Holocaust: Almost six million Jews (including 1,500,000 children) of all nationalities were murdered during the Nazi Holocaust; Himmler saw the destruction of European Jewry as 'a glorious part of our history' and the 'Final solution' to the 'Jewish problem'; 250,000 survivors sought a place where they could go to rebuild their lives; many turned to Palestine, the promised Jewish homeland, and were instrumental in establishing the State of Israel, a nation dedicated to ensuring—'Never again'.

Zion and Zionism;

The State of Israel Today.

Unit 17: Jews believing together about God

Core Values and Key Concepts: 1, 2.

Jewish beliefs about the nature of God: The heart of Judaism and its chief contribution to religion is the doctrine of the One, living God who rules the world through law and love. In Him all existence has its creative source and human beings their ideal of conduct. Though transcending time and space, He is the indwelling Presence of the world. Jews worship Him as the Lord of the Universe and as their merciful Father.

Unit 18: Jews believing together about revelation

Core Values and Key Concepts: 1, 2.

Jewish beliefs about the Torah: God reveals Himself not only in the majesty, beauty and orderliness of nature, but also in the vision and moral striving of the human spirit. Revelation is a continuous process, confined to no one group and no one age. Yet the people of Israel, through its prophets, achieved unique insight in the realm of religious truth. The Torah, both written and oral, enshrines Israel's ever-growing consciousness of God and the moral law. It preserves the historical precedents, sanctions and norms of Jewish life, and seeks to mould it in the patterns of goodness and holiness.

Unit 19: Jews believing together about the world, human society and the People of Israel (Kelal Yisra'el)

Core Values and Key Concepts: 4, 6, 7, 8.

Jewish beliefs about the creation of the world: created by God and loved by Him.

Jewish beliefs about human society: As God is the Creator of all, all human beings are His children and bound together in the bond of brotherhood; rabbinic Judaism teaches that the term 'neighbour' is to include Jew and Gentile; *'Thou shalt love thy neighbour as thyself'*; the Ten Commandments are universal laws; the moral commands of God are obligations for all peoples, races and religions; Jewish sacrifices in ancient times were offered on behalf of all humanity; Judaism proclaims the fatherhood of God and the universality of the divine love.

Jewish beliefs about the People of Israel (Kelal Yisra'el): God chose the People of Israel to fulfil a special place in His divine purpose; because God is moral, holy and righteous, His People are required to be so too; the People of Israel are co-workers with God in building a better world and bringing the Divine Plan to its fruition. *'Throughout the ages it has been Israel's mission to witness to the Divine in the face of every form of paganism and materialism. We regard it as our historic task to co-operate with all men in the establishment of the Kingdom of God, of universal brotherhood, justice, truth and peace on earth. This is our Messianic goal.'* (*The Columbus Platform of Reform Judaism, 1937*).

Unit 20: Jews believing together about human spirituality and the goals of human spiritual development

Core Values and Key Concepts: 3, 5, 8.

Jewish beliefs about the nature of the human person: Body, soul/spirit;
Jewish beliefs about human freedom;
Jewish beliefs about holiness and righteousness;
Jewish beliefs about repentance and forgiveness;
Jewish beliefs about the resurrection of the righteous;
Jewish beliefs about the Messianic Age.

(E) Sikhism: A Sikh Life-World Curriculum

(i) Using the Core Values Criteria to identify the 'essential minimum' key-concepts from Sikhism

Core Values Criteria	'Essential Minimum' Key Concepts
1. Providential source of order, meaning and purpose in the universe; The Sacred; Source of Revelation and Truth;	God—The One, the Only One (Ik Oanker: Akal Purakh: Sat Nam: Sat Guru);
2. Agent or agencies of Revelation; records of Revelation; experience of Revelation;	Gurmat—the teaching of the Guru; Guru Nanak; The Ten Gurus; Guru Granth Sahib; God cannot be discovered but only 'known by the Guru's Grace' (gur prasadi—God's grace);
3. View of the human;	Human beings are part of the endless cycle of birth, death and rebirth (samsara); Actions in one life determine rebirth or release (law of karma); The goal of life is release from the round of births (moksha); Human beings are neither good nor bad but in their natural condition (manmukh) are self-willed, self-reliant and attached to the world;
4. View of a just society;	Following the teachings of the Gurus; One class (or caste)—ie, humanity; One stage of life (ashrama)—ie, being a householder; One duty (dharma)—ie, serving God through one's everyday life;

5. Individual self-fulfilment through:	The ascent of the soul to God through God's grace and by constant remembrance of God through the practice of nam simaran (repeating the name of God) and following the teachings of the Guru; Living in the company of enlightened people (ie, The Panth);
6. Ethical perspective;	Following the teachings of the Gurus; The ethic of hard work (kirt karna); The ethic of giving alms to anyone in need (wand chakna); The ethic of service to others (sewa);
7. Community of faith;	The Panth (ie, the world-wide community of Skihs); The Sangat (ie, the local community of Sikhs); The Khalsa (ie, 'Pure Ones'—those Sikhs who have been initiated through taking Amrit (amrit sanskar) and must vow to live according to the Khalsa code of conduct (rahit);
8. Spiritual values;	'adore the Divine Name, practise one's livelihood, and share its fruits'; peaceful but strong to defend the faith; serving others; living a virtuous life.

(ii) *Applying the four organising categories of Family, Faith Community, Plural Society and World-Wide Community to the phenomena of Sikh faith.*

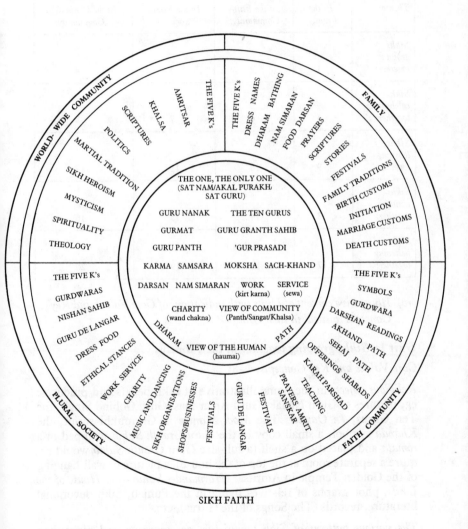

Figure Sixteen: The phenomena of Sikh Faith

(iii) *Applying the Spiral Curriculum Matrix to content drawn from the phenomena of Sikh faith.*

Sikhs

Theme:	In the Family:	In the Faith Community:	In the Plural Society:	In the World-Wide Community:
Sikhs growing together:	1	2	3	4
Sikhs celebrating together:	5	6	7	8
Sikhs learning together:	9	10	11	12
Sikhs acting together:	13	14	15	16
Sikhs believing together:	17	18	19	20

(iv) *Illustrative content of Units with indications of Core Values and Key Concepts 'visited' in each Unit*

Unit 1: Sikhs growing together in the Family

Core Values and Key Concepts: 1–8:

Religious objects in the home illustrative of Sikh beliefs and practices: eg, pictures of Guru Nanak, Guru Amar Das, Guru Gobind Singh, the Ten Gurus, *Ik Oanker*, The *Mool Mantra* in Gurmukhi script, the *Khanda* symbol, a small copy of the *Guru Granth Sahib* wrapped in a *romala* and placed on a shelf (a full-size *Guru Granth Sahib* would require a separate room at the top of the house), a picture or wall-hanging of the Golden Temple in Amritsar (*Harmander Sahib—the House of the Lord*), photographs of relatives living in the Punjab, Sikh devotional literature, records (The Songs of the Gurus), etc.

The various patterns of Sikh family life: eg, morning and night-time prayers, visiting the Gurdwara for *darshan* (an audience) with the Guru Granth Sahib and assisting in the *Guru de Langar* (The Guru's kitchen), personal devotions, visits to and from relatives, etc. (NB the 'extended' nature of the Sikh family; for many Sikhs in Britain the 'family home' is still that of the senior male member in the Punjab.)

Food, dress and family customs: First reference to the *'Five K's'—kesh* (uncut hair), *kangha* (comb), *kirpan* (sword), *kara* (steel bangle), and *kaccha* (short trousers/underpants); also the *pagri* (turban) for adult male Sikhs, the *dupatta* (scarf) for female Sikhs, the *jura* (top-knot covered with a square of cloth called the *patka*) for Sikh boys; Sikh women and girls also wear *salwar* (trousers) and *kameeze* (tunic top), and Sikh men *churidar pyjamas* (tight fitting trousers) and a *kurta* (a loose overshirt).

Birth customs: birth ceremony (*janam sanskar*): Naming ceremony (*nam sanskar*):

Initiation rites: Initiation into the *Khalsa* (*amrit sanskar*); (see Unit 13).

Marriage customs: (*Anand wedding service*): the arrangement of a marriage between families; the betrothal ceremony before the Guru Granth Sahib; exchanging of gifts; the gift of a red head scarf (*chunni*) to the bride from the groom; the wedding ceremony in the Gurdwara; marriage as a union of two souls; the tying of the bride's *chunni* to the groom's scarf; the singing of the wedding hymn (*Lavan*) during which the bride and groom walk four times round the Guru Granth Sahib; the sharing of *karah parshad*.

Death customs: the Psalm of Peace (*Sukmani*) is read at the death bed; the body is washed and dressed complete with the Five K's and taken to the Gurdwara; cremation follows (at a crematorium in this country) and the bedtime prayer (*Sohila*) is recited as the body is placed in the furnace; the ashes are often flown back to India to be sprinkled on the Ganges; the family arranges for a continuous, slow reading of the Guru Granth Sahib to be undertaken for ten days either at the home or in the Gurdwara (*Sehaj Path*).

Unit 2: Sikhs growing together in the Faith Community

Core Values and Key Concepts: 2, 5, 6, 7, 8:

The exterior and interior of the Gurdwara (The House of the Guru): The Sikh flag (*Nishan Sahib*), the prayer hall, the dais, the *takht* (throne), the *palki* (canopy), *romalas* (embroidered cloths covering the Guru Granth Sahib), the *chauri* (fly-whisk of yak hair), pictures of the Ten Gurus, the bedroom of the Guru Granth Sahib, etc.

The organisation, use and facilities of the Gurdwara: eg, ritual, social, cultural, educational. The *Guru de Langar* (The Guru's Kitchen).

The role of the Granthi (not a priest but anyone, man or woman, who can read the Guru Granth Sahib) and the Management Committee.

What going to the Gurdwara means for Sikhs.

Unit 3: Sikhs growing together in the Plural Society

Core Values and Key Concepts: 2, 3, 4, 6, 7, 8:

The variety of Sikh communities in Britain: Differences of caste and settlement patterns; eg, Kumhar, Khatri, Jats, Ramgarhias and Bhatras; the majority of Sikhs from the Punjab, mainly Jats; Ramgarhia Sikhs also from East Africa; caste related to occupation: eg, Jats—peasant, land-owners; Ramgarhia—artisans, craftsmen, professionals; Khatri—urban business and professional classes (the caste to which all the Ten Gurus belonged); Bhatras—lower caste, shop keepers, workers; additionally, Balmikis (sweepers) and Ravidasis (leatherworkers), two further Punjabi castes, but with closer links with Hinduism.

The contribution of Sikhs to cultural, social and economic life: The persistence of traditional roles; professional and commercial enterprises, etc.

Unit 4: Sikhs growing together in the World-Wide Community

Core Values and Key Concepts: 4, 7, 8:

The main centres of the Sikh 'diaspora': United Kingdom, Canada and the United States of America; 80% of Indian Sikhs concentrated in the Punjab.

The five seats (takhts) of Sikh spiritual authority: The *Akal Takht* in Amritsar, and those at Anandpur, Patna, Nander, and Damdama.

The birthplace of Guru Nanak: Nankana Sahib now in Pakistan.

The Punjab as the main focus of Sikh consciousness; the partition of the Punjab in 1947 with the founding of Pakistan; the division of the Punjab into two new states (Punjab and Haryana) in 1966.

Contemporary life in the Punjab; agricultural, social, cultural (eg, *Bhangra* and *Gidha* dancing; Sikh music (*ragas*)).

Unit 5: Sikhs celebrating together in the Family

Core Values and Key Concepts: 1, 2, 3, 5, 7, 8.

Sikh family celebrations: eg, birth of a baby, initiation into the *Khalsa*, a visit from relatives from the Punjab, a marriage or wedding anniversary, etc. (Or in Unit 1).

Daily religious observance in the home: The concept of *dharam*—duty; early rising, bathing, dressing, reciting the *Japji Sahib* (or just '*Satman Waheguru*'), meditating, reading a hymn (*shabad*); morning prayers, evening prayers (*Rehiras*), bedtime prayers (*Sohila*).

Visiting the Gurdwara for darsan—an audience with the Guru Granth Sahib.

Celebrating festivals in the home: Diwali, The Gurpurbs (ie, the birthdays of Guru Nanak and Guru Gobind Singh and the martyrdom of Guru Arjun Dev); special food and attendance at the Gurdwara.

Unit 6: Sikhs celebrating together in the Faith Community

Core Values and Key Concepts: 1–8.

The Sikh 'Sangat' at worship in the Gurdwara: The ceremony (at around 5.00 am) of awakening the Guru Granth Sahib and carrying the Sacred Book from the bedroom to his place on the *Takht*; the adoption of Sunday in Britain as the main day for Sikh congregational worship; actions of Sikhs upon entering the Gurdwara; prostration before the Guru Granth Sahib and making an offering; the Sikh musicians (*rajis*); *kirtan*—the singing of hymns (*shabads*) from the Guru Granth Sahib; *ketha*—the sermon or exposition; *Anand Sahib*—the Hymn of Guru Amar Das; *Ardas*—'The Sikh Prayer'; distribution of *Karah Parshad*; taking a meal together in the *Langar* (Kitchen).

Unit 7: Sikhs celebrating together in the Plural Society

Core Values and Key Concepts: 1–8.

The major festivals of the Sikhs: The celebration of any festival begins with the *Akhand Path*—a continuous reading of the Guru Granth Sahib taking forty-eight hours; the reading of the last five pages is made to coincide with the beginning of the festival; *Baisakhi Day* (celebrating the founding of the Khlasa by Guru Gobind Singh in 1699; on this occasion the flag pole of *Nishan Sahib* is taken down and cleaned and a new yellow cloth wound round it); *Diwali; Hola Hohall Mela* ('attack and place of attack'—originally a mock battle but now an opportunity for Sikhs to display their martial tradition, especially that of the *Nihangs*, Sikh warriors who were established by Guru Gobind Singh); *Gurpurbs*: the Birthday of Guru Nanak, the Birthday of Guru Gobind Singh, the Martyrdom of Guru Arjun Dev, the Martyrdom of Guru Tegh Bahadur, the Martydom of the two little sons of Guru Gobind Singh.

Unit 8: Sikhs celebrating together in the World-Wide Community

Core Values and Key Concepts: 1–8.

Celebrating Sikh Festivals in the Punjab: eg, Maghi Fair at Muktsar near Ferozepore; the Death of Baba Deep Singh, martyr, commemorated at Amritsar; Cheharta Fair, near Amritsar; Achal Sahib Batala Fair at Gurdaspur; plus those universally celebrated (see unit 7).

Visiting the Golden Temple (Harmander Sahib or Darbar Sahib—the First Holy Place) at Amritsar. Although Guru Nanak disapproved of 'pilgrimage', thousands of Sikhs visit the Golden Temple, often at the times of festivals.

Unit 9: Sikhs learning together in the Family

Core Values and Key Concepts: 1, 2, 3, 5, 6, 8.

Stories told to young children in Sikh homes: eg, stories from the *Janam Sakhis* about Guru Nanak, and stories about the Ten Gurus;

Nurturing children in Sikh faith and identity through symbols and actions: The Five K's; their involvement in the life of the faith community and their attendance at the Gurdwara from an early age.

Unit 10: Sikhs learning together in the Faith Community

Core Values and Key Concepts: 1, 2, 5, 6, 7, 8.

The Sikh Scriptures: The Guru Granth Sahib contains Gurbani or Gurmat—'The Word of the Gurus' or 'The Teachings of the Guru'; it is the 'Living Word of God' and the means through which God reveals himself. It consists of a collection of 3,384 hymns, each hymn (*shabad*) being set to a musical tune (*raga*) of which there are thirty-one. It was written over a period of 200 years from the time of Guru Nanak (1469–

1539) to that of Gobind Singh (1666–1708); nearly 1,000 hymns are by non-Sikhs—ie, Hindus and Muslims. It is written in *Gurmurkhi* script ('the Guru's word'), invented by Guru Angad, the second Guru; every copy is identical; sometimes called the *Adi Granth* ('*first book*') in order to distinguish it from the *Dasam Granth*, the book of Guru Gobind Singh, the tenth Guru. It became the permanent Guru for Sikhs after the death of Guru Gobind Singh, who did not choose a person to succeed him.

The Teaching of the Guru: God: The dominant theme is the praise of One God, NAM or SAT, the Truth. The Guru Granth Sahib opens with the *Mool Mantra*, and Guru Arjan decreed that each section was to begin with it. It is believed to be Guru Nanak's first composition after he returned from 'the court of God' (his call experience); it leads into the *Japji*, another of Guru Nanak's humns.

Unit 11: Sikhs learning together in the Plural Society

Core Values and Key Concepts: 3, 4, 5, 6, 7, 8.

Safeguarding Sikh culture, identity and ideals in the plural society: The importance given to transmitting Sikh cultural norms to Sikh young people born in the UK and subject to non-Sikh influences and values.

Sikh education: The importance attached to mother-tongue teaching/ bilingualism; the attitudes of Sikh parents to state education and to religious education in state schools.

Sikh organisations: eg, the Sikh Missionary Society.

Sikhism and other faiths: The attitudes of Sikhs to other religious traditions and cultures.

Unit 12: Sikhs learning together in the World-Wide Community

Core Values and Key Concepts: 1–8.

The lives and the achievements of the Ten Gurus: The geographical, social, religious and historical context of the birth and growth of Sikhism; the sixteenth and seventeenth centuries—the age of the Gurus; Guru Gobind Singh and the founding of the Khalsa and the Sikh *Panth*; the seventeenth and eighteenth centuries—the heroic age; the development of the martial tradition of Sikhism.

Unit 13: Sikhs acting together in the Family

Core Values and Key Concepts: 3, 4, 5, 6, 7, 8.

The centrality of family life within Sikhism: The fundamental obligations of the Sikh male to feed himself and his dependents and the needy through his own efforts; the concept of *sewa* (service)—giving money (Guru Gobind Singh suggested that one tenth of one's income should be given to others in need), giving time and effort to serve others, talking to others about God, not to convert them but to encourage them to believe in and love God; although one's prime responsibility is to the family, to the Sikh community and to oneself for the attainment of salvation (ie, release from samsara) through the grace (*karam*) of the Guru (ie, God), one also has a responsibility to all human beings (and animals); respect for all people and reverence for the elderly; the equality of all people.

Initiation into the Khalsa: Open to any person, man or woman, about sixteen years or over; can belong to any religion, race and nationality but should be able to read the Sikh prayers and understand their meaning; essential that initiates do not smoke or drink; willing to change and observe fully the Sikh Code of Conduct and Discipline (*rahit*); obligatory to observe the Five K's; Sikh children under sixteen can be initiated if their parents take full responsibility to see that they follow and keep the Code; Sikhs who do not become initiated are called 'Sahajdhari' (ie, a Sikh who believes the Gurus' teachings without observing the full Khalsa discipline incumbent upon a baptised Amritdhari Sikh). The ceremony always takes place in the presence of the Guru Granth Sahib, usually in the Gurdwara; conducted by five men who are themselves initiated and observe the Code; these are called *Panj Pyare* (*The Five Beloved Sikhs*); family and friends not allowed to be present; the Code is explained to the initiate who drinks *amrit* five times, has it sprinkled five times into the eyes, and five times on the hair; on each occasion are said the words, '*Waheguru ji ka khalsa, Waheguru ji ki Fateh*' ('*The Khalsa is dedicated to God, Victory ever is of Almighty Lord!*').

Unit 14: Sikhs acting together in the Faith Community

Core Values and Key Concepts: 2, 3, 5, 7, 8.

The Sikh concept of the human: Human beings are part of the cycle of rebirth (samsara); the influence of *karma*, the law of cause and effect, determines the form of the next rebirth; human beings are *manmukh*—neither good nor evil but self-willed and self-reliant; their attachment to material and worldly things can only lead to misery and rebirth; the way of release (*moksha*) is to become *gurmukh*—God-oriented; this can be attained through God's grace (*gur prasadi*) and assisted by meditating on God's Name (the practice of *nam simaran* or God-remembrance); this leads to perfection and ultimately to bliss (*moksha*).

Spiritual development in the Sikh Way: The five *khands*—piety (*dharam*), knowledge (*gian*), spiritual effort (*saram*), grace (*karam*), and truth (*sach*)—lead to the soul ascending to God; '*Jo bole so nihal: Sate Sri Akal*'—(*He who says this is saved: Truth is the immortal Lord*'.)

Sikh 'spiritual' values: Adore the Divine Name, practise one's livelihood, and share its fruits'; peaceful but strong to defend the faith; serving others; living a virtuous life.

Unit 15: Sikhs acting together in the Plural Society

Core Values and Key Concepts: 4, 6, 8.

The attitudes of Sikhs to contemporary personal, social and moral issues: eg, wealth and poverty, racism, war and peace, defence, human rights, sexism, sexuality, abortion, contraception, euthanasia, gambling, divorce, animals, conservation, materialism/consumerism, etc.

Unit 16: Sikhs acting together in the World-Wide Community

Core Values and Key Concepts: 3, 4, 6, 8.

Sikhism and politics: Political developments and conflicts in the Punjab since 1947 (the year of Partition—'the Hindus got Hindustan, the Muslims got Pakistan, what did the Sikhs get?': Master Tara Singh); internal divisions within Sikhism over the question of an independent Sikh State (Khalistan—the State of the Khalsa); the Shiromani Gurdwara Parbandhak Committee (managing Sikh gurdwara and shrines) and its relations with the Akali Dal ('Army of Immortals'); conflict between the Akali Dal and the India Congress Party; unhappy alliances and coalitions with the right-wing Hindu Jan Sangh, etc; the influence of Sant Fateh Singh on the movement for independence; the rise of Sant Jarnail Singh Bhindranwale and the growth of Sikh militantism; the seige of the Golden Temple and the martyrdom of Bhinranwale on June 6, 1984; the assassination of Mrs Gandhi (October 31, 1984) and subsequent Hindu revenge on Sikhs (eg, 2,150 Sikhs killed in Delhi); repercussions among Sikh communities throughout the world.

Unit 17: Sikhs believing together about God

Core Values and Key Concepts: 1, 2.

Sikh beliefs about the nature of God: '*Being is One, by name SAT, Truth Eternal*'; God is Creator and Sustainer but is separate from what He creates and sustains. He, however, is also immanent—God pervades all but is not identical with all; He is immanent in the human heart and He takes the initative in revealing Himself. His Word is the Guru and the human mind must become the disciple of the Word; *Akal Purakh* is also used of God, ie, The Eternal One.

Unit 18: Sikhs believing together about revelation

Core Values and Key Concepts: 1, 2.

Sikh beliefs about Guru Nanak, the Ten Gurus and the Guru Granth Sahib: In an ultimate sense God is unknowable; there is, however, a sufficient revelation communicated by the grace of the Guru (ie, God), the 'voice' of God mystically uttered within; the term 'Guru' is identified with the inner voice of God, thus the human 'guru' represents the divine presence, mystically apprehended and inwardly guiding the truly devout along the path to *sach-khand* (the 'Realm of Truth'—when all becomes harmonious); because Nanak communicated this essential truth with unique clarity he, as the human vehicle of the divine Guru, received the title of Guru; this role was transmitted to each of his nine successors, the divine spirit successively inhabiting ten enlightened individuals; the immortal Guru dwells eternally in the Guru Granth Sahib.

Unit 19: Sikhs believing together about the world, human society and the Sikh Panth

Core Values and Key Concepts: 4, 6, 7, 8.

Sikh beliefs about creation: although God is *narankar* (without form), his presence is visible to the enlightened believer, for God is immanent in all creation. The creation constitutes God's Name (*Nam*) and those who comprehend the *Nam* grasp the essential means of release from the round of births.

Sikh beliefs about human society: The concept of *manmukh* applies to all human beings; while the world is good because it was made by God, attachment to material things and reliance on one's own efforts means that people are continually reborn and never attain the bliss of *sach-khand*. While there are other paths to learning of God, the Gurus teach how to love God; it is, however, only through God's grace (*gur prasadi*) that human beings can live a virtuous life (ie, become *gurmukh*) and attain release from the round of births which is the goal of life itself.

Sikh beliefs about The Sikh Panth: *Panth* is a Sanskrit word meaning 'path' or 'road'; Sikhism is a brotherhood of 'learners' and the *Panth* is commonly used to describe the community of Sikhs. Those Sikhs who are baptised into the *Khalsa* (*Pure Ones*) are required to follow the Code of Conduct (*Rahit Maryada*) which defines a Sikh as one who believes in *Akal Purakh*, the ten Gurus and their teachings, the *Adi Granth*, and the initiation (*amrit*) instituted by Guru Gobind Singh; it adds that they should believe in no other religion. Many Sikhs are *sahaj-dhari* (not initiated) and not *amrit-dhari* (initiated); while all Sikhs belong to the *Panth*, only *amrit-dhari* Sikhs belong to the *Khalsa*.

Unit 20: Sikhs believing together about human spirituality and the goal of human spiritual development

Core Values and Key Concepts: 3, 5, 8.

Sikh beliefs about the human being: Body, soul/spirit.

Sikh beliefs about salvation: The concepts of *samsara*, *karma*, *moksha* (or *mukti*), *sahaj* (*bliss*), *sach-khand*.

Sikh beliefs about nam simaran: Constant remembrance of God through meditating on the Divine Name, greatly aided by participation in congregational worship during which the Guru Granth Sahib is read and sung; this, plus living a virtuous life, may (but only with the grace of the Guru) bring *darshan*—vision of God.

Sikh beliefs about the goal of spiritual development: Summarised in the following hymn from the Adi Granth (661):

> As is the Lord's glance, so becomes the mortal,
> Without the Lord's gracious glance no one is saved.
> If God shows mercy, then one remembers Him.
> His soul is softened and he remains in the Lord's love;
> His soul is made one with the Supreme Soul.
> His mind's duality is reabsorbed in the True mind.
> By the Guru's grace the Lord is attained.

---

3. The religious education curriculum in practice

Learning about and learning from religions

(A) *What do you think of babies?*
(Unit 1: Birth customs in the Family)

(B) *What going to church means for me*
(Unit 2: Christians growing together in the Faith Community)

(C) *Why is this night different from all other nights?*
(Unit 5: Jews celebrating together in the Family)

(D) *'Jo bole so nihal. Sat sri akal'*
(Unit 6: Sikhs celebrating together in the Faith Community)

(E) *The Goal of Life*
(Unit 8: Muslims celebrating together in the World-Wide Community)

(F) *Lord Krishna, Hero and Saviour*
(Unit 9: Hindus learning together in the Family)

(G) *War, Peace and Religion*
(Unit 15: Religions in the Plural Society)

(H) *Who is my neighbour?*
(Unit 16: Christians acting together in the World-Wide Community)

(I) *What can you trust to be true?*
(Unit 18: Revelation in the World's Religions)

The objectives of the schemes of work

While it is useful and desirable for schemes of work to be prefaced by identified and stated aims and objectives, each of the schemes of work which follow have been devised to further 'The Concerns of Religious Education' identified in Chapter Six. They have also been devised in such a way as to enable content drawn either from *Traditional Belief Systems* or *Shared Human Experience* to illuminate one or more of the Core Values, also identified in Part One. Accordingly each scheme is prefaced by an indication of those Core Values which are to be explored, the Key Religious Concepts which relate to these, and the

Belief/Value Issues in the pupils' life-worlds which may be illuminated as a consequence of studying the content. In most schemes, the distinction between *learning about* and *learning* from religions—discussed in detail in Part One—is reflected in the organisation of the content and learning experiences. I have not considered it necessary, therefore, to refine these statements of intent and translate the learning processes that follow from them into more specific aims and objectives.

(A) (Unit 1) 'What do you think of babies?'

A scheme of work for pupils aged 11–13

Belief/Value Issues: 3.

Core Values and Key Religious Concepts: 1, 2, 3, 5, 8.

Preparatory work: Unit 1 of the Adolescent Life-World Curriculum.

Learning about religions:

Use the following questions to enable pupils to investigate in groups the topic of birth customs by referring to written material, slides, artefacts illustrative of practices in Christianity, Hinduism, Islam, Judaism and Sikhism; each group to work on a different religion with learning outcomes to be shared through discussion and display with the whole class.

1. Where does the ceremony take place?
2. Who is present at the ceremony?
3. What is used during the ceremony?
4. What is said during the ceremony?
5. What happens after the ceremony?
6. For what reasons do families observe this custom?
7. What religious beliefs do the members of the religion hold about the baby?

(a) Christian birth customs:

(i) Dedicating and naming a baby in the Baptist Church; (ii) christening or baptising a baby in some Nonconformist, Anglican, Roman Catholic and Eastern Orthodox churches:

Artefacts to be made available in the classroom: Oil of chrism, a christening robe, a christening spoon and cup, a candle, a baptismal certificate, a prayer book, a Bible received by a child at its dedication, water, etc; pictures of fonts; slides showing the ceremony of baptism, etc.

Infant baptism: The baby is taken to the church by the parents: godparents, friends and the church congregation also attend. The parents and godparents promise to bring the child up in the Christian faith: using the baby's 'Christian names' the minister or priest pours water in the sign of the cross on the baby's forehead and says: '*I baptise you in the Name of the Father, and of the Son, and of the Holy Spirit. Amen.*' While one of the godparents holds a lighted candle, the minister says: '*This is to show that you have passed from darkness into light. Shine as a light in the world to the glory of God the Father.*' Everyone says The Lord's Prayer: the congregation welcome the newly baptised member of the Christian Church: a Bible and/or prayer book may be given to the baby: photographs may be taken: the family and friends may have a celebratory meal at home together: 'Christening' presents may be given to the baby: a certificate of baptism will be given to the parents.

Christian parents may have their baby baptised:
  —to give thanks to God for the baby and to dedicate it as a 'child of God';
  —so that the baby can be welcomed by members into the 'family of the Church';
  —so that the baby receives God's blessing and help (grace) as it grows up;
  —so that the baby can receive its Christian names;
  —to enable the parents and god-parents to promise that they will bring the child up in the Christian faith and way;
  —because Jesus was Himself baptised and told His disciples to baptise everyone;
  —because it is customary in their society to do so.

The beliefs Christians may hold about the baby are:
  —that all human beings belong to God;
  —that God is the creator of all life;
  —that all human beings are in need of God's forgiveness and help;
  —that the Church is open to everyone through baptism;
  —that the Church is continuing the work of Jesus Christ.

(b) Hindu birth customs:

Resources needed: Slides, photographs, a pot of honey, a spoon (or a pen), a razor, a Hindu horoscope.

Samskaras 3–9: Even before the birth certain ceremonies take place. One ritual encourages the birth of a baby boy because Hindu families believe they should have at least one son to carry out family traditions, including the death rites. Parents may give the baby a secret name which the father whispers in the baby's ear at the moment of birth:

sacred *mantras* are then said. All the ceremonies take place at home. The baby is washed to purify it: *mantras* are said for the child to be given understanding, strength and protection from evil forces: the priest writes the sacred syllable OM on the baby's tongue with a golden pen dipped in honey: passages from the *Vedas* are read: the parents tell the priest the exact time of the child's birth and he prepares a horoscope and suggests suitable syllables to the parents from which they can choose a name for the child (ie, the baby's public name). Ten or twelve days after the birth, the baby is placed in a swinging cradle; the baby is passed under and over the cradle once for each name it has been given; the women of the family then sing lullabies, and a special food, *prasadam*, is eaten: the sixth *samskara* is when the baby is taken outside and shown the sun for the first time, and the seventh when it has its first solid food; for the eighth it has its ears pierced. The ninth *samskara* takes place when the baby is one year old: the child's hair is completely shaved off so that he or she is clean and ready to start life free from evil.

Hindu parents may observe these ceremonies:
—to thank God for the gift of a child;
—to fulfil the *dharma* (duties) of their caste;
—to seek God's blessing on the child so that it grows in goodness and resists evil;
—to set the child on the path which leads to *moksha* (release from the round of births);
—because it is customary in Hindu society to do so.

The beliefs Hindus may hold about the baby are:
—that the *atman* (soul) of the baby has previously existed in other lives;
—that the *atman* (soul) is divine and immortal (one with Brahman— Ultimate Reality);
—that the goal of life is for the baby's *atman* to be absorbed into Brahman;
—that fulfilling the *samskaras* (ceremonies) of life assists the baby in being aware of God and growing towards Him;
—that all life is sacred, for God is in everything.

(c) Muslim birth customs:

Resources needed: Slides, photographs, sugar, honey, a razor and scales, etc.

Immediately after the baby is born it is bathed and the father says the *Adhan* (*the call to prayer*) into the baby's right ear:

> *Allah is the Greatest:*
> *I bear witness that there is no God but Allah:*
> *I bear witness that Muhammad is Allah's Messenger:*
> *Rush to prayer:*
> *Rush to success:*
> *Allah is the Greatest:*
> *There is no God but Allah*

Next the *Iqamah* (which is similar to the *Adhan*) is said into the baby's left ear. A few days later the *Tahneek* ceremony takes place in the home: an older member of the family places sugar and honey in the baby's mouth so that the child will be sweet tempered and obedient: a prayer follows. When the baby is a week old, the *Aqeeqah* ceremony takes place: the Prophet Muhammad (p.b.u.h.) said that this ceremony would help to protect a child from dangers in its life: the baby's head is shaved completely, the cut hair is weighed and the equivalent weight in silver is given to the poor; the baby is then given a name belonging to the Prophet Muhammad (p.b.u.h) and his family. The *Khitan* ceremony (male circumcision) normally takes place at the same time: this is followed by a feast; friends and neighbours are invited, and the feast normally involves the sacrifice of a goat(s); the meat is cooked so that it is sweet (another way of making the child sweet-tempered) and some of it is given to the poor.

Muslim parents may observe these ceremonies:
—to praise Allah for His gift of a child;
—to follow the example and practice (ie, *The Sunnah*) of the Prophet Muhammad (p.b.u.h);
—to admit the child to the Brotherhood of Islam;
—to affirm their own obedience to the Will of Allah;
—because it is customary in the Islamic community to do so.

The beliefs Muslims may hold about the baby are:
—that all life, including that of the baby, is given by Allah and is under His direction;
—that the baby, like all human beings, is utterly dependent upon Allah;
—that the goal of all human beings, including that of this child, is to be the '*abd* (slave) of Allah's will, for then human beings are free from enslavement to their own will and the wills of others;
—that the Word of Allah was revealed to the Prophet Muhammad (p.b.u.h) and that the first words the baby hears should be in praise of Allah and teach him/her that the Prophet is God's Messenger.

(d) Jewish birth customs:

Resources needed: Slides, photographs, a kiddush cup, wine, five silver coins.

If the baby is male, on the eighth day after birth the ceremony of *Brit Milah* (Covenant of circumcision) takes place in the home, in a hospital, or in a special *brit* room which some synagogues have. For each Jew circumcision is a sign that Jews have kept the covenant with God (see Genesis 17:9–14): covenants in Judaism are 'cut' not made: the ceremony is performed by a *Mohel*; the godfather/godmother (*kvater/ kvaterin*) brings the baby into the room; the person who sits in Elijah's chair and holds the baby is the *sandek*; everyone says '*Baruch Ha-Ba*' (a blessing and a welcome to the child); the father says a prayer and the mohel says: '*Blessed are you, Lord our God, King of the Universe, who sanctified us with his mizvot and commanded us concerning circumcision.*' After the foreskin is removed, the father says a blessing: '*Blessed are you, Lord our God, King of the Universe, who sanctified us with his mizvot and commanded us to enter my son into the covenant of Abraham.*' Everyone then says: '*Even as he has been entered into the covenant, so may he enter into Torah, Chuppah (marriage) and a life of good deeds.*' The ceremony is a *mitzvot* (ie, obligation/commandment); a boy is traditionally named (usually after a deceased close relative) at his *brit*; a party (*Shalom Zachar*) is given on the Friday night before the *brit milah* and another party (*Seudat Mitzvah*) afterwards; *kiddush* is said and the child given a few drops of wine. If the child is a first-born son, thirty days after his birth his father 'redeems' him (*Pidyon Haben*) by paying money (five shekels—see Numbers 18:16) to a *Cohen*; in the Reformed tradition girl babies have a covenant ceremony called *Brit Banot*.

Jewish parents may observe these ceremonies:
  —to thank God for the gift of a child;
  —because it is a *Mitzvot* (a religious obligation/commandment);
  —because it admits the child to God's covenant with Abraham;
  —because it is the traditional mark of male Jewish identity;
  —because it marks the beginning of the child's growth in the Jewish faith;
  —because it is customary in the Jewish community to do so.

The beliefs Jews may hold about the baby are:
  —that all life, including that of the baby, is given by God;
  —that, like all Jews, the baby, through the ceremony, becomes part of the Community of Israel (*Kelel Yisra'el*);

—that the baby, like all Jews, through the Covenant between God and Israel, has an obligation to be holy and moral by obeying the Commandments of the Torah.

(e) Sikh birth customs:

Resources needed: Slides, photographs, honey, '*karah parshad*' (made from mixing flour, sugar and butter), '*amrit*' (sugar dissolved in water), pictures or models of a *khanda* and *kirpan*, a *kara* (steel bracelet).

Birth ceremony (janam sanskar): The first words a baby hears, the *Mool Mantra*: '*There is One God, Eternal Truth is His Name; He made everything. He is not afraid of anything and is not fighting anything. He is not affected by time; He was not born, He Made Himself: we know about Him from the teachings of the Guru.*' Honey is placed on the baby's tongue.

Naming ceremony (nam sanskar): The baby is taken to the Gurdwara and presented before the Guru Granth Sahib. The parents take the ingredients (flour, sugar, ghee) for making *karah parshad*; they may take a *romala* (an embroidered cloth used to cover the Guru Granth Sahib) as a gift. The family gather round the Guru Granth Sahib in the Gurdwara; *amrit* (nectar) is made by dissolving sugar in water and stirring it with a double-edged sword (*khanda*); five verses of the *Japji* are recited and a prayer called the *Ardas* is offered; a prayer is said that the child '*May be a true Sikh*'; a smaller sword (*kirpan*) is dipped into the *amrit* and a drop placed on the baby's tongue; the mother drinks the rest. The *granthi* (guardian and reader of the Guru Granth Sahib) opens the Holy Book at random; the first letter of the hymn at the top of the left-hand page becomes the first letter of the child's name; the parents choose a name beginning with this initial; '*Singh*' ('Lion') is added for a boy and '*Kaur*' ('Princess') for a girl. The *granthi* says: '*Jo bole so nihal*' ('*He who speaks His name will find eternal happiness*'), and everyone replies, '*Sat sri akal*' ('*Truth is Eternal*'). Everyone then shares the *karah parshad*, indicating that all are equal. The *granthi* usually gives the child its first *kara* (steel bracelet).

Sikh parents may observe these ceremonies:
   —to thank God for the gift of a child;
   —to take the child for its first *darsan*—audience with the Guru Granth Sahib;
   —to receive God's guidance in the choice of the child's name;
   —to pray for God's grace for the child;
   —because it starts the child in the Sikh Way;
   —because it is customary in the Sikh community to do so.

The beliefs Sikhs may hold about the baby are:
   —that all life, including that of the baby, is given by God;

—that the soul of the baby is immortal and that the goal of life is the release of the soul from the round of births;

—that, with God's grace, the child will come to an awareness of God and, ultimately, blissful union of its soul with God;

—that the child is to be taught Sikh beliefs and the Sikh way of life.

Learning from religions:

Discussion points and related activities:

The value of human life: All the five religions teach that human life has value or that it is 'sacred'. What reasons do each of them give for holding this view? How are they the same and how do they differ? Do they all teach that every human life is equally valuable? What do you think about this idea? Is a baby's life as valuable as an adult's? Is a handicapped child's life as valuable as that of someone who is not handicapped? Is a child's life as valuable as that, for example, of a monarch, an important minister of state, a gifted composer, a brilliant brain surgeon? Work out a few arguments for and against the idea that people are equally valuable.

The effect of holding religious beliefs about the baby: Look at the different beliefs members of these religions hold about their babies: choose one or two of these beliefs and discuss whether parents holding them are likely to treat their children differently from parents who do not hold these religious beliefs about their children. What beliefs do you hold about babies and children?

The effect of being born into a family which holds religious beliefs: None of the babies in these families is given a choice about going through a ceremony or not: indeed, none of them know what is happening to them! Are the ceremonies really for the children or are they really for the adults? What does having these ceremonies and customs do (a) for the babies, and (b) for the parents? Do you think it is better to follow a birth custom or not to have one at all? For many babies who are not born into a religious family the custom is for relatives and friends of the parents to come and see the baby, to say how nice it is, and to bring it a present. What does this do for the baby and the parents?

The effect of having a religious faith: Most religious birth customs admit babies into a faith community in which people hold a common religious faith: most start the babies off on a pattern of life (a life of religious faith) which has a meaning for most things that will happen to them. Which is easier for people—to live by a pattern (which may involve observing rules and trying to be a particular type of person) or to take life as it comes? What things do you like about the birth customs you have been studying and what things don't you like? Do you think life is meant to be easy?

Starting a birth custom: Discuss in your group what beliefs you hold about babies and children (and about adults too, if you like) then make up a birth ceremony which expresses these beliefs through words and actions. What would need to happen for your birth ceremony to become a custom?

(B) (Unit 2) 'What going to church means for me'

A scheme of work for pupils aged 11–13

Core Values and Key Religious Concepts: 2, 5, 8.

Belief/Values Issues: 2, 5, 8.

Preparatory work: Units 1 and 2 of the Adolescent Life-World Curriculum and Unit 1 of A Christian Life-World Curriculum.

Materials to be available in the classroom: case-studies of individual Christians explaining what going to Church means for them; these may be written accounts derived from contact with Christians, tape-recordings of interviews with Christians, visits from Christians to speak to pupils in the classroom or visits by pupils to Christians in their homes, accounts brought in by pupils through their own contact with Christians, etc, etc.

Learning about Christians

Examples of case-studies

(a) *What going to Church means for me: a girl aged 11 years*:

> *My brother and I have always gone to Church, right from the time we were very young. We go with our Mum and Dad on a Sunday morning to 'Family Worship' at the Baptist Church. It starts at 11 o'clock and we go into 'Family Worship Groups' to begin with. Now that I'm 11 I go into the senior group; but my brother, who is 9, is still in the Junior Group.*
> *We do all sorts of things in our groups. Sometimes we make up plays about what it means to be a Christian today. A few weeks ago we made up a dance which our minister asked us to perform in church for everyone to see. We made it say that God loves everyone, whether you're black, like me, or white, and that everyone should do the same. After we have*

358

been in groups for half an hour or so we all go into the church and sit with our families. Even the babies come in out of the creche. We then have our 'Sharing Time' when anyone can say anything. You can tell the others about someone who is ill or who wants a bit of help, and if it's your birthday everyone sings 'Happy Birthday'! Our minister then says a prayer about all the things we've talked about. After that we sing a hymn (one I like is 'Give me oil in my lamp, keep me burning') and then we make coffee for everyone in the Church Hall. I enjoy going because everyone is very friendly and we have a good time.

Discuss the following:

1. What are the reasons why this girl goes to church?
2. Do you think her reasons for going are different from the reasons why her parents go?
3. Do you think she will keep going to church when she is older?
4. In what ways might this girl be different from someone who has never gone to church?

(b) *What going to Church means for me: a boy aged 11 years:*

I go to Church because my best friends go. We're all in the choir at St Luke's, which is Church of England. Most of the boys and girls in the choir wear blue cassocks and white surplices with a frilly white collar, but those who haven't been going long only wear cassocks and collars. I will be given a surplice and a medallion when I've finished my probation and am made a full chorister.

We have to sit in the choirstalls near the altar so everyone in the church can see us. That means we have to be well-behaved! Sometimes we try and make each other laugh, and that makes the choirmaster cross.

We sing at Matins at 11 o'clock on a Sunday and sometimes at Evensong too. I like singing some of the hymns but I don't like the psalms. I can't read music yet and it's difficult to know how to fit all the words into the tune. I can't understand the words either. The worse part is the sermon. Sometimes we sing a special anthem and that means practising a lot. We have choir practice on Friday nights at half past six so really I go to church three times every week. It's good when we have a wedding on a Saturday because we get a pound then, although sometimes I'd rather be watching the football on TV.

I'm nearly 12 now and I suppose my voice will break soon. Some boys become servers when that happens but I'm not sure I want to, but I don't much like the idea of just sitting in the congregation. I might leave then, but I'll see what my friends do.

Discuss the following:
1. What are the reasons why this boy goes to church?
2. Do you think his parents go to church too?
3. Do you think he will keep going to church after his voice breaks?
4. Do you think that going to church is having any effect on the sort of person he is?

(c) *What going to Church means for me: a youth aged 16 years*:

I'm 16 and a Roman Catholic. I go to the Catholic Church of Our Lady of Lourdes. Since my confirmation and first communion when I was eight I've always attended Mass on a Sunday and on Feast Days such as Ascension Day, the Feast of Corpus Christi and the Feast of the Assumption of the Blessed Virgin Mary. These are what we call 'Holy Days of Obligation'.

At our service the priest repeats what Jesus Christ did and said at the Last Supper on the night before he was betrayed by Judas. In this way he consecrates the bread and wine and we believe that they become the Body and Blood of Christ. When this happens we believe that Christ Himself is present on the altar and so when we take communion we are receiving Jesus into our bodies. I find this a very important thing to do. It makes me feel close to Our Lord and afterwards it's as if I'm taking Jesus with me wherever I go. This helps me to live a better life and be a better follower of Jesus.

Going to Mass also gives me a chance to thank God for all He has done for me, especially for sending His Son Jesus Christ to this world to take away our sins. I also sometimes go into the church during the week to say my prayers in front of the Blessed Sacrament—that's the consecrated bread left over after Mass which is kept in the Tabernacle on the altar. This makes me feel close to Jesus too.'

Discuss the following:
1. What are the reasons why this youth goes to church?
2. What are the ways in which he finds he comes close to Jesus?
3. Why is this important to him?
4. If you met him, what would you like to ask him more about?
5. How does being a Catholic affect the sort of person you become?

(d) *What going to Church means for me: a woman aged 24 years*:

When I was a teenager I believed that you could be a Christian without going to church. When I went, I didn't always find church interesting: in fact, to be honest, sometimes I was bored stiff! But now that I'm older, meeting with other Christians has become important to me. You see, I've learnt that believing in God and trying to put into practice what the Bible teaches isn't very easy. You need to work really hard at it to make it easy! There are always doubts creeping in and if you let this happen what faith you have soon goes and you forget all about it.

Being with other Christians, some with the same doubts as me, helps me along. Worshipping together and then sharing some of my doubts and worries with others keeps my faith alive. Once a month a number of us meet in each other's homes to discuss some of these things. We argue a good deal! Everyone gets a chance to give their point of view and share their own experiences, and although we rarely all agree on anything we do all feel that meeting in this way brings us nearer to God. It seems to prove that it is true that when two or three meet together in Jesus's name He is present. You can't be a Christian on your own. I didn't realise that when I was young.

Discuss the following:

1. What are the reasons why this young woman goes to church?
2. What things might have happened to her to make her want to be with other Christians?
3. Do you think it matters that the Christians in her church 'rarely all agree on anything'? Shouldn't all Christians have the same beliefs?
4. What difference, if any, is there between a group of Christians meeting for discussion, and any other sort of discussion group?

(e) *What going to Church means for me: a woman aged 74 years:*

I've been going to the Methodist Church in our road for over seventy years. Mother and father used to take us to the Sunday services when we were children and we all went to Sunday School. I've still got some of the 'star' cards we were given for good attendance in those days, and some of the books I was presented with at the Scholars' Prize Giving. The Sunday School Anniversary was our big occasion, and, of course, the Sunday School Treat when we would all be taken to the countryside for a picnic. One year we went to the seaside: it was the first time I'd seen the sea and I can remember us all standing on the beach singing choruses like, 'I will make you fishers of men' and 'I'm H-A-P-P-Y'.

A lot of things have happened to me since then—some very happy and some very sad. I often find myself thinking of those times when I am at church. Although they have been dead many years, I have vivid memories of my parents. Both of them loved our church. I still sit in the place where we used to sit as a family. And, of course, I remember my wedding day. I thank God for the many years of happiness my husband and I had together before he died. Of course there are lots of young families who come to our Church: they've all got a kind word for me and they're all so full of life. I like being part of that. But when I see all the children up there on the anniversary platform singing their hearts out, I can't help thinking back to when my own children were up there. They were such happy times.

So when you ask me to say what going to church means for me, it's like asking me to tell you the story of my life! We are part of that church, part of the bricks and mortar. It has held my family together for more than three-quarters of a century, and, I suppose, in a funny sort of way, we have held it together—by just being there, Sunday after Sunday—like so many other folk of my generation.

Discuss the following:
1. What are the reasons why this elderly lady goes to church?
2. What is it about being in the church which causes her to relive her memories?
3. What does she mean when she says that the church has 'held her family together'?
4. Would you have liked to have been her when she was young, or a member of her family?

Learning from Christians

Help pupils to reflect on the motives people have for doing things and on how motives change as they grow older. Would you say all these people are 'Christians'? Can children be 'Christians'? What does being a 'Christian' mean? Is it possible to be growing in the Christian way without really knowing you are? When might the two young people of eleven—case-studies (a) and (b)—have to make a conscious choice to be Christians or not? How would they do it? What is involved in making such a decision? When might you have to make a conscious choice to grow in a particular way? How will you do it? If you don't make a conscious choice, will you still keep on growing? In what direction? If you could swap places with any of the people in the case-studies, who would you choose to be? Why? Choose an experience you have of belonging to a group and try to write a description of what it means for you to belong to that group.

(C) (Unit 5) 'Why is this night different from all other nights?'

A scheme of work for pupils aged 11–13

Core Values and Key Religious Concepts: 1–8.

Belief/Value Issues: 1–8.

Preparatory work: Unit 5 of the Adolescent Life-World Curriculum.

Materials to be available in the classroom: Ingredients and religious objects required for a Seder, viz, white table cloth, candles in candle sticks, wine cups, matzah, a Seder Dish, roasted shank bone, roasted egg, horseradish, parsley or lettuce, 'red wine' (ie, Ribena), Haggadah.

The lesson involves a re-enactment of the main features of a Seder, preferably by a Rabbi, Minister, Jewish male, Jewish female, or, if no Jewish person is available, the teacher. Multiple copies of a useful but inexpensive Haggadah can be obtained from the Jewish Education Bureau, 8 Westcombe Avenue, Leeds, LS8 2BS.

Learning about the Seder

The main features of the Seder are:

1. All 'leavened' food (*chametz*) and all dishes and utensils that have been connected with it, are removed from the house for the duration of the festival. Traditionally, '*searching for the chametz*' takes place on the eve of the Passover. Leavened food is replaced by *Matzah*.

2. Apart from the religious basis of the festival, important features include good company and good food. Non-Jews may be invited to the ceremony.

3. As on the Sabbath Eve, the ceremony begins with the mother of the family lighting the candles and saying a blessing.

4. To set the Seder Table for the ceremony the following items are required:

—*matzah*;
—bitter herbs (*maror*)—grated horseradish in memory of the 'bitterness' of slavery in Egypt;
—*haroset*—a sweet paste made of apples, nuts, cinammon, grated fine and mixed with a little wine, simulating 'mortar' used by the Jews to undertake Pharaoh's building work during their slavery in Egypt;
—part of a roasted shankbone of a lamb, with a little meat on it, in memory of the ancient Temple sacrifice;
—a baked egg—symbolising the new life of spring but also a symbol of mourning for the lost Temple;
—lettuce, parsley or celery—to be dipped in salt-water as part of the ceremony;
—these items are placed on a traditional Seder Plate and three slices of *matzah* are placed on a second dish.

The ceremony:

'*Haggadah*' means 'a recital'—Jews are required to tell their children the story of the ancient Exodus from Egypt; the Passover festival celebrates that deliverance. 'Seder' means 'order' or 'programme' and this, traditionally, consists of fifteen steps:

1. Recite the *Kiddush* (blessings over the wine to consecrate the Festival);
2. Wash the hands (prior to partaking of the green herbs);
3. Partake of the green herbs;
4. Divide the *Matzah* (so that the *Afikoman* may be put away)
5. Read the *Haggadah*;
6. Wash the hands (for the meal proper);
7 & 8. Recite the two blessings over the *Matzah*;
9. Recite the blessing over the bitter herbs;
10. Eat the *Hillel sandwich*;
11. Serve the meal;
12. Eat the *Afikoman*;
13. Say the Grace after meals;
14. Conclude the Hillel Psalms (Psalms 113–118—The Psalms of Praise);
15. Pray that God will accept your Seder service with favour.

Some explanatory notes:

(a) The *Afikoman*: the middle *matzah* of the three is broken in two and half put away for the afikoman—ie, a 'savoury' or 'desert' after the meal; it is customary for the children to 'steal' the afikoman at some point and only give it back in return for a present.

(b) The *matzahs* are uncovered, the Seder plate is lifted and everyone says:

This is the bread of affliction which our ancestors ate in the land of Egypt. Let all who are hungry come and eat. Let all who are in need come and celebrate the Passover. This year we are here; next year, in the land of Israel. This year we are slaves; next year, free men.

(c) 'The story' described in the Haggadah is introduced by four questions, asked by the youngest child of the family; these are:

1. Why is this night different from all other nights? On all other nights we can eat bread or matzah: why tonight only matzah?
2. On all other nights we can eat any kind of herbs; why tonight bitter herbs?
3. On all other nights we don't dip the herbs even once; why on this night do we dip them twice? (ie, in salt water and charoset)
4. On all other nights we can eat either sitting up straight or reclining; why tonight do we all recline?

(d) The answer begins with the following words:

> *Our Ancestors were slaves to Pharaoh in Egypt but God brought us out from there with a strong hand and outstretched arm. If the Holy One, Blessed be He, had not brought our ancestors out of Egypt, we, and our children, and our children's children would still be slaves in Egypt. So even if we were all wise and clever and old and learned in the Torah, it would still be our duty to tell the story of the Exodus from Egypt. The more one talks about the Exodus, the more praiseworthy it is.*

(e) After the story of the Exodus has been told, the *'Three Essentials'* are pointed to:

> 1. *Pesach*—pointing to the shankbone;
> *Why did our ancestors eat the Passover sacrifice when the Temple still stood? Because God 'passed over' the houses of our ancestors in Egypt.*
> 2. *Matzah*—pointing to the matzah;
> *Why do we eat this matzah? Because when our ancestors in Egypt were trying to escape, God revealed himself to them and saved them before the bread they were baking had time to rise.*
> 3. *Maror*—pointing to the bitter herbs;
> *Why do we eat this bitter herb? Because the Egyptians embittered the lives of our ancestors in Egypt; as it says: They made their lives bitter with hard labour, in mortar and brick, and all manner of hard work in the fields.*

(f) Then is said:

> *In every generation, every Jew must feel as if he himself came out of Egypt. God did not only redeem our ancestors but he redeemed us with them.*

(g) Lifting up the cup of wine, the following is said:

> *At this moment, then, we thank God; we praise, glorify, exalt and bless the Power that did all these miracles for our ancestors and for us. He brought us from slavery to freedom, from sorrow to joy, from mourning to holiday, from darkness to a great light, from servitude to redemption. Let us then sing a new song; Halleluyah!!*

(h) Lifting up the cup of wine a second time, the following toast is made to 'freedom':

> *'Let us pray to God, the God of our Fathers, that He bring us to other festivals and holy days that will come to us in peace—joyful in building God's City, and happy in His service. Let us sing a new song of thanks to God for our salvation and freedom. Blessings to God who has saved Israel.'*

(i) Before the proper meal is served, hands are washed, two blessings are said, and the *'Hillel Sandwich'* is eaten: this consists of *charoset* and *maror* placed between two pieces of *matzah*.

(j) After the proper meal is eaten, the *afikoman* is produced and everyone eats a little of it—'at least the size of an olive'—the meal is then officially over; the Grace follows.

(k) A third and a fourth cup of wine are taken: the first is a toast 'To Peace' and traditionally the door of the house is then opened 'for Elijah' (the herald of the Messiah), for whom a chair at the table is provided throughout the ceremony and a cup of wine is now poured; following the Hillel Psalms the fourth cup of wine is a toast 'To Jerusalem'.

(l) The rest of the Seder consists of traditional songs.

(m) The Seder is repeated the following night; on this occasion it may take the form of a community Seder.

Learning from the Seder

The Seder is the most universally observed and therefore the most unifying of all Jewish ceremonies. In millions of Jewish homes the same observance brings Jews together not only with their contemporaries all over the world but with countless generations of Jews of the past. Why, in the light of the tragic history of the Jews, has this ceremony survived? How does the story of the Exodus as told in the Seder still unite and inspire Jewish people today? What benefits do Jewish families have from celebrating such festivals? What is the effect of being brought up in a family which has such celebrations? Do other families have occasions when members become conscious of their family's roots? How far back can you go in naming your own family? Does it matter if you can't go much beyond your grandparents? Why, do you think, are more and more people today interested in tracing their family trees? What good does it do to know about the history of your ancestors?

In what ways are the central themes of the Passover—remembrance, thanksgiving, oppression, deliverance, liberation, hope, peace, new life, etc—not only important in the lives of Jews but in all human beings? Consider if you have had an 'exodus' experience (eg, being taken to somewhere different, fulfilling a desire, enjoying a sense of freedom or of liberation, learning something new about yourself and other people which has changed the way you previously thought, etc). What would the modern equivalent of the 'Ten Plagues' of the Exodus be today? (eg, crime, disease, hunger, ignorance, intolerance, racial hatred, materialism, poverty, war, etc.) How might human beings be liberated from these?

(D) (Unit 6) 'Jo bole so nihal. Sat sri akal'

A scheme of work for pupils aged 11–13

Core Values and Key Religious Concepts: 1, 2, 7, 8.

Belief/Value Issues: 1, 2, 3, 8.

Preparatory work: Units 5 and 6 of the Adolescent Life-World Curriculum and Unit 5 of A Sikh Life-World Curriculum.

Materials to be available in the classroom: This scheme of work uses the first part of the Videotext/Exmouth School Video Number Three: *Aspects of Sikhism*. The advantage of using this video is that the deliberate exclusion of a spoken commentary enables the lesson to be focused on the interpretative processes which pupils use in order to try to give meaning to what they are observing. Thus the lesson is concerned to bring to the consciousness of pupils their own way of seeing things, and then to contrast this with Sikh consciousness.

The first part of the video, entitled *Worship in the Gurdwara*, depicts the events in the following order:

1. The exterior of the Gurdwara; *Nishan Sahib*.
2. The bedroom of the *Guru Granth Sahib*; the *Guru Granth Sahib* is taken from the bed.
3. Procession of the *Guru Granth Sahib* from the bedroom to the congregational hall: the *Guru* is covered with *romalas* and carried on the head; great care is taken to purify everything with which the *Guru Granth Sahib* comes into contact, including spraying the air; the *Guru* is installed on the *takht*, under the canopy; the Sikhs in the procession sing reverently to the *Guru Granth Sahib*.
4. The morning reading is taken at random, preceded by *Ardas*.
5. The congregational service: the reciting of *Gurbani* (compositions of the Guru), the singing of *Kirtan* (hymns from the *Guru Granth Sahib*); the musicians.
6. Prostrations: members of the *Sangat* bow to the *Guru Granth Sahib* on entering the prayer hall and make an offering.
7. Seating: All members are equal before the *Guru Granth Sahib*; the *Guru* is elevated above the level of the congregation, who sit on the floor with heads covered, footwear removed, and with feet pointing away from the *Guru*; men and women sit separately.
8. Making the *Karah Prashad* which is then placed, covered, beside the *Guru* until the time comes for its sanctification and distribution.
9. Preparation of the *Langar*; making *chapattis*.
10. Sermon: any member of the *Sangat* may address the congregation.

11. The *Ardas*: the *Guru* is asked for guidance and given thanks for directing the lives of Sikhs.

12. Sanctification of the *Karah Parshad* and *Langar* with a touch from the *Kirpan* (sword).

13. Prostrations: the congregation perform two full prostrations before the *Guru Granth Sahib* as a symbol of total obedience.

14. The *Hukam* (a random reading for guidance); this is the *Guru's* last command for the day.

15. Distribution of the *Karah Parshad*: received in both hands as a gesture of humility.

16. The *Langar*; eaten by all as a symbol of equality.

17. At the end of the day the *Guru Granth Sahib* is returned to the bedroom with appropriate respect.

An approach to learning about and learning from Sikh Worship

The above sequence of events on the video takes approximately 30 minutes; there is considerable benefit in viewing each event separately. Encourage pupils to watch an event and then express *in their own words* what they have seen; also encourage them to interpret the actions of the Sikhs *as they have perceived them*. List these comments for future reference: eg, 'They keep their Holy Book covered up all the time' (Why?); 'They keep it in a double bed over night'; 'No-one turns their back on it—some of them were walking backwards' (Why?); 'They use a "fly-whisk" all the time' (Why?); 'A boy was spraying water all over the place' (Why?) etc, etc.

The *respect* shown by Sikhs towards the *Guru Granth Sahib* is very apparent during the video. List all the different ways in which Sikhs express their respect; think of any other occasions on which people express their respect (eg, to royalty). What conclusions might we draw about how the Sikh sees the *Guru Granth Sahib*? (the Living Guru—as a person). Why are Sikhs so respectful towards their Holy Book? Compare the attitudes of adherents to other faiths towards their Holy Book. What conclusions might we draw about the place of Sacred Scriptures in religions? Why are they so venerated? (moving onto an understanding of the nature of revelation): is there anything else on earth which human beings have so much respect for? What is respect? To what should we be respectful? For what reasons?

The above are illustrations of how an *inductive approach* (based on that used by Berger, which we discussed in Chapters Two and Six) may be used to enable pupils to learn about and from religions. Once the pupils have begun to agree a framework within which they both perceive and interpret what is happening and form some view of its significance (both for Sikhs and for themselves), then new information may be given of an explanatory kind which enables the distinctiveness of

Sikh consciousness (ie, how Sikhs see things) to be more readily appreciated by the pupils. The comments made earlier by pupils may then be revised. I suggest that this approach is preferable to one in which the teacher seeks to instruct pupils about Sikhism by merely making certain statements about what Sikhs believe and do. The aim is to *engage* pupils imaginatively and existentially in their observation of Sikh behaviour, attitude and, subsequently, belief.

(E) (Unit 8)   The Goal of Life

A scheme of work for pupils aged 13–16

Core Values and Key Religious Concepts: 1–8.

Belief/Value Issues: 3, 5, 8.

Preparatory work: Units 5–8 of the Adolescent Life-World Curriculum and, preferably, Units 1–7 of A Muslim Life-World Curriculum.

Materials to be made available in the classroom: Preferably a video of the Hajj, or, alternatively, slides, film-strips or a dramatised documentary account on audio cassette. Following completion of the scheme, a *Hajji* or *Hajjin* might be invited to speak about their experience to pupils.

Learning about Muslim pilgrimage

The following information is essential to an understanding of the Hajj: one of the five Pillars of Faith; every Muslim 'if wealth and health permit' hopes to undertake the Hajj once in a life time; the word *Hajj* means 'to set out with a definite purpose'; it recalls to mind the willingness of Abraham and Ishmael to sacrifice and be sacrificed, thus the pilgrimage is the Muslim's act of sacrifice; it is a matter of the heart and the mind just as much as undertaking a physically-demanding journey; it is a visit to the most holy place of Islam during the twelfth month of the Muslim year, *Dhul-Hijjrah*.

The stages of the pilgrimage: Before entering Mecca all pilgrims put on *Ihram*—white, unsewn cloth symbolising equality, single-mindedness and self-sacrifice:

1. The pilgrimage begins with a circling of the *Ka'ba* seven times in an anti-clockwise direction; the pilgrims say:

> *O God, you are peace and the giver of peace; so our Sustainer, give us peace and admit us to the Garden, Paradise, the abode of peace.*

As they pass the *Black Stone* in one of the walls of the *Ka'ba*, those who are near enough kiss it or touch it; the rest raise their hand towards it.

2. From the *Ka'ba* they proceed to two small hills in the centre of Mecca—*as-Safa* and *al-Marwa*. Abraham, at God's command, left Ishmael amd his mother Hagar there; she ran between the two hills searching for water, and the pilgrims imitate her by going along the same path seven times. Now the ground is paved, and a roofed corridor links the two hills. They drink from the well called *Zam-Zam*, found by Ishmael (at the end of the pilgrimage they wash their *ihram* in the well, and this will eventually be worn again as their shroud when they die.) Bottles of *zam-zam* water are often take home for relatives and friends who have been unable to make the Hajj.

3. After sunrise on the ninth day of the month the pilgrims set out for *Mount Arafat*, some thirteen miles away. Some will walk, others will ride. The *Hill of Mercy* is said to be the place where Adam and Eve met and were reconciled after their expulsion from the Garden of Eden; here the pilgrims offer the noon and mid-afternoon prayers. They turn back towards Mecca and assemble at *Muzdalifah*, about eight miles from the city, to say their evening prayers and camp for the night.

4. Next morning they journey to the village of *Mina*, in which there are three stone pillars; these mark the spot where the devil tried to persuade the prophet Ishmael to rebel against his father Abraham and refuse to be offered as a sacrifice; it is said that the boy drove off the devil with stones. In imitation, the pilgrims throw stones at the three pillars. Stoning of the first pillar is followed by the killing of a sheep, goat or camel in remembrance of Abraham's sacrifice of a ram instead of Ishmael. The day of this sacrifice is one of the feast days of the Muslim year throughout the world, ie, *Eid-ul-Adha*—the Feast of Sacrifice.

5. The pilgrims return to Mecca for a second circling of the *Ka'ba* and they are then free from the restrictions of the Hajj. Many then visit the Prophet Muhammad's tomb (p.b.u.h), the mosque at Medina and other historic sites of Islam before returning home.

A man or woman who completes the pilgrimage may then add the title *Hajji* or *Hajjin* to his or her name; they are very respected persons in Islam.

Presentation of the content

It is important that the above content is presented from the point of view of the Muslim pilgrim—hence the desirability of using a video which is sensitive to this perspective, and of inviting a *Hajji(n)* to speak to the pupils. A 'detached' presentation of 'the facts' as given above is likely to convey little of the intense spiritual experience which is characteristic of Muslim pilgrimage. Indeed, divorced from this the actions of the pilgrims may appear wholly bizarre to non-Muslim pupils.

It is important, especially with older pupils (and especially those taking GCSE Religious Studies) that the study of the Hajj is placed within the context of Islamic Theology. Islam's first requirement is *belief* and its second, *action*. Out of its concepts and beliefs, a certain attitude toward life, toward one's own self, toward other human beings, toward the universe; a certain kind of personhood; a distinctive type of human interaction; a particular mode of worship, of family, manners, living habits, etc, in relation to all aspects of life, takes its development. The Hajj is an *action* which stems from particular beliefs about the nature of Reality. Some of these fundamental beliefs are:

(a) The two realms of existence—*al-Ghaib* and *ash-Shahadah*. (See Unit 18 of 'A Muslim Life-World Curriculum' given earlier).

(b) God is *the* Reality.

(c) Human nature has its own reality. (See Unit 20 of 'A Muslim Life-World Curriculum' given earlier.)

(d) Hajj constitutes a form of worship with the totality of the Muslim's being: with body, mind and soul, time, possessions, the temporary sacrifice of all ordinary comforts, conveniences and tokens of status and individuality which human beings normally enjoy, to assume for a few days the condition of a pilgrim totally at God's service and disposal—His slave who seeks only His pleasure.

Another important consideration in the presentation of content is to examine the symbolism of the Hajj. For example:

(a) All the rites of Hajj centre on complete submission and devotion to God. They commemorate as an example of such total submission and obedience the willingness of Abraham to sacrifice his son Ishmael and the willingness of Ishmael to be sacrificed.

(b) Hajj brings together millions of pilgrims from all parts of the world. Putting on *ihram* divests them temporarily of all marks of status, individuality and nationality. They are united by their common will, beliefs, actions and language; they become humanity as God intended it to be.

(c) The *Ka'ba* is the visible symbol of God's Unity, representing in concrete form His centrality in the life of the Muslim, the focal point for Muslims of all times and places to turn towards (itself a symbol) in their worship as a symbol of their unity as one community submitting to the One God, a part of the endless stream of worshippers facing and circling it unceasingly since remote antiquity to the glorification of God Most High.

(d) Describing the experience of Hajj, Suzanne Haneef, a Muslim, writes:

When the worshipper joins the host of Muslims circling the Ka'ba, a sense of timelessness sweeps over him as he realises that he is one atom in an endless ocean of those who have worshipped in that place since nearly the beginning of recorded history. A deep sense of his smallness and insignificance comes to him; under the blazing sun of Mecca he comes face to face with his own nothingness, his creatureliness, his utter dependence on his Creator, grasping, in a brief but intense encounter with the sublimity of God, that all the movements and efforts which men make on this earth are as nothing. They and he will pass away, and then he will come alone before the One who gave him life to receive His judgment and the recompense for all he did. (What Everyone Should Know about Islam and Muslims, Lahore, Kazi Publications, 1979, pp51–59.)

(e) Circling (or circumambulating) the *Ka'ba* symbolises God being placed at the centre of human life. Running between Safa and Marwah (*sa'i = hastening*) is symbolic of the efforts and movements of human beings, of their ceaseless striving throughout life; but constantly, as they run, pilgrims catch glimpses of the *Ka'ba*, the focal point on earth for the worship of God, and long to return there. Thus the centrality of the *Ka'ba* in Mecca represents in concrete form the centrality of God in the life of the Muslim individual and community.

(f) The climax of the Hajj occurs on the ninth day of *Dhul-Hijjrah, The Day of Arafat.* Arafat is the name of a vast, empty plain outside Mecca; it is treeless and barren, without any shelter from the blinding sun, and encircled by stark, jagged purple-black lava peaks. As many as two million people may assemble there and spend the afternoon until sundown engaged in penitence and supplication to God. Thousands of tents are erected there to shelter them. This gathering brings to mind the immense gathering on the Day of Judgment when Muslims believe bodies will be brought out of the graves and rejoined with their souls and all will stand in utter humility before God to await His judgment.

(g) Although the stoning of the three pillars at Mina symbolises rejection of Satan, it also serves to illustrate the endless human struggle against evil.

(h) Hajj, for a Muslim, provides the ultimate experience in human brotherhood. Muslims are not required merely to be present but to behave with kindness and consideration to all their fellow pilgrims; indeed, one's entire pilgrimage can be rendered void by acts of harshness or hostility to others.

(g) The pattern of the Hajj was prescribed by the Prophet Muhammad (p.b.u.h), and in following it Muslims follow in his steps and in his example.

Learning from Muslim pilgrimage

Impersonal evaluation

As is the case with most religious practices, evaluation involves consideration of what adherents regard as authoritative. In this case a consideration of the Muslim's acceptance of the Holy Qur'an as the Final and Universal Revelation of Allah, and of the importance of the Hadith and the Sunnah in interpreting it, is necessary.

Muslims insist that meaningful answers to questions posed by the human condition must be compatible with the observed phenomena of the universe and with reason. They also insist that human beings cannot arrive at the objective *Truth*, at a correct knowledge of the meaning and purpose of existence, the nature of the Creator of all things, and of the role and ultimate destiny of human beings, etc, by their own efforts since it concerns what is totally outside the realm of human observation or deduction. The only possible means by which human beings can have access to an unquestionably true understanding of such matters is if the Source of everything, the Power whom Muslims call *Allah*, Himself imparts this knowledge by whatever means He may deem fit. It is here that the second part of Islam's declaration of Faith—*Muhammad (p.b.u.h) is the Messenger of God*—is a necessary foundation for all Muslim belief and practice, including Hajj.

Although a proper evaluation of these claims will include an examination of the internal consistency of the Qur'an (which Muslims claim is entirely consistent, no part of it being contradictory of any other part) and the means of its transmission both to the Prophet Muhammad (p.b.u.h) and subsequently in written form, this may be more appropriately considered in Unit 10 of 'A Muslim Life-World Curriculum'. In the present Unit, sociological and psychological considerations, such as the effect of pilgrimage upon the outlook of adherents and its role in strengthening commitment, both of the individual and the Muslim community, are likely to be seen as more relevant. Such questions which might be considered are, therefore:—

1. What factors combine to make the Hajj one of the essential Pillars of Faith of Islam?

2. What functional value does the Hajj have in the lives of individual Muslims and in the Islamic community?

3. Is exertion of a physical kind necessary for spiritual development? (This question might include reference to the physical elements involved in some of the other Pillars, eg, *salat, sawm, zakat.*)

4. Does Islam allow for individuality?

Personal evaluation

The events and actions of the Hajj are remote from the immediate experiences of non-Muslim pupils. In learning about these, how might pupils also learn from them about themselves?

An approach whereby 'parallels' are sought between pupils' experiences and those of Muslim pilgrims is unlikely to be very productive (eg, the outcomes of engaging in some of the schemes leading to the Duke of Edinburgh's Award, especially those which are physically demanding, etc). While it may be the case that some pupils belonging to religious traditions within which the pilgrimage experience is given prominence (eg, Catholicism, Hinduism) may be able to recognise something of their own experience in the Hajj, the majority of pupils will not have access to this personal resource or the necessary religious consciousness to make this a possibility. Any attempts to use 'secular' equivalents is likely to be misleading and may even be offensive to Muslims.

A more productive approach is one which, while giving attention to the events of the pilgrimage, also explores the human situation to which Muslim beliefs are addressed. As indicated earlier, central to Islamic Theology is the view that human nature is made up of various elements which must be brought together into a harmonious whole. We might ask if this is a view with which we can agree, and if so, how might such harmony be achieved? Such a question prompts us to examine a wide range of possible techniques—medical, social, psychological and religious—which aim to promote personal well-being and mental health. Related to this is the question of the 'goals of life'. Are they necessary? How might they be chosen? What are the likely consequences of choosing/not choosing them? 'Goals' imply 'values' and 'values' imply 'commitments'. The Hajj is a dramatic example of all three. Muslims are committed to particular values. What are these values? To what extent are these values shared with non-Muslims? A powerful concept in Islam is that of 'submission'; the ideal is to be the slave of Allah, for only then can one become fully human—as one was intended to be. We might compare and contrast this ideal with that of the 'autonomy' of the individual which exercises a normative influence on Western conceptions of the human being. Does the West have anything to learn from the Islamic conception of what it means to be human? Do I, myself?

(F) (Unit 9)   Krishna, Hero and Saviour

A scheme of work for pupils aged 11–13

Core Values and Key Religious Concepts: 2, 4, 8.

Belief/Values Issues: 2, 4, 8.

Preparatory work: Unit 9 of the Adolescent Life-World Curriculum.

Materials to be available in the classroom: This scheme focuses on stories about Lord Krishna, especially on those with which Hindu children are likely to be familiar as a result of story-telling at home. One of the difficulties presented by this topic is that of finding contemporary translations of Hindu Sacred Scriptures which bring these stories within the comprehension of children and young people but retain their authenticity as sacred texts. For example, *The Srimad-Bhagavatam of Krishna-Dwaipayana Vyasa* has been translated into English prose from the original Sanskrit text by J M Sanyal (Calcutta, Oriental Publishing Co), but few pupils of secondary age are likely to find it compulsive reading! While this text retains its authenticity, it can hardly be said to present the Hindu Scriptures in a way which makes them available for classroom use. On the other hand, Nigel Frith's book *The Legend of Krishna* (London, Sheldon Press, 1975) is written in a most engaging style; but his blending of the stories of Krishna into a continuous narrative which incorporates material from other Hindu sources and does not follow the traditional chronology means that for Hindus this text is far from authentic. Proceeding on the assumption that it is better that pupils should have some familiarity with the stories of Krishna than none, the four incidents which follow are based on Frith's adaptations and do not purport to be literal translations of the original Sanskrit text.

Learning about Lord Krishna

1. *Lord Krishna's birth*:

A priest told Vasudeva and Devaki that their eighth son would kill the tyrant King Kamsa and rule as Raj in the city of Mathura. When Kamsa heard of this he threw Vasudeva and Devaki into prison, and there they stayed until this son was born. That night Vasudeva heard a voice say: 'Take up your baby and go into the land of Braj. Leave the baby there, and he will be safe from the tyrant. Up, now, quick, now, away!' Vasudeva told what happened like this:

> '*I took up the baby, my little son Krishna, I wrapped up his little blue limbs in a blanket and cradled him against the cold. When I came to the barred gates at the end of the corridor, all slid open silently as I approached and all the guards were fast asleep. Soon I was out in the dark streets of the city on my way to the snowy plain.*
>
> '*But I came then to the river Jumna, and swollen with the melted snow it roared between its banks. Just as I was about to turn back in*

despair my baby son Krishna stuck out his little blue foot towards the river, and at once the roaring waves went down and the river sank, and running quickly on the wet sand of the bottom I was able to get across and come to safety. I blessed the gods who were helping me that night.

'And so I came to the village of Braj, where I found the house of Nanda the faithful herdsman, and I found the baby girl, a child just born that night to his wife Jasuda, and I swapped my little Krishna for the girl and laid him instead of her in the wooden cradle. Back to Mathura I went, and all went well until I was safe again in prison. All that remained was to show Kamsa the girl and make him believe that it was my wife's baby, and he would think that what the priest said could not be true.

'Kamsa was enraged to see the little girl and picked her up to dash her to the ground, but the baby turned into the goddess Devi, and roaring up to heaven in a sheet of blue flame she spoke to us in a voice of thunder: 'Your son is safe, your little blue child, for he is no ordinary baby: he is the highest god come to earth again to save mankind, he is the keeper of the universe, Vishnu'.

'Kamsa still kept us in prison, and although my wife and I were sad at losing our little son, we were happy enough to know that he would live. And with the knowledge that he is indeed Vishnu, the almighty, how can we be sad?' (pp72–73)

2. Lord Krishna's boyhood

Krishna went for a walk by the river. It happened that some cowfolk children were playing there and Kaliya, the snake-demon, had poisoned the water. When the children drank the water they became very ill. When Krishna saw this he ran to the water's edge and looked down. And from the depths of the river the great snake Kaliya came up, twirling and winding his body round. And the water grew dark as he came to the surface, and suddenly the snake's head reared up out of the water, dripping with yellow poison. Kaliya had seven heads, and all of them hissed and spat at Krishna, and his neck and head towered out of the water as huge as a great palm tree that bends and streams in a hurricane wind. And Kaliya's heads rocked to and fro, waiting to dive and snatch Krishna from the bank.

But Krishna leapt up and swung himself onto Kaliya's heads, and danced on them, banging them each with his feet, thumping a dance. And Kaliya grew weak and dizzy, and his eyes went misty with pain. Out of the water then came Kaliya's wife, and bowing to Krishna, she cried out: 'O Krishna, spare my husband's life and we will run away and trouble you no more.' And Krishna felt sorry for the snake and jumped onto the shore and said: 'Go, Kaliya, you and your wife and your little ones, and I shall not harm you.' And Kaliya went with his wife and children far away to the realm of Varuna, the god of Ocean. (pp35–36)

3. Lord Krishna's youth

And Radha came to her room and sat down looking out of the window on the trees outside. And it was so still that she seemed to see in the blue moonlight pictures of Krishna in the trunk of a tree or in the glittering of lilies or in the lotuses on the pond. But then she heard thunder as another storm came on. But amid the rumbling of the thunder she heard another sound, a fluting coming from the depths of the forest, and she knew it was Krishna's flute.

Out then into the rain she ran, without fearing the snakes or the bangs of thunder. The anklets of her mud-spattered ankles jangled as she ran on, following the silvery fluting among the trees, and climbed up the mountain. And she found that she was being led to the enchanted lake where Krishna and she had strolled. But although she looked around the lake, and though she could still hear the fluting nearer than ever before, she could not see Krishna anywhere among the trees.

And Radha gazed out to the island and wished that she had gone with him to that place, that enchanted spot, and left the world to go on alone into whatever grim-faced fate awaited. At that moment she saw Krishna on the island, playing his flute among the branches of a tree, and she leapt up and called with all her heart: 'Krishna!' And all the hills around the lake echoed with 'Krishna, Krishna' like the voices of a thousand nymphs.

Krishna looked up when he heard his name, and saw Radha on the bank and cried out: 'Radha!' and leapt down from the tree. And he dived into the water and struck towards the bank. All the woods and hills that were echoing still with Radha's call of 'Krishna' now echoed Krishna's call of 'Radha', so that each tree and rock seemed to cry together, 'Radha, Krishna, Radha, Krishna', as though the very stars were singing the tune. And Krishna swam to the weedy shore and embraced Radha, saying, 'Radha, my darling, deep-hearted Radha, my soul, my love. I heard you call me from the depths of the ocean. My heart was struck with love and I was helpless, yearning for you on the very bottom of the sea, and you called to me. O my love, never leave me more, O my heart's joy, my life, my self.' And Radha lifted her hands to his face and said: 'O my dear darling, you are my soul.' (pp182–185)

4. Lord Krishna the King

And after Krishna had killed Kamsa he went back to Vasudeva and the others and said: 'I have spoken with my friends and considered all that you have said. If indeed I am not the son of Nanda, but am the son prophesied to be the end of Kamsa, than I shall be your King, and guard you from your foes.' The councillors rejoiced, and took Krishna into the courtyard and told the people: 'People of Mathura, today you have lost a King. But he that rid you of your King shall be your King. Krishna shall now be Raj of Mathura.'

And as he said this the people cheered, and Krishna went and joined them and soon they were all feasting happily. And the gods in heaven all agreed that Krishna the champion of the cowherds was now King of Mathura, and had begun on a great reign that was to bring peace to the warring land of India, and usher in another age of wisdom and of light. (pp225–226)

Learning from Hindu devotion to Lord Krishna

Lord Krishna is depicted simultaneously in Hindu Sacred Scriptures as a naughty child, a mighty hero and demon-slayer, a daring lover and (in his instruction to Arjuna in the *Bhagavad-Gita*) a great teacher. Non-Hindus find this a strange combination and have difficulties in reconciling one with the other, not least the eroticism of Krishna's exploits with the *ghopis*. The material thus provides a useful entry point for exploring the differences between Western religious consciousness and Hindu religious consciousness.

Possible approaches include comparing the hero figures (and their demon counterparts) of Hindu mythology with contemporary hero figures of Western popular culture, especially those which appeal to young people, eg, *He-Man* and *Masters of the Universe*. Although the parallels are, of course, far from exact, there is sufficient similarity between them to permit some comparison; for example, both present through a range of characters ranging from gods to humans to animals to demons and monsters a dramatised account of the eternal conflict between good and evil. In this battle the possession of special knowledge (or a special instrument or power) is an important factor in ensuring victory and avoiding defeat, and there is often a clear representation of the hero as not only the restorer of goodness but as the revealer of truth. It is the cosmic scale of the battle which is significant in both types of mythology—this being seen particularly clearly, for example, in the figure of *Superman* (and also *Superwoman*). Without in any way wishing to trivialise the Hindu epics, their appropriateness as a medium for the expression of religious truth is not impaired by their fulfilling, in the culture of which they are a significant part, an important role as entertainment. While none of the contemporary heroes of popular Western culture fulfils a religious role (although characters as diverse as Mary Poppins and Bananaman do display all the qualities of moral, revelatory agents), and all fall predominantly into the realm of entertainment, a consideration of why in both Hindu and Western cultures such heroes are 'popular' does have the potential of raising important questions about the needs of human beings, eg, why *are* hero figures so popular?; why is it necessary for human beings to seek 'help' from models embodying 'superhuman' rather than 'human' qualities?; and so on.

Secondly, stories such as these raise questions about the nature of religious language and symbolism which can be explored with profit by young people who are prone to favour scientific rather than allegorical conceptions of truth. Despite the uniqueness of the Hindu mythological genre, some parallels may be drawn between, for example, the birth stories of Krishna and those of Jesus and Gautama. Similarly, there is value in examining the symbols and images in such stories which enable complex doctrines (such as that of Paramatman-Atman) to be expressed through the story of the love of Radha for Krishna and vice-versa. We have already considered the value of exploring ways in which 'signals of transcendence' may be discerned within everyday experiences; the legend of Krishna, although presenting them in a stylised manner, is full of incidents which show how such signals are 'sedimented' into that tradition. Finding them and releasing them from the culture in which they are fixed so that they can speak to contemporary Western youth is not without its educational and religious value.

(G) (Unit 15)   War, Peace and Religion

A scheme of work for pupils aged 13–16

Core Values and Key Religious Concepts: 4, 6, 8.

Belief/Value Issues: 1–8.

Preparatory work: Units 13–15 of the Adolescent Life-World Curriculum and, preferably, Units 9, 10, 13 and 14 of the Religious Life-World Curriculum of several religions.

Materials to be available in the classroom: Sheets providing quotations from the Sacred Scriptures of the world's religions; cuttings from newspapers reporting incidents locally, nationally and internationally relating to war and peace, especially those having some connection with religion (eg, incidents in Beirut, the Lebanon, the Punjab, Northern Ireland, etc).

Learning about religious attitudes to war and peace

1. *Christianity*:

   (a) *'Repay no one evil for evil, but take thought for what is noble in the sight of all. If possible, so far as it depends on you, live peacefully with all. Beloved, never avenge yourselves, but leave it to God; for it is written: "Vengeance is mine, I will repay, says the Lord," No, "If your enemy is hungry, feed him; if he is thirsty, give him drink; for by so doing you will heap burning coals upon his head." Do not be overcome by evil, but overcome evil with good.' (Romans 12:17–21)*

(b) *'Love is patient and kind; love is not jealous or boastful; it is not arrogant or rude. Love does not insist on its own way; it is not irritable or resentful; it does not rejoice at wrong, but rejoices in the right. Love bears all things, believes all things, hopes all things, endures all things.'* (1 Corinthians 13:4–7)

2. Hinduism:

(c) *'You should not retaliate when another does you injury. Good conduct is the adornment of those who are good. Even if those who do wrong deserve to be killed, the noble ones should be compassionate, since there is no one who does not transgress.'* (The Ramayana)

(d) Arjuna, who is about to go into battle against the Kauravas, turns to Krishna (his charioteer who is also an avatar of Vishnu) and says:

'It is not right that we slay our kinsmen. . . How can we be happy if we kill our own people? . . . Alas, what a great sin have we resolved to commit in striving to slay our own people through our greed for the pleasures of the kingdom! Far better would it be for me if the sons of Dhritarashtra, with weapons in hand, should slay me in battle, while I remain unresisting and unarmed.' (Bhagavad-Gita 1, 26–47)

But Krishna replies:

'Just as a person casts off worn-out garments and puts on others that are new, even so does the embodied soul cast off worn-out bodies and take on others that are new. Weapons do not cleave this self, fire does not burn him; waters do not make him wet; nor does the wind make him dry. He is uncleavable. he cannot be burnt. He can be neither wetted nor dried. He is eternal, all-pervading, unchanging and immovable. He is the same for ever.' (Bhagavad-Gita 2, 22–24).

Later Krishna adds:

'Further, having regard for your own duty (dharma), you should not falter; there exists no greater good for a warrior (kshatriya) than war enjoined by duty. Happy are the warriors, Arjuna, for whom such a war comes of its own accord as an open door to heaven. But if you do not engage in this lawful battle, then you will fail in your duty and your glory, and incur sin.' (Bhagavad-Gita 2, 31–33)

3. Islam:

(e)*'And when the sacred months are passed, kill those who join other gods with God wherever ye shall find them; and seize them, besiege them, and lay wait for them with every kind of ambush; but if they shall convert, and observe prayer, and pay the obligatory alms, then let them* go their way, for God is Gracious, Merciful. If any one of those who join gods with God ask an asylum of thee, grant him an asylum, that he may hear the Word of God, and then let him reach his place of safety.' (The Holy Qur'an, Surah 9, 5–6)

(f) 'Let those then fight on the path of God, who exchange this present life for that which is to come; for whoever fighteth on God's path, whether he be slain or conquer, we will in the end give him a great reward.' (The Holy Qur'an, Surah 4, 76–77)

(g) 'Say to the infidels: If they desist from their unbelief, what is now past shall be forgiven them; but if they return to it, they have already before them the doom of the ancients. Fight then against them till strife be at an end, and the religion be all of it God's.' (The Holy Qur'an, Surah 8, 39–40)

(h) 'Every soul tastes of death, and we test you with evil and with good as a trial, and to us you will return.' (The Holy Qur'an, Surah 21, 36)

4. Judaism:

(i) 'I will sing to the Lord, for he has triumphed gloriously;
the horse and his rider he has thrown into the sea.
The Lord is my strength and my song,
and he has become my salvation;
. . . The Lord is a man of war: the Lord is his name.
Pharaoh's chariots and his host he
cast into the sea;
and his picked officers are sunk in
the Red Sea;
. . . Thy right hand, O Lord, glorious in power.
thy right hand, O Lord, shatters the enemy.'
(Exodus, 15: 1–6)

(j) 'Take a census of all the congregation of the people of Israel . . .
from twenty years old and upward, all in Israel who are able to go
forth to war. . .' (Numbers, 1: 2–3)

(k) 'You shall not kill'. (Exodus, 20: 13)

(l) 'When a man causes a disfigurement in his neighbour, as he has done it shall be done to him, fracture for fracture, eye for eye, tooth for tooth. . . He who kills a man shall be put to death.' (Leviticus, 24: 19–21)

(m) 'Pray for the peace of Jerusalem:
May those who love you prosper;
peace be within your ramparts
and prosperity in your palaces. (Psalm 122: 6–7)

5. *Sikhism:*

   *(n) 'I wear two swords as symbols of spiritual and temporal authority.
   In the Guru's house religion and wordly enjoyment shall be combined—
   the cauldron to supply the poor and needy, and the scimitar to smite
   oppressors.' (Guru Har Gobind, the sixth Guru)*
   *(o) 'Eternal God, our shield, O Lord,
   our daggar, arrow, spear and sword.
   To us for our defence is given
   the timeless, deathless Lord of heaven;
   to us, All-steel's unconquered might;
   to us, All-time's resistless flight;
   and you, All-steel, in all will render
   valiant service as our Defender.
   (Guru Gobind Singh, the tenth Guru)*

   *(p) 'I bow with love and devotion to the Holy Sword.
   Assist me that I may complete this work.'
   (Guru Gobind Singh, the tenth Guru).*

Learning from religions about our own attitudes to war and peace

The teachings of all the world's religions have been appealed to, at one
time or another, to justify war or to plead the case for peace; in uniting
people religions also divide them. Is this inevitable or could the religions of the world become the most powerful influence for peace known
to humankind? Why do most religions use imagery which reflects war-
fare, fighting and being a soldier? Are there any religions, or traditions
within a religion, which are entirely committed to non-violence? Find
out about Jainism, especially the concept of *ahimsa*. Does this religion
offer an example to the others? Find out about Quakerism within the
Christian tradition. Do Quaker beliefs have anything to offer in working out a basis for harmony between the religions? Consider the same
question in the light of the beliefs of Baha'ism. What influences your
view of war and peace?—what the religions teach?—what the politicians say?—what your parents think?

(H) (Unit 16)   Who is my neighbour?

A scheme of work for pupils aged 13–16

Core Values and Key Religious Concepts: 3, 4, 6, 8.

Belief/Value Issues: 3, 4.

Preparatory work: Units 15 and 16 of the Adolescent Life-World Curriculum and, preferably, Unit 15 of A Christian Life-World Curriculum.

Materials to be available in the classroom: Visuals of Christians involved in overseas relief and development projects sponsored by Christian organisations such as Christian Aid, the Catholic Fund for Overseas Development (CAFOD), the Tear Fund, the Church Missionary Societies, etc; pamphlets and booklets from Christian relief organisations, from the British Council of Churches and the World Council of Churches describing their organisation and work.

Learning about Christianity
(a) *The work of ecumenical councils and the World Council of Churches.* Help pupils to learn about the co-operative response of the Christian churches to human interdependence in working for human rights and the liberation of oppressed people throughout the world.

Possible approaches: a brief survey of the growth of the unity movement from the first World Missionary Conference in Edinburgh in 1910 to the creation of the World Council of Churches in 1948; consideration of the six basic human rights approved by the Nairobi Assembly of the World Council of Churches in 1975, viz:

1. The basic human right to life.
2. The right to enjoy and maintain a cultural identity.
3. The right to protest (ie, dissent; 'to preserve a community or system from hardening into authoritarian rigidity').
4. The right to participate in decision-making within the community.
5. The right to personal dignity—which involves condemnation of torture or of protracted imprisonment without trial.
6. The right to choose freely a religion or belief which includes freedom to practise and teach one's religion or belief.

Discuss the meaning of these six human rights; show how they relate to Christian beliefs about the human; consider, with examples, why in some countries these rights are denied to some people; discuss ways in which such countries can be persuaded to respect human rights; consider to what extent an organisation like the World Council of Churches should support (both morally and financially) 'freedom-fighters' and 'liberation armies' (which others might define as 'guerrillas' and 'terrorists') using force to restore human rights in these countries; consider the meaning that Christians engaged in this struggle may give to 'salvation'.

Learning from Christianity

Consider why these six human rights should have been identified. How were they decided upon? Who is to say that they are *basic* requirements for human beings? Do they depend upon the acceptance of Christian beliefs or can they be justified by reference to other ways of thinking and believing? Why is it important that human beings commit themselves to these values? What effect does making a commitment to basic human rights and values have upon the way in which people live and think? What other important human values might be derived from these?

Learning about Christianity

(b) *The work of Christian relief organisations with special reference to Christian Aid*

Help pupils to learn about the co-operative response of the Christian churches to human interdependence through their involvement in relief and development projects throughout the world. (Literature and study kits from Christian Aid, PO Box No 1, London SW9 8BH.)

Possible approaches: Using published literature from Christian Aid, present a series of case studies of people who have benefitted from the relief and development work of this organisation; distinguish between 'relief' and 'development' projects and emphasise the importance Christian Aid gives to the principle of encouraging self-help; consider the Christian beliefs underlying Christian Aid's view that rich nations are morally and economically obliged to share their wealth with the poor nations and that they should change their trade policies accordingly, even though this may be economically disadvantageous to the West; without such a change voluntary efforts offer the only way out of misery for millions.

Learning from Christianity

Encourage pupils to reflect on the relationship of human interdependence to human obligation; the notion that if the rich get richer the poor get poorer is an example of human interdependence; should we have a lower standard of living so that other people in the world can have a more reasonable one?; what are the difficulties of fulfilling an obligation to people we have never met and are unlikely to do so? Read Matthew 25:31–46 and Luke 16:19–31 and consider whether these passages have a message only for Christians. Using the following modern version of the passage from Matthew, discuss possible meanings that can be given to 'sin', 'salvation', 'resurrection' and 'faith':

> 'I was hungry and you fed your animals with my food;

*I was hungry and your multi-nationals planted your winter tomatoes on
our best land;*

I was hungry and you wouldn't give us steak from South America;

*I was hungry and they grow tea for you where rice might grow for my
daily meal;*

*I was hungry and you turned our sugar cane and manioc into fuel for
your cars;*

*I was hungry but the waste from your factories is poisoning the fishing
grounds of the earth;*

I was hungry but with your money you bought up my food;

I was hungry while my land grows exotic fruits for your table.

What are you afraid of?

Forgoing excessive and harmful consumption?

Having to change your attitudes?

The power of the politicians?

The work involved in achieving greater self-sufficiency?

The disapproving looks of your neighbours?

What are you afraid of?

I was hungry and you gave me no food.

(*Translated from Brot Fur Die Welt*, Education Newsletter, No 3,
1981, World Council of Churches, Geneva.)

Devise a series of posters which prompt people to examine their attitudes to people in other countries. See if you can find ways of including
reference to the fact of human interdependence. How might the following statement be translated into visual forms?

'*Our lives are inextricably linked by the common thread of humanity. If
we break it, we are all undone.*'

(I) (Unit 18)   What can you trust to be true?

A scheme of work for pupils aged 16

Core Values and Key Religious Concepts: 1, 2, 8.

Belief/Value Issues: 1, 2, 8.

Preparatory work: Units 1–18 of both the Adolescent Life-World Curriculum and the Religious Life-World Curriculum.

Preparatory work: Units 1–18 of both the Adolescent Life-World Curriculum and the Religious Life-World Curriculum.

Materials to be available in the classroom: This scheme envisages pupils working in groups exploring the concept of 'revelation' either as it is understood in one religion or as a concept which is common to all religions. The two approaches suggested below both require resource material to be readily available in the classroom, ranging from encyclopaedia of world religions to copies of sacred texts, commentaries and any other suitably informative literature (eg, personal 'testimonies' to religious experience).

Learning about revelation in the world's religions

Approach One:

This approach uses phenomenological methods of study and envisages each group studying one of the religions; viz:

Group 1. Revelation in Christianity;
Group 2. Revelation in Hinduism;
Group 3. Revelation in Islam;
Group 4. Revelation in Judaism;
Group 5. Revelation in Sikhism.

Groups should decide how best to deploy their members to research the subject. The following questions are offered as possible guidelines for undertaking research:

1. What are the written sources (sacred texts, scriptures or otherwise) which provide an account of revelation or revelatory experience in the religion?

2. Is it possible to identify passages or references in these texts which indicate the medium/modes through which the revelation manifests itself in human consciousness?

> eg, a place of revelation (always the same place or anywhere?); a person who is the recipient of the revelation through dreams, visions, trances (natural or self-induced); an ecstatic encounter in nature or with the natural elements; and event in history; an incarnation in human or animal form; as a result of engaging in rituals, physical/mental exercises, abstinence or excess; through prophecies or miracles, etc. List such instances with an outline account of the event.

3. What is the content of the revelation in each instance? ie, what is disclosed?: the character/nature of the deity?; the will/purpose of the deity?; a set of commandments?; a message for humankind?; an instruction to a person, group or nation? Note the contents in each instance.

4. Using the sacred texts and commentaries, attempt to summarise the dominant conception of revelation found in the religion. Is it a conception of revelation as *once and for ever* or as *progressive, continuous, and subject to change*? Are there conflicting estimates of the nature of revelation in the same religion? Is the religion divided into 'sects', 'denominations', 'schools', 'parties', 'movements' each with its own distinctive way of understanding revelation? Are they divided on what revelatory experience is to be regarded as authoritative? Compare and contrast 'orthodox', 'conservative', 'fundamentalist' conceptions of revelation with 'reformed', 'progressive', 'liberal', 'modernist' conceptions.

5. Compare the view of revelation found in the religion's sacred texts and traditions with 'popular' conceptions held by adherents. By what means does the follower of a religion appropriate 'revealed truth'— through initiation rites?, by following a set of precepts / duties / rituals / exercises—through a 'conversion' experience? What authenticates the experience? Is there room for individual interpretation or are all interpretations the responsibility of the faith community?

It is envisaged that the outcome of this approach will be a series of summarises which enable comparisons of important revelatory experiences to be made between the religions and between traditions within the religions.

Approach Two:

This approach is similar to the one suggested above but makes use of 'typologies' as a means of collecting and collating information about revelation from all five religions viz:

Group 1. People experiencing revelation;
Group 2. Places of revelation;
Group 3. Methods of revelation;
Group 4. Messages of revelation;
Group 5. Effects of revelation.

Thus, possible objectives are that the pupils will:
Group 1. Learn about the lives and backgrounds of certain individuals (selected from various religious traditions) who have had revelatory experiences;
Group 2. Identify places of revelation and consider what, if anything, these places have in common;
Group 3. Identify different types of revelatory experience;
Group 4. Identify the meaning of revelation as understood by the recipients of revelation;
Group 5. Discern the effect of the revelatory experience in the life of the individual and its subsequent historical importance.

Learning from revelation in the world's religions

Do people have 'revelations' today?—consideration of contemporary literature giving an account of 'religious experiences'; a useful introduction is provided by Ronald Lello's book *Revelations: Glimpses of Reality* (Shepheard-Walwyn, 1985), which includes autobiographical accounts of such experiences by Michael Bentine, Dr Sheila Cassidy, Sir Fred Hoyle, Yusuf Islam (formerly Cat Stevens), P J Kavanagh, Krishnamurti, Sarah Miles, Iris Murdoch, Doug Scott, Paul Tortelier, Sir Laurens van der Post and Kenneth Williams. None of these is a founder of a religion as a consequence of such an experience, and not all are happy to use the term 'religious' of it; but all consider their lives to have been enriched and even changed as a consequence of it.

Encourage pupils to reflect on any 'moments of truth' they may have had in which they have experienced a sense of learning more about themselves. While respecting the essential privacy of such experiences, encourage them to consider the different meanings that might be given to their lives as a consequence of seeing these as 'revelations' of truth. Poetry, story or artwork might be used as a means of expressing these meanings. Consider the view that human beings are endowed with a 'spiritual capacity' and explore its expression through music, drama and dance. Discuss the view that without belief in an ultimate source of truth that reveals itself to human beings, human life is meaningless and the human condition absurd.

Notes and references

PREFACE

1. Peters (1972) p111

CHAPTER ONE

1. Compare, for example, the contrasting views of Althusser (1971) and those of Bantock (1965), (1967), (1968).
2. See Moore (1982) Chap 3.
3. Hirst (1974).
4. Hirst and Peters (1970) p64.
5. Hirst (1974) p44.
6. Hirst (1974) p87.
7. Hirst and Peters (1970) p65.
8. Grimmitt (1973) pp26–29.
9. Phenix (1964) p5.
10. Phenix (1964) p5.
11. Phenix (1964) p5.
12. Phenix (1964) pp193–194.
13. Phenix (1964) p7.
14. Berger and Luckmann (1967).
15. Times Educational Supplement, 17th September, 1976.
16. Berger (1969) pp3–4.
17. Postman and Weingartner (1969) p101.
18. Postman and Weingartner (1969) p102.
19. See, for example, Young (1971).
20. Freire (1974) pp154–155.
21. Peters (1966) in Archambault (1966) p107.
22. Peters (1972) in Dearden, Hirst and Peters (1972) p11.
23. Hirst (1974) p31.
24. First published in Archambault (1965) pp113–138, and subsequently in Hirst (1974) pp30–53.
25. Jeffreys (1950) pp86–87.
26. Lawton (1973) pp43–44.
27. Sharpe (1983) p126.
28. Education 2000 (1983) Introduction, px.
29. Habermas (1975) title.

30. Shell Survey (1982) and Nipkow (1984).
31. For example, M Apple, B Bernstein, G Whitty, R Williams, M Young *et al.*
32. Apple (1982) p1.
33. Dolbeare and Dolbeare (1976) cited by Elias (1982).
34. Seaman, Esland and Cosin (1972) pp133–135.
35. Grace (1978) Chap 3. *passim.*
36. Seaman, Esland and Cosin (1972) p149.
37. Lawton (1973) pp22–24.
38. Lawton (1973) p24.
39. Reid (1981) pp160–167 and *passim.*
40. This is the position of Apple (1979).
41. Reid (1981) p166.
42. This is the position of Pinar (1975).
43. Reid (1981) p167.
44. Compare, for example, Avon Education Committee (1976).
45. For a typical example of a conception of education and religious education based on the value assumptions of 'Christian Absolutism', see Jeffreys (1950) and (1969). For a critique of Jeffreys' work and position, see Grimmitt (1984).
46. 'It (ie, phenomenology) is not just concerned with how a faith manifests itself or appears in this sense, but with how it actually js. Its aim is to give insight and understanding of the substance of men's faiths, the way they actually operate, impinge upon institutions, exist in human consciousness, and so on.' Smart (1973) p69.
47. 'Equal' in the sense that judgments are not made about the claims but all are regarded as equally worthy of attention.
48. See, for example, Hardy (1975) pp10–16, (1976) pp55–62, (1979) pp102–119 (and in Hull (1982) pp109–118).
49. For a more detailed treatment of the implications of this view for religious education, see Grimmitt (1981).
50. Halstead (1986) Foreword, pvi.
51. A view endorsed by the Swann Report—see HMSO (1985) Chap 8, para 2.11.
52. Newbigin (1977) and in Hull (1982) pp97–108.
53. City of Birmingham Education Committee (1975) pp4–5.
54. City of Birmingham Education Committee (1975) p5.
55. City of Birmingham Education Committee (1975) p4.
56. But see note 57.
57. Although Newbigin, unlike Jeffreys, takes sympathetic cognisance of the truth claims of religions other than Christianity, his position does not in actuality appear to be significantly different from that of Jeffreys. Both are opposed to the relativisation of religious beliefs and values which is a characteristic of modernity, which they also oppose. See, for example, Newbigin (1983) and (1986).
58. Newbigin (1977) p84 and in Hull (1982) p100.
59. Halstead (1986) p20.
60. See, for example, Hull (1984) pp227–285.
61. Postman and Weingartner (1969) p86.
62. See Gammage (1982), Chap 1, Cleverley and Phillips (1976), Aries (1962).
63. See Boas (1966) cited in Gammage (1982).
64. Froebel (1826).
65. See Eisenstadt (1968) cited in Gammage (1982).
66. Skinner (1972), p184.
67. See Gammage (1982) pp68–78.
68. Skinner (1974) p104.
69. See Wheldall and Merrett (1984) in Fontana (1984), p15.
70. Wheldall and Merrett (1983).

71. Fontana (1984) pp16–17.
72. Piaget (1932): Kohlberg (1976) in Lickona (1976) and in Munsey (1980).
73. Flavell (1963) p296: also Cohen (1983) pp52–65.
74. Bergling (1981) p30.
75. Bergling (1981) pp26–42.
76. Bergling (1981) p42.
77. Bergling (1981) p29.
78. Piaget (1932) p404.
79. See Grimmitt (1973) pp33–48.
80. Dearden (1984) p141.
81. Fontana (1984) p18.
82. Skinner (1948).
83. Rogers (1969) p152–154.
84. Rogers (1968) pp265–280.
85. Rogers (1959) in Koch (1959) p221.
86. Hodgkin (1970) p5.

CHAPTER TWO

1. Bach (1975) p1.
2. I fully acknowledge the undesirably sexist implications of the word 'man' in this sentence. I have sought to be sensitive to the gender issue throughout this book. In this chapter, however, I am unable to use my preferred terms of 'human being', 'human person' or 'people' (or to use plural forms) as I am seeking to identify the process by which the species of primates which are called 'homo sapiens' acquires those characteristics which are represented by terms like 'human being' and 'person' and which are implied when we speak of 'people'. Of the alternatives—'homo sapiens' and 'man'—I have chosen to use the latter.
3. Cited by Buber (1961) p149.
4. Buber (1961) p150.
5. Compare Cox, H (1974) p94; *'I lose my soul if I become merely the sum total of all the external inputs'*.
6. See Trigg (1982) for a critique of the view that culture is determined by genetic factors (ie, the view of sociobiologists).
7. Bhagavad-Gita 17 v3.
8. Heinemann, F H (1953) p39.
9. I am unable to attribute this statement. It was brought to my attention in 1974 by G T Read, my former colleague and collaborator, who also contributed to the elaboration of its meaning developed in section (v).
10. For a similar view, compare Peters (1966a): *'It is a grave error to regard the learning of a language as a purely instrumental matter, as a tool in the services of purposes, standards, feelings and beliefs. For in a language is distilled a view of the world which is constituted by them. . . In learning a language the individual is initiated into a public inheritance which his parents and teachers are inviting him to share'. p53.*
11. Berger (1967) p3.
12. I am indebted to Robert Witkin for these observations, and also for the distinction between 'object knowing' and 'subject knowing' as developed in Witkin (1974).
13. Compare, however, Segundo (1982), p25: *'In the light of the three basic facts brought out by our previous analysis, we now come to our first conclusion:* faith, *understood in the broadest, secular sense, is an* indispensable component, *a dimension, of every human life. It is an anthropological dimension. . .'*
14. I am indebted to Dr Wilna Meijer of Rijksuniversiteit, Groningen, Netherlands, for

presenting this argument to me in a personal communication dated 14th January, 1985.

15. Compare Segundo (1982), p25: *'Contrary to what we might have assumed, every human being needs referential witnesses to articulate his or her realm of values; and we cannot help but give the designation,* faith, *to the criterion which prompts them to accept or reject those witnesses. . . What we call "faith" in the religious sense is a particular instance subsumed under this more universal anthropological dimension of faith. In religious faith, too, we have human referential witnesses. But if that is the case, then from an anthropological standpoint it is not proper to set up a meaning-based division between "believers" and "nonbelievers" (the latter presumably being scientific and rational), since both groups base their values-structure on a type of knowledge that we must call* faith.'

16. Compare Segundo (1982), p5; *'In so far as free will is concerned, every option which is positive (in intent) becomes limiting (in result). In other words, to choose one path is to close ourselves to other paths.'*

17. Erikson (1963) *passim*; the further three phases, characteristic of adult experience, which Erikson identifies are the struggle to achieve: 6. A sense of intimacy and solidarity while avoiding a sense of isolation (a realisation of love); 7. A sense of generativity while avoiding a sense of self-absorption (a realisation of care); 8. A sense of integrity while avoiding a sense of despair (a realisation of wisdom).

18. Wall (1977) p228.
19. Powell (1976) pp68–69.
20. Powell (1976) pp74–75.
21. Wall (1977) p39.
22. Wall (1977) pp31–32.
23. Wall (1977) p230.
24. Wall (1977) p231.
25. Wall (1977) p226.
26. See Witkin (1974) pp17–29.
27. Wall (1977) pp232–233.
28. Keen (1970) p39.
29. Keen (1970) pp99–100.
30. Edwards, D L: I am unable to locate the source of this quotation, nor is its author, although in a private communication he acknowledges it to be his own.
31. Cox, H (1974) p108.
32. Berger (1970) p17.
33. Berger (1970) p13–14.
34. Berger (1970) p42.
35. Berger (1970) p63.
36. Berger (1970) p63.
37. Berger (1970) p65.
38. Berger (1970) p65.
39. Berger (1970) p76.
40. Berger (1970) p72.
41. Berger (1970) p92.
42. Berger (1970) p71.
43. Berger (1970) p71.
44. Berger (1970) p73.
45. Berger (1970) p75.
46. Berger (1970) p84.
47. Berger (1970) p85.
48. Berger (1970) p85.
49. Berger (1970) p87.
50. Berger (1970) p88.

51. Berger (1969) pp88–89.
52. Smart (1977) pp74–91.
53. Berger (1970) p100.
54. Read, P P (1969) pp138–139.

CHAPTER THREE

1. Pring (1976) pp68–69.
2. Jaynes (1976); cited by Marsella, Devos & Hsu (1985) p75.
3. Crook (1980) p31.
4. Crook (1980) p31.
5. Martin and Pluck (1977).
6. Martin and Pluck (1977) p46.
7. Martin and Pluck (1977) pp46–47.
8. Martin and Pluck (1977) p47.
9. Martin and Pluck (1977) p48.
10. Martin and Pluck (1977) p48.
11. Martin and Pluck (1977) p49.
12. Martin and Pluck (1977) p49.
13. Berger (1977) p101.
14. Berger (1979) p103.
15. Berger, Berger and Kellner (1973) p18.
16. Berger, Berger and Kellner (1973) pp42–43.
17. Berger, Berger and Kellner (1973) p30.
18. Berger, Berger and Kellner (1973) p42.
19. Hull (1986).
20. Hull (1985); see also Berryman (1985), Elias (1985), Hay (1985), King (1985), Lealman (1982) and (1985), Priestley (1982a) and (1985), Webster (1982).
21. Lawrence (1980).
22. As I write this section, the front-page of the *Birmingham Evening Mail* (5th August, 1986) reports Mr Rajiv Ghandi's comment on the British Government's refusal to co-operate with sanctions against South Africa, as *'We see now that Britain is compromising on its basic values for some economic gain'*.
23. I am indebted to my former colleague, G Robson, HMI, for this illustration.
24. See Stopes-Roe (1976): *'. . . if any reader feels that he would prefer to replace every use I make of "stance for living" and "life stance" by "faith", he is welcome to do so.' p25.*
25. DES (1977) p42.
26. Whorf (1965) pp213–214.
27. Peters (1966a) p53.
28. DES (1977) p6.
29. In a two page Supplement to DES (1977) alternative descriptions of 'the spiritual' are offered: viz

   (i) *'The spiritual area is concerned with the awareness a person has of those elements in existence and experience which may be defined in terms of inner feelings and beliefs that affect the way people see themselves and throw light for them on the purpose and meaning of life itself. Often these feelings and beliefs lead people to claim to know God and to glimpse the transcendent; sometimes they represent that striving and longing for perfection which characterises human beings but always they are concerned with matters at the heart and root of existence.'*

   (ii) *'The spiritual area is concerned with everything in human knowledge or experience that is connected with or derives from a sense of God or of Gods. Spiritual is a meaningless adjective for the atheist and of dubious use to the agnostic. Irrespective of personal belief or disbelief, an unaccountable number of people have believed and*

> *do believe in the spiritual aspects of human life, and therefore their actions, attitudes and interpretations of events have been influenced accordingly.'*

An eighth area of experience, 'the technological', is also offered.

30. See Wilson (1972) p16.

CHAPTER FOUR

1. See, for example, Abrams (1961), Musgrove (1964) and (1974), Hargreaves (1967), Flacks (1971), Larkin (1979), Ishwaren (1979), Roberts (1983), Bibby & Posterski (1985), King (1986).
2. Kitwood (1980).
3. Martin and Pluck (1977).
4. Henriksson (1983).
5. Henriksson (1983) pxi.
6. Henriksson (1983) p30.
7. Henriksson (1983) pp32–33.
8. Henriksson (1983) p33.
9. Henriksson (1983) pp35–37.
10. Henriksson (1983) p41.
11. Henriksson (1983) p46.
12. Henriksson (1983) pp55–56.
13. Henriksson (1983) pp60–63.
14. Henriksson (1983) pp70–72.
15. Henriksson (1983) pp75–86.
16. Henriksson (1983) p89.
17. Henriksson (1983) p89.
18. Henriksson (1983) p90.
19. Kitwood (1980) p45.
20. Kitwood (1980) p49.
21. Kitwood (1980) pp48–49.
22. Kitwood (1980) p79.
23. Kitwood (1980) p87.
24. Kitwood (1980) p113.
25. Kitwood (1980) p115.
26. Kitwood (1980) p116.
27. Kitwood (1980) p117.
28. Kitwood (1980) p167.
29. Kitwood (1980) p122.
30. Kitwood (1980) p122.
31. Kitwood (1980) p279.
32. Kitwood (1980) p166.
33. Kitwood (1980) p258.
34. Kitwood (1980) p244.
35. Kitwood (1980) p258.
36. Kitwood (1980) p280.
37. Martin and Pluck (1977) piii.
38. Martin and Pluck (1977) p12.
39. Martin and Pluck (1977) p20.
40. Martin and Pluck (1977) p28.
41. Martin and Pluck (1977) p28.
42. Martin and Pluck (1977) p12.
43. Martin and Pluck (1977) pp14–15.
44. Martin and Pluck (1977) pp24–25.

45. Martin and Pluck (1977) pp22–23.
46. Hull (1985) p27.
47. Kitwood (1980) p167.
48. Wall (1977) p230.
49. See, for example, Burns (1979), Crook (1980), Kegan (1982), Lasch (1984), Leeper (1967), Loevinger (1976), Marsella, Devos & Hsu (1985), Moustakas (1975), Ruddock (1972).
50. See, for example, Wheeler (1967).

CHAPTER FIVE

1. City of Birmingham Education Committee (1975).
2. Inner London Education Authority (1984).
3. Hardy (1979) in Hull (1982) p113.
4. Hardy (1979) in Hull (1982) p116.
5. Hardy (1985) in Felderhof (1985) p113.
6. Hardy (1985) in Felderhof (1985) p110.
7. Hardy (1985) in Felderhof (1985) p111.
8. Hardy (1985) in Felderhof (1985) p104.
9. Hardy (1985) in Felderhof (1985) p105.
10. Hardy (1985) in Felderhof (1985) p113.
11. Schools Council (1971).
12. Weil (1951) pp137–138.
13. Fowler (1981) pp135–173.
14. Hardy (1979) in Hull (1982) pp117–118.
15. Robinson (1977) p15.
16. Paffard (1973) p35 and *passim*.
17. Cited by Paffard (1973) p108.
18. Hay (1982a) p122.
19. Hay (1982a) p131.
20. Hay (1982a) p151.
21. Hay (1982a) p161.
22. Hay (1982a) pp161–162.
23. Robinson (1977) p11.
24. Robinson (1977) p11.
25. Robinson (1977) p16.
26. Robinson (1977) p8.
27. Sanders (1986) p10.
28. Robinson (1977) p85.
29. Robinson (1977) p101.
30. Hay (1982a) p152.
31. Hay (1986) (*Inside Information*, April, 1986) p23.
32. Cited from a personal communication.
33. Hay (1986) (*Inside Information*, April, 1986) p23.
34. Hay (1985a) pp140–147.
35. Hay (1985a) p142.
36. Hay (1985a) p142.
37. Hay (1985a) p145.
38. Hay (1985a) p146.
39. Hay (1985a) p146.
40. Robinson (1977) p87.
41. Surin (1980) p103.
42. Hay (1985b) unpublished paper.

43. Grimmitt (1973) especially pp52–58, 93–96, 101–102.
44. While I recognise this to be an important matter of principle, this exploratory study focuses on the contribution that the study of *religions* makes to pupils' learning. I see no reason why the educational rationale which I offer in Chapter Six and the framework for curriculum decision-making which derives from this study could not equally embrace the study of naturalistic stances for living. Similarly it can also accommodate the study of other religious traditions and movements not represented here because of limitations of time and space; for example, Baha'ism, Buddhism, Confucianism, Taoism, Zorostrianism, etc.
45. Starkings (1986) unpublished manuscript.

CHAPTER SIX

1. Hartshorne (1970) p29.
2. See, for example, Schutz (1967) and Schutz and Luckmann (1973).
3. Kitwood (1980) p244.
4. See Powell (1976) pp68–75.
5. Grimmitt and Read (1977) p4: See also Langford (1986) p60.
6. See Musgrove (1982): *'The first business of schools is to educate children but this cannot be divorced from its social consequences. . . The school curriculum must be transformational.'* pp137–138.
7. See, for example, Rutter, Maughan, Mortimore & Ouston (1979) pp66–94: 177–205.
8. Berger (1970) p76.
9. See Wall (1977) pp91–102.
10. Freire (1974) pp154–155.
11. See, for example, Hubery (1960), Goldman (1964) and (1965), Loukes (1961) and (1965), Hull (1975), Holm (1975), Grimmitt (1973).
12. Goldman (1964) pp220–246: (1965) pp192–223.
13. See, for example, the writings of Kierkegaard, Nietzsche, Sartre, Berdyaev, Marcel, Jaspers, Merleau-Ponty, Ricoeur.
14. See, for example, Curtis and Mays (1978).
15. Pring (1976) p84.
16. See Burns (1979) and (1982).
17. Martin and Pluck (1977) p12.
18. Grimmitt (1980) in Lealman (1980) pp16–21, and Castles & Rossiter (1983) pp12–18.
19. Wakefield (1983) p251.
20. Secondary Examinations Council (1986).
21. See Dearden (1972).
22. Bruner (1960) p18.
23. Bruner (1960) pp23–26.
24. Bruner (1960) pp52–53.
25. Bruner (1960) p13.
26. Cantwell-Smith (1978) p17. Compare Hick (1973), pp108–119, especially the following statement:

> *'I am suggesting, then, that in its essence Christianity is the way of life and salvation which has its origin in the Christ-event.* (which Hick has earlier defined as: *'a phrase which has been coined in modern times to refer to the complex of happenings constituting the life, death and resurrection of Jesus and the birth of the persisting community which was created by its response to Him') It* (ie, the Christ-event) *will continue as a way of salvation so long as men and women continue to find salvation—that is, spiritual life and health—through it. And so long as there is a community of people, however closely or loosely organised, who find salvation in the Christian way, and who continue to take the name of Christian, their*

religious beliefs will be part of the history of Christian theology. Christian belief consists in the beliefs of Christians, and the Christians of one age cannot legislate for the Christians of another age, either past or future. Christianity, then, is an open-ended history which has taken varying forms in varying circumstances, and which has at its essence the way of salvation that was initiated by the Christ-event' (p119).

27. See Bellah (1970), pp20–50, especially his differentiation of *primitive, archaic, historic, early modern and modern religion.*
28. Smart (1968) p98.
29. Cantwell-Smith (1978) pp200–201.
30. Secondary Examinations Council (1986).

POSTSCRIPT

1. For a more detailed discussion of this issue, see Grimmitt (1981).
2. Hull (1984), p231.
3. It is to this that Hardy and Newbigin appear to object.
4. This tradition has its roots in the writings of the early Christian Apologists and Fathers, especially Justin Martyr, Clement of Alexandria and St Augustine, and enabled the Christian Church to incorporate Greek, Roman and Jewish thought and culture largely on the basis that it was 'paving the way towards perfection in Christ'. For a more contemporary expression of this view see the writings of Jeffreys (eg, 1950).
5. Cited by Davies (1973), p94.
6. See Copley (1976).

Bibliography

Abrams, M
1961: *The Teenage Consumer*, London, London Press Exchange.

Althusser L
1971: *Lenin and Philosophy and other essays*, London, New Left Books.

Annand, J B (ed)
1977: *Education for Self-Discovery*, London, Hodder & Stoughton.

Apple, M W
1979: *Ideology and Curriculum*, London, Routledge & Kegan Paul.
1982 *Education and Power*, Boston Mass., Routledge & Kegan Paul.

Archambault, R D
1965: *Philosophical Analysis and Education*, London, Routledge & Kegan Paul.

Aries, P
1962: *Centuries of Childhood*, London, Jonathan Cape.

Armstrong, D M and Malcolm, N
1984: *Consciousness and Causality*—a debate on the nature of mind, Oxford, Basil Blackwell.

Avon Education Committee
1976: *Religious Education: Avon Agreed Syllabus*, Bristol.

Bantock, G H
1965: *Education and values*: essays in the theory of education, London, Faber.
1967: *Education, culture and the emotions*: further essays in the theory of education: London, Faber.
1968: *Culture, industrialisation and education*: London, Routledge & Kegan Paul.

Beck, C M, Crittenden, B S, and Sullivan, E V (eds)
1971: *Moral Education*, Ontario, Toronto University Press.

Bellah, R M
1970: *Beyond Belief:*—essays on religion in a post-traditional world, New York, Harper and Row.

Berger, P L
1967: (with Luckmann, T) *The Social Construction of Reality*, Harmondsworth, Middx, Penguin Books.
1969: *The Social Reality of Religion*, London, Faber & Faber.
1970: *A Rumour of Angels*, Harmondsworth, Middx, Penguin Books.
1977: *Facing Upto Modernity*, Harmondsworth, Middx, Penguin Books (1979).

Berger, P, Berger B and Kellner, H
1973: *The Homeless Mind*, Harmondsworth, Middx, Penguin Books (1974).

Bergling, K
1981: *Moral Development: the validity of Kohlberg's theory*, Stockholm, Almquist & Wiksell International.

Bernbaum, G
1977: *Knowledge and Ideology in the Sociology of Education*, London, Macmillan.

Berryman, J W
1985: 'Children's spirituality and religious language', in *British Journal of Religious Education*, Vol 7, No 3, pp120–127.

Bibby, W and Posterski, D C
1985: *The Emerging Generation*—an inside look at Canada's teenagers: Toronto, Irwin Publishing.

Boas, G
1966: *The Cult of Childhood*, London, Warburg Institute.

Brake, M
1980: *The Sociology of Youth Culture and Youth Subcultures*, London, Routledge & Kegan Paul.

Bridges, D and Scrimshaw, P (eds)
1975: *Values and Authority in Schools*, London, Hodder & Stoughton.

Brittan, A
1973: *Meaning and Situations*, London, Routledge & Kegan Paul.

Bruner, J S
1960: *The Process of Education*, Cambridge, Mass, Harvard University Press (1966 edition).

Brunner, E
1964: *Truth as Encounter*, London, SCM Press.

Buber, M
1961: *Between Man and Man*, London, Collins Fontana.

Burns, R B
1979: *The Self Concept*—theory, measurement, development and behaviour, London, Longman.
1982: *Self-Concept Development and Education*, London, Holt, Rinehart & Winston.

Cantwell-Smith, W
1978: *The Meaning and End of Religion*—a new approach to the religious traditions of mankind, London, SPCK.

Carmody, D L and Carmody, J
1983: *Religion: The Great Questions*, New York, The Seabury Press.

Castles, G M and Rossiter G M (eds)
1983: *Curriculum Theory and Religious Education*, Sydney, Australian Association for Religious Education.

City of Birmingham Education Committee
1975: *Agreed Syllabus of Religious Instruction*, City of Birmingham.

Clasby, M
1971: 'Education as a tool for humanisation and the work of Paulo Freire', *Living Light*, Vol 8, Spring, pp48–59.

Cleverley, J and Phillips, D C
1976: *From Locke to Spock*, Melbourne, Melbourne University Press.

Cohen, D
1983: *Piaget: Critique and Reassessment*, London, Croom Helm.

Copley, T
1976: 'Graveyard for the RE Teacher? The "Statutory Period" in the fourth and fifth forms', *Learning for Living*, Vol 16, No 1, pp34–35.

Cosin, B R (ed)
1972: *Education, Structure and Society*, selected readings, London, Penguin Books in association with the Open University.

Cox, H
1974: *The Seduction of the Spirit*, England, Wildewood.

Crook, J H
1980: *The Evolution of Human Consciousness*, Oxford, Clarendon Press.

Curtis, B and Mays, W (eds)
1978: *Phenomenology and Education*, London, Methuen.

Davies, J G
1973: *Every Day God*, London, SCM Press.

Dearden, R F
1972: 'Education as a process of growth' in Dearden, R F, Hirst, P H, and Peters, R S (eds), *Education and the Development of Reason Part One: A Critique of Current Educational Aims*, London, Routledge & Kegan Paul, pp63–82.
1981: 'Controversial issues and the curriculum', *Journal of Curriculum Studies*, Vol 13, No 1, pp37–44.

1984: *Theory and Practice in Education*, Chap 11, 'Behaviour modification: towards an ethical appraisal', London, Routledge & Kegan Paul, pp138–148.

DES/HMSO
1977: *The Curriculum 11–16*—working papers by HM Inspectorate: a contribution to current debate, London, HMSO.
1980: *A View of the Curriculum*, HMI series: 'Matters for Discussion' No 11, London, HMSO.
1985: *Survey of Religious Education in Years 4 and 5 of the Secondary School*, (HMI Report ref 57/85), London, HMSO.

Dixon, K
1980: *The Sociology of Belief*, London, Routledge & Kegan Paul.

Dolbeare, K M and Dolbeare, P
1976: *American Ideologies*, Third Edition, Chicago, Rand McNally.

Dykstra, C and Parks, S (eds)
1986: *Faith Development and Fowler*, Birmingham, Alabama, Religious Education Press.

Education 2000
1983: *A consultative document on Hypotheses for Education in AD 2000* co-chaired by Thwaites, B, and Wysock-Wright, C, Cambridge, Cambridge University Press.

Egan, K
1979: *Educational Development*, New York, Oxford University Press.

Eggleston, J
1977: *The Sociology of the School Curriculum*, London, Routledge & Kegan Paul.

Eisner, E W and Vallance, E (eds)
1974: *Conflicting Conceptions of the Curriculum*, USA, McCutchan.

Eisenstadt, S N
1968: *The Protestant Ethic and Modernisation*, New York, Basic Books.

Elias, J L
1979: *Psychology and Religious Education*, Second Edition, Bethlehem, Pennsylvania, Catechetical Communications.
1982: 'Ideology and Religious Education', *Lumen Vitae*, Vol 37, No 4, pp383–395.

Elliott, J and Pring, R (eds)
1975: *Social Education and Social Understanding*, London, University of London Press.

Erikson, E H
1968: *Identity: Youth and Crisis*, New York, Norton.
1974: *Dimensions of a New Identity*, New York, Norton.

Felderhof, M C (ed)
1985: *Religious Education in a Pluralistic Society*—papers from a consultation on Theology and Education, London, Hodder & Stoughton.

Flacks, R
1971: *Youth and Social Change*, USA, Markham Publishing Co.

Flavell, J H
1963: *The Development Psychology of Jean Piaget*, New York, D Van Nostrand Co Inc.

Flude, M and Ahier, J
1974: *Educability, Schools and Ideology*, London, Croom Helm.

Fontana, D (ed)
1984: *Behaviourism and Learning in Education*, monograph of the *British Journal of Educational Psychology*, Edinburgh, Scottish Academic Press in association with the British Psychological Society.

Fowler, J W
1981: *Stages of Faith: The Psychology of Human Development and the Quest for Meaning*, San Francisco, Harper and Row.
1986: 'Faith and the structure of meaning' in Dykstra and Parks (1986) pp15–42.

Francis, L J
1982: *Youth in Transit*—a profile of 16–25 year olds, Aldershot, Gower Publishing Co.

Freire, P
1972: *Pedagogy of the Oppressed*, Harmondsworth, Middx, Penguin Books.
1974: *Education for Critical Consciousness*, London, Sheed and Ward.

Froebel, F
1826: *The Education of Man*, London, Appleton (1894 edition).

Fromm, E
1949: *Man for Himself*—an enquiry into the psychology of ethics, Ark Paperbacks, Routledge & Kegan Paul, London.

Gammage, P
1982: *Children and Schooling*, London, George Allen & Unwin.

General Board of Education
1977: *Young People's Beliefs*: an exploratory study commissioned by the General Synod Board of Education of the views and behavioural patterns of young people related to their beliefs, London, General Board of Education.

Geuss, R
1981: *The Idea of a Critical Theory: Habermas and the Frankfurt School*, Cambridge, Cambridge University Press.

Gilbert, R
1984: *The Impotent Image*:—reflections on ideology in the secondary school curriculum, London, The Falmer Press.

Goldman, R
1964: *Religious Thinking from Childhood to Adolescence*, London, Routledge & Kegan Paul.
1965: *Readiness for Religion*—a basis for developmental religious education: London, Routledge & Kegan Paul.

Gosling, D and Musschenga, B
1985: *Science Education and Ethical Values*—introducing ethics and religion into the science classroom and laboratory, Geneva, The World Council of Churches/ Georgetown University Press.

Gouldner, A W
1976: *The Dialectic of Ideology and Technology*: the origins, grammar and future of ideology, New York, Seabury Press.

Grace, G
1978: *Teachers, Ideology and Control*—a study in urban education, London, Routledge & Kegan Paul.

Grene, M
1966: *The Knower and the Known*, London, Faber & Faber.

1969: (ed) *Knowing and Being*, London, Routledge & Kegan Paul.

Grimmitt, M H

1973: *What Can I Do in RE?*—a consideration of the place of religion in the curriculum with suggestions for practical work in schools, Essex, Mayhew-McCrimmon.

1977: (with Read, G T) *Teaching Christianity in RE*, Essex, K. Mayhew.

1980: 'What does RE contribute to the curriculum?' in Lealman (ed) (1980), pp16–21: also in Castles and Rossiter (1983), pp12–18.

1981: 'When is "commitment" a problem in religious education?', *British Journal of Educational Studies*, Vol 29, No 1, pp42–53.

1982: 'World Religions and Personal Development', in Jackson, R (ed) *Approaching World Religions*, London, John Murray, pp136–149.

1983: *Religious Education and Humanisation*—lectures given at the Seventh National Conference of the Australian Association for Religious Education in the University of Queensland, 1978, Sydney, AARE, pp13–124.

1984: 'Glaucon re-visited: a consideration of the educational thought of Professor M V C Jeffreys, CBE', *British Journal of Religious Education*, Vol 6, No 2, pp68–74.

1986: 'Contemporary Issues in Religious Education in England', *World in Life Journal of Religious Education*, Sydney, Australia, Vol 34, No 4, pp4–9.

Habermas, J

1975: *Legitimation Crisis*, translated by McCarthy, T, Boston, USA, Beacon Books.

Halstead, J M

1986: *The Case for Muslim Voluntary-Aided Schools*—some philosophical reflections, Cambridge, The Islamic Academy.

Hardy, D W

1975: 'Teaching religion: a theological critique', *Learning for Living*, Vol 15, No 1, pp10–16.

1976: 'The implications of pluralism for religious education', *Learning for Living*, Vol 16, No 2, pp55–62.

1979: 'Truth in religious education: further reflections on the implications of pluralism', *British Journal of Religious Education*, Vol 1, No 3, pp102–107: reprinted in Hull, J M (1982).

1985: 'Religious Education—Truth-claims or Meaning-giving?', in Felderhof, M C (1985), pp101–115.

Hargreaves, D

1967: *Social Relations in the Secondary School*, London, Routledge & Kegan Paul.

1972: *Interpersonal Relations and Education*, London, Routledge & Kegan Paul.

1982: *The Challenge for the Comprehensive School*: Culture, curriculum and community, London, Routledge & Kegan Paul.

Harris, K

1979: *Education and Knowledge*, London, Routledge & Kegan Paul.

Hartshorne, C

1970: *Creative Synthesis and Philosophic Method*, London, SCM Press.

Hay, D

1982a: *Exploring Inner Space*—Is God still possible in the twentieth century?, Harmondsworth, Middx, Penguin Books.

1982b: 'Teaching the science of the spirit', in Priestley (1982) pp37–53.

1985a: 'Suspicion of the spiritual: teaching religion in a world of secular experience', *British Journal of Religious Education*, Vol 7, No 3, pp140–147.

1985b: 'Experiential Learning in Religious Education', unpublished paper.

1986: 'Experiential education in religion as de-indoctrination', *Inside Information* (April), Nottingham, Religious Experience Research Project.

Heinemann, F H
1953: *Existentialism and the Modern Predicament*, London, Adam & Charles Black.

Henriksson, B
1983: *Not For Sale: Young People in Society*, translated from the Swedish by Davies, S and Scobbie, I, Aberdeen, Aberdeen University Press.

Hick, J
1973: *God and the Universe of Faiths*—essays in the philosophy of religion, London, Macmillan.

Hill, B
1973: *Education and the Endangered Individual*—a critique of ten modern thinkers, Columbia, USA, Teacher's College Press.

Hirst, P H
1965: 'Liberal education and the nature of knowledge', in Archambault (1965), pp113–138.
1970: (with Peters, R S) *The Logic of Education*, London, Routledge & Kegan Paul.
1974: *Knowledge and the Curriculum*, a collection of philosophical papers, London, Routledge & Kegan Paul.

HMSO
1985: *Education for All: The Report of the Committee of Inquiry into the Education of Children from Ethnic Minority Groups* (The Swann Report), London, Her Majesty's Stationery Office.

Hodgkin, R A
1970: *Reconnaissance on an Educational Frontier*, London, Oxford University Press.

Holm, J
1975: *Teaching Religion in School*, London, Oxford University Press.

Hubery, D S
1960: *The Experiential Approach to Christian Education*, London, National Sunday School Union.

Hull, J M
1975: 'Perennial symbols: preparing to teach religion through life themes', *Education 3–13*, Vol 3, No 2, pp104–109.
1982: (ed) *New Directions in Religious Education*, Basingstoke, Falmer Press.
1984: *Studies in Religion and Education*, Basingstoke, Falmer Press.
1985a: *What Prevents Christian Adults from Learning?*, London, SCM Press.
1985b: (ed) *Spirituality Across the Curriculum, British Journal of Religious Education*, Vol 7, No 3.
1986: 'Ideologies and the Consciousness-Creating Industries: Religious Education in the Public Schools of Late Capitalistic Society', unpublished paper delivered in the University of Calgary, Canada, May, 1986.

Inner London Education Authority.
1984: *Religious Education for Our Children*: The Agreed Syllabus of the Inner London Education Authority, London.

Ishwaren, K
1979: *Childhood and Adolescence in Canada*, Canada, McGraw-Hill Ryerson Ltd.

Jaynes, J
1976: *The Origin of Consciousness in the Breakdown of the Bicameral Mind*, New York, Houghton Mifflin.

Jeffreys, M V C
1950: *Glaucon*, London, Sir Isaac Pitman.
1969: *Truth is Not Neutral*, London, The Religious Education Press.

Jenks, C (ed)
1977: *Rationality, Education and the Social Organization of Knowledge*, London, Routledge & Kegan Paul.

Josselyn, I M
1952: *The Adolescent and His World*, New York, Family Service Association.

Keen, S
1970: *To a Dancing God*, London, Collins Fontana.

Kegan, R
1982: *The Evolving Self*—problem and process in human development, Cambridge, Mass, Harvard University Press.

Kelly, G
1955: *The Psychology of Personal Constructs: Vol 1*, New York, W W Norton and Co.

King, A J C
1986: *The Adolescent Experience*, The Research Committee of the Ontario Secondary School Teachers' Federation.

King, U
1985: 'Spirituality in secular society: recovering a lost dimension', *British Journal of Religious Education*, Vol 7, No 3, pp135–137.

Kitwood, T
1976: 'On values and value systems: evidence from interviews with adolescents', *Educational Review*, Vol 18, pp223–31.
1977: 'What does "Having Values" mean?', *Journal of Moral Education*, Vol 6, No 2, pp81–89.
1978: 'The morality of inter-personal values; an aspect of values in adolescent life', *Journal of Moral Education*, Vol 7, pp189–198.
1980: *Disclosures to a Stranger: Adolescent Values in an Advanced Industrial Society*, London, Routledge & Kegan Paul.

Kleinig, J
1982: *Philosophical Issues in Education*, London, Croom Helm.

Koch, S
1959: *Psychology: A study of Science*, Vol 3, New York, McGraw Hill.

Kohlberg, L
1976: 'Moral stages and moralization: the cognitive developmental approach' in Lickona, T (ed) (1976).
1980: 'Stages of Moral Development as a Basis for Moral Education', in Munsey, B (1980) pp15–100.

Langford, G
1968: *Philosophy and Education*, London, Macmillan.

Larkin, R W
1979: *Suburban Youth in Cultural Crisis*, New York, Oxford University Press.

Larrain, J
1979: *The Concept of Ideology*, London, Hutchinson University Library.

Lasch, C.
1984: *The Minimal Self: Psychic Survival in Troubled Times*, London, Picador, Pan Books.

Lawn, M and Barton, L
1981: *Rethinking Curriculum Studies*—a radical approach: London, Croom Helm.

Lawrence, I
1980: *Linguistics and Theology*, New York, Scarecrow Press.

Lawton, D
1973: *Social Change, Education Theory and Curriculum Planning*, London, Open University/Hodder & Stoughton.

Lealman, B
1980: *The Total Curriculum in Relation to RE*, London, CEM.
1986: 'Grottos, Ghettos and City of Glass: Conversations about Spirituality', *British Journal of Religious Education*, Vol 8, No 2, pp65–71.

Leeper, R R (ed)
1967: *Humanizing Education: The Person in Process*, Washington DC, Association for Supervision and Curriculum Development.

Lehmann, P L
1962: *Ideology and Incarnation*, Geneva, John Knox Association.

Lickona, T (ed)
1976: *Moral development and behaviour: theory, research and social issues*, New York, Holt, Rinehart & Winston, pp31–53.

Loevinger, J
1976: *Ego Development*, San Francisco, Jossey-Bass Press.

Loukes, H.
1961: *Teenage Religion*, London, SCM Press.
1965: *New Ground in Christian Education*, London, SCM Press.

Marsella, A J, Devos, G and Hsu, F L K
1985: *Culture and Self: Asian and Western Perspectives*, London, Tavistock Publications.

Martin, B and Pluck, R
1977: *Young People's Beliefs*: an exploratory study commissioned by the General Synod Board of Education of the views and behavioural patterns of young people related to their beliefs, London, General Board of Education.

Mol, H
1976: *Identity and the Sacred*, Oxford, Basil Blackwell.

Moore, T W
1982: *Philosophy of Education*, London, Routledge & Kegan Paul.

Moustakas, C E
1975: *The Self: Explorations in Personal Growth*, New York, Harper & Row.

Munsey, B
1980: *Moral Development, Moral Education, and Kohlberg*—basic issues in philosophy, psychology, religion, and education, with a response by Kohlberg, Birmingham, Alabama, Religious Education Press.

Musgrove, F
1964: *Youth and the Social Order*, London, Routledge & Kegan Paul.
1966: *The Family, Education and Society*, London, Routledge & Kegan Paul.
1974: *Ecstasy and Holiness*, London, Methuen.
1979: *School and the Social Order*, Chichester, John Wiley.
1982: *Education and Anthropology: other cultures and the teacher* Chichester, John Wiley.

Newbigin, L
1977: 'Teaching religion in a secular, plural society', *Learning for Living*, Vol 17, No 2, reprinted in Hull, J M (1982) pp97–107.
1983: *The Other Side of 1984*, London, The British Council of Churches.
1986: *Foolishness to the Greeks: the Gospel and Western Culture*, London, SPCK.

Nipkow, K E
1984: 'Education's responsibility for morality and faith in a rapidly changing world', unpublished paper presented to the Fourth International Seminar on Religious Education and Values, Kemptville, Ontario.

Paffard, M
1973: *Inglorious Wordsworths*, London, Hodder & Stoughton.
1976: *The Unattended Moment*, London, SCM Press.

Peters, R S
1966a: *Ethics and Education*, London, George Allen & Unwin.
1966b: 'Education as Initiation' in Archambault (1965), pp87–111.
1972: 'Education and the educated man', in Dearden, R F, Hirst, P H, and Peters, R S (eds), *Education and the development of Reason, Part 1*, London, Routledge & Kegan Paul, pp1–16.

Phenix, P
1964: *Realms of Meaning*, New York, McGraw Hill.
1975: 'Transcendence and the Curriculum', in Pinar (1975), pp323–327.

Piaget, J
1932: *The Moral Judgement of the Child*, London, Routledge & Kegan Paul.

Pinar, W F
1975: *Curriculum Theorizing: the Reconceptualists*, Berkeley, McCutchan.

Plantinger, A
1974: *The Nature of Necessity*, Oxford, Clarendon Press.

Polyani, M
1958: *Personal Knowledge*, London, Routledge & Kegan Paul.
1975: (with Prosch, H) *Meaning*, Chicago, University of Chicago Press.

Poole, R
1972: *Towards Deep Subjectivity*, Harmondsworth, Middx, Penguin Books.

Postman, N
1969: (with Weingartner, C.) *Teaching as a Subversive Activity*, Harmondsworth, Middx, Penguin Books.

Powell, J
1976: *Fully Human, Fully Alive*, Illinois, Argus Communications.

Priestley, J
1982a: (ed) *Religion, Spirituality and Schools*, Exeter, School of Education, University of Exeter.
1982b: 'Teaching Transcendence', in Tickner, M and Webster, D, (1982) pp5–21.

1985: 'Towards finding the hidden curriculum: a consideration of the spiritual dimension of experience in curriculum planning', *British Journal of Religious Education*, Vol 7, No 3, pp112-119.

Pring, R
1984: *Personal and Social Education in the Curriculum*, Sevenoaks, Kent, Hodder & Stoughton Educational.

Read, P P
1969: *Monk Dawson—a novel*, London, Alison Press Books, Secker & Warburg.

Reid, W A
1978: *Thinking about the Curriculum*—the nature and treatment of curriculum problems, London, Routledge & Kegan Paul.
1981: 'The Deliberative Approach to the Study of the Curriculum and its Relation to Critical Pluralism', in Lawn, M and Barton, L (eds), (1981) pp160-187.

Remmling, G W (ed)
1973: *Towards the Sociology of Knowledge*, London, Routledge and Kegan Paul.

Roberts, K
1983: *Youth and Leisure*, London, George Allen & Unwin.

Robinson, E
1977: *The Original Vision*, Manchester College, Oxford, The Religious Experience Research Unit.

Robinson, P
1981: *Perspectives on the Sociology of Education*, London, Routledge & Kegan Paul.

Rogers, C
1959: 'A Theory of Therapy, Personality and Interpersonal Relationships', in Koch, S (1959).
1968: 'Interpersonal Relationships: USA 2000', *Journal of Applied Behavioural Science*, No 4, pp265-280.
1969: *Freedom to Learn*, Columbus, Ohio, Merrill.

Rokeach, M
1970: *Beliefs, Attitudes and Values*—a theory of organisation and change, San Francisco, Jossey-Bass Inc.
1973: *The Nature of Human Values*, New York, The Free Press.

Rolston, H
1985: *Religious Inquiry—Participation and Detachment*, New York, Philosophical Library, Inc.

Rosenberg, M
1979: *Conceiving the Self*, New York, Basic Books.

Ruddock, R
1972: 'Conditions of personal identity' in Ruddock, R (ed) *Six Approaches to the Person*, London, Routledge & Kegan Paul pp93-125.

Rutter, M, Maughan, B, Mortimore, P & Ouston, J
1979: *Fifteen Thousand Hours*—secondary schools and their effects on children, London, Open Books.

Sadler, W A (Jr)
1969: *Existence and Love*:—a new approach to existential phenomenology, London, Cambridge University Press.

Sanders, J
1986: 'Thoughts on experiential learning in the classroom', *Inside Information* (July), Nottingham, Religious Experience Research Project.

Schools Council
1971: Working Paper 36: *Religious Education in Secondary Schools*, London, Evans/ Methuen Educational.

Schutz, A
1967: *The Phenomenology of the Social World*, translated by Walsh, G, and Lehert, F, USA, Northwestern University Press.
1973: (with Luckmann, T) *The Structures of the Life-World*, translated by Zaner, R M, and Egelhardt, H T, London, Heinemann.

Seaman, P, Esland, G, and Cosin, B
1972: *Innovation and Ideology*, London, The Open University.

Segundo, J L
1984: *Faith and Ideologies*, translated by Drury J, New York, Orbis Books.

Sharpe, E J
1983: *Understanding Religion*, London, Duckworth.

Shell Survey
1982: *Lebensentwurfe, Alltagskulturen, Zukunftsbilder*, Opladen, West Germany, Leske and Budrich.

Skinner, B F
1948: *Walden Two*, New York, Macmillan.
1972: *Beyond Freedom and Dignity*, London, Jonathan Cape.
1974: *About Behaviourism*, London, Jonathan Cape.

Smart, N
1968: *Secular Education and the Logic of Religion*, London, Faber.
1973: *The Phenomenon of Religion*, London, Macmillan.
1977: *The Science of Religion and the Sociology of Knowledge*, New Jersey, Princeton University Press.
1981: *Beyond Ideology: Religion and the Future of Western Civilisation*, London, Collins.

Stopes-Roe, H V
1976: 'The concept of a 'life-stance' in education', *Learning for Living*, Vol 16, No 1, pp25–28.

Starkings, D
1986: 'Approaches to Christianity', unpublished manuscript.

Surin, K
1980: 'Can the experiential and the phenomenological approaches be reconciled?', *British Journal of Religious Education*, Vol 2, No 3, pp99–103.

Taylor, P H (ed)
1975: (with Tye, K) *Curriculum, School and Society*, Windsor, NFER.
1979: *New Directions in Curriculum Studies*, Lewes, Falmer Press.

Tickner, M and Webster, D H (eds)
1982: *Religious Education and the Imagination*, Aspects of Education Number 28, Hull, University of Hull Institute of Education.

Thomas, J B
1980: *The Self in Education*, Slough, NFER Publishing Co.

Thompson, J L
1984: *Studies in the Theory of Ideology*, Cambridge, Polity Press/Basil Blackwell.

Trigg, R
1982: *The Shaping of Man*—philosophical aspects of sociobiology; Oxford, Basil Blackwell.

Wakefield, G S (ed)
1983: *A Dictionary of Christian Spirituality*, London, SCM Press.

Wakeman, B E
1984: *Personal, Social and Moral Education*, Tring, Lion Publishing.

Wall, W D
1975: *Constructive education for children*, London, Harrap/UNESCO.
1977: *Constructive education for adolescents*, London, Harrap/UNESCO.

Webster, D H
1980: 'Creativity within Religious Education: a note towards the significance of a dialogue between Christian Theology and Humanistic Psychology', *British Journal of Religious Education*, Vol 2, No 4, pp129–135.
1982: 'Spiritual growth in religious education', in Tickner and Webster (1982) pp85–95.

Weil, S
1951: *Waiting on God*, London, Collins Fontana.

Wheeler, D K
1967: *Curriculum Process*, London, University of London Press.

Wheelis, B
1973: *The Quest for Identity*, New York, Norton.

Wheldall, K and Merrett, F
1983: *Postive Teaching: the Behavioural Approach*, London, George Allen & Unwin.
1984: 'The behavioural approach to classroom management', in Fontana, D (1984).

Williams, B
1973: *Problems of the Self*, London, Cambridge University Press.

Whitty, G
1985: *Sociology and School Knowledge*—curriculum theory, research and politics, London, Methuen & Co.

Whorf, B L
1965: *Language, Thought and Reality*, Cambridge, Mass, MIT Press.

Wilson, J
1971: *Education in Religion & The Emotions*, London, Heinemann.
1972: 'Religious Education and Ultimate Questions', *Learning for Living*, Vol 11, No 5, pp16–18.
1973: *The Assessment of Morality*, Slough, NFER Publishing Co.

Wren, B
1977: *Education For Justice*, London, SCM Press.

Young, F D (ed)
1971: *Knowledge and Control*, London, Open University/Collier Macmillan.

Index

THE DIAGRAMS

CHARTS SHOWING THE APPLICATION OF THE CORE VALUES CRITERIA TO SHARED HUMAN EXPERIENCE, THE ADOLESCENT LIFE-WORLD AND TRADITIONAL BELIEF SYSTEMS

410

ILLUSTRATIVE CURRICULUM UNITS ARISING FROM THE APPLICATION OF THE SPIRAL CURRICULUM MATRIX TO CONTENT DRAWN FROM SHARED HUMAN EXPERIENCE AND TRADITIONAL BELIEF SYSTEMS

Names

Hume, D, 19

Ishwaren, K, 394n

Jeffreys, M V C, 30, 389n–390n, 397n
Jung, C, 65

Kant, I, 18, 19, 70–71, 161–162
Keen, S, 99–100
Kegan, R, 395n
King, A J C, 394n
King, U, 393n
Kitwood, T, 8, 143, 148–153, 158, 162–163
Kohlberg, L, 60, 61–62, 254
Korzybski, A, 26

Langford, G, 396n
Larkin, R W, 394n
Lasch, C, 395n
Lawton, D, 8, 30, 35–37
Lawrence, I, 393n
Lealman, B, 393n
Leeper, R R, 395n
Lehmann, P L, 261
Leibnitz, G W, 18
Locke, J, 19
Loevinger, J, 395n
Luckmann, T, 30, 389n, 396n
Loukes, H, 208

Marsella, A J, 393n, 395n
Martin, B, 8, 113–115, 143, 153–156, 166
Maslow, A H, 65
Meijer, W, 391–392n
Merrett, F, 54–55, 64
Moore, T W, 389n
Moustakas, C E, 395n
Musgrove, F, 394n, 396n

Newbigin, L, 42–43, 45, 80, 390n, 397n
Nipkow, K E, 390n

Paffard, M, 180, 189
Peters, R S, 9, 20–21, 29, 133, 255
Phenix, P, 22–23, 133, 159
Piaget, J, 52, 60–63, 65, 210, 212
Pinar, W, 390n
Plato, 18, 72
Pluck, R, 8, 113–115, 143, 153–156, 166
Popper, K, 19
Posterski, D C, 394n
Postman, N, 8, 26, 50–51
Powell, J, 94
Priestley, J, 393n
Pring, R, 109

FURTHER ACKNOWLEDGEMENTS

Basic Books, Inc, USA: Excerpts from *Facing up to Modernity*
by Peter L Berger Copyright © 1977 by Peter L Berger
reprinted by permission of Basic Books, Inc.

Doubleday Publishing: Excerpts from *THE SACRED
CANOPY* by Peter L Berger copyright © 1967 by
Peter L Berger reprinted by permission of
DOUBLEDAY PUBLISHING a division of Bantam,
Doubleday, Dell Publishing Group, Inc.